Reading Romans within Judaism

Other volumes in this series:

Reading Paul within Judaism: Collected Essays of Mark D. Nanos, Vol. 1

Reading Galatians within Judaism: Collected Essays of Mark D. Nanos, Vol. 3

Reading Corinthians and Philippians within Judaism: Collected Essays of Mark D. Nanos, Vol. 4

"Over the years, Nanos has exposed many unexamined and problematic assumptions readers often bring to their reading of Paul. In this collection of essays, we are given a chance to trace how Nanos further developed his thoughts on Paul's letter to the Romans since the publication of *The Mystery of Romans* (1996). Consider this, then, Nanos' sequel to that award-winning monograph. Unlike most sequels, this one did not let me down."

—Tat-siong Benny Liew, College of the Holy Cross

"The 'Paul within Judaism' approach is dedicated alike to reading Paul as a Jew, writing to congregations still affiliated with Diaspora synagogues, and to rooting out Christian supersessionist assumptions wherever they appear in scholarship on the apostle. Meticulous exegetical and historical precision have been as characteristic of Nanos' work as has the daring of his guiding hypotheses. These close readings of key aspects of Romans stand as testaments to his achievement and challenges to the research ahead."

—Neil Elliott, author of *The Arrogance of Nations: Reading Romans in the Shadow of Empire* (2008)

"These essays will remind readers why Mark Nanos is rightly regarded as one of the chief architects of the Paul within Judaism perspective. Paradigm shifts in biblical studies often involve fresh, challenging, and credible exegetical insights, and one will find a plethora of them here. Even when I'm not fully convinced by a particular rereading, I always come away feeling like my hermeneutical horizons have been profitably expanded by what Mark has to say. I look forward to discussing these essays with students for years to come!"

—Mark D. Given, Missouri State University

"These essays, the fruit of close attention to the text of Romans, are indicative of Nanos' unique contribution to the interpretation of Romans. Significantly, both Paul and the Christ-following groups in Rome are viewed as part of Jewish community life. This challenges traditional approaches, and standard translations, and offers a fresh analysis of the historical context. Nanos opens up exciting avenues to further explore one of the most influential documents of Christian tradition in relation to Judaism."

—William S. Campbell, University of Wales

Reading Romans within Judaism

Collected Essays of Mark D. Nanos, Vol. 2

MARK D. NANOS

CASCADE Books • Eugene, Oregon

READING ROMANS WITHIN JUDAISM
Collected Essays of Mark D. Nanos, Vol. 2

Copyright © 2018 Mark D. Nanos. All rights reserved. Except for brief quotations in critical publications or reviews, no part of this book may be reproduced in any manner without prior written permission from the publisher. Write: Permissions, Wipf and Stock Publishers, 199 W. 8th Ave., Suite 3, Eugene, OR 97401.

Cascade Books
An Imprint of Wipf and Stock Publishers
199 W. 8th Ave., Suite 3
Eugene, OR 97401

www.wipfandstock.com

PAPERBACK ISBN: 978-1-5326-1756-0
HARDCOVER ISBN: 978-1-4982-4233-2
EBOOK ISBN: 978-1-4982-4232-5

Cataloguing-in-Publication data:

Names: Nanos, Mark D., 1954–, author.

Title: Reading Romans within Judaism : collected essays of Mark D. Nanos, vol. 2 / Mark D. Nanos.

Description: Eugene, OR: Cascade Books, 2018 | Includes bibliographical references and index.

Identifiers: ISBN 978-1-5326-1756-0 (paperback) | ISBN 978-1-4982-4233-2 (hardcover) | ISBN 978-1-4982-4232-5 (ebook)

Subjects: LCSH: Bible. Romans—Criticism, interpretation, etc. | Paul, the Apostle, Saint—Relations with Jews | Paul, the Apostle, Saint | Judaism—Relations—Christianity | Jews in the New Testament | Gentiles in the New Testament | Judaism (Christian theology)

Classification: BS2665.52 N36 2018 (print) | BS2665.52 (ebook)

Manufactured in the U.S.A.   07/06/18

Contents

Preface | vii
Permissions | xxxiii

PART I: **A New Approach to Romans: Paul's Synagogue Correspondence**

1   To the Churches within the Synagogues of Rome | 3

PART II: **Exegetical Support for Non-Jews within the Synagogues of Rome as Paul's Target Audience**

2   Some Problems with Reading Romans through the Lens of the Edict of Claudius | 23

3   The Jewish Context of the Gentile Audience Addressed in Paul's Letter to the Romans | 40

4   A Rejoinder to Robert A. J. Gagnon's "Why the 'Weak' at Rome Cannot Be Non-Christian Jews" | 65

PART III: **A New Exegetical Approach to Romans 9–11 and Christian-Jewish Relations**

5   Romans 9–11 from a Jewish Perspective on Christian-Jewish Relations | 103

6   "Broken Branches": A Pauline Metaphor Gone Awry? (Romans 11:11–24) | 112

7 "Callused," Not "Hardened": Paul's Revelation of Temporary Protection until All Israel Can Be Healed | 153

8 Romans 11 and Christian-Jewish Relations: Exegetical Options for Revisiting the Translation and Interpretation of This Central Text | 179

9 The Translation of Romans 11 since the Shoah: What's Different? What's Not? What Could Be? | 200

10 "The Gifts and the Calling of God are Irrevocable" (Romans 11:29): If So, How Can Paul Declare that "Not All Israelites Truly Belong to Israel" (9:6)? | 214

Part IV: **Special Occasions**

11 Challenging the Limits That Continue to Define Paul's Perspective on Jews and Judaism | 237

12 Implications of Paul's Hopes for the End of Days for Jews and Christians Today: A Critical Re-evaluation of the Evidence —co-authored with Philip Cunningham | 249

Appendix: Translating Romans 11:11—12:1a within Judaism: Literal-Oriented and Expanded Versions | 285

Index of Ancient Sources | 293

Preface

WAS ROMANS WRITTEN BY a Paul who practiced and promoted a Jewish way of life, and read by its original recipients within Judaism? The idea first dawned on me when trying to follow Paul's seemingly contradictory arguments about the fate of Israel in chapter 11. The year was 1977; ironically, I was taking a class studying Jewish eschatological texts, not "Christian" ones. In these Jewish texts it was common for prophetic predictions about a promising future for Israel to be mixed with judgments about the prophet's various contemporaries, often fellow Israelites (= Jews).[1] Having recently read Romans, it struck me that Paul's widely-cited arguments in chapters 9–11, although containing a jarring mixture of disparaging yet ultimately positive statements about the fate of his fellow Jews, were, on the surface anyway, *no less Jewish* than the other texts we had read, and were less vitriolic than some, especially texts from the Dead Sea Scrolls community. What was I missing? Could Paul have been an advocate for Jews and Judaism—albeit representing the new, contested perspective of a few minority Jewish subgroups—rather than the opponent of the interests of Jews and Judaism he is commonly understood to be? Moreover, could Paul, reread from this historical perspective, offer a positive contribution to Christian-Jewish relations today, instead of the divisive and harmful role his voice is often made to serve? I began a paper exploring whether his argument might represent an intra- or inter-Jewish discourse, rather than a Christians-*in-place-of*-Jews (or *as-enemies-to*-Jews) discourse. Forty years later I am still pursuing

---

1. I use the terms "Jew" and "Israelite" and cognates interchangeable to discuss Paul's period, unless exploring some nuance among the tribal affiliations, which I will signal; see the discussion in chapter 1 in volume 1 of this series of collected essays.

this intriguing historical question and its profound ideological implications, although now with many more researched reasons to be convinced of the merits, both historical and contemporary.

Yes, it was immediately apparent that Romans contained descriptions of and predictions *about* Israelites who did not share the author's conviction that Jesus was the Messiah (Christ) who now should be announced to the nations. That could indicate that the writer now perceived *them* as the *other* with respect to himself and the followers of Christ to whom he wrote, which is indeed how the received view of Paul has interpreted this rhetoric. The consensus has been that the author no longer regarded himself to be a spiritual "brother" to such Israelites, although still admittedly kin through genealogical birth (in the "flesh"), about which he had no choice.[2] And although Paul may have exhibited some Jewish cultural habits because of his *past* life, this was certainly no longer because he wanted to express continued responsibility to observe Jewish Torah-based interpretations of covenantal obligations. But it seemed to me that Paul—like the other Jewish prophets—described *himself*, and *his* and his *audience's* best interests, to be bound together inextricably with those of the *them* he was passionately describing, even if he disapproved of their present negative response to the message he proclaimed.

The premises from which Paul attempted to stir the non-Jews he addressed to graciousness rather than indifference to *these Jews'* present plight, or resentment toward *these Jews*, seemed to me to be palpably empathetic. The arguments in these chapters were predicated upon Paul reasoning that *their* destinies together with those of *himself* and *his addressees* were *one*; the *them* was for him and for his addressees also the *us*. The letter was to ensure that his addressees recognized this fundamental oneness, which stands in stark contrast to the received reading of this letter, to say the least. In my view, Paul sought to instruct the non-Israelite Christ-followers in Rome that they must choose to live *for* these Israelites as brothers and sisters in the family of God, as fellow heirs of Abraham's promises, such as he still chose to live *for* rather than *against* these Israelites. Their fate was *our* fate, however "mysterious" that may presently seem to the non-Jews to whom Paul targeted his arguments. The observation that the target audience or implied readers were probably *non-Jews* who followed Christ proved to be important when trying to decode Paul's arguments in their pre-Revolt first-century context: while they were made *to* and *for* non-Jews, they concerned how to *think about* and

---

2. The continual objections to my readings of the "brothers" in Rom 14–15 and 1 Cor 8 to refer non-Christ-followers, as if self-evident, makes plain that this remains the case four decades later; see ch. 4 in this volume.

live among Jews in ways that suggested the audience were still members of *subgroups within the Jewish communities* of Rome.

In summary, I basically surmised that just as one would approach the reading of other texts written by Jews (= Israelites), one should expect to read Romans *within* Judaism (= a way of life designed by and for Jews/Israelites). At very least, one should begin to fashion hypotheses for reading the letter from this perspective, consider and test various lexical alternatives, weigh the results, and compare them to the received views. But was this assumption about how to proceed even warranted? Was Romans Jewish correspondence, rather than Christian, at least as usually categorically differentiated?

Naturally, I did not formulate my initial reactions in precisely the conceptual and terminological ways that I present them now following years of studying and writing about these texts and their historical contexts, interacting with many others scholars and students. I nevertheless intuited that approaching Paul's arguments as intra-Jewish critique (even though directed to non-Jews), based upon appeals to the presumably shared ideals and destiny of all Jews (to which Paul sought to persuade these non-Jews), including those Jews being criticized for their present behavior (*mutatis mutandis*, of course), would profoundly alter the historical and ideological ways that Paul's arguments were interpreted and used by Christians (who were [usually] non-Jews themselves), not least to formulate their perceptions of Jews and Judaism.

The immediate challenge has been the making of the *necessary changes*, indicated by the *mutatis mutandis* above, to interpret Paul in the most probable way. The quest involves many elements, including the need to carefully consider all the options for translating and interpreting his language, comparing and contrasting Paul and his groups with other Jews and their viewpoints and practices and groups (especially related to non-Jews), evaluating the rhetoric and lifestyles of other Jews and Romans, and exploring every other relevant factor available. This process also involves constant vigilance to avoid the traps of anachronism and ideological bias and the constraints of traditional as well as consensus perspectives (and that list now includes the need for suspicion about the perspectives I have crafted over the years too!), and extends to how one conceptualizes the possibilities to explore and tests them, and to why one chooses one conclusion over another. Today, after many years of research, *mutatis mutandis*, these remain the challenges for anyone proposing to construct an historically probable reading of Paul, whether proposing to read his letters within Judaism, as I do, or not!

Before we turn to the history of the specific essays included in this volume, I want to return to the story of my initial effort to read Romans within

Judaism for that class paper in 1977. I knew just enough Greek (having lived in Crete for two years as a teenager) to consult the lexicons in addition to reading the secondary sources. The title I selected was based upon the conclusion that Paul, in 11:26, insisted was beyond doubt: according to God's promise, "all Israel will be saved!" I wanted to understand what Paul (most likely) meant, and also what he (most likely) wanted that assertion and the surrounding arguments to motivate his original readers towards thinking and doing differently than he apparently feared they would arrive at otherwise. I gave it my best shot. While completing a degree in Judaica within the history department and in the years after that while operating an advertising agency, I pondered the prospects in the direction I imagined most probable.

The more I thought about this idea, the more I concluded that this alternative perspective on Paul's historical voice could helpfully challenge the prevailing Christian discourses about Jews and Judaism, not least the ways of talking and behaving derived from his texts that were factors in shaping a Christian, European cultural world that could carry out the atrocities of the Holocaust. Challenging the essentialized thinking involved in the othering of Jews and Judaism that seemed instinctually mixed with the quest for Christian self- and group-esteem would logically challenge the basis for the traditional othering aimed at non-Christians in general, but also the pattern of othering women, people of other colors and places, and other orientations of all kinds, even alternative ways of being Christian. The thought of pursuing this research interest someday in the future became more and more compelling as the years ticked off, for both the historical and the ideological benefits that I imagined it could offer. One sleep-challenged night some fifteen years later, in 1992, I searched for that paper in my school files.

At the time, I had begun to read advocates of the emerging New Perspective on Paul as well as the latest dialogues on Christian-Jewish relations. Both of these developments appeared to present an opportunity to reread Paul, Romans in particular, in the direction I had imagined worth pursuing some fifteen years earlier, largely because the traditional representations of Judaism (e.g., the essentializing of works-righteousness and legalistic values in contrast to grace, faith, and integrity of purpose) as the negative-Christian-binary-other were beginning to be recognized as mistaken by Christian interpreters of Paul. This was a profoundly important development.

When I originally wrote the research paper and considered the prospect of pursuing the thesis in graduate studies, the idea of tackling such essentialized Christian misrepresentations of Judaism appeared to be an insurmountable obstacle, yet one that had to be overcome before it would be possible to construct a portrait of Paul practicing and promoting Judaism such as I imagined. But now there was a new paradigm for interpreting the Judaism of Paul's time that appeared to be gaining wide acceptance in Pauline studies. At the same time, however, I was struck by the frustrating realization that the interpretation of Paul remained relatively unchanged. (Although, importantly, I did encounter a few exceptions, especially the essays by Krister Stendahl, who, when I met him years later, interestingly enough, told me that he was deeply influenced by his teacher Johannes Munck, from whose books I had gained the most insight and encouragement when writing that initial school paper!)

It was immediately clear that in spite of new perspectives on Judaism and challenges to certain elements of the traditional theological paradigms for interpreting Paul, Pauline specialists still categorically portrayed him as the champion of a movement that rejected Judaism, even the continued value of Jewish identity, although some of the reasons for his supposedly having done so had shifted. This seemed illogical to me. Does it not follow that, if what Paul was supposed to have opposed did not exist as conceptualized, then what Paul probably meant to communicate in Romans and every other letter, not least with respect to decoding the targets of his polemical language—including the people and ideas or practices often portrayed by him in either-or terms—would also need to be re-conceptualized? I wondered: could it be, to borrow a popular metaphor, that the tail was—or better, as far as this logical failure persists, *is*—wagging the dog?

To finish up the story, although I did not have a post-graduate degree, and was far from certain how to proceed, in 1992 I decided to write an essay about Romans 11 starting from insights in that school paper, even if no one ever read it. I did not know whether I could complete such a project, of course; or where the undertaking would lead. The process was hardly easy, and I did not imagine that the essay I had begun to research would result in a book-length manuscript, much less that it could or would be published by an esteemed publisher of scholarly books about Paul, Fortress Press, in January of 1996, entitled *The Mystery of Romans: The Jewish Context of Paul's Letter* (how that came about is a story of its own). Of course, in the process I discovered many other texts and topics of great interest and of importance to that text that I wanted to understand and communicate (i.e., Romans 11). The detailed investigation of chapter 11 now followed four other chapters. Although my interpretation of this text continued to develop, and yes, to change, I remained convinced that decoding the arguments Paul made there was fundamental to sorting out Paul and related historical matters, and just as importantly, to constructing a very different way forward for Christian-Jewish relations where his voice is concerned. The gracious reception of this book by specialists and others interested in these matters, and its receipt of the 1996 National Jewish Book Award for Jewish-Christian Relations, were two of several encouraging developments that subsequently led me to sell my business and seek a PhD to pursue testing this hypothesis and sharing the results as a full-time second career.

Today, I remain animated by the challenge to figure out what Paul meant to disclose in the "mystery" of chapter 11 as well as the letter overall. And, where Christian-Jewish relations are concerned, I still find this to be the most critical text, and context, for ascertaining Paul's views of Jews and Judaism. Moreover, as you will discover herein, some twenty-plus years after the publication of that monograph I still keep adjusting what I think Paul most likely meant, or would most likely have been understood by his first audience to mean, and, moreover, what he can mean for those who seek to understand him for today, as well as the best terminology to use to discuss his messages. I probably always will. Historical and ideological criticism can be exciting, but done well are also humbling; they deal in possibilities and probabilities as well as sensibilities and perceptions, but there are few to no certainties; the enterprise requires continual questioning of what we think we know about what must have been, as well as about what is taking place today, and why; and even the impact of our own work, if there is any, can be very different than imagined or intended.

As explained more broadly for Paul in volume 1 of this series of collected essays, I now more confidently contend that it is historically responsible as well as helpful to refer to *Paul's Judaism*, to his letters as *Jewish correspondence*, and thus to interpret his arguments *within Judaism*—at least that we should continue to test and modify the hypotheses according to the highest standards of historiography, that this was the most likely original context. The essays in this volume explain the case for reading Romans according to this conviction, and the benefits for doing so.

I want to bring attention to some changes in terminology you will encounter as you read essays that were published over the course of more than two decades, which, except for formatting and minor editorial adjustments, have been reproduced without adjusting the terminology to that which I prefer to use today, although the two that were not published previously have been updated to do so. This will allow the reader to trace the development of my thought and presentation of the material since the completion of *The Mystery of Romans*, for which the appendix included herein as chapter 2 was written. In that monograph as well as the essay for the *Catholic Biblical Quarterly* that constitutes chapter 3, both completed in the mid-90s, I attempted to avoid anachronism and assist myself and the reader to think in more mid-first century terms by using the word "Christian" only as an adjective (hence, Christian Jews/gentiles or non-Christian Jews/gentiles), although sometimes for simplicity I found it useful to retain the substantive form when describing the views of others and some topics that were usually presented as Christian/Christianity. At the time the effort was innovative, but by the end of the 90s I found it to be inadequate for the task. In order to help the reader and myself think with Paul in more relevant historical ways I began to use "Christ-believer," then settled on "Christ-follower" and cognates by the mid-00s. For the same reasons I eventually eschewed the use of "gentiles," opting for "non-Jews" or "members of the other nations," and while I had already avoided the use of "church," using "gatherings" or "assemblies," I regularly began to qualify these as *Jewish subgroup* gatherings, since it remains common to read of "gentile churches," which plays to the traditional constructions that are being questioned. Along the way I coined several terms to try to capture the historical dynamics more clearly and concisely, but the practice of avoiding the usual terminology—although an important element for undertaking critical re-thinking that is appropriately cross-cultural—unfortunately produces a more cumbersome writing style (e.g., instead of "Paul wrote to Christians" or maybe "to gentile Christian churches," I would write something like "Paul's arguments targeted Christ-following non-Jews meeting in Jewish subgroups"). These and related efforts to find terminology that is more precise and at the same time defamiliarizes, so that we can undertake to investigate and discuss these historical texts less anachronistically and with appropriate historical distance from our own interests, are discussed at various points when introduced in these essays and others in this series.

I sincerely hope you will find the research and reflections in this volume both warranted and helpful, even if you are not always persuaded to change your mind from what you thought before reading my arguments. I welcome your feedback to the cases I have made. You can reach me by email through the contact tab at my website (www.marknanos.com), which also provides more information about my other publications and activities, and makes available a number of downloadable files.

THE ORGANIZATION OF THIS VOLUME

This volume is arranged into four sections, followed by an appendix; the chapters within each section are presented in the order of their publication dates. Two essays are published here for the first time and arranged according to their original venue dates (earlier drafts of both have been available on my website): one (ch. 4) was written in 2000 as a rejoinder to an essay published that year to contest a major argument made in *The Mystery of Romans*; the other (ch. 5) is the English version from which an Italian translation was published in 2009. All but one post-date the publication of *The Mystery of Romans* in 1996. The appendix presents a new translation of Romans 11 that reflects the research discussed in these chapters.

The first section consists of one chapter, a summary-style, lightly annotated essay introducing many of the basic elements involved in constructing the context for a "new approach to Romans" as "synagogue correspondence," a proposition to which every essay in this volume contributes.

The second section contains three chapters. Each essay offers "Exegetical Support for Non-Jews within the Synagogues of Rome as Paul's Target Audience." The first essay (ch. 2) reproduces an appendix from *The Mystery of Romans* that explains my reservations about the recent popularity of certain construals of the Edict of Claudius to construct the context for interpreting Romans. The next essay (ch. 3) discusses the factors for constructing the rhetorical and historical settings for interpreting Paul's arguments in more detail than undertaken in the summary-style essay comprising chapter 1. Chapter 4 is a previously unpublished essay written as a rejoinder to Robert Gagnon's 2000 *Catholic Biblical Quarterly* essay challenging my arguments for the identities of the "weak" and "strong" made in chapter 3 of *The Mystery of Romans*, which completes this section with a very detailed discussion of the likely social tensions in Rome that provoked Paul to write just this letter.

Under the third section heading, "A New Exegetical Approach to Romans 9–11 and Christian-Jewish Relations," six chapters (5–10) revisit the details of Paul's arguments. The first chapter (5), written for non-specialist readers of an Italian magazine about Paul, is a summary survey of my reading of these chapters that also signals the promising implications for Christian-Jewish relations. The next two essays (chs. 6 and 7) explore many new ideas that arise from detailed exegetical explorations of the language in Romans 11, to which I returned after roughly fifteen years. Chapter 6 focuses on why I propose that Paul's references to *branches* is better understood to refer metaphorically to the present case of some Israelites as *temporarily injured* in order to signify being *temporarily estranged*, thus the Greek would be better translated as *broken* or *bent (aside)* rather than *broken off*. The proposed alternatives undermine the traditional way of conceptualizing Paul's message here, which has been understood to signify a permanent state of removal, reflecting the supersessionistic and replacement-based theological paradigms that have prevailed. Chapter 7 investigates the word usually translated as *hardened*, which has been interpreted to indicate intentional resistance to God's grace. I instead propose that Paul was playing off of the olive tree allegorical imagery of temporarily injured branches, and thus to metaphorically signify the formation of a protective *callus* (which involves a process of hardening, but one that represents a positive, healing-based activity). The callus was formed to protect Israel (being "natural branches" in the tree signifying the people of God through Abraham, with some presently injured among those who are healthy, and now joined by a "wild branch" grafted among them, signifying non-Jews who are Christ-followers and thus also related to Abraham) during this mysterious period of disagreement about the gospel. These two detailed exegetical essays are followed by a more programmatic essay in chapter 8, which summarizes the research and discusses the positive implications for Christian-Jewish relations. Chapter 9 continues the discussion of matters of interest for Christian-Jewish relations, specifically, how the translations since the revolutionary Catholic statements made in *Nostra Aetate* 4, which signaled the need for a re-evaluation of just such texts and topics, still fail to reflect such sensibilities, but, as my research demonstrates, certainly could (dare I say now, *should*?), since there are more promising lexical alternatives readily available. The final essay in this section, chapter 10, explores translation and related interpretive alternatives to the received view of Paul's language in Romans 9:6, where his argument has been understood to indicate that Paul no longer regarded many of his fellow Israelites as *truly* Israelites, but rather as "cut off." This text has been used to conclude that the "all Israel" of 11:26 now signifies "the church," although such interpretive decisions, and the replacement theological thinking that depends upon them, contradict Paul's assertion in 11:28–29 that these genealogical descendents of the patriarchs remain God's "beloved," for whom "the gifts and calling of God are irrevocable." This essay challenges those contradictory interpretive moves, which are ineluctably dismissive of Jews, and shows how these texts can work together to offer a more coherent argument, and a more promising reading of Paul's position for Christian-Jewish-relations critics to build upon.

The two chapters in the fourth section, "Special Occasions," represent essays that were developed in collaboration with others. Chapter 11 was a response to papers by William S. Campbell and Guenter Wasserberg at the 1998 Society of Biblical Literature Annual Meeting. Chapter 12, the final essay in this volume, was co-written with Philip Cunningham, a Catholic theologian specializing in Christian-Jewish-relations criticism. Published in 2014, this essay explores how the exegetical decisions discussed in the previous chapters, combined with post-*Nostra Aetate* 4 Christian-Jewish-relations-based theological reasoning, challenge current ways of thinking about and discussing the eschatological dynamics of Paul's expectations for the future of Israel and the church.

The Appendix provides a working translation of Romans 11:11—12:1a. In addition to the literal-oriented translation, which is offered alongside the Greek text, a second, expanded version details additional translation options, explanations, and paraphrases that clarify how I believe the original reader most likely understood Paul's language.

A SHORT HISTORY OF THESE ESSAYS

The essays in this volume were written between 1992 and 2016, and some were updated for this volume; the appendix is new. The earliest reproduces an excursus from *The Mystery of Romans*; the latest was published the year I started this series of collected essays. During the years 1995 to 2008, my research often focused on other letters, first Galatians, then certain flashpoint texts in 1 Corinthians and Philippians that are central to the traditional view that Paul negatively valued Jewish identity and ways of life, especially Torah. Thereafter, as the other volumes in this series attest, these research projects often overlapped with my return—once again, after several years and armed with new questions and information and methodologies—to exploring certain texts of Romans.

I discovered many new things about Paul and Romans during the research for each of these essays. Some naturally build on the work begun in the first monograph; some were unanticipated discoveries; and some are in tension with earlier decisions, resulting in continual adjustments to my working translations and interpretations. The order of the essays in sections two and three largely reflect the flow of the research as it developed. Those in Part II were written between 1994 and 2000; those in Part III, between 2008 and 2016. Naturally, there is some repetition, especially within essays exploring the same themes or texts, which range from the historical and rhetorical elements for constructing the context in the first and second Parts, to the translation and interpretation of topics and texts in chapters 9–11 in the Parts III and IV, to the implications of the proposed readings for Christian-Jewish relations, which arise within all of these research projects.

For the reader who might be interested in additional projects on Romans in particular, there are a few to mention that are not included in this volume. I wrote the introduction and annotations for "Romans" in *The Jewish Annotated New Testament*.[3] Those comments and notes provide a good survey of my reading of the letter overall. Two other studies are included in

---

3. "Romans" in *The Jewish Annotated New Testament*, rev. ed., edited by Marc Brettler and Amy Jill Levine, 285–320 (Oxford: Oxford University Press, 2017). Note also the first edition in 2011, for which I did the research in 2009–10.

Volume 1 of this series of collected essays, where they serve as examples of the overall proposal for *Reading Paul within Judaism*: chapter 5 therein is entitled, "Paul's Non-Jews Do Not Become 'Jews,' But Do They Become 'Jewish'?: Reading Romans 2:25–29 within Judaism, alongside Josephus"; and chapter 6 is entitled, "Reading Paul in a Jewish Way: 'Oh be joyful all you peoples, with God's People' (Rom 15:10): Who are the people?" In addition, two planned projects on Romans are at various stages of development: one is the revision for publication of a paper presented at the 2015 Paul within Judaism session of the Annual Meeting of the Society of Biblical Literature in San Antonio, entitled "Are Jews Outside of the Covenants If Not Confessing Jesus as Messiah? Questioning the Questions, the Options for the Answers too," which includes a re-reading of the connotations of *sōzō* in Paul's argument (a topic briefly discussed in chapter 10 of this volume); the other is a commentary that the research undertaken for each of these essays brings me one step closer to being able to complete, although still a few years in the future, *To the Synagogues of Rome: A Jewish Commentary on Paul's Letter to the Romans* (Eerdmans).

Part I. A New Approach to Romans: Paul's Synagogue Correspondence

"To the Churches Within the Synagogues of Rome," the first chapter of the first section, introduces the thesis at work throughout all of the essays in this volume—namely, that Romans was Jewish correspondence, and should be read accordingly, at least that this approach should be tested for a number of probable historical reasons. The essay focuses on the elements related to the setting and audience in Rome. Paul's rhetorical approach suggests that he is targeting non-Jews who are followers of Christ, but just as importantly, that these non-Jews are gathering (with Jews) within subgroups of Christ-followers that are still under the authority of the larger Roman Jewish community and their gatherings/synagogues.

The essay was developed initially for a collection edited by Jerry Sumney, to whom I am grateful for including my contribution, thereby making readers aware of an alternative to most of the other essays in the volume. The purpose of his volume, published by the Society of Biblical Literature in 2012, was to introduce college and seminary students to recent developments in the study of Romans. The project offered me a chance to revisit the evidence some fifteen years after completing the manuscript for *The Mystery of Romans*. The annotations are minimal, so the essay herein serves the additional benefit of introducing the non-specialist to major elements of my thesis for how to read Romans within Judaism. More detailed argumentation follows in the other essays herein, especially in the chapters of the second section.

Part II. Exegetical Support for Non-Jews within the Synagogues of Rome as Paul's Target Audience

Part II opens with chapter 2 of the volume, "Some Problems with Reading Romans through the Lens of the Edict of Claudius." The essay was written in 1994 as an appendix for *The Mystery of Romans*. I also presented a paper based on this research in 1996 at the Mid-Central States Regional Meeting of the Society of Biblical Literature in St. Louis. I would like to explain why I think this matter was important, although developed to be an appendix, and why I wanted to include it here, even though it appeared in a book rather than as an independent essay.

I originally added this appendix to the monograph because I discovered, as I neared the completion of the manuscript, just how consequential a certain way of construing the evidence was becoming for defining the historical options for contemporary interpreters of Romans. I was aware of the construct, to be sure, but I had not found it compelling, and had planned to discuss a few of the shortcomings in various footnotes. But at the 1993 Annual Meeting of the Society of Biblical Literature, a chance encounter with a leading scholar on the first-century historical context for reading Romans convinced me that I had to deal with the topic in detail.

What happened? While we were both awaiting appointments with Fortress, I explained to this eminent scholar that I was completing a book for which I did not have a publisher, which was the reason I was there to seek to speak to an acquisition editor. He kindly listened as I explained that I did not have formal training in New Testament, much less Romans (I had neither a PhD nor was I enrolled, at the time, in a program toward gaining one), and that I was a businessman rather than a professor and, moreover, that I was Jewish. I enthusiastically discussed how I was working on a book proposing to read Romans as a letter written to non-Jews within subgroups of the Jewish communities of Rome, and other elements of my proposed interpretation, not least the idea to read chapter 13 to call for subordination to synagogue authorities rather than imperial ones. He graciously expressed interest all along the way in this "intriguing" approach, granted that it offered a new and interesting as well as coherent reading of the rhetoric in the letter—but he also made it clear that this approach was not viable historically. I naturally asked him, "Why?" The answer astonished me: "Because of the edict of Claudius," he replied.

I was stunned, really, to think that what had seemed to me to be merely one way to construe the evidence, one I found unconvincing, was considered *a priori* evidence against any reading that did not proceed from that construct's implications, even though that historical construal required several tenuous interpretive decisions and had only become a common refrain for constructing the setting of Romans in the previous two decades. This essay represents my response. I am pleased to report that there is a growing awareness of the tenuousness of the construction, even that some now eschew the approach as unlikely. Nevertheless, it continues to represent the most common way to set up the context for Romans among recent commentators, especially for those who argue that the churches to whom Paul wrote were already operating entirely independent of Jewish communities, which has been a characteristic of the *Christian theological* Paul addressing his *Christian gentile churches'* supposedly *theological* rather than intra-Jewish-communal-based concerns, which are then naturally reflected in the many interpretive decisions concomitant with these working hypotheses. In view of the construction's continued influence, I am grateful to Fortress for letting me reproduce it here.

The second section continues in chapter 3, an essay first published in the *Catholic Biblical Quarterly* in 1999 with the title, "The Jewish Context of the Audience Addressed in Paul's Letter to the Romans." I am grateful to the general editor, Aelred Cody, for his kind help and patience with me on this project, which was my first journal submission. Neil Elliott helped me rewrite the essay to fit the requirements of the journal, especially making a number of arguments more concisely; thank you so much, Neil, for your invaluable help and continual encouragement.

In addition to being my first published journal essay, I presented my first society paper from this research at the 1995 Southwest Regional Meeting of the Society of Biblical Literature in Dallas, which I entitled, "It Takes Real Jews to Make Real Sense of Romans." I developed the paper before *The Mystery of Romans* was published, but after the manuscript was completed, in order to explain how I conceptualized the basic situational context that Paul sought to address in Romans. I had not known about this scholarly society until well into the research for the book, and I was interested in discussing my thesis with students and specialists.

It seemed logical to me when writing this essay, and still does, that to make sense of Paul's concerns and aims requires communal interaction with Jews who were not Christ-followers. Otherwise, how could Paul have expected those Jews to be influenced positively toward the gospel (not least, to want to emulate Paul's ministry to the nations; see 11:13)? The prevailing church-separate-from-the-synagogue scenarios did not account adequately for Paul's expectations; they still don't. How could Paul expect Jews to be in a position to witness behavioral changes among non-Jews, and all the more to be expected to interpret these as expressions of righteousness according to their own Jewish communal norms, if they would learn of them only second-hand, and thus likely through negatively fashioned rumors about groups that had separated from their communities intentionally, even as groups that rejected Judaism? Paul's expectations are even harder to understand if Paul's recipients represented "gentile churches" that existed precisely because the Jews had been expelled from Rome over conflicts about the meaning of Jesus, which is required by the edict of Claudius constructions (as discussed in the previous chapter).

For chapter 4, which completes Part II, I updated a rejoinder initially written in 2000 to respond to an essay by Robert Gagnon published earlier that year in *Catholic Biblical Quarterly*. Gagnon argued against the case I made in *The Mystery or Romans* for the identity of the so-called "weak" of Romans 14–15. The rejoinder I submitted to *CBQ* was entitled, "A Rejoinder to Robert A. J. Gagnon's 'Why the "Weak" at Rome Cannot Be Non-Christian Jews,'" which remains the title for this slightly updated version.

I hoped that *CBQ* would publish my rejoinder, but they declined to do so, stating that I already had made my arguments in the monograph. I maintained that the publication of my rejoinder was warranted for several reasons: a) Gagnon challenged specific arguments that I raised, to which I wanted to respond; b) he introduced new proposals that should be addressed through further discussion; c) the way he set up his criticisms often misrepresented my arguments, even if sometimes only in the sense of choosing certain elements that he wished to critique, which can make an enormous difference for anyone who might read his essay but not my book; d) along the same line, many of Gagnon's challenges actually constituted informal, and sometimes even formal, fallacies rather than an appropriate engagement of the elements in my arguments; and e) one could easily reason that in the future those who wished to proceed without engaging my arguments would likely find grounds to do so by simply appealing to Gagnon's essay; that likely would shut down discussion rather than facilitate it, which a rejoinder published in the same journal might help to avoid. Indeed, that predictable outcome can now be observed in the footnotes of those wishing to dismiss my reading of the evidence. They frequently appeal to Gagnon's essay without engaging my arguments, often seemingly without bothering to even read them (a conclusion reached based on the fact that they repeat his misrepresentations and other fallacies). The rejoinder has the added benefit of also offering a response to others who have critically engaged certain elements in my arguments as well, whether in reviews of the monograph or in discussions of the relevant topics, which usually have offered the same objections raised by Gagnon, and also often similarly proceed as if I had not already anticipated and argued for alternative ways to understand these textual details, albeit from a different overall perspective on Paul, his audiences, and the message of the letter.

When I developed a web page with some of my papers in 2003, I updated the essay slightly and made it available there. For this volume, I have updated the essay yet again, primarily to reflect my current terminological preferences. I believe that this rejoinder strengthens the case for which I argued; the final judgment, naturally, remains yours to make.

Part III. A New Exegetical Approach to Romans 9–11 and Christian-Jewish Relations

Chapter 5 was initially written in the spring of 2009 in response to an invitation to explain the implications of my reading of Romans 9–11 for Christian-Jewish relations in *Paulus: An International Magazine on Saint Paul*, an Italian-language magazine published by Società San Paolo for non-specialist Catholics. This was one of several welcome opportunities to present my views on Paul from a Jewish perspective that arose from Pope Benedict XVI's declaration of 2009 as a Celebration of the Year of St. Paul (see also chapters 4 and 7 in volume 1 of this series of collected essays).

I submitted the English manuscript under the title, "Romans 9–11 from a Jewish Perspective on Christian-Jewish Relations," which I have retained for this chapter; the Italian title was modified to, "Le relazioni cristiano-giudaiche: Il punto di vista ebraico," and published in June of 2009. I made the original English version available on my website. By the time this was written, I had made several of the discoveries about Paul's argument in Romans 11 that are discussed in detail in the next two chapters. A few adjustments were made for this chapter, primarily to conform to my current terminological preferences. Although the essay targets non-specialist readers, and more specifically Catholic readers, clergy as well as laity, I trust it will be of interest to other readers, since it summarizes some of the major elements of my reading, and because it offers new, more promising ways to enlist Paul's voice for Christian-Jewish relations that might help reverse the inhibitive role his voice has played as traditionally interpreted. I am grateful to Daniela D'Andrea, who was my contact throughout the process, and to my colleague at the time at Rockhurst University, Daniel Stramara, who looked over the translation and made several suggestions. I regret that I do not know the name of the translator, to thank him or her personally, and it appears that the magazine is no longer published.

The essay in chapter 6, begun as a paper in 2008 and revised in 2009 for the subsequent conference volume, represents a major new stage of my research on Romans, especially for chapter 11, since after completing the manuscript for *The Mystery of Romans* in 1994 I primarily turned to investigations of Paul's other letters. The research agenda arose in part from puzzling over a startling disconnect in Paul's argument as usually translated and interpreted, including in my own earlier work, which became especially striking when reading the usual terminology in student papers that were otherwise exploring a more promising way to read the text. I especially puzzled over the translations of Paul's metaphorical identification in chapter 11 of branches *broken off*, which, if connoting the fate of Paul's fellow Jews, undermines the metaphorical point he had just made, having emphatically insisted that while some had stumbled, they had *not fallen*. But branches broken or cut *off* corresponds to affirming that they have *fallen*. Moreover, in the midst of the allegory of the tree Paul seems to mix the metaphors by mentioning that some who had *fallen* could be grafted *back in*. And similarly, as the next chapter herein discusses in detail, to state that those who are stumbling or broken are *hardened* is also jarringly inconsistent. Have we mistranslated something here, or has Paul contradicted himself within a few sentences? "'Broken Branches': A Pauline Metaphor Gone Awry? (Romans 11:11–24)," which constitutes a major reinvestigation of this language since writing *The Mystery of Romans*, explores these questions and related topics in conjunction with the research in the next chapter.

I commenced this project in response to the welcome invitation of Ross Wagner and Florian Wilk to present a paper at an International Symposium in Göttingen, Germany, entitled, "Romans 9–11 at the Interface between the 'New Perspective on Paul' and Jewish-Christian Dialog," in May of 2008. The symposium brought together exegetes and theologians to present and discuss papers that systematically analyzed the flow of the arguments in these three chapters of Paul's letter. I enjoyed meeting and engaging in discussion with many scholars from many different countries holding many different views on Paul and how to best understand his arguments in these passages. As a Jewish exegete of Paul, the opportunity to present my research in dialogue with German scholarship was especially gratifying. I continually find that many people of good will want to find new, more promising ways to understand Paul's texts where the topics of Jews and Judaism arise. The revised papers were published as a conference volume in 2010. During the time I was updating the paper for that volume,

I also presented the research to my peers in the Ancient Jewish-Christian Relations section of the Society of Biblical Literature at the Annual Meeting in New Orleans in November 2009.

The next few chapters are extensions of the insights associated with the research for the olive tree allegory, which became much more comprehensive than I could complete for the original venue (I was, in fact, still in the process of discovering potential options to investigate when the symposium convened). For example, the research into ancient oleicultural practices relevant to decoding this allegory could constitute a project of its own, which I had not anticipated. Although this chapter and others related to the olive tree in particular focus on the language in Romans 11, as you will see in subsequent chapters, these new insights have led me to reconsider the arguments of chapters 9 and 10 as well as several others throughout the letter (for some of the results to date, not least for 9:6, see chapters 5 and 10 in this volume, and chapter 6 in volume 1 of this series, as well as my annotations for "Romans" in *The Jewish Annotated New Testament*).

As the title of chapter 7 signals, "'Callused,' Not 'Hardened': Paul's Revelation of Temporary Protection until All Israel Can Be Healed," continues the investigation of metaphors drawing on the olive tree. If Paul was seeking to communicate the present status of branches in terms of being injured—*bent* or *cracked*, or more likely, *bent aside* to provide some room to make a graft, rather than detached (as in *broken off*)—then it occurred to me that the more natural way to read the terminology usually translated and interpreted in terms of *hardening* would be in terms of a *callus* that forms on an injured tree branch, or limb of a body. A callus is hard, to be sure, but in a different sense than hardened has been used to connote here. A plant forms a callus, after all, to preserve the health of an injured branch, but also the health of the entire tree, which brings both a positive valence to the imagery, and a corporate focus, which is otherwise central to the allegory Paul had developed around the olive tree metaphor, and the stumbling metaphor too. The opportunity to complete this essay commenced with the welcome invitation by Kathy Ehrensperger and Brian Tucker to contribute to a Festschrift they edited for a dear friend, William S. Campbell. This seemed like the perfect opportunity to explore this idea in Romans 11, since Bill has been a leading figure in the effort to reconsider Paul's texts, especially Romans, in ways that challenge prevailing Paul-against-Judaism paradigms. In fact, after reading a draft of parts of the manuscript for *Mystery of Romans* in 1994, Bill had invited me to teach university courses to his students in Birmingham, England, in order to expose them to my perspective, and he has inspired and encouraged me in the years since. The initial work on this essay overlapped with the completion of the revisions for the essay focused on "Broken Branches," which not only helped me anticipate the outcomes for this project, but also helped me to think through the implications for both essays, and others. I presented a paper based upon this research to my peers at the 2010 Central States Regional Meeting of the Society of Biblical Literature.

Chapter 8 was originally written for the *Criswell Theological Review*, in response to the welcome invitation by the editor Alan Streett to contribute to a 2012 issue that would focus on Jewish studies. This afforded the opportunity to bring together the more detailed research on the olive tree allegory and related matters into a more concise essay, as well as to articulate more of the implications for Christian-Jewish relations. Addressing the target audience for this journal also offered a new opportunity to present this research to evangelical readers.

I developed several lectures in the general direction of the arguments in the essay prior to completing it: especially notable were the King Lecture at Washburn University in Topeka, Kansas, in April of 2010, by the welcome invitation of Barry Crawford, entitled, "Images of Jews and Judaism in Paul's Letter to the Romans: Challenging Translation Decisions That Subvert Paul's Message"; and the inaugural lecture for the MJTI Center for Jewish-Christians Relations at the Skirball Cultural Center in Los Angeles in October of 2010, by the welcome invitation of Mark Kinzer, entitled, "Paul, Judaism, and Christian-Jewish Relations: Revisiting the Evidence from Romans." I developed this information in yet another direction for a conference at Baylor in April 2011, discussed below for chapter 9. The challenge to pull these various research elements together for various audiences continued after the essay was completed. These reflections formed the basis for several lectures and seminars at Lutheran Theological Seminary of Hong Kong in 2013, thanks to the invitation by Simon Chow and Dieter Mitternacht, the latter serving also as my host for several days of adventure. In October of 2013, John Pawlikowski kindly invited me to give the Shapiro Lecture at the Catholic Theological Union, which was entitled, "Translating Paul in the Light of *Nostra Aetate*." I have presented versions adapted to various audiences in the years since, mostly at university settings, including Azuza Pacific, Pepperdine, Westmont, and Lund, for which I am grateful to each of the hosts and institutions.

Excerpts from this *Criswell* essay were also translated into German by Volker Haarmann for a booklet developed for German Evangelical Lutheran pastors preparing sermons for the 2014 lectionary reading of this text from Romans 11. The translation was entitled, "Römer 11 und christlich-jüdische Beziehungen: Exegetische Optionen für eine andere Übersetzung und Interpretation des Textes," published as pages 18–25 in

"*So wird ganz Israel gerettet werden*": *Arbeitshilfe zum Israelsonntag 2014: 10. Sonntag nach Trinitatis*.[4] I am very grateful to Volker for undertaking this task, and to Alan for the permission to reuse the elements from the essay in translation. That German as well as English-speaking evangelical pastors would be informing their congregations to think and talk about Paul's reflections on Jews and Judaism in the ways that I propose to be more historically probable and more hermeneutically respectful is a special honor that brings me great pleasure.

Chapter 9, "The Translation of Romans 11 Since the Shoah: What's Different? What's Not? What Could Be?" reflects on the way that Romans 11 is accessed by most English readers fifty-plus years after Vatican II's *Nostra Aetate* 4 appealed to this text to reorient the way it envisaged and communicated the Catholic Church's relationship to Jews and Judaism following the Holocaust. The essay was published in the centennial festschrift of the Lutheran Theological Seminary of Hong Kong, based on the lecture there in October of 2012. I am grateful especially to Dieter Mitternacht for the opportunity to present this research in Hong Kong, and its inclusion in their centennial volume. An earlier, exploratory version of this paper was developed for a seminar entitled "Paul, Jewishness, and Otherness after the Holocaust" at Baylor University in April, 2011; I am grateful to Todd Penner and Davina Lopez for including me in that useful program, which prompted me to try to sort out the hows and whys of the present conundrum. What conundrum?

When researching the texts and secondary sources on Romans 11, I was surprised and dismayed to discover that English translations, and also those into other languages that I consulted, not to mention most interpretations of them, had not changed to reflect the new sensibilities that were being expressed about Jews and Judaism in *Nostra Aetate* 4 and similar official statements by other Christian organizations. Those who heard or read more promising ways for Christians to talk about the Jewish people and their religious practices would find it difficult to retrace these arguments directly when they consulted the texts in Romans 11 in their native languages, whether to reflect upon them or share them with others. In fact, even more troubling, I discovered that the translations for some phrases and verses had become even more incompatible with the new sensibilities: for example, the NRSV, widely heralded as the translation of choice for university courses and mainline Christians, had introduced a new level

---

4. Edited by Hanna Lehming, Volker Haarmann, and Ursula Rudnick (Hannover/Düsseldorf: Evangelisch-Lutherische Landeskirche Hannover, Evangelische Kirche im Rheinland, Evangelisch-Lutherische Kirche in Norddeutschland, Begegnung von Christen und Juden Bayern, 2014).

of replacement theology ("in their place" for "among them" in v. 17) in direct contradiction of the Greek phrasing, and added a phrase expressing opposition to God that is unattested in any Greek manuscripts ("enemies *of God* for your sake" for "enemies [better, 'estranged'] for your sake" in v. 28). This is a counter-intuitive development *in our time*, to say the least; this essay reflects an attempt both to understand why that might be the case, and to call attention to the more promising alternatives detailed in the previous chapters (and demonstrated in the Appendix) in the hope that future translation committees will reconsider new ways to capture Paul's more probable and more promising message.

Chapter 10 reflects research begun in late 2015, in response to Volker Haarmann's request whether I might have research he could translate for a chapter in the handbook he was editing for German Evangelical Lutheran pastors to consult when preparing sermons for the 2016 lectionary reading of Romans 9:1-16 (cf. chapter 8, for an earlier example). I did not (at the time), but I concluded that this would be a very useful exegetical project to pursue. I am pleased to say that I discovered several new translation and interpretive alternatives that help make Paul's arguments in Romans 9 much more continuous with those in Romans 11, as I had come to understand the latter, and completed the research and manuscript for him in early 2016. This research was undertaken immediately after I developed a paper for the "Paul within Judaism" Session of the Society of Biblical Literature Annual Meeting in Atlanta, Nov. 23, 2015, entitled, "Are Jews Outside of the Covenants if Not Confessing Jesus as Messiah?: Questioning the Questions, the Options for the Answers too," so it offers the reader the reasoning for my recent change of mind about how to best translate and understand the phrasing in 11:26 that is usually translated "all Israel will be saved," which I had suggested (as attested in several of the essays herein) be translated to indicate "restored" or "rescued," but now realized is better translated "protected" or "kept/made safe," in keeping not only with the usual meaning of *sōzō*, but also the thrust of Paul's argument. I hope to complete a publication on this topic, but this essay offers an introduction to the insight, even though the focus is the translation of Romans 9:1-16. Volker's translation was entitled, "'Gottes Gaben und Berufungen können Ihn nicht gereuen.'— Wie, also, sollten wir Römer 9,1-16 (insbesondere V. 6) übersetzen und verstehen?," and was published as pages 14-23 in *"Die Gotteskindschaft des jüdischen Volkes (Röm 9,1-16)": Arbeitshilfe zum Israelsonntag 2016: 10. Sonntag nach Trinitatis.*[5] I am grateful to Volker for his careful translation,

---

5. Edited by Volker Haarmann, Ursula Rudnick, and Axel Töllner (Düsseldorf/Hannover: Evangelische Kirche im Rheinland, Evangelisch-Lutherische Landeskirche Hannover, Begegnung von Christen und Juden Bayern, 2016).

and to Ginny Miller and Dieter Mitternacht for helping me proof it. Afterwards, I submitted an expanded version of the English manuscript to the *Studies in Christian-Jewish Relations (SCJR)* for peer review in 2016. The essay was published as, "'The Gifts and the Calling of God are Irrevocable' (Romans 11:29): If So, How Can Paul Declare That 'Not All Israelites Truly Belong to Israel' (9:6)?" I dedicated this version to Lloyd Gaston, who pioneered the idea that Paul's language indicates his concern that Israel carry out the mission of bringing the gospel to the nations.

Part IV: Special Occasions

The essay for chapter 11 represents the revision of a paper originally composed to respond to papers by William S. Campbell and Guenter Wasserberg for the Interpretation of Romans section of the 1998 Society of Biblical Literature Annual Meeting in Orlando. Although their papers are not presented here, they are readily available in the same edited volume in which mine first appeared, and my response includes discussions of their arguments, with some citations from their papers. In addition to discussing the superb cases they presented, from which I learned much, I ventured several interpretations as well. One of my interests was to offer a new way to think about the hermeneutical question of what Paul would likely think and say today about Jews and Judaism in light of the logic at work in his arguments in Romans 9–11 for his own time, since things did not turn out as he supposed, at least according to the way that I read him. Following my original paper presentation, I was deeply honored to have Krister Stendahl discuss with those in attendance that he found my presentation of the solution both clear and convincing, one that he could draw on to explain his own perspective, which had been largely misunderstood. He wanted to disassociate his view from the paradigm that had come to be known as the two-covenant or *Sonderweg* perspective, although he had been regularly counted among its proponents because of his positive, respectful statements about Jews who were not Christians in a way that challenged the traditional Lutheran discourse. Oddly, I have experienced a similar misrepresentation of my position.

There are three elements from the original essay's context that are not represented in the chapter in this volume. First of all, as already noted, one should read the essays of those to whom I responded on their own terms, which is not possible herein. Secondly, Daniel Patte offered a post-Holocaust biblical critique to each of these essays as a co-editor of the conference volume, which offers many rich insights that can only be accessed by reading his response essay. Thirdly, this chapter does not include the sophisticated notes that the editors, Daniel Patte and Cristina Grenholm, added in the margins to each of our essays to call attention to the analytical, contextual, and hermeneutical frameworks of our arguments.

Chapter 12, the final essay in this volume, is entitled "Implications of Paul's Hopes for the End of Days for Jews and Christians Today: A Critical Re-evaluation of the Evidence." This essay was written jointly with Philip Cunningham, a Catholic theologian and professor at Saint Joseph's University who specializes in Christian-Jewish relations, indeed, who was the President of the International Council of Christians and Jews while we were collaborating on this project, which commemorates the fiftieth anniversary of *Nostra Aetate* 4. Phil and I had been discussing a shared concern about certain elements of eschatological reasoning that we regularly encountered: in his case, in response to Catholic statements about the fate of Jews and Judaism; in my case, in exegetical as well as hermeneutical observations on the same topics among Pauline scholars, especially when dealing with Romans 9–11. We shared compatible sensibilities about what was problematic yet often seemed to us to go unrecognized, as well as common ground for offering new ways to conceptualize the issues and alternatives to consider. I enjoyed working with Phil on this project, to whom I am grateful for permission to reproduce the essay.

Appendix: Translating Romans 11:11—12:1a within Judaism: Literal-Oriented and Expanded Versions

The appendix was written after completing the rest of the work for this volume in order to present a translation of Romans 11 that reflects the exegetical details and sensibilities for which the various chapters have argued. The basic elements were initially developed to offer a handout for the various papers and lectures associated with chapters 6 through 9 in this volume, and modified over the years as I made new discoveries. The handouts included the NRSV translation followed by literal translation alternatives and clarifying comments in brackets. For this venue, the NRSV has not been included; instead, the reader can evaluate this translation on its own terms and compare it to any other on offer. In addition to the literal-oriented translation, which is offered alongside the Greek text as arranged by the translation committee for the Nestle-Aland 28th edition, a second, expanded version offers additional interpretive comments and paraphrases. I am grateful to Neil Elliott and Paula Fredriksen for helpful, last minute reviews of the proposed translation(s). The task remains a work in progress; as new discoveries are made, I will no doubt continue to revise the translation as well as my understanding of Paul's argument here and throughout the letter. Again, I welcome your feedback.

A WORD ABOUT THE COVER IMAGE

Vincent van Gogh, *Olivenhain* (Olive Orchard), June 1889; Kröller-Müller Museum, Otterlo, Netherlands (F585). The National Gallery of Art webpage offers the following commentary about the series of olive tree paintings van Gogh completed in 1889: "In the olive trees—in the expressive power of their ancient and gnarled forms—Van Gogh found a manifestation of the spiritual force he believed resided in all of nature. . . . These strong individual dashes do not seem painted so much as drawn onto the canvas with a heavily loaded brush. The energy in their continuous rhythm communicates to us, in an almost physical way, the living force that Van Gogh found within the trees themselves, the very spiritual force that he believed had shaped them."

Paul also drew attention to the forces at work in the tree, not least that the root nourishes the branches, not the other way around, and that it is more natural to successfully nourish natural branches than a grafted wild shoot; moreover, that the tree creates a callus to protect injured natural branches so that they can still produce fruit. Paul called attention to these dynamics to confront the potential emergence of arrogant suppositions among Christ-following non-Jews toward Jews who did not share their convictions about Jesus: they were to see themselves as precariously placed among the recipients of God's favor in a divine scheme that was far more inclusive than it might presently seem to them to be. Ironically, however, Paul's allegorical appeal to the olive tree in Romans 11 has had a profound influence on Christian theological formulations that subvert the thrust of Paul's call to humility and compassionate concern for the suffering other, and, in addition, do so by way of appeal to this imagery as if not requiring decoding out of the language used to describe trees when seeking to describe human communal affiliations, thereby exemplifying what literary theorists call a "dead metaphor." We thus hear the common refrain, including in otherwise formal theological discourses, that "gentiles are grafted into Israel," even though people are not grafted into communities, and in spite of the fact that Paul never calls the tree Israel as well as insisting that those from the other nations remain non-Israelites (to not complete the ethnic transformation rites signified by male circumcision); moreover, Paul analogizes the Israelites to branches, some broken (bent aside), and indicates that the (singular) non-Jew Christ-follower wild shoot takes its place "among them," not, as the NRSV's replacement-theology loaded brush stroke shapes the phrase, "in their place." The imagery is gnarled—dare I say gnarly; so too is its reception history.

EDITORIAL NOTES

The reader will encounter numbers in brackets ("[oo]") in the text of each article. These indicate the page numbers in the original publication of the essay.

Other essays included as chapters in this volume are indicated in the bibliographic information listed for them at the end of each chapter. For example "(See chapter x in this volume of collected essays)" or "(See volume x in this series of collected essays)."

ACKNOWLEDGEMENTS

Having recounted how my research interest in Paul began with texts from Romans, and that the letter continues to be a central element of my research agenda to this day, it follows that there are many to thank along the way in addition to the few I have noted specifically: for all of you who have been a part of this journey—thank you! I want to express once again a special thanks to my editor at Cascade, Robin Parry, and to my wife, Vicky, for helping me proof this manuscript, and for discussing and reading countless versions of each of these projects all along the way. I can only wonder if I would have ever been able to undertake this journey if not for the model of inter-faith dialogue I learned from my primary undergraduate Judaic studies professor, Joseph P. Schultz, to whom I am indebted not only for the inspiration to ask hard questions and respect the other's intentions, but also for the advice to pursue the course of the gentleman-scholar in rabbinic tradition, which would allow me the freedom to challenge the consensus views; thank you for the gift of wisdom you have given to so many of us who had the privilege of studying with you.

This volume *is dedicated to Lela*, my second granddaughter, an observant, caring person already at ten. Lela loves to read, although admittedly not books of this kind (yet?). These essays represent my feeble but sincere effort to contribute to a way of being in the world that seems to come naturally to Lela: empathy for the other, accompanied by action on their behalf. Thank you for the example you set.

I am finishing this manuscript in Carpinteria while a visiting scholar at the University of California, Santa Barbara, an area that has just suffered the worst fire recorded in the state, followed by devastating mudslides, especially in neighboring Montecito, for whom we hope for relief and recovery soon. As I reflect on their present plight, I find the empathetic logic at work in Paul's Jewish message to the non-Jews addressed in Rome about his fellow Jews instructive, at least as I read him, *mutatis mutandis*: due to the precariousness of life it is wise to enjoy the successes, accept the defeats, and always live graciously toward the other, whose present state may involve suffering far beyond that which we realize. Moreover, regardless of the reality or the extent of the other's suffering—past, present, or future—we should always seek to enable the same success (i.e., blessing) for everyone else that we wish for ourselves and our own, all the more if claiming them as gifts from the Divine.

Mark D. Nanos, February 13, 2018

Permissions

"To the Churches within the Synagogues of Rome." In *Reading Paul's Letter to the Romans*, edited by Jerry L. Sumney, 11–28. Resources for Biblical Studies Series 72. Atlanta: Society of Biblical Literature, 2012.

"Some Problems with Reading Romans through the Lens of the Edict of Claudius." In *The Mystery of Romans: The Jewish Context of Paul's Letter*, Appendix 2. Minneapolis: Fortress, 1996.

"The Jewish Context of the Gentile Audience Addressed in Paul's Letter to the Romans." *Catholic Biblical Quarterly* 61 (1999) 283–304.

"Romans 9–11 from a Jewish Perspective on Christian-Jewish Relations." Published in Italian as "Le relazioni christiano-giudaiche: Il punto di vista ebraico." *Paulus: An International Magazine on Saint Paul* 1.12 (2009) 271–73.

"'Broken Branches': A Pauline Metaphor Gone Awry? (Romans 11:11–24)." In *Between Gospel and Election: Explorations in the Interpretation of Romans 9–11*, edited by Florian Wilk and J. Ross Wagner, 339–76. Tübingen: Mohr Siebeck, 2010.

"'Callused,' Not 'Hardened': Paul's Revelation of Temporary Protection until All Israel Can Be Healed." In *Reading Paul in Context: Explorations in Identity Formation*, edited by Kathy Ehrensperger and J. Brian Tucker, 52–73. London: T. & T. Clark, 2010.

"Romans 11 and Christian-Jewish Relations: Exegetical Options for Revisiting the Translation and Interpretation of This Central Text." *Criswell Theological Review* N.S. 9.2 (2012) 3–21.

"The Translation of Romans 11 Since the Shoah: What's Different? What's Not? What Could Be?" In *Exploring Bible, Church and Life: Essays in Celebration of the 100th Anniversary of Lutheran Theological Seminary*, edited by Dieter Mitternacht and Nicholas Thai, 167–77. Theology and Life 36. Hong Kong: Lutheran Theological Seminary, 2013.

"'The Gifts and the Calling of God are Irrevocable' (Romans 11:29): If So, How Can Paul Declare that 'Not All Israelites Truly Belong to Israel' (9:6)?" *Studies in Christian-Jewish Relations* 11.1 (2016) 1–17; http://ejournals.bc.edu/ojs/index.php/scjr/article/view/9525.

"Challenging the Limits That Continue to Define Paul's Perspective on Jews and Judaism." In *Reading Israel in Romans: Legitimacy and Plausibility of Divergent Interpretations. Vol. 1: "Romans through History and Cultures: Receptions and Critical Interpretations,"* edited by Cristina Grenholm and Daniel Patte, 212–24. Harrisburg, PA: Trinity, 2000.

"Implications of Paul's Hopes for the End of Days for Jews and Christians Today: A Critical Re-evaluation of the Evidence." Co-authored with Philip Cunningham. *Studies in Christian-Jewish Relations* 9.1 (2014) 1–45; http://ejournals.bc.edu/ojs/index.php/scjr/article/view/5793/5165.

PART I

A New Approach to Romans

Paul's Synagogue Correspondence

1

To the Churches within the Synagogues of Rome

[11] PAUL DID NOT use the label "Christian" in his letters, and it is widely recognized that in Paul's time "Christianity" did not exist in a formal, institutional sense. Instead, Christ-followers were still identifying themselves in Israelite/Jewish terms based on covenant affiliation with the one God who created a people from Abraham's descendants. Those who shared Paul's commitment to Christ were addressed and discussed, in terms of ethnicity, as Jews or non-Jews/Greeks, Israelites or members from the other "nations" (*ethnē*, usually translated "gentiles"),[1] circumcised or foreskinned, and so on.

In spite of the common recognition of such historical factors, for the most part Romans continues to be discussed as if it represents a time when Christianity, however labeled, is understood to have been something other than Judaism, and Christians to have been something other than Jews. On this reading, Jews who became Christians no longer hold their identity as Jews to be of covenantal value (the Mosaic covenant having been fulfilled and thus made obsolete). In other words, they are no longer Jews religiously, even if they remained ethnically Jews because of birth. If some Christ-following Jews "also" attended Jewish communal meetings (i.e., "synagogues"), these are separate from attending Christ-followers' meetings

---

1. We derive ethnic and ethnicity from *ethnē*, which translates as "peoples" or "nations" (i.e., "members from the nations" other than Israel); it can refer to members of the nation of Israel too.

(i.e., "churches"): Christians and Jews represented separate group identities; they met separately and they upheld different foundational norms.

[12] The traditional position is generally presented in binary (this or that) theological terms, thus Christ *or* Torah (often labeled "law"),[2] concluding that Christ replaced Torah, making the latter obsolete for guiding life among Christ-followers—or that is how it should be (i.e., traditionally "Paulinism" is defined as a "law-free gospel").[3] Within a few centuries, no Christians—even (former) Jews who "converted"—were permitted to attend Jewish meetings or practice Jewish rites or ways of life[4] and this was apparently the view of some (although by no means all) Christ-following non-Jews already in the early second century (e.g., Ignatius of Antioch).[5]

Following from these premises, the primary problems Paul addressed in Rome are understood to have arisen from the failure of some Christ-followers to respect this change of eons and to live "free of Torah" and Jewish identity (as most interpreters understand the "weak" in Rom 14), or alternatively, from the misguided teaching of those who promoted Torah and Jewish identity alongside of commitment to Christ. Secondarily, however, Paul called for his audience to avoid offending any "weak" Christ-following Jews (and perhaps "Judaized" non-Jews), and also not to think that God had rejected those Jews who did not (yet) share their commitment to Christ.

Those traditional ways of approaching Paul as well as Romans are easily challenged. I propose that Paul and his communities—including the community he did not found but wrote to in Rome—were *subgroups* of the Jewish communities that believed Jesus represented the dawning of the awaited age.[6] The Jews in these subgroups, Paul included, observed [13] the covenantal obligations of Torah, for they were Jews involved in a fully Jewish movement.[7] They argued that the awaited-age gift of the Holy Spirit now

---

2. "Torah" is a Hebrew word that denotes "teaching" rather than simply "law," including laws/commandments but also many other teachings, stories, warnings, consolations, etc. For Paul, "Torah" is not the opposite of "love" or "freedom" but embodies "teaching" about important values, including "commandments" that clarify how those whom God has "freed" from Egypt, from sin, and so on, are to treat ("love") others.

3. Nanos, "The Myth of the 'Law-Free' Paul Standing between Christians and Jews."

4. Second Council of Nicea, Canon 8; see Parkes, *The Conflict of the Church and the Synagogue*, 394–400.

5. See Ignatius, *Phld.* 6.1 for the first extant reference to "Christianity *[Christianismos]*" as a religious system, apparently coined to set it out in antithesis to "Judaism *[Ioudaismos]*" (see also Ign., *Magn.* 9.1).

6. See Nanos, *The Mystery of Romans*.

7. See Tacitus, *Ann.* 15.44. Ambrosiaster in the fourth century, in his commentary *Ad Romanos* (ed. H. J. Vogels; CSEL 81:1), described the earliest Christ-followers in Rome being taught to keep Torah by Christ-following Jews.

enabled them to practice their commitment to the God of Israel according to the highest ideals of Torah. The non-Jews who joined them did not become Jews and were thus not under the Mosaic legislation (Torah) on the same terms as Jews; however, they were committed to lives of righteousness defined in Jewish communal terms and thus by Torah, for they met in Jewish groups—and thus according to the Jewish norms for these groups—and were enabled by the same Spirit of God.

Those in the Jewish community who did not appreciate non-Jews claiming full identity and rights within the Jewish community apart from proselyte conversion, a tradition providing inclusiveness, might react with confusion and disapproval. If such identity claims continued, such "guests" and Jews advocating such policies would likely be deemed dangerous and subject to discipline. Reactions along that line might stem from a desire to protect divinely commanded covenantal norms, including circumcision. Sociopolitical concerns would also arise, including fear that the community's rights would be compromised, resulting in punishment and perhaps elimination of these rights. In addition, consideration must be given to the simple cultural observation that in antiquity one's identity in a community was more central to one's sense of self than the cultural norms shaping post-Enlightenment notions of self. Complicated? Yes, but Paul's letters indicate just such complexities existed for these non-Jews in terms of how to negotiate Jewish communal identity while remaining non-Jews, rather than that they were experiencing the kind of already fully "gentilized," separated communities and values usually championed in Paul's name.[8]

[14] What happens if we read Romans anew based on the proposition that the audience to which Paul addressed the letter met together as

---

8. By way of analogy, consider the dynamics likely to arise if some small group within the Amish community began to teach non-Amish neighbors that they could avoid military service if they but attended Amish meetings without actually becoming Amish. Non-Amish neighbors who believed this would eventually find that this proposition was controversial. Amish leaders, upon learning of it, would likely seek to stop this breach of policy, for it posed a threat to their rights if they did not maintain compliance with the government's definition of who was Amish and thus entitled to avoid service, and it undermined communal identity standards. At the same time, the non-Amish boy seeking this right would be challenged by his family, friends, and civic leaders, for unpatriotic, misguided, and dangerous behavior. The Amish subgroup leader upholding this deviant policy, like Paul, would teach him to hold fast in the face of social pressure. How this would unfold in different local contexts would of course be different, yet certain developments would likely be common. Similarly, these are the kinds of complexity that I propose were faced by the non-Jews within the Christ-following Jewish subgroups. In his letters we see Paul's responses to those who have been persuaded by him and others to uphold a social identity that deviates from the prevailing Jewish and non-Jewish communal norms.

subgroups of the larger Jewish community (or communities) of Rome? Do features of Paul's letter make better sense when approached from this contextual vantage point? Besides avoiding the disapproval and dismissal of the value of Judaism, what might be at risk for Christian identity and guidance? In this essay, we can only begin to explore why this approach is compelling. It is my opinion, granted, as a Jew and outsider, that in addition to the concern for historical probability being served, there are theological and spiritual gains for Christians when they are no longer tied to the negative binary (either/or) categories traditionally posed in terms such as Christians *or* Jews, Christianity *or* Judaism, Christ *or* Torah, freedom *or* obligation, grace *or* responsibility, faith *or* works (deeds/actions), moral *or* ritual, spiritual *or* physical, and so on. In keeping with Paul's own arguments, these categories are more realistically approached in this-*and*-that rather than this-*or*-that terms. Paul's beliefs and actions (his concepts of faithfulness to Torah and Christ) were not conceptualized in a Christianity *or* Judaism framework. Rather, for Paul and those under his influence, surprising though it may seem, being a Christ-follower was the ideal way to live out *Judaism* in the awaited age-to-come, which they believed had begun.

THE HISTORICAL CONTEXT

Despite our wealth of information about Rome in the mid-first century C.E., surprisingly little is known about the Jewish communities there, and outside of Romans and Acts of the Apostles, which can be variously interpreted, nothing is known about relationships between the Jewish communities and Christ-followers there. Nevertheless, there are several topics to discuss.

[15] There is no evidence of any buildings from the time used for meetings of Jews or Christ-followers. There is no reason to suppose that Paul's use of the term "gatherings/churches" (*ekklēsia*) distinguishes his group from any other Jewish subgroup or its gatherings, which could equally be referred to as *ekklēsia*. The terms community, meeting, gathering, and assembly were general terms, just as they are today. Only later did "church/*ekklēsia*" come to refer specifically to Christian gatherings and buildings, while "synagogue/*synagōgē*" referred to Jewish gatherings and buildings.[9]

Paul appears to use *ekklēsia* not, as often claimed, to distinguish his groups from *synagōgē*, but rather to signify their identity as subgroups "meeting" specifically *within* the larger Jewish communities. The point

---

9. In general, non-Jews used *synagōgē* to refer to any kind of gathering together, including of animals, and *ekklēsia* was used to refer to many different kinds of gatherings, most formally to indicate the assembling of the citizens of a city to cast votes as equals.

was not to indicate a rival movement, but to indicate that these gatherings demonstrated that Christ had begun the restoration of Israel and the reconciliation of the nations already in the midst of the present age, as promised in Scripture. Interestingly, Paul does not use the term *ekklēsia* in Romans to refer to the overall community but only to one specific "gathering" in the house of Prisca and Aquila (16:3–5); almost certainly there were other gatherings in other locations.

Paul addressed households where meetings took place, and households were also the likely venue for many meetings among Jews. Of the few synagogue buildings that are dated to Paul's time or before, there are none in Italy.[10] There may have been some buildings in Rome, even large ones, that were referred to as *proseuchē* or *synagōgē*, but there is no evidence of it. Even if there were several large public structures, there were likely hundreds more small meetings to facilitate reading and discussing Scripture, worship and prayer, celebrating Sabbaths and other holidays, and other mutual interests and causes as well as social life in general.

In addition, the Jewish community of Rome, as elsewhere, likely consisted of many independent communities or subgroups, often unaware of, if not intentionally distinct from, each other for any number of reasons. [16] These might include the distance between each other in this large city, differing interpretation and practice of Torah or level of acculturation, different cultural and ethnic backgrounds, dissimilar economic standing, and so on. Inscriptions in the catacombs of Rome suggest that there were at least eleven distinct synagogue communities by the third or fourth century C.E.; however, none of these synagogues have been dated as early as Paul's period.[11]

Similarly, Rom 16 indicates that there were already a number of small groups of Christ-followers, although only one household "gathering [*ekklēsia*]" is specifically noted (16:3–5). The total number of people addressed might have been as few as fifty based on Paul's greetings to less than thirty specific individuals. Even if there were several hundred, they would easily fit within the larger Jewish communities of Rome as subgroups. They may have still been largely unnoticed and probably not well understood. Their subgroup identity is suggested all the more if most or all of the members of the groups confessing Christ were composed of the non-elite, and thus likely dependent upon existing Jewish communal leadership and other communal resources. In other words, when we think about the "churches" of Rome we can think in terms similar to those of the "synagogues" of Rome, as

---

10. See Runesson, "The Synagogue at Ancient Ostia: The Building and Its History from the First to the Fifth Century," esp. 81–82.

11. Rutgers, "Jewish Ideas about Death and Afterlife: The Inscriptional Evidence."

"house-churches/assemblies" or "house synagogues." That remains the case whether or not there were also other more formal buildings. But this still does not tell us much about the relationships between the Christ-following subgroups and the larger Jewish communities of Rome.

The Romans had granted Jewish communities certain privileges since the time of Julius Caesar (Josephus, *Ant.* 14.190–212; 16.52–53). Jews were permitted "to live in accordance with their customs and to contribute money to common meals and sacred rites," "to assemble and feast in accordance with their native customs and ordinances" (*Ant.* 14.214–16 [Marcus, LCL]; reiterated by Augustus, *Ant.* 16.162–65, 172). These rights for Jewish communities continued under Claudius and Titus. When these rights were occasionally denied, Jewish communities successfully appealed to the reigning emperor for judgment according to this precedent (Josephus, *Ant.* 14.213–67; 16.160–78, 278–312; 19.304–6).[12]

[17] This distinctive treatment leads us to ask whether the kind of anti-Jewishness found in Roman authors after the Judean Revolt was already prevalent among Romans when Paul wrote this letter in the mid-50s. There seems to have been a decisive negative shift after 70 C.E., following the Revolt. Vespasian and Titus appealed to their victory over the Judeans to legitimate the beginnings of their new (Flavian) dynasty—with unavoidable implications for Jews in general.[13] Even if the Jews of Rome were not directly involved in the Judean Revolt, such distinctions often become blurred in times of political crisis involving an ethno-religious group's identity (cf. Josephus, *J.W.* 5.2; 7.420).[14]

When Paul wrote Romans, however, Jews were in general still respected and held in high regard as good citizens who exemplified high ideals, even if upholding some seemingly strange ideas and practices.[15] This general respect toward Jews and Judaism, albeit mixed with some ambivalence, has seldom been factored into interpretations of Romans.

It is easy to see the attractiveness of joining Jewish subgroups for non-Jews who turned from the worship of other gods to the worship of the God of Israel in Christ. However, apart from "full" identification with the Jewish community by becoming Jews themselves through proselyte conversion, their ostensible "atheism" for not worshipping the Roman gods and their traitorous refusal to participate in familial and civic cult

---

12. See full discussion in Ben Zeev, *Jewish Rights in the Roman World*.

13. Goodman, *Rome and Jerusalem*, 366–76, 428–77.

14. Consider, e.g., some today who fail to distinguish clearly between Islamic nations or so-called "insurgents/terrorists" and Muslim people, regardless of how vehemently these Muslims might be opposed to such people and policies.

15. Consider again the analogy with common opinions of the Amish.

would be inscrutable if not dangerous (cf. Tacitus, *Hist.* 5.4-5; Juvenal, *Sat.* 14.96-106). That issue arose in the second century C.E. when the Romans began to identify Christians as something other than Jews and to develop punishments for neglect of proper behavior for Roman subjects who were not Jews (cf. the correspondence between Pliny the Younger and the emperor Trajan in ca. 110-12 C.E., *Ep.* 10.96.1-10; 10.97.98-117). But no similar evidence indicates that Roman authorities knew about "Christians" as a separate socio-religious group independent of Jewish communal life during the time Paul wrote to Rome.

[18] The earliest mention of *christiani* arises in accounts of them being blamed by Nero for the fire of 64 C.E., language that probably indicates a subgroup identity within the Jewish community that was vaguely understood by non-Jewish Roman authorities rather than an independent religious association ("a 'superstition' of Jewish origin").[16] If Christ-following non-Jews were already neglecting familial and civic cult apart from affiliation with the Jewish communities of Rome, it seems highly unlikely that they were not known about immediately as a threat to the welfare of Rome, as well as to the interests of the Jewish communities and their relations with Roman authorities. The Jewish community's own rights to refrain from civic cult would be brought into question for not bringing any non-Jews into compliance with communal norms. I propose that the language in Romans suggests the beginnings of just such tensions regarding the non-Jews in these subgroups, but also that it implies that no hard break between the larger Jewish community and these subgroups had already been made. Paul sought to address intra-Jewish communal developments.[17]

In the past forty years or so, the traditional interpretations of Romans have argued that the Christ-followers Paul addressed in the mid- to late-50s C.E. were (presumably) already meeting separately from the Jewish communities of Rome as a result of an expulsion of the Jews from Rome during the reign of Claudius (usually dated to 49 C.E.). According to the construct, conflicts between Christ-followers and the larger Jewish community precipitated this expulsion.

This construct is based upon a reading of two early second-century C.E. accounts. Suetonius briefly mentions a conflict regarding someone named *Chrestus* (Suetonius, *Claud.* 25.4), which led to an expulsion of the Jews for turbulence within their communities and, in Acts 18:2, Luke notes

---

16. Benko, *Pagan Rome and the Early Christians*, 16, 20.

17. I read Rom 13:1-5 to be calling for subordination to the synagogue authorities (rather than Roman authorities) and payment of the temple tax by these non-Jews is just such an effort to demonstrate their commitment to the Jewish communities, albeit apart from becoming proselytes (*Mystery of Romans*, 289-336).

that Aquila and Priscilla were expelled from Rome along with "all" the Jews. The conclusion is then drawn that since the Jews were forced to leave Rome, the only Christ-followers who remained were non-Jews. Even if some Jews remained, the Christ-following communities were no longer a part of the Jewish community, by choice or default, because they were [19] responsible for a cataclysmic disruption of life for, if not the expulsion of, some estimated twenty to fifty thousand Jewish people.

According to this view, the Christ-followers who remained developed their own identity as "Christians" and their ethos became more "gentile" in contrast to "Jewish" values. Thus, when Jews began to return under Nero (beginning in 54 C.E.), those who were Christ-followers, including those who were formerly leaders within the Christ-following subgroups of the Jewish community, were not welcomed back without reservations. Rather, they were being greeted with the proposition that they needed to adopt a more "strengthened" (i.e., non-Judaism based) approach to Christian values, such as Paul is generally imagined to have upheld, for example, in Rom 14. This new lifestyle revolved around rejection of the Torah-defined ways of life that distinguished Jews from non-Jews, such as circumcision, Sabbath and other calendrical observances, kosher dietary customs, and so on.

There are many reasons to be suspicious of this construction: the sources are unclear and conflict with each other, and it is doubtful that Paul would have approached that level of ethnicity-based discrimination in the name of Christ with the arguments we meet in Romans.[18] Let us examine a few details.

First, it is highly unlikely that all or even much of the Jewish community was expelled from Rome by Claudius. Suetonius's report can be understood to indicate an expulsion of only those Jews involved in a disturbance, in direct conflict with the statement in Acts 18:2 that all the Jews were expelled. The silence of Jewish and Roman writers about this expulsion is all the more suggestive when we note that citizens, which at least a number of Jews in Rome were, could not be expelled without due process. Moreover, Dio Cassius writes specifically that Claudius did not expel the Jews of Rome but only restricted their meetings (*Hist. Rom.* 60.6.6–7). Further, while the author of Acts notes that the Jewish leaders in Rome have little firsthand knowledge of the Christ-followers and mentions the wholesale expulsion, he does not link this expulsion to a disturbance over Christ (18:1–4). The author of Acts may well know that it had nothing to do with disturbances related to claims about Christ. Whatever his source, it seems to have exaggerated the extent of any such edict. Luke's notice simply explains why Aquila and Priscilla,

---

18. For a more detailed discussion, see my *Mystery of Romans*, 372–87.

who are not explicitly identified [20] as already Christ-followers, were in Corinth when Paul met these fellow Jews and leather workers, whom he stayed with "because he was of the same trade."

Second, it is unlikely that the expulsion mentioned was precipitated by disputes about Jesus Christ. Suetonius elsewhere discusses the *christiani* under Nero rather than the *chrestiani* (*Nero* 16.2), following Tacitus, who already knew of the *christiani*. This spelling suggests that Suetonius knew the difference and that he was not under the impression that the expulsion under Claudius had anything to do with Christ or Christ-followers, but with someone in Rome named *Chrestus*, a relatively common name in Rome.[19]

Third, it is curious to suppose that Romans would have expelled Jews without also expelling the non-Jews meeting in their midst. Would these non-Jews be left in Rome to carry on meetings involving the name Christ and avoiding civic cult, including to Caesar, if such groups had provoked disturbances that had led to the expulsion of the Jewish community in the first place?

Fourth, most importantly, Paul's approach to the non-Jews in Romans is not what one might expect if they were in positions of power and using that power to exclude or discriminate against Jewish Christ-followers. If they appealed to the teaching of Paul or other leaders to legitimate such behavior, we could expect Paul to challenge these teachings and teachers much more directly, just as he had in other writings (cf. 1 Cor 1:10—6:20). We might also expect some direct instruction about respecting at least the five Jews mentioned in chapter 16, instead of just extending simple greetings and acknowledging their positions of authority in the community (two holding meetings in their house, which suggests a problem with the construction, and two others are "apostles").

Although a relatively new twist on this historical data, many recent interpreters matter-of-factly relay this construction in their introductions to Romans. Yet, the data do not provide a reliable foundation to build upon. Someone coming upon this construct who did not think it supported an interpretation of Romans already held would not likely be impressed that it constituted a reliable historical measure by which to limit the options for exploring the context for or meaning of Paul's message.

---

19. Suetonius also appears to be unaware that this supposed *Christus* was not actually in Rome at the time of Claudius, if that was to whom he meant to refer.

THE RHETORICAL IMPLICATIONS FROM THE LETTER

[21] In the formal opening of the letter, Paul introduces himself in language that would make little sense to a Greco-Roman person apart from learning the story of Christ within the context of the Jewish communal narrative, one that can be developed from Jewish Scriptures but not elsewhere. He not only cites Jewish Scriptures, which he will continue to do more than in any other extant letter, some fifty-plus times, but he alludes to these Scriptures many more times. He apparently assumes that the recipients would be competent to follow his line of thought. Yet copies of these Jewish texts were expensive and apparently not well known outside of Jewish communities. How then would they know the Scriptures upon which his arguments were based apart from being socialized into Jewish communal life?

If these non-Jews attended Jewish communal meetings, they would hear the Scriptures read, translated, and interpreted in regular, weekly sermons.[20] Or are we to suppose that Paul expected those raised on Greek and Roman stories (but not those of the Bible) were meeting in households independent of Jewish communal affiliation, and that each already possessed these expensive scrolls (or had attendees who already knew them well enough from earlier exposure that they could now recite and explain them)? In addition, would they have competent readers and the educational programs sufficient to prepare them to understand Paul's Scripture-based arguments? Alternatively, are we to suppose that Paul simply overshot the competence of his recipients, playing on their respect for the authority of this source as a persuasive advantage?

Paul approaches his audience as if they are familiar with many concepts that would be foreign to non-Jews. In the first sentence, he makes the significance of the lineage of David central, that is, the idea that a king (i.e., messianic leader) as promised in Scripture was now on the throne of Israel, even though his descendants had been living under occupying empires for over six hundred years, and now lived under Roman rule. Paul presents the one who fills that role as having been killed by crucifixion, which was reserved for slaves and feared terrorists and carried out by the regime of Caesar, the one ruling the world from his home city, Rome. Roman readers would recognize that Paul's argument challenges the claims of the Roman [22] empire; but how deeply would they resonate with this Jewish tradition apart from familiarity with Jewish communal interpretations and ways of negotiating the paradoxes such aspirations created?

20. Cf. Philo, *Hypothetica* 7.12–13; Josephus, *Ant.* 16.43; *Ag. Ap.* 2.175; *J.W.* 2.291; Luke 4:16–22; Acts 13:14–15; 15:21.

There is not space to discuss many similar topics in the letter that seem to suggest a Jewish communal context, since for many interpreters they simply suggest some familiarity with Jewish Scriptures, as indeed did come to be the case in Christianity. Such topics are found throughout the letter. Several features in chapter 11, which discusses the topic of those Israelites/Jews who do not share Paul and his target audience's convictions about Jesus, support a strong case for intimate interaction, as well as the improbability of the kind of break that is central to the edict-of-Claudius constructions of the situation in Rome. Let us take a closer look at this particular chapter.

THE IMPLIED JEWISH COMMUNAL CONTEXT OF THE NON-JEWS ADDRESSED IN CHAPTER 11

The identity of the Christ-followers Paul addressed is a critical factor in determining how to approach the implications of his comments. Regardless of the actual makeup of the audience in Rome, it is important to hypothesize the makeup of the audience Paul imagined he would influence. More specifically, we need to identify whom he targeted with his various comments, perhaps even different groups at different points in different arguments. These specific people or subgroups are referred to variously as the author's "target" or "implied" or "encoded" or even "rhetorical" audience—that is, the ones whom the author seeks to persuade directly when the letter is read. When an author seeks to influence, the construal of the audience may already be shaped by how the author wishes for them to conceptualize themselves and their circumstances. This "rhetorical" dynamic can mislead the later reader who does not know the actual makeup of the original historical audience, author, and situation, including exactly how the author sought to influence that audience, and how the author chose to address them, or intentionally refrained from doing so. The author may also target different specific constituents among the audience imagined to receive the text, and do so disproportionately, either by ignoring certain other groups among the recipients, or addressing them and their concerns less or indirectly, even implicitly.

Throughout the letter there are indications that the members of Paul's target audience—the ones to whom he directs his attention specifically—[23] are non-Jews, because he describes some people as his Jewish compatriots in chapter 16. These audience members are identified as those from among "the nations" (*ta ethnē*) to whom Paul is specifically called to proclaim the message of Christ (e.g., 1:5–6, 13; 11:13–32; 15:15–16).

Furthermore, in the midst of Paul's arguments, these non-Jews are often differentiated from "them," Jews about whom Paul writes, and in many cases "they" are Jews who are not Christ-followers (e.g., 3:1–3; 9:1–5; 10:1–2; 11:1, 11–32; 15:25–32). Although there is controversy about whether Paul was always targeting non-Jews throughout the letter, in 11:13 he writes explicitly that he is targeting non-Jews, members from the nations other than Israel ("now I am speaking to you Gentiles"; NRSV), and this remains the case throughout this chapter.

Chapter 11 represents the culmination of the arguments Paul began in chapter 1, followed by the "therefore" of 12:1, which initiates a transition to the instructions that occupy the rest of the letter. Paul seeks to explain to non-Jewish Christ-followers the present anomalous situation in which many Jews (members of the nation Israel) are not persuaded about the meaning of Jesus at the same time that a number of members of the other nations, such as his addressees, are persuaded. This is the case even though the Scriptures, as Paul understands them, uphold the covenant promise that "all Israel will be restored," "removing godlessness from Jacob" (i.e., Israel), and "taking away their sins" (11:26–27).

Throughout the argument Paul instructs these non-Jews to resist any temptation to grow arrogant or suppose that they have replaced those Israelites who are "stumbling," that is, those Jews not joining Paul as heralds who proclaim the message of Christ to the nations. These non-Jews should not be concerned only about their own success. Rather, they are to recognize humbly the generosity (grace/favor/benefaction) of God toward themselves and, in reciprocity, to think and to live generously toward those who are temporarily suffering this fate, which is somehow, mysteriously, tied up with how God is bringing about the promised restoration of these members of Israel. Nevertheless, those Jews remain in the covenant relationship, albeit in some kind of disciplinary state. He seeks to clarify that, however inscrutable the plan may be, it involves some Israelites now requiring God's mercy for their present failure to be persuaded to proclaim Christ to the nations alongside Paul. This is similar to the mercy extended to these former idolaters from the other nations for their failure to be persuaded about the one Creator God. Now, although for different reasons, all are joined in equal need of God's mercy (vv. 25–32).

[24] In making his case, Paul develops an allegory in which the non-Jewish audience is one shoot cut off of a wild olive tree and grafted among the many branches natural to a cultivated olive tree, which represent members of Israel (vv. 17–24).[21] By way of the olive tree allegory, Paul argues that

---

21. See Nanos, "'Broken Branches': A Pauline Metaphor Gone Awry? (Romans

God will not tolerate arrogant attitudes or behavior toward those branches suffering some kind of temporary state of harm, which are being cloaked in a divine "callus [*pōrōsis*]" to keep them, and the overall tree, protected until they are prepared to produce fruit.[22]

Paul's language presupposes that these non-Jews are involved in personal contact with Jews who do not share their views about Jesus, but whom Paul believes will, in due time. At the same time, these non-Jews must avoid behaving in arrogant ways that might turn these Jews away from considering this proposition. Moreover, if that should occur, God will punish these non-Jews severely; in metaphorical terms, they will be cut off from the tree, to which they were not natural in the first place. The image in the allegory of one wild shoot among many natural branches suggests a social situation in which the non-Jews are the minority group among a much larger and more diverse body of Jews; the non-Jews are not the majority or separated socially from the Jews whom they might negatively affect—although we must be careful not to make too much out of allegorical elements. In any case, the social connections implied in spelling out the role of these non-Jews in the divine plan for the restoration of these Israelites, and the price to be paid for failing to perform their part, are palpable. Actually, Paul makes them plain just before beginning this allegory.

Paul introduces the idea in verses 11–12 that some Israelites were suffering a temporary setback in their divine role as messengers of God enlisted to bring God's words to the nations. That has been to the immediate benefit of these non-Jews, but ultimately, Paul argues, their best interests will actually be served when these Israelites are restored to carrying out their special task. In his two uses of the metaphor of messengers running [25] but some temporarily tripping (which Paul draws on both before and after the tree allegory, and elsewhere throughout the letter), they are characterized as "stumbling," but forcefully declared "not fallen!" Thus, non-Jews should not think their own success is best gained by these Jews remaining unconvinced about taking the gospel message to the nations. In verse 12 and again in verse 15, Paul makes the comparative point that the return of those Jews will be exponentially more advantageous for non-Jews than it has been to date. Paul declares that these non-Jews' own aspirations will actually only be realized following the restoration of these Jews to their role as heralds of the gospel.

11:11–36).''

22. See Nanos, "'Callused'; Not 'Hardened': Paul's Revelation of Temporary Protection until All Israel Can Be Healed."

In verses 13–14, Paul tells these non-Jews that even his efforts toward them were motivated by his commitment to the ultimate restoration of those fellow Israelites. In other words, these non-Jews' interests are not even the ultimate goal of Paul's ministry! Rather, his work among them is a means to accomplish another end: "Now I am speaking to you Gentiles. Inasmuch then as I am an apostle to the Gentiles, I glorify my ministry in order to make my own people jealous, and thus save some of them" (NRSV).[23]

Note that it is not jealousy of these non-Jews that Paul promotes, as if he would have expected Jews to understand these non-Jews to be replacing them. That would have hardly made sense to any Jews who rejected this message as mistaken, since they would not then have seen themselves as missing out or supposed that these non-Jews have gained something worth gaining; they have decided already that this is not the case. Moreover, Paul seeks to make his fellow Jews "jealous," and, specifically, jealous *of his ministry*," that is, of Paul's successful work among non-Jews. Jealousy bespeaks the desire to "emulate" (Gk.: *zēlos*; to want to gain for oneself), not to deny to the other per se; it is very different from wanting to provoke "envy" (Gk.: *phthonos*), a begrudging reaction to the good gained by another.

Paul wants his fellow Jews to join him in declaring the good news among the non-Jewish nations when they see the successful results of his ministry. He imagines that the Jews will recognize that his success [26] represents their own promised destiny, the hope of Israel, so that they will then conclude that they are not "yet" participating with him in this special, covenant privilege, because they have not shared his conviction that the age to come has begun with Christ. It is Israel's special calling to declare God's words to the world (see 3:1–2!), at least when the day arrives to initiate this special task. Paul believes that day has dawned with the resurrection of Christ and calling of himself and others to be "sent" (i.e., apostles) to the nations with this news, followed then by the full light of that day.

Thus, in Paul's way of thinking, when he gains a positive response to his ministry among non-Jewish nations, his fellow Jews who witness the turning of these non-Jews from idolatry to the one God will see that a new, promised stage has arrived. They will then recognize that the awaited day has indeed begun among these subgroups composed of Jews and non-Jews celebrating Christ. Israel must be in the stage of being restored (i.e., "saved," in common theological terms), and made ready to announce this news, but

---

23. The case can be strengthened by alternative translation, but it is not necessary in order to make the point: "But I am speaking to you members of the nations: inasmuch then as I am an apostle to the nations, I think (about how to carry out) my ministry, if somehow I may make my flesh (i.e., fellow Israelites) jealous of me, and restore some of them."

some of them have excluded themselves. Rather than envy, that is, begrudging Paul or his audience's claims of gaining good, they will judge this behavior legitimate (i.e., "justified;" *"righteoused,"* in common theological terms) and want to be a part of this awaited fulfillment of Israel's covenant expectations (i.e., "to evangelize"). In Paul's terms, they will join him in trusting that God has raised Jesus from the dead and announce that God has initiated the dawning of the age to come with this act.

Paul's relating of his motivation and plan for success among the non-Jewish nations reveals much, but what does it suggest about the state of the social situation in Rome? If a cataclysmic separation of the Christ-followers into separate meetings, indeed, into rival and specifically non-Jewish-oriented meetings, has already developed (as the traditional and edict-of-Claudius constructions contend), then Paul's hopes for the positive reaction of Jews to his ministry among the nations would seem to be misguided. How could he suppose that they will assess his mission in self-authenticating terms? Would not any Jews who would learn of his mission consider it independent of Jewish communal aspirations and dangerous? Is this not even more the case if he claims to represent a Greco-Roman "Christian" rather than a Jewish movement, which could be dismissed as irrelevant? Could such activity result in the positive reconsideration that Paul seems to anticipate and desire?

If the communal life of Christ-followers took place in groups that were [27] no longer operating within the larger Jewish community, all the more if by definition purposefully separated from it, Paul could not reasonably suppose that they would assess these later developments positively. Jews who had already dismissed the claims of these groups would probably not only remain generally unaware of such non-Jewish communal activity, but would also regard any such news that reached them with indifference if not hostility. But Paul does not think that will be the outcome, and he glories instead in imagining how his ministry among the non-Jews will provide the positive catalyst for his fellow Jews to reconsider his message, moreover, to want to emulate his ministry.

I approach Paul's texts with the assumption that he was able to reason well, regardless of whether I agree with his conclusions, and in spite of the fact that it seems things did not turn out as he hoped they would. Nevertheless, it takes real, intimate contact within the community of those who practice Judaism for Paul to expect that his readers will understand his meaning and identify their own interests and experiences with these aspirations, as well as to suppose that his fellow Jews will react in the manner he describes. I do not understand how Paul could imagine this scenario, or expect his audience to do so, apart from continued identity within the Jewish communities as subgroups, as those who understand themselves to be models of the practice of Judaism, albeit as non-Jews. That conclusion is in keeping with how Paul interprets the significance of incorporating non-Jews within these Jewish subgroups as equal members of God's people, although they do not become Jews/members of Israel but rather represent those from the other nations who join alongside of Jews/Israelites. For Paul, this communal gathering thereby exemplifies the arrival of the end of the ages, when, according to Scripture, the wolf will graze with, rather than devour, the lamb (Isa 65:25).

FOR FURTHER READING

William S. Campbell, *Paul and the Creation of Christian Identity*. LNTS 322. London: T. & T. Clark, 2006. Campbell's approach to Paul and to the message of Romans, which is the focus of most of his monograph, is in many ways compatible with mine. Because he did not seem to me to share the view that the audience was still in the synagogues or that Paul was Torah-observant, his arguments may be especially relevant for those who are interested in aspects of my interpretation of Paul or Romans, but not convinced of those elements.

[28] Bruce N. Fisk, "Synagogue Influence and Scriptural Knowledge among the Christians of Rome." In *As It Is Written: Studying Paul's Use of Scripture*, edited by Stanley E. Porter and Christopher D. Stanley, 157–85. SBLSymS 50. Atlanta: SBL, 2008. Fisk challenges interpreters of Romans to consider the logical strengths of constructing the situation in Rome and the message of the letter in the way proposed herein. His additional insights, largely drawn from intertextual observations, offer further support for exploring this hypothesis.

Mark D. Nanos, "The Jewish Context of the Gentile Audience Addressed in Paul's Letter to the Romans." *Catholic Biblical Quarterly* 61 (1999) 283–304. In this essay, I detail the historical and rhetorical bases for understanding the audience of Romans to be composed of gentiles who are a subgroup within the Jewish synagogue.

―――, *The Mystery of Romans: The Jewish Context of Paul's Letter*. Minneapolis: Fortress, 1996. In this book, I offer an examination of some of the many new interpretive options that arise from reading Romans as targeting Christ-following non-Jews in synagogue subgroups whom Paul seeks to bring to a better understanding of who they are and how they fit into God's larger plan for themselves as well as "all" Israel.

Leonard Victor Rutgers, *The Jews in Late Ancient Rome: Evidence of Cultural Interaction in the Roman Diaspora*. RGRW 126. Leiden: Brill, 1995. Rutgers evaluates the material and literary evidence important to any construction of the context of the recipients of Romans.

H. Dixon Slingerland, *Claudian Policymaking and the Early Imperial Repression of Judaism at Rome*. SFSHJ 160. Atlanta: Scholars Press, 1997. Slingerland provides a comprehensive study of the expulsion by Claudius that challenges the conclusions upon which the prevailing constructions are based. His conclusions support the position advocated in this essay.

BIBLIOGRAPHY

Benko, Stephen. *Pagan Rome and the Early Christians*. London: Batsford, 1985.
Ben Zeev, Miriam Pucci. *Jewish Rights in the Roman World: The Greek and Roman Documents Quoted by Josephus Flavius*. TSAJ 74. Tübingen: Mohr Siebeck, 1998.
Goodman, Martin. *Rome and Jerusalem: The Clash of Ancient Civilizations*. New York: Knopf, 2007.
Nanos, Mark D. "'Broken Branches': A Pauline Metaphor Gone Awry? (Romans 11:11–36)." In *Between Gospel and Election: Explorations in the Interpretation of Romans 9–11*, edited by Florian Wilk and J. Ross Wagner, 339–76. WUNT 257. Tübingen: Mohr Siebeck, 2010. (See chapter 6 in this volume of collected essays.)
———. "'Callused'; Not 'Hardened': Paul's Revelation of Temporary Protection until All Israel Can Be Healed." In *Reading Paul in Context: Explorations in Identity Formation*, edited by Kathy Ehrensperger and J. Brian Tucker, 52–73. London: T. & T. Clark, 2010. (See chapter 7 in this volume of collected essays.)
———. *The Mystery of Romans: The Jewish Context of Paul's Letter*. Minneapolis: Fortress, 1996.
———. "The Myth of the 'Law-Free' Paul Standing between Christians and Jews" *Studies in Christian-Jewish Relations* 4 (2009) 1–21. Online: http://escholarship.bc.edu/scjr /vol4/iss1I 4/. (See volume 1, chapter 3, in this series of collected essays.)
Parkes, James. *The Conflict of the Church and the Synagogue: A Study in the Origins of Antisemitism*. New York: Atheneum, 1979.
Runesson, Anders. "The Synagogue at Ancient Ostia: The Building and Its History from the First to the Fifth Century." In *The Synagogue of Ancient Ostia and the Jews of Rome: Interdisciplinary Studies*, edited by Birger Olsson, Dieter Mitternacht, and Olof Brandt, 29–99. Jonsered, Sweden: Åströms, 2001.
Rutgers, Leonard Victor. "Jewish Ideas about Death and Afterlife: The Inscriptional Evidence." In *The Hidden Heritage of Diaspora Judaism*, 2nd ed., 45–71. CBET 20. Leuven: Peeters, 1998.

PART II

Exegetical Support for Non-Jews within the Synagogues of Rome as Paul's Target Audience

2

Some Problems with Reading Romans through the Lens of the Edict of Claudius

[372] LUKE UNDERSTOOD THE leadership of the Jewish communities in Rome to be aware of, yet to have relatively little firsthand negative knowledge about, the Christian message and movement at the time of Paul's arrival (ca. 58–62 C.E.; cf. Acts 28:17–22). They do not appear to harbor any personal hostility; however, they are concerned about this "sect," having heard some disturbing news. When Paul concluded the introductory defense of his unwarranted imprisonment in the context of suffering "for the sake of the hope of Israel," he received the following response from the Jewish leadership in Rome:

> We have neither received letters from Judea concerning you, nor have any of the brethren come here and reported or spoken anything bad about you. But we desire to hear from you what your views are; for concerning this sect, it is known to us that it is spoken against everywhere.[1] (Acts 28:21–22)

This raises an interesting question concerning the historical backdrop of the conflict between Christians and Jews that is presumed by modern scholars to have led to the complete, or at least extensive, expulsion of the

---

1. Note that Luke understands them to have some knowledge of this message and group that causes concern; however, what they know does not completely put them off and preclude their interest, which would be likely if what they did know led them to believe that it represented an entirely new religion.

Jews (including Christian Jews and God-fearing [judaized] gentiles in most constructs) from Rome in 49 C.E. during the reign of Claudius, followed by their presumed return to Rome after the death of Claudius in 54 C.E.[2] The framework for the *Sitz im Leben* [373] of Romans projected through this historical construct[3] highlights a dramatic separation of "Christianity" and Judaism by the time of Paul's letter to and arrival in Rome in the late 50s or early 60s, although, interestingly, some interpreters allow that prior to the edict of Claudius the social setting in Rome was as I have argued in this study. That is, some interpreters recognize that operating in the background of Romans was the fact that the Christians in Rome had met prior to the edict "as a 'special synagogue' under the protection of the Jewish religious and legal privileges."[4]

---

2. The dates for the reign of Claudius are fixed (41–54 C.E.); however, the later histories of Luke, Suetonius, and Dio Cassius do not include dates for the incidents recording the so-called edict of Claudius or its withdrawal, or even if it was withdrawn. It is assumed to have been no longer operative after the death of Claudius in 54 C.E.

3. There are many modern proponents of the edict-of-Claudius construct I am discussing, many with their own unique twist. However, almost all share the same basic views I am generalizing herein. Some modern scholars use a good deal of caution, recognizing the possibility of this construct but also the paucity of the information and corroborating evidence, as well as the various ways the information could be construed to make quite different points. For example, Scramuzza, "Policy," 295–96, drew careful conclusions similar to those I argue herein. Some scholars note that these tensions should or could be located between Jews and Christians as early as the beginning of the reign of Claudius in 41 C.E. See Smallwood, *Jews*, 210–16, who argues decidedly that Suetonius's Chrestus reference is to Christianity (p. 11), but also cautions that it need not suggest that more than some (i.e., the actual rioters) were expelled (p. 216); see Dunn, *Romans*, xlviii–liv, for an excellent discussion. For Dahl, *Studies in Paul*, 142, it constituted a three-sentence note to consider. Many modern scholars, however, appeal to the construct extensively, often without a substantial caveat, and it has become extremely influential for outlining the development of Christianity in Rome as well as for interpreting Romans. See Kümmel, *Introduction*, 217–19, for an essential standard treatment. For historical development of the implications see Wiefel, "Jewish Community," 92–96, an often-noted article that develops the "possibility" this construct holds for specifying the *Sitz im Leben* of Romans (e.g., R. Jewett, *Tolerance*, 27–29, builds on the reconstruction of Wiefel). Other recent examples of the importance of this construct for interpreting Romans include: Watson, *Paul*, 88–98; Wedderburn, *Reasons*, 54–59, 64–65; Campbell, *Intercultural Context*, 180–82, and n. 96, 185–87, 200–204 and nn. 18, 20 (it is interesting to note the change in tone from Campbell's 1972 dissertation at Edinburgh, "Purpose of Paul," 467–75, wherein he balanced the ideas of Wiefel's construct with the very different observations of Judge and Thomas and drew highly nuanced conclusions where the implications of this construct are concerned). J. Walters, *Ethnic Issues in Paul's Letter to the Romans*, has built an entire book around this construct and its historical significance for interpreting Romans.

4. Stuhlmacher, *Paul's Letter to the Romans*, 7; Dunn, *Romans*, xlviii–liv.

The edict-of-Claudius construct suggests that house-churches, composed largely of Christian gentiles, developed rapidly in Rome and functioned independently of and at considerable distance from the synagogues and Jewish communities after the expulsion of 49 C.E. [374] This construct is derived by harmonizing information provided in three references to the so-called edict of Claudius.

1. Luke's account in Acts 18:2:

> And he [Paul] found a certain Jew named Aquila, a native of Pontus, having recently come from Italy with his wife Priscilla, because Claudius had commanded all the Jews to leave Rome.

2. The second-century note in Suetonius *Claudius* 25.4:

> Since the Jews constantly made disturbances at the instigation of Chrestus, he [Claudius] expelled them from Rome.[5]

This note may also be interpreted:

> He [Claudius] expelled from Rome the Jews constantly making disturbances at the instigation of Chrestus.

3. The third-century note in Dio Cassius 60.6.6–7:

> As for the Jews, who had again increased so greatly that by reason of their multitude it would have been hard without raising a tumult to bar them from the city, he [Claudius] did not drive them out, but ordered them, while continuing their traditional mode of life, not to hold meetings.[6]

This expulsion is assumed by many modern scholars to lie behind the tensions addressed in Romans,[7] particularly between the "weak" and the "strong" (14:1—15:3).[8] The conflicts Paul addressed presumably [375] grew

---

5. Loeb Classic Library translation by J. C. Rolfe of Suetonius, *The Lives of the Caesars*: "'Iudaeos impulsore Chresto assidue tumultuantes Roma expulit.'"

6. Loeb Classic Library translation by E. Cary of Dio Cassius, *Roman History*.

7. D. Slingerland extensively, and I think convincingly, undercuts the tentative foundations upon which these "arbitrary" harmonizations of the citations and their historical importance rest. See his detailed arguments in "Suetonius *Claudius* 25.4, Acts 18, and Paulus Orosius' *Historiarum Adversum Paganos Libri VII*: Dating the Claudian Expulsion(s) of Roman Jews," 127–44; "Suetonius *Claudius* 25.4 and the Account in Cassius Dio," 305–22; and "Chrestus: Christus?," 133–44.

8. This construct, however, ignores the condescending and anti-Judaic implications of Luther's trap by suggesting that the "weak" are Christian Jews presumably weak because of their continued practice of Torah and Jewish customs as meaningful

out of the resocialization of Christian Jews (the "weak"), who were formerly in the majority and in prominent positions when Christianity was beginning in Rome, particularly when a synagogue environment is assumed for the earliest Christians who were Jews and God-fearing (judaized) gentiles. However, they were now returning to Rome only to find the Christian communities functioning independent of the synagogues, which were supposedly not operative again until this same time (54 C.E. and thereafter) since all (or almost all) of the Jews were banished from Rome. The newly formed house churches, with Christian gentiles (the "strong") in the majority and in authority, had developed their own patterns of Christian practice that were presumably not very Jewish, perhaps even anti-Judaic. These Christian gentiles did not entirely welcome the returning Christian Jews, rejecting their continued practice of Jewish Law and customs, not to mention their desire to continue to be a part of the larger Jewish community(s), which they did not see being supplanted because of their new Christian persuasion, but rather restored. Nor did the Christian gentiles care to comply with their Jewish opinions about applicable halakhah for "righteous gentiles."

However, if the historical situation had been as profoundly affected by the edict of Claudius as is assumed in such a construct, then why does Luke not build on the irreconcilable animosity of the Jewish community(s) toward the Christian message (particularly as this would fit with the assumption of many scholars that it was Luke's intention to show Jews rejecting the gospel, thereby losing their place among God's people),[9] or at least, why doesn't Luke make the logical connection between their *firsthand, extensive, and extremely negative* knowledge of the gospel and its proclaimers and the situation in Rome upon Paul's arrival.[10] After all, Paul approached the very Jews who would have been severely affected and only recently returned to Rome when the edict expired. The Jewish leaders in Rome would certainly not have forgotten such a group if they had been victims of an expulsion [376] because of them![11] Yet Luke portrays the Jewish leaders in

---

expressions of faith for those who believed in Christ. See Nanos, *The Mystery of Romans*, chapter 3 for the many problems with this view for both Paul and his audience.

9. Cf. J. T. Sanders, *Jews in Luke-Acts*. See the summaries of Gager, *Origins*, 149–51; Kümmel, *Introduction*, 115. For a full discussion of the flaws in these assumptions see the reading of Luke's intentions by Jervell, *Luke*, 41–74; Evans, "Is Luke's View"; see also Nanos, *The Mystery of Romans*, chapter 5.

10. Some might argue that Luke is intentionally avoiding such a scenario for political reasons, but then why did Luke include the comment regarding the expulsion in the first place? Was it really necessary? Wouldn't this reference actually suggest that Luke does not connect the expulsion with any Jewish-Christian tensions?

11. This point is similarly noted by S. Benko, "The Edict of Claudius of A.D. 49 and the Instigator Chrestus," 417–18.

Rome as essentially aware of this "sect" yet unfamiliar with the reasons that it is "spoken against everywhere," nor have they heard specifically of Paul's message (Acts 28:22). Would the same Luke who communicated the information upon which the lens of the Claudian-edict constructs are ground (Acts 18:2) have been so totally blind to the extensive results that it would have precipitated in Rome (which are clear to modern scholars), namely, that the Jewish communities in Rome were highly aware of and antagonistic toward the Christian communities and their gospel by the time of Paul's arrival in the late 50s?[12]

Following the modern scholars' development of the programmatic nature of Luke's intentions in constructing Acts, one must surely ask why Luke would not use this for all its worth, setting up the Jewish community in Rome as already rejecting, or at least predisposed to reject, on the basis of its own experience, the Pauline gospel. At least one must ask why Luke does not acknowledge such a highly agitated situation between Jews and Christians if he knew the expulsion under Claudius to have been the result of disturbances arising from the proclamation of the gospel in the synagogues of Rome. In other words, any historical inferences drawn with regard to the cause or extent of the expulsion under Claudius must address the internal contradiction they create within Luke's own account of the situation in Rome, regardless of Luke's historical reliability.

First of all, is it possible that Luke did not mean to communicate that *all* Jews had been expelled under Claudius? Perhaps "all the Jews" refers to a specific group of Jews in Rome: *pantas tous Ioudaious*, with *pantas* in the predicate position, need not imply "every"; it may be translated indefinitely as "Jews," that is, "*some* Jews," or definitely as "the Jews," that is, *"all* the Jews."[13] This reading is supported by the alternate translation of Suetonius's report, which does not suggest that all the Jews were expelled; only "the Jews constantly making disturbances" would have been affected. Along the same lines, where does Luke suggest that the expulsion had anything [377] to do with Christian matters, or that Aquila and Priscilla were "Christian" Jews? Luke identifies them as Jews and by trade tentmakers with whom Paul stayed "because he was of the same trade" (Acts 18:3), but not as Christians per se.[14] Note that after they met in Corinth Paul was engaged in preaching within the synagogue there (v. 4); he met them while he was working in the context of the synagogues, not churches. It certainly

---

12. The cunning, or at least purposed, intentions of Luke in his development of Luke-Acts presupposed by modern scholarship would seem to preclude such naiveté on Luke's part regarding the extensive knowledge of this expulsion among his readers.

13. Slingerland, "Suetonius *Claudius* 25.4, Acts 18, and Paulus Orosius," 134.

14. Similarly noted by Benko, "Edict," 413.

takes no stretch of the imagination to see them learning of and believing in Christ in response to Paul's influence.

To press this point further, Luke does not even indicate that all the Jews who were expelled included Christians among them; for that matter neither does Suetonius or Dio. Perhaps it was only the members of the offending synagogue (which likely would have constituted no more than a house meeting),[15] or even only the *offending* members of a particular synagogue, who were expelled. After all, Jews had been expelled several times from Rome well before Christ or Christianity were on the scene.[16] Even more likely, Luke may have seen clearly (known?) that the edict of Claudius had nothing to do with a negative Jewish response to Christ or to the Christian message or even to the Christian Jews among the synagogue communities, even if some "Christian" Jews (and Christian gentiles) may have been included among the members expelled (as Jews or judaized gentiles). Luke appears to believe that the Jewish leaders in Rome are largely (but not completely) unaware of the gospel message at the time of Paul's arrival, at least with respect to why this "sect" is spoken against elsewhere, [378] though apparently not among their own congregations in Rome. For that matter, Luke appears to know of an expulsion of Jews from Rome that does not seem to include any Christian involvement and that does not result in any direct knowledge of the dangers of this group among the Roman authorities with whom Paul deals: Gallio, Felix, Agrippa, or the prison authorities in Rome, where even as a prisoner he appears to be involved in the kind of behavior that is assumed to have stirred up exactly such riots: they regard Paul's activities as a purely intra-Jewish affair outside the confines of normal official Roman action. This is a startling circumstance, for if they did not know of such an extensive expulsion resulting from the tumultuous nature of this faction in Rome (is that really possible?), Paul's accusers would have certainly made them aware of such former incidents in seeking

---

15. There is no evidence of independent synagogue structures in the Diaspora during this period. Private homes were adapted for meetings, and since the Jews of Rome of this period were not often wealthy, most if not all of their homes would have accommodated only small groups. See White, *Building God's House*, 60-101; Meyers and Kraabel, "Archaeology, Iconography," 177-89, cf. 184-85, and Meyers and Strange, *Archaeology, the Rabbis*, 140-54; Zeitlin, "Origins," 14-26; Lampe, *Die stadtrömischen Christen*.

16. See Rutgers, "Roman Policy," 56-74, for a discussion of the various expulsions during the first century C.E. Also discussed by Benko, "Edict," 412-17, who notes on p. 412: "The only reason why the expulsion of the Jews from Rome by Claudius may be connected with the Christian movement is because of the occurrence of the name Chrestus in Suetonius. Otherwise the years leading up to the Jewish revolt of A.D. 66-70 are filled with Jewish-Gentile clashes in various parts of the empire and with various measures against Jewish excesses which had absolutely nothing to do with Christianity."

Paul's conviction (cf. 24:5), that is, if they applied.[17] Luke indicates that the leaders of the Jewish communities of Rome have firsthand knowledge of this faction, yet this knowledge provides no basis for understanding why they have heard that it is spoken against in other locations.

Further, perhaps "Chrestus" is not a reference to Christ or the Christian message or Christians at all, since Chrestus was a common Greco-Roman name, and in the case of Suetonius he does write later of the *christiani*, not *chrestiani*, when referring to this new religion:[18] "a consideration which might lead to the conclusion that Suetonius saw no association between the previously mentioned Chrestus and the religion of the christianorum."[19] We must also consider that Tacitus, who [379] was "active before Suetonius, already knew the origin of the name and its correct spelling,"[20] and initially introduced the Christians only under the reign of Nero in 64 C.E. in a way that "rules out any prior treatment of them in his work,"[21] thus corroborating the possibility that "the Chrestus of Suetonius may therefore safely be left as some religious star whose appearance at Rome caused an upheaval among the Jews, but whose fame was sufficiently ephemeral for his precise identity to have been lost."[22]

Besides the obvious possibility that Chrestus was the name of a person in Rome, there is the possibility that it refers to a messianic person or movement, but not necessarily Jesus or his followers.[23] For example, Judge

---

17. See Acts 18:12–17 for Gallio, proconsul of Achaia; chaps. 23–26 for Felix, governor, and King Agrippa II, son of Herod Agrippa I; chap. 28 for his freedom to move among the Jewish communities in Rome while still a prisoner for allegedly stirring up dissension (24:5). This point bears weight because Luke does report the expulsion in 18:2 (it does not appear necessary to have done so—was Luke so naive that he would include unnecessarily this historical point in 18:2, yet so cunning as to seek to obscure its significance for his reader at these other places in his narrative?), yet he does not link it with either official Roman or Jewish knowledge of the Christian movement as the source of riots in the Jewish communities that have been so threatening to the pax Romana that they have already resulted in expulsions such as the one by Claudius. Cf. Judge and Thomas, "Origin," 88; Campbell, "Purpose of Paul," 470. See also Gill and Winter, "Acts and Roman Religion," 98–103.

18. *Nero*, 16.2. See Benko, "Edict," 410–12.

19. Slingerland, "Chrestus: Christus?" 136–37, and the complete article for a very strong argument against taking the reference to Chrestus as a reference to Christ or Christians, including a discussion of the fact that the text does not indicate that the issue is with those *preaching about* Chrestus: Suetonius appears to believe that this Chrestus is *personally present* in Rome (pp. 137–38). See also Benko, "Edict," 406–18.

20. Benko, "Edict," 412.

21. Judge and Thomas, "Origin," 86.

22. Ibid., 87.

23. Borg, "New Context," 211–12, points out "that Chrestus should be read as

and Thomas argue that "Chrestus" should be understood as a messianic title that was

> taken by Suetonius or his source as a personal name. But if the Messiah concerned had been Jesus, we not only sharpen the problem of Suetonius' failure to see the point (even if his source did not), but come up with a quite different obstacle . . . we have to suppose that the Jewish lobby completely missed a unique opportunity of settling their account with the Christians by laying the blame firmly where it belonged. They failed to have the Christians as such named as political agitators, and at the same time allowed to pass into the record the title that implicitly conceded to Jesus the status they were at most pains to deny.[24]

Was Luke, who included such a specific detail as the expulsion of Jews from Rome under Claudius in Acts 18:2 (the very basis for this construct) completely unable to see the reasons for or implications of [380] the expulsion as they applied to Paul's arrival in Rome, or even how this detail could have been woven into his supposedly programmatic (even anti-Jewish?)[25] legitimization of Christianity as Israel's true heir?[26] Furthermore, we should not overlook the fact that this important historical detail apparently escaped the notice (or at least notations) of several important historians of the time, such as Josephus, the Jewish historian concerned with just such Jewish matters,[27] and Tacitus, who officially documented this period of

---

Christus (= Messiah) . . . [which] suggests that Suetonius' reference is to Jewish messianic agitation in Rome, provoked both by the expulsion of the Roman Jews and sympathy with the contemporaneous aspirations of and outrages suffered by Palestinian Jews." Benko, "Edict," 412ff., suggests that Chrestus "was a rabble-rouser who incited the Jews to various riots" and links him with extreme nationalists who "expected the kingdom of God to come through violence" (pp. 413ff.), concluding that "Chrestus, in all probability, was an extremist ('zealot') leader in the Jewish community of Rome" (p. 418).

24. Judge and Thomas, "Origin," 86.

25. Cf. J. Sanders, *Jews in Luke-Acts*. But see Evans, "Luke's View."

26. In Acts 28, the Jews of Rome are represented as honorable truth-seekers, not contentious or riotous. Constructs that suggest a replacement theology for Luke should expect to find the Jews hardened against and rejecting violently the message of Paul, particularly in view of the edict of Claudius, shouldn't they? See the various essays (particularly on the twelve thrones of Israel) in Jervell, *Luke*; C. A. Evans and J. A. Sanders, *Luke and Scripture: The Function of Sacred Tradition in Luke-Acts*.

27. Josephus does, however, mention the expulsion of 19 C.E. under Tiberius (*Ant.* 18.3.4-5 [65, 81–84]). For a discussion of the many problems with the reference attributed to Josephus by Orosius (fifth-century Christian writer), and thus why it should be disregarded in the constructs we are exploring, see Slingerland, "Suetonius *Claudius* 25.4, Acts 18, and Paulus Orosius," 136–42.

Roman history.[28] Neither mentions this Jewish expulsion in Rome under Claudius. This fact seems particularly strange since the Jewish residents of Rome numbered 20,000 to 50,000 at the time,[29] a sizable number of people to expel without significant historical notice, particularly if many Jews in Rome were citizens (freed slaves), as is noted by Philo.[30] Consider also that Dio appears to be denying just such a (mis)understanding of these events in stating that "he [Claudius] did not drive [381] them out," although Dio may be discussing an entirely different event in the reign of Claudius.[31]

While there are tensions in Rome according to both Luke's account and Paul's letter, they do not seem to have degenerated to the perilous and irreversible degree suggested by such a construct.[32] There is not the monolithic

28. Tacitus, *Annals*, a second-century Roman historian's account of 47-54 C.E. As Slingerland points out, Tacitus would have been able to make excellent use of this information in his diatribe (*Hist.* 5.5.9); instead he is silent (Slingerland, "Suetonius *Claudius* 25.4, Acts 18, and Paulus Orosius," 128-29, 135-36).

29. Leon, *Jews*, 135-37, and Nanos, *The Mystery of Romans*, chapter 2.

30. *Legatione Ad Gaium* 23.155, which was composed most likely after the death of Gaius (14.107) and the assumption of power by Claudius (30.206), according to Slingerland, "Suetonius *Claudius* 25.4 and the Account in Cassius Dio," 314-15. On the status of Jews with respect to citizenship, etc., see Rutgers, "Roman Policy," 59-60. See also Scramuzza, "Policy," 296, who points out also the "practical difficulty of expelling all the Jews" in concluding that "only those individuals were expelled who took part in the disorders" and "the main body of the Jews was left unmolested." The obvious question is: How were those Jews who were citizens expelled on other than an individual-by-individual basis and with great difficulty in each case at that?

31. It seems a curious negative comment for Dio at this point. Why would he note what did not happen when writing the history of what did happen unless he was challenging another version of the event(s) at this point? But see Slingerland, "Suetonius *Claudius* 25.4 and the Account in Cassius Dio," 305-22, who argues for separate incidents by demonstrating several problems, including the circular reasoning involved in arbitrarily harmonizing the references (pp. 317-22): Dio describing an event in 41 C.E. and Suetonius an event that took place at another (uncertain) time under Claudius, Suetonius having written in a topical rather than annalistic style. See also Slingerland, "Suetonius *Claudius* 25.4, Acts 18, and Paulus Orosius," 127-44, in which he argues further that it is not certain that Luke and Suetonius refer to the same incident (pp. 132-36), and if they do it provides only a range of dates between late 47 and 54 C.E. (p. 134 n. 31).

32. Slingerland, "Suetonius *Claudius* 25.4 and the Account in Cassius Dio," 321, notes that the following harmonizations have been proposed: "Claudius restricted Roman Jewish worship and expelled rioters [Scramuzza]; he closed one synagogue and expelled some of its members [Penna, Luedemann]; he closed some synagogues and expelled rioters [Haenchen]; he closed all synagogues but expelled no one [Juster, Guterman]; he closed all synagogues and threatened expulsion [Harnack]; he closed all synagogues, threatened expulsion, and some Jews did leave or were expelled [Stern]; he closed all synagogues, and religious Jews left the city [Bruce, Schürer, Vogelstein, Suhl]; he closed all synagogues and expelled rioters [Leon, Berliner, Hoerber, May]; he

hostility we would expect; there is instead the strain of different opinions developing within communities concerned with proper belief and behavior for the people of God. Nor do Christian gentiles (wild olive branches) appear to be in positions of authority in Rome to a greater degree than Christian Jews (the root that supports the branches) as this construct suggests, either by way of Paul's argument[33] or by way of the list of individuals in Romans 16. In fact, of the [382] five Christian Jews mentioned, two (Aquila and Prisca) have meetings in their house (16:3-5) and two are apostles who were in Christ before Paul (16:7). Thus 80 percent of the Christian Jews mentioned are associated with authority roles in Rome within a few years after the edict of Claudius would have expired.

Moreover, if Christian gentiles were indistinguishably connected to the synagogues of Rome, or at least so from the standpoint of the Roman officials who apparently did not know much about the situation, (mis)citing *Chrestus* as though this individual was present (not to mention the obvious misspelling if they meant to refer to *Christus* or *Christiani*),[34] why wouldn't

---

closed synagogues and expelled all Jews [Benko; Smallwood in 'Jews and Romans' but not in *Jews*]; all Jews were simply expelled [Zielinski, Janne, Borg]" (brackets added for footnote references). To these many can be added from modern interpreters of Romans who largely see the complete, or at least extensive, expulsion of Jews in 49 C.E. as a result of Christian controversies in the synagogues of Rome (usually assuming a monolithic development of relations between Jews and Christians in Rome).

33. See the discussion of Rom 13:1-7 in Nanos, *The Mystery of Romans*, chapter 6, that proposes that the situation addressed suggests Christian gentiles are to subordinate themselves to the synagogue authorities. Note also that while the Christian gentiles are challenged for their arrogant and high-minded attitudes toward Jews or the "weak" they are not confronted with the kind of instructions that would be directed to those guilty of abusing positions of power. They are dealt with rather as those who were resentful of the sustained privileges of Jews who have not "seen" what they have now seen so that they might recognize the awful error of nurturing such an uninformed and ungrateful attitude toward those whose very blindness has paradoxically served their own clarity of vision (11:1; 11:11—12:3). Note also that the "weak" are in the position to legitimately "approve" or "blaspheme" the behavior of the "strong" and not the other way around (14:16-18). It is also notable that Romans does not address any officials in Rome directly or even indirectly with respect to their position of authority or its proper execution (except full service of gifts in 12:6-8), not even among the many addressed in chap. 16, with the exception of Phoebe, a διάκονον of the church at Cenchrea, the port city of Corinth (v. 1), who was sent by Paul, and the two Christian *Jewish* apostles Andronicus and Junias (v. 7). See examples in Paul's other letters of those in authority and the continued expression of their responsibilities (e.g., throughout 1 Corinthians; apostles in 2 Cor 8:23; 11:5, 13; 12:11; elders in Phil 1:1; Titus 1:5-9; 1 Tim 3:2; responsibilities of those in power, e.g., 2 Thess 5:12—14; 1 Tim 3; see Burtchaell, *From Synagogue to Church*, 288-312, for full discussion of early church authorities).

34. But see Wiefel, "Jewish Community," 92-93, who argues that *Chrestiani* was commonly used for *Christiani* in the first two centuries, citing Tacitus, *Ann.* 15.44.2-4. See also Tertullian, *Apol.* 3.5; Justin, *Apol.* 1.4. Later Christian writers also played with

the (judaized) gentiles have been expelled along with the Jews?[35] Why would (Jewish or semi-Jewish [judaized]) gentiles have been permitted to remain in Rome, particularly when [383] they were supposedly at the center of the controversy? Was the Roman government able to make such a highly nuanced distinction at such an early date between the gentile adherents to the synagogues that they could expel gentile God-fearers and proselytes who were not Christians, but not those who were? Could they distinguish Christians from Jews at any level?[36] Would they even bother to try?[37] If so, this would suggest a heightened discriminatory policy on the part of the Romans toward Jews and Judaism, a viewpoint that modern scholarship has challenged.[38] Further, it necessitates a far more extensive knowledge of the Christian movement than even the proponents of this construct otherwise suggest.[39]

Along the same line, were the leaders of the synagogues even able to make such a clear distinction among the gentile sympathizers in Rome, for example, between gentiles believing in Christ and other God-fearing gentiles who did not? Even if they could, would they have done so to the benefit

the nuance provided by intentionally switching the ι for an η, for example, Clement of Alexandria in *Stromata* 2.5 writes: "Now those who believe in Christ both are and are called Chrestoi (good)," but this only proves that they were not confused about such a misspelling (Benko, "Edict," 410).

35. Cohen, "Crossing the Boundary," 13–33, especially 20–21, discusses the indications that even in the second and third centuries gentiles who practiced Jewish rituals or lived in Jewish ways were still being referred to as Jews by gentile writers such as Juvenal, Plutarch, and Dio Cassius, even if they were not necessarily considered Jews by members of the Jewish community.

36. The continuing uncertainty among modern scholars about the identity of Clemens and Domitilla as referred to by Dio Cassius for the charge by Domitian in 95 C.E. of "'atheism,' for which also many others were condemned who had drifted into the practices of the Jews" (*Roman History* 67.14) bears witness to the unlikelihood that there was a clear distinction between Christians and Jews among the Roman rulers or historians of the period. The (arguable) conclusion that Domitilla's "crime" was actually conversion to Christianity based on late documentary evidence (Eusebius) and especially archeological evidence is discussed at length by Jeffers, *Conflict*, chaps. 1–4; cf. pp. 25–28.

37. Rutgers, "Roman Policy," 67–69, 70ff., 73–74, argues that Roman authorities primarily persecuted Roman Jews to suppress unrest and maintain law and order and not because of their religious practices and beliefs: Roman authors reflect a "general antipathy to un-Roman religious practices" (p. 67). In order to research these details at the level necessary to make such discriminating choices they would have had to operate with great care and effort in matters probably of minor interest.

38. Cf. Gager, *Origins*, and see discussion in Nanos, *The Mystery of Romans*, chapter 2.

39. Most of these same scholars can be found recognizing that Roman authorities do not identify or appear to formally recognize Christianity as a separate movement until 64 C.E. at the earliest.

of Christian gentiles (with whom the hostility had supposedly become so fierce) so that they were excluded from the expulsion? This is counter-intuitive and highly unlikely. In other words, it follows logically that if the Jews were expelled, so too were the Christian gentiles,[40] who would most likely have been classified at this time as Jews or semi-Jews (judaized gentiles) by both the synagogue leaders and Roman officials.

[384] In addition, this construct still leaves open the problem of how the Christian gentiles would have procured official Roman permission to meet during this time. They had no rights if they operated outside the jurisdiction of the synagogues and their recognized privileges,[41] a problem that quickly came into focus in later years when Christians did meet outside such sanctions at great expense. Even if they had wanted to operate under the authority of the synagogues during this period, it would have been entirely impossible if all the Jews had been expelled, because naturally all synagogue privileges would have been suspended.

The tensions addressed in Romans are better explained when we recognize that these are precisely the kinds of tensions that would have been unfolding in synagogues as the Christian adherents grew in number and developed a subgroup identity (with additional meetings in their homes for worship and instruction). This would particularly be the case when more and more gentiles sought association as equals, without becoming Jews, with some even questioning the need to comply with the requirements of "righteous gentile" behavior in view of their perceived freedoms in Christ.

I suggest, for Luke, that the expulsion of Jews from Rome and the lack of extensive familiarity with the gospel among the Jewish leaders are compatible because (1) the expulsion had nothing to do with Christians and their message; or (2) if the expulsion was related to Christians and their message, it was a minor incident involving a specific and limited group of people (a house-synagogue?) so that it did not significantly affect the larger Jewish community(s). This makes sense of the situation addressed in Romans, the interpretation of which is perhaps best served apart from

---

40. See Scramuzza, "Policy," 296, for a similar conclusion.

41. See the discussion in Nanos, *The Mystery of Romans*, chapter 2. Wiefel, "Jewish Community," 92–96, sees this shaping the situation in Rome; however, he fails to note the political problems involved in forming a new assembly outside the synagogue's privileges, which he sees under the ban, not to mention his problematic view of the early Christians' intentions: "Christians could only assemble in Rome if they, as a group, had broken ties with the synagogue" (p. 94) and thus: "House churches provided a setting similar to that of congregations in the East who had also formed them in order to be independent of the synagogue" (p. 95).

constructs dependent upon the harmonization of the limited historical details of the so-called edict of Claudius.[42]

[385] This suggestion also makes better sense of later evidence for positive Jewish and Christian interaction in Rome,[43] and the observation that Christianity in Rome developed with a distinctively Jewish *bent* (Ambrosiaster, ca. 375), which included loyalty to its Jewish heritage[44] and perhaps even continued synagogue involvement (cf. *Shepherd of Hermas* 11.9–14),[45] as well as the fact that Christian people do not appear to have an identity distinct from Jewish people in Roman sources until possibly 64 C.E., and even then they appear to have been regarded only as members of a faction *within* Judaism.[46]

It is likely that the Christians in Rome (gentiles as well as Jews) were much more Jewish and much more involved within the normal context of synagogue association than has been recognized in the past. Further, the tensions known to both Paul and the Jewish leadership, not to mention Luke, were perhaps much more intra-Jewish and manageable within the context of Judaism, precluding a parting of the ways as early as the Claudian-edict-dependent constructs seem logically, and necessarily, to promote.[47]

---

42. In fact, the evidence is so limited that it is not really clear that Jews were involved in any disturbances. The report by Suetonius, who was often given to sensationalism, the contrary report of Dio, and the absence of comment by Josephus and Tacitus all lead one to wonder if this accusation was grounded in any real disturbance in the Jewish community. Perhaps it was an entirely false or fabricated accusation to serve some other purpose, or perhaps the report of Suetonius itself should be questioned.

43. Rutgers, "Archaeological Evidence," 101–18, discusses a wide range of third- and fourth-century evidence pointing to extensive positive interaction.

44. See Brown and Meier, *Antioch and Rome*, and the discussion in Nanos, *The Mystery of Romans*, chapters 1, 2, and 4, including indications of continued application of some of the food concerns of the apostolic decree.

45. There are several references to synagogue meetings in *Shepherd of Hermas* (ca. 100–140 C.E.). Perhaps even Hebrews was written to the Christians in Rome still meeting in synagogues; cf. Glaze, *No Easy Salvation*, 22–28; Brown and Meier, *Antioch and Rome*, 139–58; Judge and Thomas, "Origin," 92; Lane, *Hebrews 1–8*, xviii–lx, cxxv–cxxviii.

46. The persecution and fire of the 64 C.E. are the first indications of the Roman government's awareness of a separation between Christians and Jews, and even this may be simply the awareness of a new sect of Judaism known as "Christiani" (Tacitus, *Annals*, 15.44.2–8; Grant, *Nero*, 151–61; Benko as cited by Dunn, *Romans*, 1). Benko, *Pagan Rome*, 16, notes that "Tacitus saw Christianity as a 'superstition' of Jewish origin. . . . It seems that he drew no distinction between Jews and Christians"; and on p. 20 he summarizes: "In 64 Christians were still known as Jews."

47. Paul was, after all, close to Aquila and Priscilla and thus would have been well aware of the profound implications of the Claudian-edict construct's proposed cataclysmic separation between Jews and Christians. Judge and Thomas, "Origin," 88, note

This would make sense of Paul's [386] appeal in Romans to the unifying essence of the Shema as the central governing principle of their obligation no longer to entertain potentially crippling behavior in the assertion of their special place in God's design, but rather to welcome and serve each other in the same grace that the One God has acted in toward themselves, without discrimination, as equals—as one:

> Now may the God who gives perseverance and encouragement grant you to be of the same mind with one another according to Christ Jesus; that with one accord you may with one voice glorify the God and Father of our Lord Jesus Christ. Wherefore, accept one another, just as Christ also accepted us to the glory of God. (Rom 15:5-7)

By way of contrast, reading Romans through the lens of the edict of Claudius projects an irreversible hostility and separation between Jewish and Christian communities by the time of Paul's letter,[48] not to mention an unforgivable level of self-serving intentions between those Jews and gentiles believing in Christ.[49] Such scenarios fail to make sense of Paul's optimism and light-handed treatment of the implied tensions (e.g., 1:8; 15:14; 16:19),[50] believing, in spite of the emergence of alarming trends, that progress could be made, by way of this reminder and his imminent trip, toward the restoration of all Israel in Rome.

When we look closely at the details of Luke's understanding of the situation in Rome wherein the synagogue leaders were aware of but not alienated from the Jewish faction believing Jesus to be the Christ, [387] even in the light of the expulsion of some of the Jews of Rome by Claudius,

---

the issue similarly. A most instructive example of the depth of synagogue involvement allowed before the edict of Claudius construct impacts the assumptions of the social setting in Rome is found in Stuhlmacher, *Romans*, 7: "They [gentile Christians] now no longer had any possibility of meeting in their congregational gatherings as a 'special synagogue' under the protection of the Jewish religious and legal privileges, but had to form their own freely constituted assemblies without leaning on the Jewish synagogues."

48. A point that, at the very least, ought to cause proponents of this construct to reconsider Paul's projected role as the catalyst for the separation of Christianity from its Jewish roots, since he has not been to or personally influenced these developments in Rome. In this case, he is clearly the one seeking to mitigate differences and bridge a gap that others have already widened ostensibly beyond repair.

49. Watson, *Paul*, 94-98.

50. Interpreters relying on this construct often note Paul's oblique handling of the tensions, including indirect labels, such as "weak" and "strong," yet they fail to see the logical inconsistency of this approach for Paul if the hostilities were among Christian Jews and gentiles and were as heightened as they suggest (e.g., Walters, *Ethnic Issues*, 86-92).

we perhaps gain a new insight into the historical situation confronting Paul as he wrote to and later visited the Christians living within the context of the synagogues of Rome. Perhaps Paul's bold reminder of the need to continue to observe "the teaching" of the apostolic decree ("the obedience of faith") with the intention of winning the respect of the synagogue leaders was initially heeded by those he addressed in Romans. Perhaps Paul's letter actually succeeded in convincing the Christian gentiles in Rome to "serve Christ in a manner acceptable to God *and* approved by men" (Rom 14:18), making them coworkers in the mystery designed to ensure simultaneously both of Paul's ultimate goals: "the fullness of the gentiles" and the certain restoration of "all Israel."

BIBLIOGRAPHY

Benko, Stephen. "The Edict of Claudius of A.D. 49 and the Instigator Chrestus." *Theologisthe Zeitschrift* 25.6 (1969) 406–18.

Borg, Marcus. "A New Context for Romans XIII." *New Testament Studies* 19 (1972–73) 205–18.

Brown, Raymond Edward, and John P. Meier. *Antioch and Rome: New Testament Cradles of Catholic Christianity*. New York: Paulist, 1983.

Burtchaell, James Tunstead. *From Synagogue to Church: Public Services and Offices in the Earliest Christian Communities*. Cambridge: Cambridge University Press, 1992.

Campbell, William S. *Paul's Gospel in an Intercultural Context: Jew and Gentile in the Letter to the Romans*. Frankfurt am Main: Lang, 1992.

———. "The Purpose of Paul in the Letter to the Romans: A Survey of Romans I–XI with Special Reference to Chapters IX–XI." PhD diss., University of Edinburgh, 1972.

Cohen, Shaye J. D. "Crossing the Boundary and Becoming a Jew." *Harvard Theological Review* 82 (1989) 13–33.

Dahl, Nils Alstrup. *Studies in Paul: Theology for the Early Christian Mission*. Minneapolis: Augsburg, 1977.

Dunn, James D. G. *Romans 1–8*. WBC 38a. Dallas: Word, 1988.

Evans, Craig A. "Is Luke's View of the Jewish Rejection of Jesus Anti-Semitic?" In *Reimaging the Death of the Lukan Jesus*, edited by Dennis D. Sylva, 29–56. Athenäums Monografien 73. Frankfurt am Main: Hain, 1990.

Evans, Craig A., and James A. Sanders. *Luke and Scripture: The Function of Sacred Tradition in Luke-Acts*. Minneapolis: Fortress, 1993.

Gager, John G. *The Origins of Anti-Semitism: Attitudes Toward Judaism in Pagan and Christian Antiquity*. New York: Oxford University Press, 1985.

Gill, David W. J., and Bruce W. Winter. "Acts and Roman Religion." In *The Book of Acts in Its Graeco-Roman Setting. Vol. 2: The Book of Acts in Its First-Century Setting*, edited by David W. J. Gill and C. Gempf, 79–104. Grand Rapids: Eerdmans, 1994.

Glaze, R. E., Jr. *No Easy Salvation*. Nashville: Broadman, 1966.

Grant, Michael. *Nero*. London: Weidenfeld and Nicolson, 1970.

Jeffers, James S. *Conflict at Rome: Social Order and Hierarchy in Early Christianity.* Minneapolis: Fortress, 1991.
Jervell, Jacob. *Luke and the People of God: A New Look at Luke-Acts.* Minneapolis: Augsburg, 1972.
Jewett, Robert. *Christian Tolerance: Paul's Message to the Modern Church.* Philadelphia: Westminster, 1982.
Judge, E. A., and G. S. R. Thomas. "The Origin of the Church at Rome: A New Solution?" *Reformed Theological Review* 25.3 (1966) 81–94.
Kümmel, Werner Georg. *Introduction to the New Testament.* Rev. ed. Nashville: Abingdon Press, 1966.
Lampe, Peter. *Die stadtrömischen Christen in den ersten beiden Jahrhunderten: Untersuchungen zur Sozialgeschichte.* WUNT 2.18. Tübingen: Mohr Siebeck, 1989.
Lane, William L. *Hebrews 1–8.* Word Biblical Commentary 47A. Dallas: Word, 1991.
Leon, Harry J. *The Jews of Ancient Rome.* Philadelphia: The Jewish Publication Society of America, 1960.
Meyers, Eric M., and A. Thomas Kraabel. "Archaeology, Iconography, and Nonliterary Written Remains." In *Early Judaism and Its Modern Interpreters,* edited by Robert A. Kraft and George W. E. Nickelsburg, 175–210. Philadelphia: Fortress, 1986.
Meyers, Eric M,. and James F. Strange. *Archaeology, the Rabbis, and Early Christianity: The Social and Historical Setting of Palestinian Judaism and Christianity.* Nashville: Abingdon, 1981.
Nanos, Mark D. *The Mystery of Romans: The Jewish Context of Paul's Letter.* Minneapolis: Fortress Press, 1996.
Rutgers, Leonard Victor. "Archaeological Evidence for the Interaction of Jews and Non-Jews in Late Antiquity." *American Journal of Archaeology* 96 (1992) 101–18.
———. "Roman Policy towards the Jews: Expulsions from the City of Rome during the First Century C.E." *Classical Antiquity* 13.1 (1994) 56–74.
Sanders, Jack T. *The Jews in Luke-Acts.* Philadelphia: Fortress, 1987.
Scramuzza, Vincent M. "The Policy of the Early Roman Emperors towards Judaism." *The Beginnings of Christianity. Part 1: The Acts of the Apostles.* Vol. 5. Additional Notes: XXV, edited by F. J. Foakes Jackson and Kirsopp Lake, 277–97. London: Macmillan, 1933.
Slingerland, Dixon. "Chrestus: Christus?" In *New Perspectives on Ancient Judaism. Vol. 4: The Literature of Early Rabbinic Judaism: Issues in Talmudic Redaction and Interpretation,* edited by Alan J. Avery-Peck, 133–44. Lanham, MD: University Press of America, 1989.
———. "Suetonius Claudius 25.4, Acts 18, and Paulus Orosius' Historiarum Adversum Paganos Libri VII: Dating the Claudian Expulsion(s) of Roman Jews." *Jewish Quarterly Review* 83.1–2 (1992) 127–44.
———. "Suetonius Claudius 25.4 and the Account in Cassius Dio." *Jewish Quarterly Review* 79.4 (1989) 305–22.
Smallwood, Mary E. *The Jews under Roman Rule: From Pompey to Diocletian: A Study in Political Relations.* SJLA 20. Leiden: Brill, 1981.
Stuhlmacher, Peter. *Paul's Letter to the Romans: A Commentary.* Louisville: Westminster/John Knox, 1994.
Walters, James C. *Ethnic Issues in Paul's Letter to the Romans: Changing Self-Definitions in Earliest Roman Christianity.* Valley Forge, PA: Trinity, 1993.

Watson, Francis. *Paul, Judaism, and the Gentiles: A Sociological Approach*. SNTSMS 56. Cambridge: Cambridge University Press, 1989.

Wedderburn, A. J. M. *The Reasons for Romans*. Edinburgh: T. & T. Clark, 1988.

White, L. Michael. *Building God's House in the Roman World: Architectural Adaptation among Pagans, Jews, and Christians*. ASOR Library of Biblical and Near Eastern Archaeology. Baltimore, MD: Johns Hopkins University Press, 1990.

Wiefel, Wolfgang. "The Jewish Community in Ancient Rome and the Origins of Roman Christianity." In *The Romans Debate*, edited by Karl P. Donfried, 85–101. Peabody, MA: Hendrickson, 1991.

Zeitlin, Solomon. "The Origin of the Synagogue." In *The Synagogue: Studies in Origins, Archaeology and Architecture*, edited by Joseph Gutmann, 14–26. New York: KTAV, 1975.

3

The Jewish Context of the Gentile Audience Addressed in Paul's Letter to the Romans

[283] Most interpreters of Paul's Letter to the Romans recognize that the roots of Christianity in Rome grew in Jewish soil. They cite, for example, Ambrosiaster's report in his commentary on Romans (ca. 375):

> It is established that there were Jews living in Rome in the times of the apostles, and that those Jews who had believed [in Christ] passed on to the Romans the tradition that they ought to profess Christ but keep the law. .... One ought not to condemn the Romans, but to praise their faith; because without seeing any signs or miracles and without seeing any of the apostles, they nevertheless accepted faith in Christ, although according to a Jewish rite [*ritu licet Judaico*].[1]

I will review a number of facts indicating the Jewish character of the Jesus movement in Rome. My overall concern, however, is to demonstrate that while many scholars describe the earliest developments of Roman Christianity within the synagogues of Rome, and most recognize that it takes Christian Jews to make sense of Romans, and some even recognize that these Christian Jews may still have attended synagogues *in addition to* church assemblies at the time of Paul's letter, none (to my knowledge) recognizes the [284] real and intimate interaction between the letter's

---

1. Cited by Wedderburn, *The Reasons for Romans*, 51. Cf. Brown and Meier, *Antioch and Rome*, 110–11.

audience and the social context of non-Christian Jewish communities that this evidence demands.²

Recent interpreters of Romans have shown how rhetorical analysis highlights the historical situation perceived by Paul, permitting us to "penetrate the fundamental problems of the letter's value as argumentation."³ Yet this approach generally remains limited by traditional assumptions that in Romans Paul confronts problems created by (Christian) Jews and Judaisms. The authors of several recent studies have challenged these assumptions, showing instead that Romans is addressed to Christian *gentiles*, and that the letter's prolonged argument is meant to dispel an early (perhaps the first?) manifestation not of "Judaizing" but of "gentilizing" among gentile believers in Jesus.⁴ Although Christian Jews were present among those addressed in Rome, they were not the intended or implied audience for Paul's remarks.

More likely, the Jews of Rome were the intended beneficiaries of Paul's instructions, as Paul sought to check initial trends in the thinking and behavior of certain gentiles over against these Jews. I suggest that these gentiles are to be found within subgroups of believers in Jesus, still entirely located within the synagogues of Rome and functioning in lively, sometimes distressing, contact in view of the expectations of the Jewish community (or communities) regarding conduct appropriate for them.⁵ In fact, I believe [285] Romans provides literary evidence predating the parting of the ways between Christians and Jews. If that is correct, we must reevaluate the presence and concerns of those whom Paul addressed wholly within the context of the Jewish synagogal community there.

---

2. Judge and Thomas ("The Origin of the Church at Rome," 91) come closest to recognizing this interaction, noting that the early Christians "had preferred to shelter under the umbrella of the synagogues rather than forming their own church." More recently, Judge ("Judaism and the Rise of Christianity," 362) argues for a sharp distinction between Jews and Christians earlier than many recent scholars suggest, yet he too notes that Paul's failure to address Romans to a "church" is "surely because the believers in Rome had still not broken with the synagogue community." Eschner (*Der Römerbrief: An die Juden der Synagogen in Rom?*) explains the situation somewhat differently.

3. Elliott, *Rhetoric of Romans*, 61; see also 18, 62.

4. Elliott, *Rhetoric of Romans*; Stowers, *A Rereading of Romans*; W. S. Campbell, *Paul's Gospel in an Intercultural Context*; Wright, *The Climax of the Covenant*, 251; Nanos, *The Mystery of Romans*, 75–84.

5. This view is sustained in Nanos, *Mystery of Romans*. See J. T. Sanders (*Schismatics, Sectarians, Dissidents, Deviants*, 129–51) for a useful discussion of deviant behavior that may help to explain the development of the subgroup identity of the Jewish and gentile believers in Christ within the synagogal community (or communities) of Rome which led eventually to strained relations with the members and leaders of the larger Jewish population who did not become believers in Christ.

I. EVIDENCE FOR CHRISTIAN GENTILES IN JEWISH SYNAGOGAL CONTEXTS

Several different lines of evidence, both material and literary, point to the synagogues of Rome as the context for the implied readership of Romans.

A. Material Evidence

Peter Lampe, in his significant study of early Roman Christianity, has shown that in the first and second centuries believers in Jesus assembled in houses, "in any rooms which had been used daily in other ways by the occupants," as did the Jews of this period, and that they did so in the same areas of the city; this is his conclusion:

> In the pre-Constantine period, the Christians of the city of Rome assembled in fractions on premises, scattered across the world-renowned city, which were provided by private persons. .... The finding concerning fractionation stands against the background of *a Jewish community in the city of Rome which had fractions* [emphasis mine]. Roman Judaism consisted of a number of independent synagogue communities. The parallelism is amazing.[6]

We should imagine many synagogues or assemblies among the estimated 20,000–50,000 Jews of Rome,[7] tens or perhaps even hundreds of meetings normally consisting of ten to fifty persons each. This suggestion respects the lack of evidence for large synagogue or church structures prior to the fourth [286] century,[8] and it recognizes that house-churches developed as a natural extension of Jewish assemblies as house-synagogues.[9] Inscriptions

---

6. Lampe, *Die stadtrömischen Christen in den ersten beiden Jahrhunderten*, part 5, chaps. 1 and 2. I am grateful to Marshall Johnson and Fortress Press for an early transcript of the forthcoming English edition quoted here. See also White, *Building God's House in the Roman World*, 60–101; Kee, "Defining the First-Century CE Synagogue."

7. Leon, *The Jews of Ancient Rome*, 135–37.

8. See Jewett, "Tenement Churches and Communal Meals in the Early Church," for development of Lampe's observations and detailed consideration of the socioeconomic implications, particularly within the limitations of tenement communities in Trastevere and Porta Capena, two densely populated sections of the city where many Jews of this period lived.

9. See the essays in Fine (ed.), *Sacred Realm*. The consensus of the scholars who wrote these essays is that during this time *synagōgē* usually refers to the social institution ("gathering") around which Jewish community life revolved in the Diaspora, while the private houses where they met were often called *proseuchai*.

found in the catacombs of Rome provide evidence of at least eleven distinct synagogues,[10] though this evidence postdates our period.[11] More likely, as Philo indicates for Alexandria, we should expect that there were very many synagogues ("group[s] of Jews who make communal decisions"),[12] and that they were found throughout the neighborhoods of Rome.[13]

Archaeological evidence of the third and later centuries indicates a close interaction between Jews and Christians continuing long after the generally assumed cataclysmic separating of the ways. This evidence includes similar burial customs and locations (in some cases sharing the same site), as well as shared imagery and materials.[14]

We must also consider political and practical obstacles to Christians meeting outside of synagogue associations during this period. Josephus indicated that Julius Caesar's decree proscribed the assembly of religious [287] societies, *except* for the Jews, in the city of Rome.[15] Suetonius tells us that Caesar had "dissolved all guilds, except those of ancient foundation."[16] How then would Christians, outside of association with the synagogues, obtain the right to congregate for fellowship and worship, even in their own homes or tenement rooms, unless they petitioned to be designated a "private club"?[17] Significantly, we have no evidence of such a petition, and

10. Leon, *Jews of Ancient Rome*, 135–66.

11. Rutgers *(The Jews in Late Ancient Rome*, xvii and *passim)* distributes the evidence chronologically from the late second century through the early fifth century C.E.

12. Feldman, "Diaspora Synagogues," 50.

13. Philo, *Embassy* 20 §132 (on Alexandria); 23 §156 (on Rome). See Rutgers, *Jews in Late Ancient Rome*. M. H. Williams ("The Structure of Roman Jewry Reconsidered," 129-41) observes, on the basis of epigraphic evidence, that the synagogues of Rome were likely as varied "in their structure and the titulature of their officials" as "those found elsewhere in the Jewish world" (141).

14. Rutgers, "Archaeological Evidence for the Interaction of Jews and Non-Jews in Late Antiquity"; Rutgers, *Jews in Late Ancient Rome, passim*. See also Meyers and Kraabel, "Archaeology, Iconography, and Nonliterary Written Remains," esp. 178–79.

15. Josephus, *Ant.* 14.10.8 §§213–16.

16. Suetonius, *Jul.* 42.3; cf. E. P. Sanders, *Judaism*, 212.

17. In this period the Roman government legally classified synagogues as "collegia," a term used because of the traits they shared with "private clubs," guilds, and other cultic associations legally recognized to have the same privileges, namely, the right to assemble and rights to common meals, common property, their own fiscal responsibilities (treasury), disciplinary jurisdiction over their members, and responsibility for the burial of their members; see Smallwood, *Jews under Roman Rule*, 133–43, 210.

In addition to the privileges usually granted to "private clubs," Julius Caesar granted to the Jewish communities special privileges "to live according to their ancestral laws"; see Josephus, *Ant.* 12.3.3–4 §§138–50; 14.10.1—11.2 §§185–276; 16.2.3 §§27–28; 16.6.2 §§162–65; 19.5.3 §§287–91; 19.6.3 §300; Philo, *Embassy* 23 §§155–58; PLondon 1912.73–105. Cf. Tcherikover, *Hellenistic Civilization and the Jews*, 83, 301–2.

we have good reason to believe that they did not pursue such a course. Instead, they may well have found the authority of the synagogue sufficient.[18] Even if they had sought a private club's right of assembly and had been granted it, this would not have extended to the practice of their religion without interference.[19] To the [288] contrary, Christians were denied just such rights early in the second century when they began to be distinguished from Jews as a separate group.

B. Literary Evidence

A number of early Christian writings to and from Rome reveal an indelible Jewish stamp. The author of *First Clement* (96 C.E.) and Hermas, in *The Shepherd* (ca. 100-140 C.E.), make pervasive use of Israel's Scriptures and Hellenistic Jewish rhetorical features.[20] Justin Martyr's *Dialogue with Trypho* indicates a close association with Jews and Jewish leaders continuing well into the mid-second century.[21] In addition, some scholars argue for the Roman provenance and Jewish character of 1 Peter, Hebrews, and James. [22] Though such symbolic and thematic connections could be explained on the premise of heavily "Judaized" Christian gentile audiences, that is, former "Godfearers" and proselytes, an even more decisive feature of some of these

18. Regarding legal status, see Lampe, *Die stadtrömischen Christen*, part 5, chap. 3, "Fractionation"; I quote from the forthcoming English translation: "For lack of evidence [that the Christian groups had organized themselves as *collegia tenuiorum* or *collegia funeraticia*] the hypothesis has long been abandoned. That the groups of Christians were not *legalized* as *corpora* or *collegia* is one of the more certain statements which we can make." See also Wright, *The New Testament and the People of God*, 355; Meeks, *The First Urban Christians*, 77-78. According to Dunn (*Romans 1-8*, lii), "the Christians were not yet clearly distinguished from the wider Jewish community.... Insofar as they had any legal status, they would meet presumably as a 'collegium' or under the auspices of a synagogue."

19. Christian gentiles still would not have had the right to observe the Sabbath, nor would they have been free from serving in civic cults; they would not have enjoyed the right to refrain from the mandatory practice of declaring Caesar as their god, as Jews, only, were exempted from this practice by the institution of a special substitutionary sacrifice (Josephus, *J.W.* 2.10.4 §§195-97; *Ag. Ap.* 2.6 §§75-77; Philo, *Embassy* 23 §157); they would not have been excluded from military service and other public responsibilities with their concomitant idolatry (Josephus, *Ant.* 14.10.6 §204; 14.10.11-13 §§225-30).

20. See Brown and Meier, *Antioch and Rome*, 169-70, 179, 203; Lampe, *Die stadtrömischen Christen*, chap. 1.

21. Remus, "Justin Martyr's Argument with Judaism," 72-74.

22. Brown and Meier, *Antioch and Rome*, 129-37, 140-58; Lane, *Hebrews 1-8*, xviii-lx, cxxv-cxxviii; Streeter, *The Primitive Church*, 196-206; Judge and Thomas, "Origin of the Church at Rome," 92 n. 69.

writings is the repeated reference to the synagogues of those addressed (Herm., *Mand.* 11:9, 13, 14; Heb 10:25 [*episynagōgē*]; Jas 2:2).

Pagan literature from the period presents a complementary picture of Christians distinguished only with difficulty from Jews. The persecution and fire of 64 C.E. are the first indications of the Roman government distinguishing between Christians and Jews, and even this is likely to be simply the awareness of a new sect of Judaism known as "Christiani" (Messianics), "a 'superstition' of Jewish origin."[23] Even later, Epictetus still seems to think of Christians (distinguished by baptism) as "acting the part" of Jews.[24] As late as 95, Domitian's niece Domitilla and her husband, Flavius Clemens, were condemned of "atheism" for being "carried away into Jewish customs"; since the practice of Judaism was not a crime at this time, it is quite possible that "Judaism here really means Christianity."[25]

[289] Most importantly, Romans itself implies the presence of Jews and "righteous gentiles" among the letter's addressees. While Paul explicitly addresses gentiles throughout Romans (1:5–6, 13; 11:13–14; 15:15–16) and implicitly indicates their gentile viewpoint (e.g., in chaps. 1, 6, 9–11, 13–15), he expects them, nevertheless, to have a high degree of familiarity with the Septuagint (explicitly in 7:1 and 15:4). Further, much of his letter revolves around issues and relations relative to the matters of boundary and purity which were of concern in Jewish communities. But how would gentiles learn the Scriptures and the way God deals with his people if they were not involved in synagogues, where alone the Scriptures were read and interpreted? [26]

Such rhetorical questions lead us to revisit Romans itself, examining indications of the character of the letter's implied audience.

---

23. Benko (*Pagan Rome and the Early Christians*, 16) notes that "Tacitus saw Christianity as a 'superstition' of Jewish origin" and that he seems to have drawn no distinction between Jews and Christians. Benko concludes (20) that "in 64 Christians were still known as Jews." On the events, see Tacitus, *Ann.* 15.44.2–8; also Grant, *Nero*, 151–61.

24. Epictetus, *Diss.* 2.9.20–21, cited by Dunn, *Romans 1–8*, 1.

25. Benko, *Pagan Rome*, 16.

26. Collins (*Between Athens and Jerusalem*, 4) notes that the Septuagint was not known in Greco-Roman literary circles.

II. A REEXAMINATION OF THE ARGUMENT OF ROMANS

A. Indications of the Jewish Context of Paul's Argument

The Jewish context of the concern leading Paul to write Romans, and of his planning to come to Rome, is evident throughout the letter.

In the letter's opening (1:1-7), Paul introduces himself, his ministry, his gospel, his Lord and theirs, in thoroughly Jewish terms: Jesus Christ, "promised beforehand through [God's] prophets in the holy Scriptures, . . . born of a descendant of David according to the flesh, . . . declared the Son of God with power by the resurrection from the dead, according to the Spirit of holiness." Many interpreters ascribe this introductory language to an earlier Jewish-Christian formula that, they assume, Paul merely mimics, because they assume that it does not express the essence of the Pauline gospel as they conceive it.[27]

Paul then sets out his plain intentions toward Rome. He plans to come to the Romans, finally, so that they may be "established" through the imparting of his "spiritual gift," the apostolic preaching of the gospel. This gospel is the "power of God for salvation to everyone who believes, to the [290] Jew *first* and *also* to the Greek"—in his particular case, strikingly, to those in Rome who clearly already believe in the gospel (1:8-15). Further, he will gather some "fruit" from among the gentiles addressed, just as he has on the eastern spiral of his ministry. That spiral will end in Jerusalem with an offering expressing the indebtedness of gentiles to Israel for having shared its spiritual benefits with them at great cost. While the completion of that work has thus far prevented his coming to Rome and points west, he intends to incorporate the Romans similarly in this economic obligation, which will demonstrate continuity and fidelity with the historic people and plan of God (1:9-13; cf. 15:15-32). Bringing the gospel "to the Jew first and also to the Greek" is Paul's pattern, because he understands it to be God's (1:16-17; cf. 2:9; 11:11-32).

The gentiles who believe in Christ in Rome have come to this belief independently of Paul's apostolic foundation. This anomalous

---

27. Garlington ("*The Obedience of Faith*," 237) provides an excellent example when he writes that Rom 1:3-4, especially when read with certain Old Testament passages in mind, "would lead one to believe that if an informed reader of Romans went no further than v. 4 of the letter, he would have no cause to suspect that Paul was championing any other than an unmodified Jewish conception of the Messiah in his relation to Israel and the Gentiles." Garlington (242-47) does go past these initial passages to inform his reader of a very different, post-Jewish Paul, one who has necessarily broken with such Jewish heritage.

circumstance may explain their inadequate grasp of the priority, privilege, and irrevocable place of Israel in the history of salvation.[28] In other words, they have come to faith in Christ without being properly "established" by the apostolic pattern, which provides for the restoration of Israel and the inclusion of the nations through faith in Israel's Christ as the savior of the world. Paul fully intends to rectify this deviation from the apostolic pattern upon his imminent arrival.

In his closing in 15:14—16:27 Paul focuses on these same features. Interestingly, they are cast in the light of his ministry through Rome toward Spain (15:24), the uttermost end of the earth, the biblical Tarshish, to which he will bring the light of the nations, as Isaiah foretold.[29] The "obedience of faith" that Paul secured among the gentiles in the East is embodied in a collection that he dearly hopes will be found acceptable to the saints of Jerusalem. The immediacy of this "bold reminder" to Rome (15:14) is somehow inextricably tied up with this offering. Paul now invites the Romans' participation in it, albeit vicariously, through their supportive prayers, until he can finally reach them and make their inclusion a reality (15:26–32; cf. 1:13). Then the Christian gentiles in Rome, like those of the East, will be established "by word and deed, in the power of signs and wonders, in the power of the Spirit" (15:18–19), so that Paul's "offering of the gentiles may become acceptable, sanctified by the Holy Spirit" (15:16).

[291] The Jewish context of Paul's concerns fills his closing greetings to some twenty-six persons, of whom five are described explicitly with regard to their Jewish status (16:3–4, 7, 11). This is a strange pattern of behavior for one whom many interpreters assume no longer to regard the distinction of Jews who believe in Christ as meaningful.[30]

The final framing construction in chapter 16 focuses attention on some group that is threatening to pull the Romans away from the "teaching" that they had learned (16:17–20). Members of this group appear to regard their freedom to eat all things higher than their concern to "serve Christ in a manner acceptable to God and approved by men" (14:18). They may best be labeled as "gentilizers," and they closely resemble those who are the source of the temptation toward arrogance that characterizes the gentiles of chapter 11 and the "strong" of chapter 14. Though the final doxology is

---

28. The possible scenarios for the earlier proclamation of the gospel in Rome are many; see Campbell, *Paul's Gospel in an Intercultural Context*, 102–6.

29. Aus, "Paul's Travel Plans to Spain and the 'Full Number of the Gentiles'"; Scott, *Paul and the Nations*.

30. Note that these greetings follow closely on Paul's use of the oblique labels "weak" and "strong" in 14:1—15:13, which some interpreters believe were coined to avoid calling attention to just such ethnic or cultural distinctions.

disputable, it faithfully summarizes Paul's concern to place his gospel—a gospel leading all the nations to the "obedience of faith"—in continuity with the revelation anticipated by the "Scriptures of the prophets, according to the commandment of the eternal God" (16:25–27).

The Jewish context of Paul's concern is evident throughout the argument of the letter's body as well. The first four chapters of Romans bear witness to an intra-Jewish debate characterized by synagogal sermons and the style of argumentation characteristic of the diatribe. In fact, the Jewish nature of the material is so contrary to the Pauline theological assumptions of modern scholars that E. P. Sanders suggests understanding 1:18—2:29 as a synagogue sermon of the Diaspora that Paul has inserted in his larger argument without any "distinctively Pauline imprint."[31] Paul clearly assumes Jewish priority and privilege (3:29a, 31), though not to the exclusion of those gentiles who are now in Christ by faith (3:29b–30). His argument is still for "the Jew first and *also* the Greek"; his intention is to bring about the certain restoration of all Israel and *also* the inclusion of the nations. Thus, Paul seeks to explain how the gentiles of Rome have entered into Israel's story, a story intended for the restoration of the whole creation.[32]

Christ's justifying work is "witnessed by the Law and the prophets" and fulfills the atoning sacrifice at the mercy seat (3:21–26), a far cry from Greco-Roman contextualizing for these gentile addressees. In Paul's discussion of [292] Jewish advantage, the "oracles of God" and the "works of the Law" provide a legitimate basis for boasting (3:27–29; cf. 9:1–5; 11:28–29),[33] yet they are held in tension with the equality of status for gentiles now offered through faith in Christ. It is this status, shared with Abraham, Israel's patriarch *par excellence,* at the point of faith, that obviates such boasting.[34] Other notable features are the catalog of pagan idolatry, the illustration of the apostrophic "Jew," the juxtaposition of circumcision and uncircumcision, and the dialectic of the hearers and doers of the Law with the positive emphasis on observing Torah—themes that Paul will develop to pull the opening Jewish perspective right through the rest of Romans.

---

31. E. P. Sanders, *Paul, the Law, and the Jewish People*, 129.

32. See Fraikin, "The Rhetorical Function of the Jews in Romans."

33. Lambrecht, "Why Is Boasting Excluded?" The "no" of Paul's response is too often overlooked.

34. Chance ("The Seed of Abraham and the People of God, 395) notes that "it was a *Jewish* concern for legitimacy which sparked the debate about Abraham and his seed. Put another way, the legitimization of gentiles as God's people by showing them to be of the seed of Abraham was not an intrinsic concern to the gentiles, or even to Paul" (emphasis his).

The Jewish focus continues to operate throughout chapters 5–11. Paul explains the positive role of the Law, contextualized differently for Jews and gentiles now in Christ, most recognizably in chapters 9–11, where Paul addresses the misguided and unacceptable triumphal notions gaining ground among the gentiles of Rome toward Jews who do not share their faith in Christ. Paul concedes that these Jews may be "stumbling" in faith, but they have not fallen, and while they may have been considered enemies, the minds of the Christian gentiles being addressed should now be "renewed" so that they are able to view these Jews as "God's beloved," suffering vicariously for a while in the very service of the gentiles themselves.[35]

This theme is equally developed in the tensions addressed in chapters 12–15 between the "weak" and "strong" as well as between the "enemies" and "neighbors" and "brethren." These tensions are unmistakably marked by lines of purity, by what is proper to eat, do, and say in the service of Christ that will be both acceptable to God *and* approved by men. The δυνατοί, those "able" to believe, are not to "destroy with [their] food him for whom Christ died," nor are they to walk in such a way that their "good things" will be legitimately blasphemed by the ἀσθενείς, the "weak" or "stumbling" who are not able (ἀδύνατοι) to believe in Jesus as Israel's Christ or to accept the equal participation of gentiles in the identity of the people of God through their faith in Jesus (14:1—15:13).[36] Notably, Paul concludes this argument by [293] calling both gentiles and Jews to welcome one another even as God has welcomed both. This echoes the Shema's call for unity of voice of both the circumcised and uncircumcised in glorifying the one God. Paul has cleverly shaped the distinctive contours of his argument around Israel's hope for that day when gentiles will be found declaring the glories of its God as the savior of all the nations, even in the midst of the congregation of Israel (15:5–12).[37]

B. The "Double Character" of the Letter

While Paul, throughout Romans, is concerned with matters Jewish, he has addressed the letter explicitly to Christian gentiles, a fact that, at the very least, "puts the letter's *rhetorical* integrity into question."[38] Consequently, many scholars have considered the question of the implied audience of Romans under the rubric of the letter's "double character." Few interpreters,

---

35. Hays, *Echoes of Scripture in the Letters of Paul*, 160–63.
36. I treat this theme at length in Nanos, *Mystery of Romans*, 85–165.
37. Hays, *Echoes of Scripture*, 70–74.
38. Elliott, *Rhetoric of Romans*, 10 (emphasis his); see also 20–21.

however, even consider the possibility that the text of Romans presupposes that the Christians whom Paul addressed in Rome actually continued to be involved in any real way with the Jewish synagogues—much less that they remained *within* the synagogues. Thus, they fail, I think, to draw out the implications of Paul's writing Romans to Christians in continuing relation to *real* Jewish communities.[39]

This point is represented most clearly, perhaps, by J. Christiaan Beker, who provides a sensitive treatment of the "Jewish problem" addressed in Romans 9–11; yet in the end he really provides no context for the letter's interaction with non-Christian Jews in Rome. While the clear presence of Jewish themes and tensions throughout Romans suggests a social setting with real non-Christian Jews, Beker describes a setting filled only with Jewish theological concerns, most likely those of Paul rather than those of his audience, but hardly a setting in which there are real, empirical Jews. Beker asks the right questions: "If Romans is a tractate evoked by historical circumstances, why does the letter address itself to a Jewish issue and present itself as a dialogue with Jews rather than with Jewish Christians—because they, and not Jews, are members of the Roman church? . . . If Paul's concern is the unity of Jewish and gentile Christians in the church, why does he carry on a [294] dialogue with synagogue Jews in Romans?"[40] But then he follows the traditional assumption that the problem that Paul addresses is the arrogance of non-Christian and Christian *Jews*,[41] concluding that

> dialogue with Jews . . . was necessary to determine not only the legitimate role of Jewish Christianity but especially that of the law-free gentile mission. The key to the dialogue is the abiding faithfulness of God in the light of the faithlessness and unbelief of Israel, manifested in its rejection of Christ. And if God's act in Christ confirms his faithfulness to Israel, God becomes as well the ground of trust for the gentiles.[42]

---

39. Brown, for example (Brown and Meier, *Antioch and Rome*, 110), declares that "the dominant Christianity at Rome had been shaped by the Jerusalem Christianity associated with James and Peter, and hence was a Christianity appreciative of Judaism and loyal to its customs." Cf. Fitzmyer, *Romans*, 36. Dunn (*Romans 1–8*, xlviii) suggests, differently, that "the Christian groups in Rome emerged from within the Jewish community itself," so that their "meetings in each others' homes would probably not, in the first instance, be thought of as opposed to the life and worship of the wider Jewish community."

40. Beker, *Paul the Apostle*, 89.

41. Ibid., 91; see Campbell, *Paul's Gospel in an Intercultural Context*, 136–41, and Elliott, *Rhetoric of Romans*, passim, for discussions of the problems with Beker's position.

42. Beker, *Paul the Apostle*, 89–91; see also Beker, "The Faithfulness of God and the Priority of Israel." See the critique of Beker's position by D. A. Campbell ("Determining

Beker's conclusions require only *theoretical* Jewish issues, and *Christian* Jews functioning independently of the Jewish communities. Furthermore, he fails to take seriously what the letter clearly implies, namely, that the gentiles in Rome are not questioning the grounds of God's faithfulness toward themselves, and certainly not of his faithfulness toward any Jews, Christian or non-Christian. Rather, they are boasting of just such a discontinuity, in that they are smugly secure in their new status, assuming that they have now both supplanted non-Christian Jews as the people of God and surpassed Christian Jews in their understanding of how to live in grace (this follows from Beker's assumption that the "weak" are Christian Jews). These gentiles in Rome may even presume that this is Paul's position.[43] Yet it is actually Paul's concern that their position casts doubt on God's faithfulness to Israel. Against their growing indifference, Paul seeks to show them the inherent error in viewing themselves as having supplanted Israel.

The failure of conventional solutions to resolve the "double character" of Romans is succinctly set out by Günter Klein. That Paul is engaged in a dialogue with Jews and Judaism is clear, but the explanations conventionally [295] offered fail to make sense of the implied character of the Christian gentile audience. It is not clear how the argument in chapters 1–11, concerned with non-Christian Jews, is supposed to prepare the audience for the paraenesis of chaps. 12–15, which is assumed to be concerned with Christian Jews. Klein cogently argues that the first eleven chapters do not provide the necessary "theological foundation of an intended peace settlement between gentile Christians and Jewish Christians," that Paul's "decisive statements" regarding the Law are "meant to shed light on the situation of the non-believing Jews, in fact on non-believers in general," not on that of the Jewish Christians, and that Romans 9–11 "cannot be regarded as a defense of Jewish Christianity in Rome" because "unconverted Israel" is the "primary reference."[44]

I suggest that Beker's intended rhetorical question is actually not so rhetorical after all,[45] and that Klein's paradox is not really a paradox. Rather, the

---

the Gospel through Rhetorical Analysis," esp. 316–18), who in the midst of his argument (317) makes the following comment: "Initially it seems incomprehensible that Paul, the apostle to the Gentiles, should compose and dictate fifteen chapters of very carefully constructed prose discoursing on *Jewish* questions, and send these to the *Gentile* Christians *at Rome*" (emphasis his). On the other hand, Campbell's conclusion that Paul writes in expectation that "Judaizers" will arrive in Rome is quite conventional.

43. Carter, "Rome (and Jerusalem)."
44. Klein, "Paul's Purpose in Writing the Epistle to the Romans," 36–37.
45. See the somewhat different critique of Beker by Elliott, *Rhetoric of Romans*, 41–43.

historical setting of Romans involves relationships between non-Christian Jews *because the early believers in Jesus were still meeting in the synagogues and functioning wholly within the larger Jewish community (or communities) of Rome.* This proposal makes sense of Paul's concerns regarding synagogue Jews, as Beker rightly observes, and as Klein upholds, making it paramount. It also explains why Paul addresses the everyday concerns and attitudes of the gentiles in Rome as they work out their faith and practices in the context of the Jewish community (or communities)—something that Beker's assumptions obscure but Klein's assumptions demand.

Given this proposal's explanatory value, why has it proved so elusive? Possibly because it goes against a number of conventional assumptions in the Christian tradition of theological interpretation. These assumptions bear closer examination.

C. The Inadequacy of Prevailing Assumptions about Romans

In spite of Paul's overwhelming concern to convey so thoroughly Jewish a perspective, the full implications for setting the letter's argument within the context of the Jewish community (or communities) are routinely overlooked. Several reasons may be identified, some involving issues presumed to have affected Rome prior to the composition and arrival of Paul's Letter to the Romans, others having to do with Paul's intentions and thought (or perhaps better, with the interpreters' prior understanding of "Paulinism").

1. House-churches in Rome are presumed to function independently of synagogues—in fact, in opposition to them. This is particularly emphasized by those who rely heavily on the so-called Edict of Claudius in reconstructing [296] the letter's historical situation. Even when these interpreters allow that prior to the edict the Christian gentiles in Rome did meet as a synagogal subgroup, they commonly presume that this was no longer the case by the time Romans was written.[46] But Paul's argument in Romans suggests that no such cataclysmic separation of the ways has taken place yet in Rome.

---

46. Stuhlmacher's comments *(Paul's Letter to the Romans,* 7) are an instructive example: "They [gentile Christians] now no longer had any possibility of meeting in their congregational gatherings as a 'special synagogue' under the protection of the Jewish religious and legal privileges, but had to form their own freely constituted assemblies without leaning on the Jewish synagogues." See also Walters, *Ethnic Issues* in *Paul's Letter to the Romans.* For a full critique of this assumption, see Nanos, *Mystery of Romans,* 372-87.

2. The theology of Galatians, and Paul's supposed Law-free gospel, is implicitly, and often explicitly, presumed to be operative for the recipients of Romans. But no evidence of such knowledge can be demonstrated in Rome, and in his letter to Rome Paul nowhere appeals to such knowledge.[47]

3. Justification by faith is assumed to obviate Jewish observance. It is often assumed that the early Christians (Jews and gentiles alike) saw their faith in Christ as a faith nullifying the observance of Torah and halakah, thus making continued contact with Jewish synagogues and worship undesirable. Against this assumption, it must be asked how the churches of Judaea could function as Law-observant, or how the temptation to "Judaize" among Christian gentiles could have been so pervasive, if this bifurcation was so necessary to Christian faith.

4. Many interpreters believe that the polemical debate with Judaism that surfaces in the text demonstrates the presence of Christian Jews opposed to Paul.[48] This explanation can be traced back to Marcion's depiction of the situation in his prologue to Romans, written in Rome in the middle of the second century: "The Romans [i.e., the Roman Christians] . . . were overcome [*praeventi sunt*] by false apostles and had been led, under the name of our Lord Jesus Christ, to the Law and the Prophets. Them the apostle recalled to the true evangelical faith, writing to them from Corinth."[49] Marcion recognizes the Jewish context of Roman Christianity, but his assumption that the [297] problem addressed in the letter is Jewish-Christian opposition raises the same questions directed earlier to interpreters like Beker: (a) How are we to reconcile the arrogant attitudes toward Jews and Judaism that Paul confronts among the Christian gentiles in Rome with the supposed attraction to Judaism that Marcion imagines?[50] and (b) How could "Judaizing" be a real threat if Jewish practices were automatically regarded as undesirable for those who believed in Jesus, as Marcion appears to suppose?

5. Many interpreters assume that by the time Paul wrote Romans, he was functioning independently of Jewish communities, setting up churches distinct and separate from synagogues. Some assert further that he intended to do the same for Rome, if churches were not already independent of synagogues there.[51]

---

47. Cf. Brown and Meier, *Antioch and Rome*, 111–14, 119; R. E. Brown, "Further Reflections on the Origins of the Church of Rome," 108–10.

48. Kümmel, *Introduction to the New Testament*, 220–22; Beker, *Paul the Apostle*; Fraikin, "Rhetorical Function of the Jews in Romans," 98.

49. Sanders, *Schismatics*, 217, translating the Latin text in Harnack, *Marcion*, 128.

50. Marcus, "The Circumcision and the Uncircumcision in Rome."

51. Watson, *Paul, Judaism and the Gentiles*; Judge and Thomas, "Origin of the

6. It is a virtually unquestioned assumption that Paul taught a Law-free gospel, that this was, in fact, the essence of Paulinism. According to this assumption, Paul's gospel diminished the value of Jewish practices and was intended ultimately to negate Jewish life within the Christian movement. Such an intention would naturally have led Paul to disregard the Jewish communities and their concerns, to distance himself from them, and to oppose any who sought to promote continued Jewish observances. It is assumed that although Paul tolerated the "weak in faith" (usually taken to be Christian Jews) for their own continued observance of Torah, he opposed any who sought to convince others either to become Jews or to observe Jewish practices.[52]

D. The Contextual Case for a Setting within the Jewish Community (or Communities)

The selected examples just seen show why, despite historical, archaeological, and literary evidence, including the argument of Romans itself, most, if not all, interpreters fail to see that the Christian movement that Paul addresses is to be located within the context of the Jewish community (or communities). The gentile believers in Christ, often presumed to have been the majority, are usually regarded as *former* God-fearers, now converted to Christ and attached to the Christian communities.[53] They are thought to [298] have abandoned Jewish convictions and customs, though perhaps not without some qualms. Some interpreters even believe that Paul writes precisely to ensure such withdrawal from Jewish community life.[54] They understand Paul to be engaging "the Jewish problem" in Rome, a problem having to do with "Judaizers" or Judaism and with the misguided views of *Jewish* Christians. Differently, for those who do not locate the letter's *Sitz im Leben* in Rome, Romans is "Paul's own thinking on the question of the Jews and the

---

Church at Rome."

52. So, for example, Brown and Meier, *Antioch and Rome*, 111–14.

53. Schmithals, *Paul and James*, 60–62; Dunn, *Romans 1-8*, xlv–liv; Lampe, "The Roman Christians of Romans 16."

54. Most of these scholars, including Judge and Thomas ("Origin of the Church at Rome"), Watson (*Paul, Judaism and the Gentiles*), and Schmithals (*Paul and James*) believe that Paul was seeking to dissuade the Romans from continuing to function within the Jewish communities as adherents, or even to continue to live a Jewish lifestyle within the Christian communities. See the criticism of Watson by Campbell (*Paul's Gospel in an Intercultural Context*, 122–30) and the criticism of both Schmithals and Watson by Elliott (*Rhetoric of Romans*, 31–36).

Law in light of his impending visit to Jerusalem."[55] Most interpreters seem content to observe that "Judaizers" and Christian Jews are present, or will soon be present, in Rome, assuming that these are referred to in Romans 14 and 15 (as the "weak in faith") and again in 16:17-20.

I argue that this assumption is not correct.[56] Even if it were correct, it still could not explain the concerns in the rest of the letter, as the following observations make clear.

1. Non-Christian Jews are clearly in view at significant points in the argument. The illustration that Paul uses in Romans 2 is that of a *non*-Christian Jew, as is the case in the argument that follows in Romans 3 and 4. In Romans 11 Paul addresses a breakdown in attitudes toward non-Christian Jews by Christian gentiles, a problem of perspective that is both real in Rome and of utmost concern to Paul. (Note that the Christian Jews constituting the "remnant" in 11:1-6 provide only the background rhetorical device in this argument.) Those perceived to be neighbors and even enemies in chapters 12-15 are likely the same. As I have noted, the entire framework of chapters 1-11 provides a renewed perspective expressly toward non-Christian Jews. In the paraenesis of chapters 12-15, Paul addresses the same tension between the "strong" (δυνατοί) Christian gentiles and the "weak" (ἀσθενείς, here better rendered as "stumbling") non-Christian Jews. In contrast to the prevailing assumptions regarding Paul's opposition to Judaism and Judaizing discussed above, I suggest that if Paul's argument throughout Romans is to make sense, it requires *real* Jews, empirical Jews with Jewish lifestyles, within [299] Jewish communities, in direct and regular (perhaps authoritative) contact with the Christian gentile audience.[57]

2. Paul says nothing explicit in Romans against Christian "Judaizing." Neither Christian Jews nor "Judaizers" appear to be the problem in Rome; Paul speaks to the dangers of "gentilizing," if anything. The Christian gentiles he addresses are tempted not toward circumcision but toward an arrogant triumphalism against the circumcised. Paul's criticism is not of the Law. He "joyfully concurs" with the Law and calls it spiritual (7:14), holy, righteous,

---

55. E. P. Sanders, *Paul and Palestinian Judaism*, 487-89; Jervell, "The Letter to Jerusalem."

56. See Nanos, *Mystery of Romans*, 85-165.

57. I do not mean to suggest that Jews who believe in Jesus are not real Jews, or that God-fearing gentiles might not also be regarded as real semi-Jews. As long as such persons continue to observe Torah and operative halakot, they are real Jews and semi-Jews. But I do mean to exclude persons in certain categories commonly adduced in discussions of Romans: *former* God-fearing gentiles, and *former* Jews, who are no longer understood to live as Jews because of their faith in Christ. Most importantly, I mean to exclude theological Jews and abstract Judaism, that is, Judaism not assumed to be real in the lives and lifestyles of those addressed.

good (7:12, 16), established by faith in Christ (3:31), even an "advantage" for Jews (3:1-2), as well as a gift of God that is forever irrevocable (9:1-5; 11:28-29). Paul is not polemical, not even guarded, in his references to Torah in Romans—which suggests that he is not concerned that the gentiles whom he addresses are in danger of embracing it in a way which he considers dangerous. Paul himself wishes to do the Law, agrees with it in his inner self, and finds in Christ the victory enabling him to fulfill Torah; he expects the same of those whom he addresses (7:7—8:4; 10:4; 13:8-10).

3. Paul does not address issues that we might expect to arise in the sort of gentile congregations, functioning independently of the synagogue, that are presumed by so many interpreters. Paul's audience is told how to get along not with gentiles, nor with Romans, but with Jews. No advice is given that would be helpful to gentiles newly in authority in these churches—nothing of ecclesiastical matters, no household codes, no instructions for baptism, marriage, burial, or evangelism.

4. Paul does address his gentile audience's behavior with regard to their close proximity to Jews, and he does so according to Jewish standards. The practice of their new faith is not contextualized with respect to pagan religions or customs or with concern for social status suddenly rendered uncertain by their new faith and behavior. Rather, they are told how to relate their faith and the practice of righteousness to the community issues prevailing among the historical people of God. They are to become "slaves of righteousness" concerned with the "obedience of faith" outlined in the teaching of proper behavior with which they are already familiar (6:16-23). They are to seek peace with those "stumbling in faith" with whom they are beginning to disagree about behavior related to purity. They are to "serve Christ in a way [300] acceptable to God and approved by men," men who, oddly enough, appear to have the power either to guarantee their faith as good, as the real thing, or otherwise to blaspheme it as evil (14:14b-23).

Paul's instruction to "renew their minds" (12:1-2) follows not the typical synagogue sermon cataloging pagan idolatry and sin in chapter 1 but Paul's explanation of the "stumbling" of Israel in chapter 11. These are Jews whom Paul's audience has come to regard as enemies of God but now must learn to see anew from God's perspective as his beloved. Paul goes to great lengths to insist that these Jews are not stumbling so as to fall: rather, they are suffering vicariously so that God's mercies will be recognized among the gentiles addressed, and (only) then among themselves. The apostrophe to the Jew guilty of hypocritically judging others (2:17-29) serves as a rhetorical gambit revealing to these gentiles their own very real conceptions and prejudices, how they themselves are hypocrites if they suppose that they have supplanted the "stumbling" of Israel (11:11-32). Regarding proper diet, they are told to accommodate Jewish notions so as not to "destroy with [their] food him for whom Christ died" (14:14b—15:3).

E. The Social Setting of Paul's Motif of "Jealousy"

The relevance of a non-Christian Jewish context for Paul's argument is nowhere more evident than in Romans 11. Ironically, it is just here that interpretation continues to be distorted by mistaken assumptions regarding Paul's theology. It is surely clear that in this argument Paul seeks to correct a misconceived triumphalism on the part of Christian gentiles in Rome over Jewish people who do not share these gentiles' faith in Jesus or accept their participation as equals. Here, precisely, Paul declares that he is seeking to provoke some of these Jews to "jealousy" by—it is to be noted—his ministry.

The jealousy Paul means to arouse in his fellow Jews is not envy or resentment but emulation,[58] a positive jealousy that will "save some of them" who have thus far not believed in Jesus as the Christ. Paul cannot mean that these Jews will be jealous of gentiles being saved. The assumption that this is what he means, seemingly unquestioned in much modern scholarship, is just not plausible. Nor is it acceptable. It appears to be predicated on one of two twisted premises: either that Jews are so selfish that they do not want gentiles to be saved, or that seeing gentiles saved would make Jews jealous because this would mean that Jews were being replaced as God's people.

[301] Such reactions would have been completely inscrutable to Paul's Jewish contemporaries. If gentiles were purportedly being saved in a new religious movement, outside of Jewish expectations and norms, then whatever else Jews thought of the proposition, it would not be seen as one jeopardizing their own salvation. As the people of covenant by God's promise, they could hardly be expected to be jealous of such gentiles. On the other hand, if one *could* imagine Jews regarding the salvation of gentiles as a threat to their own salvation—as if, for example, gentiles could be seen as a group replacing Jews as "the saved"—one might well expect Jews to denounce such a movement, to be provoked to a negative jealousy expressed in anger and contempt. But this is clearly not what Paul anticipated.

Nor does such a supposition make any sense of Paul's intentions in Romans. Instead Paul confronts the temptation of "saved" gentiles to regard themselves as a group supplanting Jews. Does it make sense that he would

---

58. Aristotle, *Rh.* 2.10.11. See Bell, *Provoked to Jealousy*, for a full discussion of the range of meanings possible for "jealousy" and a study of the roots of this motif in Deuteronomy 32. In Romans 11 Paul speaks of a positive jealousy, namely, emulation (vv. 11–14). See also Robinson, "The Salvation of Israel in Romans 9–11."

seek to persuade his Jewish brothers and sisters that this is precisely what *is* taking place? Is it not simply anachronistic to impute to Paul's Jewish contemporaries a replacement theory that was only beginning to emerge among Christian gentiles?[59]

Even more damaging to this conventional interpretation of the "jealousy" Paul seeks to arouse is its implicit contradiction of Paul's *modus operandi* for the gentile mission, that is, his eschatological notion of bearing the light of Israel to the nations. While Jewish missionary impulses and programs for this period are the subject of lively debate, Jewish eschatological notions were clearly full of the expectation that gentiles would turn to the worship of Israel's Lord in the last days, albeit according to scenarios that ranged widely, from pilgrimages to massive conversions.[60] It follows that most Jews would have viewed gentiles' turning to Israel's Lord not negatively but with delight, if they could regard those gentiles as "righteous gentiles."[61] Such conversion would have meant not that Jews were stepping down but that gentiles were stepping up and recognizing what Jews already knew; that "the Lord is our God, the Lord is one."

[302] The construct of Jewish "jealousy" of gentile salvation is based on a Christian theory of displacement that would not have occurred to Paul's Jewish contemporaries, or to Paul. It is time to abandon this assumption, almost universally held by Christian interpreters of Romans 11, as anachronistic and counterintuitive. The notion of gentiles displacing the people of Israel was in fact an error of judgment among gentiles that Paul emphatically confronted as wrong and harmful to Jews, and even dangerous to gentiles themselves: "otherwise you also will be cut off," he warns (11:22).

Most importantly, this common assumption does not reflect what Paul actually says. His aim is to make "some" of the Jews in Rome whom he and his audience consider to be "stumbling" jealous of *his* "ministry," which is a very different point. Paul expects these Jews to recognize in his ministry that *their own* positive hopes and expectations for a successful ministry with gentiles at the end of time are being realized, though without their expected participation. This is a demonstration of (un)realized eschatology on their

---

59. The first evidence of this theory of replacement is found in Justin Martyr's writings from the mid-second century; see Richardson, *Israel in the Apostolic Church*.

60. E. P. Sanders, *Jesus and Judaism*, 214; Donaldson, "Proselytes or 'Righteous Gentiles'?"; Fredriksen, *From Jesus to Christ*, 149–76.

61. It appears from most of the extant literature that Jews expected that the gentiles would remain gentiles, though they would be no longer idolaters or sinners but "righteous gentiles" at the point of their eschatological salvation; cf. Fredriksen, "Judaism, the Circumcision of Gentiles, and Apocalyptic Hope"; Donaldson, "Proselytes or 'Righteous Gentiles'?" 25–27.

part, so to speak, in that Paul intends to make his Jewish contemporaries jealous of his ministry of serving as a light to the nations. When they realize that Paul is fulfilling the role of Israel that they fully expect to participate in as well, "ministering [as priests] the gospel of God, that [their] offering of the gentiles might become acceptable, sanctified by the Holy Spirit" (15:16; cf. 1:13; 12:1–2; 15:26–29), then Paul expects their consequent jealousy to provoke them to reconsider the "good news" that he proclaims, a gospel that they have thus far been disregarding for themselves. In fact, the jealousy in view is a positive, competitive jealousy.

What can this passage tell us about the social setting addressed in Romans? I propose that it helps us realize the logical construction of a context in which the gentiles and Jews who believed in Jesus Christ were still meeting within the synagogues, those who believed in Christ forming an additional subgroup identity along lines analogous, for example, to modem charismatics within mainline Christian churches, or Wesley and his early followers among the Anglicans. There are a number of grounds for this proposal, though I am not aware of their consideration in modem scholarship.

When we reflect on the entire context of Romans 11, we surely must ask, why, in a letter usually thought to show considerable circumspection toward those who might not accept Paul's authority over themselves, would he address the growing gentile arrogance toward Jews if this were not a real problem in Rome? Paul clearly challenges this notion as though his intervention could make a difference. But how could this be a real, though not irreversible, problem, if gentiles were not still associating with non-Christian Jews?

Why, furthermore, is the gentiles' concern to validate their own self-identity as the people of God by negating and supplanting Jews so central? Why is such resentment toward non-Christian Jews evident from the letter [303] if in fact the Christian gentiles are functioning independently of the synagogues? What would these gentiles really gain from adopting such a theory of replacement, and why would Paul oppose this notion so strenuously if it had nothing to do with actual circumstances of regular contact between Christian gentiles and non-Christian Jews?

Why would Paul believe that by revealing the mystery of Rom 11:25–26 he would confront the gentiles' temptation toward conceit, if (as most interpreters believe) the idea that the eventual salvation of "all Israel" is certain really reinforces the newly conceived priority of the gentiles (i.e., gentiles first, then Jews)? If the salvation of "all Israel" required some distant, apocalyptic act of God that was quite beyond human control,[62] would

---

62. W. Campbell, *Paul's Gospel in an Intercultural Context*, 92–93

this not imply that the gentiles' certainty of salvation remained untouched by Israel's response, or (more to the point) by their own attitudes toward non-Christian Jews in their midst? Such an understanding of God's unilateral salvation of Israel, independent of any human action, would subtly imply the failure of the gospel in Israel. For Paul, this would mean shame (cf. 1:16), and it would render incomprehensible his motives for composing Romans.

How, finally, could Paul expect Jews to be acquainted with the contours of his ministry, let alone be jealous of it, if he were operating outside of the synagogues,[63] or if he was regarded as an apostate or former Jew now proclaiming a new religion?[64] Why should Paul's Jewish contemporaries care about his gentile converts—let alone consider their conversion an occasion of jealousy—unless they, and Paul himself, knew themselves to be working within Jewish communities in Jewish ways?

Paul expects that his ministry among the gentiles will be both known and acknowledged among Jews. This means that he, his ministry, and those he is seeking to persuade in Rome, must all be functioning within the context and jurisdiction of Jewish communities. Unless those with whom his readers interact know of Paul's ministry at first hand, unless they recognize it as an intended actualization of their own authentically Jewish expectations, his play to provoke jealousy will have no persuasive force at all.[65]

III. CONCLUSION

[304] If the motif of jealousy in Romans is to make sense, it requires a social setting involving regular contact with real Jews, most likely in positions of authority. Among these Jews must be some whom Paul characterizes as "stumbling," Jews who, unlike Abraham, are growing weak in faith (4:19–21), who are unable to believe in the "seed." These must be non-Christian

---

63. Watson, *Paul, Judaism, and the Gentiles*; Meeks, *First Urban Christians*, 168.

64. Barclay, "Paul among Diaspora Jews: Anomaly or Apostate?," 89–120.

65. This interpretation of the "jealousy" of 11:14 has implications for our understanding of the mystery of 11:25–26 as well. I believe that the "fullness of the gentiles" is neither the completion of Paul's ministry to the gentiles, nor the summation of the collection for Jerusalem, nor some eschatological event in the distant future such as the parousia, but rather the commencement of the mission to the gentiles in a given location after Paul's initial preaching to the Jews of that place. Paul's intention with the "bold reminder" of Romans was to call these gentiles to continued observance of applicable halakah, that is, to continue in the "obedience of faith" and thereby to "serve Christ in a way acceptable to God and approved by men," until he arrived with "his gift," the gospel which would establish them as it brought them within God's two-step pattern for the restoration of Israel and the ingathering of the nations.

Jews, whose destiny is inextricably bound up with the very "ability" of the gentiles to believe—but upon whom the gentiles' capacity to believe also unexpectedly depends.

The letter that Paul wrote to the Romans offers the modern interpreter literary evidence of Paul's thought and of the social setting of the Roman believers in Christ, before the parting of the ways between Judaism and Christianity, before believers in Christ formally functioned outside of the identity and jurisdiction of the synagogue, before they were understood by Paul as anything other than participants in a Jewish coalition.[66]

BIBLIOGRAPHY

Aus, Roger D. "Paul's Travel Plans to Spain and the 'Full Number of the Gentiles' of Rom. XI 25." *Novum Testamentum* 21 (1979) 232–62.

Barclay, John. "Paul among Diaspora Jews: Anomaly or Apostate?" *Journal for the Study of the New Testament* 60 (1995) 89–120.

Beker, Johan Christiaan. "The Faithfulness of God and the Priority of Israel in Paul's Letter to the Romans." In *The Romans Debate*, edited by Karl P. Donfried, 327–45. Rev. ed. Peabody, MA: Hendrickson, 1991.

———. *Paul the Apostle: The Triumph of God in Life and Thought*. Philadelphia: Fortress, 1980.

Bell, Richard H. *Provoked to Jealousy: The Origin and Purpose of the Jealousy Motif in Romans 9–11*. WUNT 2/63. Tübingen: Mohr (Siebeck), 1994.

Benko, Stephen. *Pagan Rome and the Early Christians*. London: Batsford, 1985.

Brown, Raymond Edward. "Further Reflections on the Origins of the Church of Rome." In *The Conversation Continues: Studies in Paul and John in Honor of J. Louis Martyn*, edited by Robert T. Fortna and Beverly R. Gaventa. 98–115. Nashville: Abingdon, 1990.

Brown, Raymond Edward, and John P. Meier. *Antioch and Rome: New Testament Cradles of Catholic Christianity*. New York: Paulist, 1983.

Campbell, Douglas A. "Determining the Gospel through Rhetorical Analysis in Paul's Letter to the Roman Christians." In *Gospel in Paul: Studies on Corinthians, Galatians and Romans for Richard N. Longenecker*, edited by L. Ann Jervis and Peter Richardson, 315–36. JSNTSup 108. Sheffield, UK: Sheffield Academic Press, 1994.

Campbell, William S. *Paul's Gospel in an Intercultural Context: Jew and Gentile in the Letter to the Romans*. Studien zur interkulturellen Geschichte des Christentums 69. Frankfurt am Main: Lang, 1992.

Chance, J. Bradley. "The Seed of Abraham and the People of God: A Study of Two Pauls." In *Society of Biblical Literature Seminar Papers 1993*, 384–411.

Collins, John J. *Between Athens and Jerusalem: Jewish Identity in the Hellenistic Diaspora*. New York: Crossroad, 1983.

---

66. I wish to express special thanks to Neil Elliott for his helpful review of this article and his comments on it.

Donaldson, Terrance L. "Proselytes or 'Righteous Gentiles'? The Status of Gentiles in Eschatological Pilgrimage Patterns of Thought." *Journal for the Study of the Pseudepigrapha* 7 (1990) 3–27.

Dunn, James D. G. *Romans 1–8*. WBC 38A. Dallas, TX: Word, 1988.

Elliott, Neil. *The Rhetoric of Romans: Argumentative Constraint and Strategy and Paul's Dialogue with Judaism*. JSNTSup 45. Sheffield, UK: Sheffield Academic Press, 1990.

Eschner, Werner. *Der Romerbrief: An die Juden der Synagogen in Rom?* 2 vols. Hannover: Eschner, 1981.

Feldman, Louis H. "Diaspora Synagogues: New Light from Inscriptions and Papyri." In *Sacred Realm*, edited by Steven Fine, 48–66. Oxford: Oxford University Press, 1996

Fine, Steven, ed. *Sacred Realm: The Emergence of the Synagogue in the Ancient World.* Oxford: Oxford University Press, 1996.

Fitzmyer, Joseph A. *Romans*. AB 33. New York: Doubleday, 1993.

Fraikin, Daniel. "The Rhetorical Function of the Jews in Romans." In *Anti-Judaism in Early Christianity 1: Paul and the Gospels*, edited by Peter Richardson with David Granskou, 91–106. Waterloo, ON: Wilfrid Laurier University Press, 1986.

Fredriksen, Paula. *From Jesus to Christ: The Origins of the New Testament Images of Jesus*. New Haven: Yale University Press, 1988.

———. "Judaism, the Circumcision of Gentiles, and Apocalyptic Hope: Another Look at Galatians 1 and 2." *Journal of Theological Studies* n.s. 42 (1991) 544–48.

Garlington, Don B. *"The Obedience of Faith": A Pauline Phrase in Historical Context*. WUNT 2/38. Tübingen: Mohr (Siebeck) 1991.

Grant, Michael. *Nero*. London: Weidenfeld & Nicolson, 1970.

Harnack, Adolf von. *Marcion: Das Evangelium vom fremden Gott; eine Monographie zur Geschichte der Grundlegung der katholischen Kirche*. TU 45. 2nd ed. Leipzig: Hinrichs, 1924.

Hays, Richard B. *Echoes of Scripture in the Letters of Paul*. New Haven: Yale University Press, 1989.

Jervell, Jacob. "The Letter to Jerusalem." In *The Romans Debate*, edited by Karl P. Donfried, 53–64. Peabody, MS: Hendrickson, 1991.

Jewett, Robert. "Tenement Churches and Communal Meals in the Early Church: The Implications of a Form-critical Analysis of 2 Thessalonians 3:10." *Biblical Research* 38 (1993) 23–43.

Judge, Edwin A. "Judaism and the Rise of Christianity: A Roman Perspective." *Tyndale Bulletin* 45 (1994) 355–68.

Judge, Edwin A., and G. S. R. Thomas. "The Origin of the Church at Rome: A New Solution." *Reformed Theological Review* 25 (1966) 81–94.

Kee, Howard Clark. "Defining the First-Century CE Synagogue: Problems and Progress." *New Testament Studies* 41 (1995) 481–500.

Klein, Günter. "Paul's Purpose in Writing the Epistle to the Romans." In *The Romans Debate*, edited by Karl P. Donfried, 29–43. Peabody, MA: Hendrickson, 1991.

Kümmel, Werner G. *Introduction to the New Testament*. Nashville: Abingdon, 1966.

Lambrecht, Jan. "Why Is Boasting Excluded? A Note on Romans 3,27 and 4,2." In *Pauline Studies: Collected Essays*, 27–31. BETL 115. Leuven: Leuven University Press, 1994.

Lampe, Peter. "The Roman Christians of Romans 16." In *The Romans Debate*, edited by Karl P. Donfried, 216-30. Peabody, MA: Hendrickson, 1991.

———. *Die stadtrömischen Christen in den ersten beiden Jahrhunderten: Untersuchungen zur Sozialgeschichte*. WUNT 2/18. Tübingen: Mohr (Siebeck), 1989.

Lane, William L. *Hebrews 1-8*. WBC 47A. Dallas, TX: Word, 1991.

Leon, Harry J. *The Jews of Ancient Rome*. Philadelphia: Jewish Publication Society of America, 1960.

Marcus, Joel. "The Circumcision and the Uncircumcision in Rome." *New Testament Studies* 35 (1989) 67-81.

Meeks, Wayne A. *The First Urban Christians: The Social World of the Apostle Paul*. New Haven: Yale University Press, 1983.

Meyers, Eric M., and A. Thomas Kraabel. "Archaeology, Iconography, and Nonliterary Written Remains." In *Early Judaism and Its Modern Interpreters*, edited by Robert A. Kraft and George W. E. Nickelsburg, 175-210. SBLBMI 2. Philadelphia: Fortress; Atlanta: Scholars, 1986.

Nanos, Mark D. *The Mystery of Romans: The Jewish Context of Paul's Letter*. Minneapolis: Fortress, 1996.

Remus, H. "Justin Martyr's Argument with Judaism." In *Anti-Judaism in Early Christianity 2: Separation and Polemic*, edited by Stephen G. Wilson, 72-74. Waterloo, ON: Wilfrid Laurier University Press, 1986.

Richardson, Peter. *Israel in the Apostolic Church*. SNTSMS 10. Cambridge: Cambridge University Press, 1969.

Robinson, D. W. B. "The Salvation of Israel in Romans 9-11." *Reformed Theological Review* 26 (1967) 92-95.

Rutgers, Leonard Victor. "Archaeological Evidence for the Interaction of Jews and Non-Jews in Late Antiquity." *American Journal of Archaeology* 96 (1992) 101-18.

———. *The Jews in Late Ancient Rome: Evidence of Cultural Interaction in the Roman Diaspora*. Religions in the Graeco-Roman World 126. Leiden, Brill, 1995.

Sanders, E. P. *Jesus and Judaism*. Philadelphia: Fortress, 1985

———. *Judaism: Practice and Belief 63 BCE-66 CE*. Philadelphia: Trinity, 1992.

———. *Paul and Palestinian Judaism: A Comparison of Patterns of Religion*. Philadelphia: Fortress, 1977.

———. *Paul, the Law, and the Jewish People*. Philadelphia: Fortress, 1983.

Sanders, Jack T. *Schismatics, Sectarians, Dissidents, Deviants: The First One Hundred Years of Jewish-Christian Relations*. London: SCM, 1993.

Schmithals, Walther. *Paul and James*. SBT 46. Naperville, IL: Allenson, 1965.

Scott, James M. *Paul and the Nations: The Old Testament and Jewish Background of Paul's Mission to the Nations with Special Reference to the Destination of Galatians*. WUNT 84; Tübingen: Mohr (Siebeck), 1995.

Smallwood, E. Mary. *The Jews under Roman Rule, from Pompey to Diocletian: A Study in Political Relations*. SJLA 20. Leiden: Brill, 1981.

Stowers, Stanley Kent. *A Rereading of Romans: Justice, Jews, and Gentiles*. New Haven: Yale University Press, 1994.

Streeter, B. H. *The Primitive Church, Studied with Special Reference to the Origins of the Christian Ministry*. New York: Macmillan, 1929.

Stuhlmacher, Peter. *Paul's Letter to the Romans: A Commentary*. Louisville: Westminster/John Knox, 1994.

Tcherikover, Victor. *Hellenistic Civilization and the Jews.* Philadelphia: Jewish Publication Society of America, 1961.

Walters, James C. *Ethnic Issues in Paul's Letter to the Romans: Changing Self-Definitions in Earliest Roman Christianity.* Valley Forge, PA: Trinity, 1993.

Watson, Francis. *Paul, Judaism and the Gentiles: A Sociological Approach.* SNTSMS 56. Cambridge: Cambridge University Press, 1986.

Wedderburn, A. J. M. *The Reasons for Romans.* Studies of the New Testament and Its World. Minneapolis: Fortress, 1988.

White, L. Michael. *Building God's House in the Roman World: Architectural Adaptation among Pagans, Jews, and Christians.* Baltimore: Johns Hopkins University Press, 1990.

Williams, Margaret H. "The Structure of Roman Jewry Reconsidered—Were the Synagogues of Ancient Rome Entirely Homogeneous?" *Zeitschrift für Papyrologie und Epigraphik* 102 (1994) 129–41.

Wright, N. T. *The Climax of the Covenant.* Minneapolis: Fortress, 1992.

———. *The New Testament and the People of God.* London: SPCK, 1992.

4

A Rejoinder to Robert A. J. Gagnon's "Why the 'Weak' at Rome Cannot Be Non-Christian Jews"[1]

IN AN ESSAY PUBLISHED in *Catholic Biblical Quarterly* in 2000, Robert Gagnon objected to the argument in *The Mystery of Romans* (1996) that "the ἀσθενέω" (usually: "the *weak*") in Romans 14–15 signified Jewish people who did *not* believe Jesus to be the Christ (Messiah), claiming that my interpretation—which challenged the probability of the traditional and prevailing views—"cannot" be correct.

It is an honor to have one's argument considered significant enough to engage in detail, all the more the kind of extensive effort Gagnon has undertaken, regardless of the fact that he intends to undermine my arguments because he perceives them to be a threat to long-standing theological viewpoints he wants to defend. In addition to seeking to respond to many of the elements in his arguments, let me begin by stating I do

---

1. Robert Gagnon's article in *CBQ* is a response to a chapter in my *The Mystery of Romans* entitled "Who Were the 'Weak' and the 'Strong' in Rome?" 85–165. I wrote this essay in 2000 to respond, although *CBQ* did not accept it for publication on the grounds that I had already had my say in *Mystery*, and have updated it slightly for publication herein. I disagreed with that judgment, and still do, for the same reason I offered then; namely, much of what might appear to be critical argumentation was misleading or fallacious, and those who wish to dismiss my case without engaging it could simply appeal to his essay as if the case was settled. That is indeed what one will find regularly exemplified in dismissive footnotes by interpreters advocating the consensus views, a habit that characterizes the commentary tradition. This matter is discussed in more detail in the Preface to this volume.

not want to claim that the situation or identities *must be* as I have argued them to be, but at the same time I do not want Gagnon's remarkable assertion that it *cannot be* possible to go unchallenged. In historical terms, we test hypotheses and argue probabilities for interpreting any document. In the case of this letter, as Gagnon explicitly recognizes, much is at stake for the interpretation of Paul and early "Christian" theology, not least the way in which Jewish identity and behavior are regarded by those who look to Romans to shape their ideology.

Gagnon frames his objection with the observation that my reading offers a more respectful view of Jews and Judaism for Paul, with helpful implications for contemporary Christian-Jewish relations. I do suppose this to be the case; Gagnon initially mentions this implication without reflecting on whether that matters to him or not when deciding between alternative interpretations on offer. Later, he brings up the topic of "politically correct standards," as if that involves a "fashionable" reshaping of how Paul might have written about his fellow Jews that compromises the quest to understand the historical Paul if he turns out to be "scandalous." This *ad hominum* is apparently introduced to signal that my approach (and others like it) is "interested," that because it articulates a position that offers more promising avenues to explore for discussions of Paul's voice with respect to Christian-Jewish relations it is thereby more suspect than the view Gagnon promotes (78). That kind of reasoning, which has become a regular refrain for those who resist the arguments to read Paul in ways that challenge the received views raises many logical and moral questions, not least: Does lack of concern about the negative implications for Jews and Judaism to which the received views have contributed (and to which they will continue to contribute if repeated without hermeneutical distance from that Paul's voice), which views Gagnon defends (without expressing such distance), logically make that viewpoint any less "interested"? Or does this make it one that instead promotes a different agenda, in this case, one proven to be harmful, and one understood by many to be at the very least historically anachronistic as well as supportive of the status quo for Christian theological reasoning? Should historical work that promises to improve the situation of someone or group other than our own be dismissed by nature as any more suspicious than that which promotes the received view when it is recognized to contribute to harmful ways of characterizing and behaving toward the other? Should we not judge the historical argumentation, remaining always aware of the location of the one who has conducted it, and ourselves, and state these explicitly so that we stay alert to where we might manipulate rather than investigate properly?

Putting aside Gagnon's and my apparently different ideological concerns, the first order of business for New Testament historical criticism is the pursuit of the probable meaning for the original author and audience. Keeping this concern central, I shall take up each of the points that Gagnon engages, allowing, for the sake of simplicity, the structure of his response to dictate the arrangement of this rejoinder, albeit not necessarily sharing his evaluation of the relative weight of the issues. In doing so I will seek to clarify issues that he has identified, at points offering additional observations that enhance the probability of the interpretation I have offered, but I will not seek to argue again all the angles originally considered, whether addressed by Gagnon, or not.

THE BASIC ISSUE

Gagnon argues from the consensus viewpoint that the parties usually identified as "the weak" were *Law-observant Christ-followers* (usually simply *Christians*)[2] and "the strong" were *Law-free* Christ-followers. Paul defined them along this binary trajectory because of their different *opinions* (*convictions* or *faith commitments*) *about the continued value of Torah-observance for Christ-followers*. Gagnon's main concern is to oppose my proposal that the division was more likely based on *different convictions about the gospel claim that Jesus was the Christ (Messiah)*, and thus to upend my conclusion that these phrases probably signified *Christ-followers* versus *non-Christ-followers* based on their *ability to trust* in the gospel claims for Jesus, or not. I maintain that for Paul and his audience, to be a Christ-follower who still valued Torah-observance as a covenantal obligation would not have logically signified "weakness," or the denial of such a position "strength" of Christian conviction, as if every Christ-follower by definition should abandon Torah in view of their faith in Christ (per the received view of Paul and Paulinism, which Gagnon defends).

---

2. In *Mystery of Romans*, I used "Christian" as an adjective (and Jew or gentile as nouns) at a time when most still used Christian as a noun, so quotations of Gagnon as well as my own arguments will reflect that, although I have updated references herein to my preferred (although still far from perfect) terminology today, Christ-following Jews and non-Jews (or non-Christ-following Jews and non-Jews), also avoiding to use "gentiles," since it was also similarly not helpful for trying to construct the mid-first-century context we seek to understand and discuss. Paul did not use the term "Christian," and there is good reason to suppose that no one did when Paul was writing this letter, or, if it was used, that it did not mean what it has come to mean and signify for most readers today, i.e., a religious way of life distinguishable not least for being something other than Judaism (a Jewish way of life).

To support resistance to my proposal that Paul's target addressees were Christ-following non-Jews in synagogue subgroups whom Paul feared were growing resentful toward the Jews in the majority groups who were not Christ-followers (which is predicated on the supposition that the Christ-movement was still a Jewish communal phenomenon), Gagnon submits that both parties—"weak" and "strong"—consisted entirely of *gentiles* divided over the value of Torah-observance (most propose that the "strong" were non-Jews, at least primarily so, and the "weak" were Jews, but might include non-Jews who were adopting Jewish lifestyles; I primarily identified the "strong" as both Jews and non-Jews who followed Christ, and likewise the "weak" could be anyone who did not, Jew or non-Jew). For Gagnon, now that the Christ-followers were entirely separated from Jewish communal life and meeting in "gentile churches," and in view of Claudius having supposedly expelled all the Jews from Rome (both represent prevailing views that I contested), there were no Christ-following Jews around anyway with whom the "strong" would have been in the conflict Paul seeks to address, and thus they were not those being referred to as "the weak" (or, as I preferred, "the stumbling").

I proposed that Paul sought to use a respectful euphemism for those whom he and the other Christ-followers in Rome considered "[in a state of] *stumbling* to trust [ἀσθενοῦντα τῇ πίστει]" (14:1) the gospel message about Jesus (i.e., the *weak*; or, more literally, "the ones in a state of *weakness/stumblingness*").[3] In this sense, Paul contrasted them with those to whom he wrote: "the *able* ones [οἱ δυνατοί]" (15:1), that is, the ones presently *able to trust* the gospel claims, referred to as "the *strong*," to use the consensus way of discussing the matter, who are instructed to understand that they are under obligation to "bear" (or "consider" or perhaps "endure" [βαστάζειν]) the *weaknesses* of the *unable*/strong ones [ἀσθενήματα τῶν ἀδυνάτων]" (15:1), a task compared to that which Christ suffered because he put the interests of the other above his own, even when suffering insults unjustly (vv. 2–3). Paul apparently believed that in time this temporary state, which he referred to as a result of God's act of *protecting* or *saving* (σῴζω) Israel (11:26), would complete its course, and that his ministry, as well as the lives of the gentiles he targeted in this letter, were somehow, in

---

3. Today I would use "trust" (or "faithfulness," "loyalty," "confidence," "steadfastness") rather than "faith" when translating *pistis*, and would argue for a translation that communicates the dative "to" when possible, as it is here, by referring to "to trust," and then filling in the referent as "in the gospel" or "in Jesus as Christ," and would challenge the views I am opposing to do the same, completing the phrasing with something like "in a state of stumbling/weakness" or "in a state of ableness" "to trust [e.g.: in the Law-free gospel]."

God's inscrutable plan, playing an integral role in the process by which these Jewish people would come to share trust in Christ with the addressees and Paul (as I read chapters 9–13 in tandem with chapters 14–15 under discussion). That the historical situation did not develop in the way that Paul's reasoned that it would is a different matter.

Gagnon classifies the arguments against my reading under two categories of evidence, *soft* and *hard*. Soft evidence is used to indicate that even if my arguments were correct they would nevertheless apply equally to Christ-followers as well, so they do not "*prove* that the 'weak' are non-Christian Jews" (65, emphasis his).[4] Hard evidence would, "if true, identify the 'weak' as non-Christian Jews rather than Christians."

I. SOFT EVIDENCE

A. The Compatibility of Romans 14:1—15:13 with Jewish-Christian Relations in Rome

Gagnon states that "it is inconceivable that the Gentile Christians had any kind of control in the synagogues, so one must assume that the 'welcoming' consisted of welcoming the 'weak' into their own meetings in house-churches. What non-Christian Jews would want to visit with Christian Gentiles instead of being visited by them?" (65–66). Gagnon suggests that the more likely situation involves Christian gentiles "free from law to welcome 'Noahide' Gentile Christians" (66). Gagnon's point is made succinctly, but there is a great deal buried in the presuppositions upon which it depends that impacts the argument and those that follow, warranting a much more detailed response.

In the first statement Gagnon finds my proposal that the action is taking place in Jewish communal contexts (synagogues) "inconceivable"; but why is this so? Because he requires my view to answer to his premises, rather than dealing with the situation as I proposed it. I argued that it was the "weak/stumbling-in-terms-of-trust-in-Christ" who were in a position to "judge" the "strong/able-to-trust-in-Christ," not the other way around, as Gagnon's "begging the question" fallacy requires. It is not my view that gentiles in the synagogues of Rome had the kind of control that Gagnon posits, and I specifically challenged constructions that suppose—on the basis of an arguable interpretation of the evidence regarding the meaning and impact

---

4. I will demonstrate that the arguments for determining the probable identity of the situation and players by way of these points are more consequential than Gagnon's qualification recognizes.

of the edict of Claudius—that this makes sense of Paul's rhetoric.[5] I argued that the so-called weak/stumbling-in-faith (i.e., Jews who are not Christ-followers) are the ones who can "approve" whether or not the way that the strong/able-to-believe (Christ-following non-Jews, but Jews like Paul who are Christ-followers can also be included under this category when Paul wants to make a broader point) behave in the service of Christ is judged to be acceptable to God (14:18). This language indicates that the "weak" are the ones in a position to "guarantee" whether the action of the "strong" is "genuine," the real thing (δοκιμάζω).

In terms of institutional power relations, ironically, my view implies that those labeled as "the strong" (the able-to-trust [in the gospel message] ones) are in *subordinate* positions to those referred to being in a state of weakness (stumbling-in-the-ability-to-trust [in the gospel message]). I argued that the distinction between them turns around that which some are "able" (i.e., have the strength") to trust in versus the some who are stumbling over (or not-yet-able-to-trust in) that, whatever that is. At issue is whether the "that" in which some trust and others do not signifies certain behavior (Torah-observance) or a certain person (Jesus as Christ). Gagnon, with the received view, sees the matter in terms of behavioral freedom from Law-observance after believing in Jesus Christ; I see it as their relative trust in the person of Jesus as Christ. Resolution of this matter in the direction I have argued would not conform to Gagnon's definition of soft evidence, since the label "weak/stumbling" would not then "apply equally" to Christ-followers; their present inability to trust the gospel of Christ is precisely what distinguishing these Jews (or non-Jews, if salient) as ἀσθενέω, as not in a state of Christ-followingness, versus those who are able to trust this propositional claim, the Christ-following "able" (δυνατόι).

The "welcoming" or "accepting" that Paul calls for in verse 1 need not signal a hard line of inside/outside that Gagnon posits, an *inter*-group development; that is, to distinguish *between* rivals. Such instruction may indicate an in-group/out-group situation, an *intra*-group tension taking place *within* a larger body of people, or even signal a division based upon categorical differences (Jew or not; Christ-follower or not) rather than formal group affiliation per se. Paul's language allows for a much more fluid situation and level of interaction than the institutional formalities that Gagnon's objection requires.

That the "weak" are "visiting" an institution alien to their own identification by definition in the sense Gagnon invokes is not stated, and far

---

5. See "Some Problems with Reading Romans through the Lens of the Edict of Claudius," *Mystery of Romans*, 372–87 (now available in chapter 2, above).

from certain. The exhortation to *welcome* or *accept* someone with a different point of view instead of immediately contending with them on the matter is not an uncommon injunction delivered *within* an organization just as it is *within* a household or family, if the speaker suspects that at least one of the members believes that there are grounds for disputing the beliefs or actions of another member. There are categorical differences within a family, but these do not by definition necessitate that they represent different groups in the way that Gagnon poses the case. The possible dynamics of an in-group situation may be more apparent if προσλαμβάνω in verse 1 is translated "accept" or "receive." Moreover, Paul uses the middle form, which can communicate a sense of "*choosing* to take/receive" someone alongside oneself. That is the kind of welcome that Paul expected to be extended to himself by Philemon, a dear friend and coworker with Paul (Phlm 17), where Paul is not a stranger or visitor, *contra* Gagnon's imposed limitation for the term's usage.

The idea of welcoming or accepting is a simple social dynamic, presuming interaction, not control; in this case, the context involves "judgments/disputes over opinions/thoughts/scruples," or, as Gagnon suggests, "judgmental evaluation of positions" (14:1). Paul calls for behavior modification on the part of the "strong/able," who are, paradoxically, in a weaker social position: they are to refrain from the usual resentful behavior toward those in stronger or dominant positions of power;[6] instead, they are to welcome them. Yet the relative strength of the "strong/able" is not set out in terms of institutional power, and it is not about the different opinions that are held, for these are not to be judged/disputed; the difference exists in terms of relative faith/trust. The issue also turns around the fact that the strong/able have the implied ability to believe that they may "eat" in a certain cavalier or resentful and judgmental way regardless of whether it might "put a stumbling block or hindrance in the way of a brother," even "destroy the one for whom Christ died" (14:13, 15). Such attitudes can develop among those that lack institutional power; indeed, precisely because they lack it, thus expressing resistance to opinions that can be resisted but that they are not in a position to legislate differently. The weak/stumbling, on the other hand, have the implied ability to judge such eating as inappropriate in the service of God, and thus not to give it the seal of approval as genuine (14:18), which suggests that in spite of being signaled by an epithet connoting relative weakness (in the subgroup terms Paul and his target audience presumably value, based on trust or not in the gospel proposition), the so-called weak/stumbling are

---

6. The cultural context of this language of weakness and strength in Greco-Roman terms of relative power is now available in Reasoner, *The Strong and the Weak*; my review is available in *RBL*: www.bookreviews.org/Reviews/0521633346.html.

actually in the position that corresponds to having relatively more strength in terms of the larger group's institutional power dynamics within which this subgroup of Christ-followers desire affirmation, and might be expected to resent lack thereof.

The majority of interpreters recognize that the instruction to "welcome" is directed to the strong/able, and Paul's argument largely targets them rather than the weak/stumbling (cf. 14:1–2; 14:14—15:4). Yet the presence of the language of mutuality in the midst of the discourse (cf. 14:3–13; 15:5–7) has led many to conclude that the weak/stumbling also constitute Paul's target audience, albeit a minority group. However, a call for mutual respect such as Paul makes can be made to a target group without implying that the "other" is also a part of the writer's/speaker's audience, that is, that the writer/speaker has the same authority or access to them as those to whom he writes/speaks. The may be present, or not, or sometimes in some ways. Whatever the actual level of mixing is or is not, an author can target a subgroup or categorical grouping without targeting other subgroups or categorical groupings that may be present. Parents at home and teachers in classrooms often address a child or certain categories or subgroups of children in a specific way about a specific matter in the presence as well as the absence of other children—whether by name, categorical qualifications (e.g., by age, by gender, by experience, by ethnicity, by natural birth versus by adoption), or without even stating the qualifications explicitly—and everyone can be expected to decode who constitutes the target audience for the instruction expressed, and who constitutes the direct or indirect beneficiary, which may include the benefit of "overhearing" that which is stated. Such expectations can be misguided, of course, and the communication fail to achieve its goals, but that is always at risk, not least when indirect language, such as Paul uses here, is employed.

Paul's even-handed appeals to mutuality reveal rhetorical aspects of both the situation and of Paul's anticipation of the desired results. Paul links the instructions that he gives to the target audience of Christ-following non-Jews to the response that he believes the weak/stumbling are in a position to determine: will they approve or reject their behavior, and thus them. This implies that the weak/stumbling are the dominant group by whom the faith claims of the strong/able are constrained. At the same time, Paul's appeals to mutuality reveal his expectation that if the strong/able-to-believe-in-Jesus-Christ whom he addresses would adopt a welcoming posture of respect toward the weak/stumbling-in-faith-in-of-Christ because of disputes about the food, wine, and days that have apparently arisen, that this will lead to the mutual welcoming of themselves by the weak/stumbling-in-faith instead of continued disapproval, and thus to the glorious fulfillment of the prophetic wish for the unity of all humankind in the worship of the One God of all (15:5–13). In other words, while not directed to the weak/stumbling, Paul's rhetoric appeals to the strong/able in the sense that he anticipates the inclusion of the weak/stumbling in the restoration that his own ministry is concerned to bring about (cf. 11:11–27).

With regard to the identity of the weak/stumbling, interpreters who consider them Christ-followers overwhelmingly recognize, *contra* Gagnon, that the rhetoric implies that they were *Jews*, or better, some combination of Jews and gentiles who were behaving *jewishly* (i.e., committed to Torah-oriented lifestyles).[7] When Paul moves in the next section to describing his priestly ministry to gentiles, not seemingly inclusive of the weak/stumbling-in-faith, this suggests the social interaction I have proposed. Gagnon breaks from the interpretive consensus when he argues that this language indicates the weak/stumbling-in-faith are *not* Jews, and the situation "consists exclusively of Christian Gentiles," and he fails to explain Paul's explicit differentiation based upon who is circumcised or not (67; see the commentaries on 15:15–16). Note also that Gagnon's proposed alternate identification of the weak as Noahide gentiles is actually an identity still based on inter- and intra-Jewish terms for classification. In fact, not only does the term Noahide bespeak a Jewish classification of social space, so too does even the term *"ethnē,"* as Paul used it to differentiate those from the nations other than Israel, even though Jews who did so considered Israel one of the nations too.

The question Gagnon poses presumes a level of group separation between Jews and Christ-followers as well as the institutional development of Christianity that are questioned by my reading of the text, introducing circularity and altering the terms of argumentative engagement. Gagnon conceives of a situation in which "visiting" another's house of worship takes place as it might across institutional boundaries of later times. However, it is not clear that any "Christianity" much less separate "Christianities" had developed such institutional form in Rome in that period, so that is precisely what must be argued, *not presupposed*.

Gagnon must answer, even for his own proposal, why there are these two types of Christ-following gentile groups in Rome, one defined in Jewish communal terms and the other not, why they normally meet separately, and why they would now be seeking to meet together, so that Paul's rhetoric appears to be addressing a live concern in Rome. Based on Gagnon's reasoning, he must answer why gentile members of supposedly non-Pauline-like "Christian" groups who still maintain the value of Jewish

---

7. The various views are succinctly set out in Reasoner, *The Strong and the Weak*, 1–23.

life (what could be called Christ-following Jewish groups) would suddenly be seeking to attend meetings of supposedly Pauline-like (Christ-following gentile) groups (although founded apart from Paul),[8] even though they do not share Gagnon's fundamental view of reality that Jewish life is now obsolete for all Christ-followers? Were there already, apart from groups founded by Paul, two other institutional forms of Christ-faith, and if so, why is one presumed to be any more likely than the other to be in a position to welcome one or the other to meetings?

Returning to my own construction of the situation, it is not difficult to imagine that non-Christ-following Jews (or Gagnon's Noahide gentiles) would want to attend (or with Gagnon, visit) subgroups consisting in part, if not largely, of Christ-following non-Jews, as long as these subgroups were part of the Jewish synagogue communities of Rome, which would be the case prior to the institutionalization of sectarian Christianity. In other words, if the proposal, on the grounds that I have argued, is kept clearly in view, then Gagnon's objection is found wanting, because it is based on appeal to the traditional premises that are at dispute, thereby begging the question. I have argued that we have no evidence—including that gained in this letter—that the Christ-following groups in Rome represented a form of institutionalized Christianity already separated from Jewish communal life. It is common for interpreters to assume that such a period of time existed prior to Romans;[9] the difference is that I propose that the rhetoric of Romans indicates that was *still* the case.[10]

Further, Gagnon states: "That Paul's few remarks to the 'weak' (14:3b, 10a, 13a; 15:7) can be explained by his ability to address the synagogue is dubious, since the letter itself is clearly addressed only to Christians, not to any in the synagogues (1:7)." It is anything but "clear" to me. The passages cited by Gagnon are not unambiguous with respect to the matter at hand. As noted above, by altering the premises rather than engaging them as set out, this informal fallacy begs the question because it fails to respect that it is precisely the issue of who was addressed or not that is under debate. His statement of the case ignores the fact that I have argued that the *target* audience of the discourse is the strong/able (Christ-following non-Jews) throughout the letter, but that they are members of Christ-following Jewish subgroups that operate in the midst of the dominant Jewish community,

---

8. Do we have any independent witness of this tradition?

9. E.g., Stuhlmacher, *Paul's Letter to the Romans*, 7.

10. See my "The Jewish Context of the Gentile Audience Addressed in Paul's Letter to the Romans."

which is controlled by the weak/stumbling (non-Christ-following Jews), to whom their own smaller and newer subgroup leaders must answer.

Paul's rhetoric expresses the viewpoints of one who represents the interests of the weak/stumbling as an insider—a reformer, not a sectarian—although he counts himself among the strong/able addressees, because he is a member of their minority coalition of Christ-followers (15:1–3). The resultant subgroup seam is evidence of an us/them inner-synagogue/Jewish communal boundary. Paul's rhetorically inclusive statements in the passages Gagnon lists embody the dynamic I have tried to capture: Paul argues from 12:1 onward that the strong/able are to learn to think with renewed minds, to see the situation of the weak/stumbling not merely from their own limited perspective, but from that of God, which is achieved in part by considering the situation from the perspective of the weak/stumbling other, whose interests even Paul's ministry to these non-Jew addressees represents (cf. 11:13–16). Paul describes the situation in chronometrical terms: as described in 15:7–12, he anticipates that time when all Israel, in concert with the rest of humankind, will be restored, in part as a result of the behavior of the addressees observing what Paul herein instructs. The interests of both parties are inextricably intertwined in Paul's rhetorical approach. This "bold reminder" aims to ensure that the strong/able addressees do not fail to grasp this fact. The inclusive rhetoric appears calculated to lead to a more empathetic viewpoint toward the weak/stumbling about the proposal to trust in Jesus as the Christ.

I was (and am) convinced that there was no institutional Christianity in Rome, and that those to whom Paul wrote were not sectarians breaking away from the fabric of Jewish communal life. They had not imagined any such move, although Paul's rhetorical approach suggests that he anticipated (presumably, in response to reports he had received) that they were growing resentful toward those who did not accept their novel faith-claims to be full members of the Abrahamic family of God as those-from-the-nations-in-Christ apart from proselyte conversion. Perhaps he simply assumed the likelihood of such a development based upon the experiences of other communities that he did found. Whatever the facts on the ground in Rome, Paul seeks to arrest the idea of growing resentful toward the so-called weak/stumbling, or behaving without concern for their welfare in a way that respects their opinions on the matters addressed.

I see Romans as the response of a reformer involved in the work of a coalition on behalf of the interests of the larger group, not a sectarian involved in the formation of a protest group.[11] Paul challenged the emer-

---

11. Sectarianism as defined, e.g., by Bryan Wilson, "The Sociology of Sects." I use

gence of judgmental attitudes among Christ-following gentiles that might lead to developments he considered unacceptable and dangerous for Jewish people, although it is likely that those to whom he wrote had not considered the issue from the point of view expressed in Romans. Sometimes rhetoric designed to avert, which is by definition anticipatory and prescriptive, if read instead as if descriptive can make situations seem to be already more developed than they might actually have been.

In my view Paul did not address "Christians," but Christ-followers who were otherwise identifiable in institutional Jewish terms, terms, in fact, that Gagnon himself must draw upon in order to make sense of the identity to which he appeals when describing the weak in his proposed way, as "Noahides." I regret my use of even the adjectival "*Christian* Jew or gentile," as the pre-Christianity level of social developments would have been better illuminated by following Paul's lead, since he did not identify anyone or any group as "Christian," but from a Jewish framework of reference as either Jews or not (those from the other nations/gentiles/non-Jews). In the years after writing *Mystery of Romans* I began to refer to "Christ-believing" Jews or non-Jews, and now prefer "Christ-following."[12] What is required of Gagnon is evidence for the unambiguous development of a non-Jewish religious institution known as Christianity; at least an argument that interprets Paul's rhetoric in terms of a social model revealing the institutionalization of sectarian dynamics in a way appropriate to this period. Gagnon's argument has not successfully addressed or undermined my construction of the situation, or the arguments made from the text in view of that construction.

B. The Credibility of Paul's Exhortations to Non-Christian Jews in Romans 14:1—15:13

Gagnon contends that the rhetorical distinction I make between the strong/stumbling, *to* whom Paul writes, and the weak/able, *about* whom he writes, cannot be maintained, since Paul calls for mutual acceptance. As with the last point, this criticism fails to recognize the natural distinction in discourse between the rhetorical target (or implied, encoded, rhetorical, authorial) audience and the larger historical audience that might be present, or perhaps not even present but that constitutes a salient contextual concern for the author and, the rhetoric presumes, for those addressed.

---

coalition here in the sense defined by Boissevain, *Friends of Friends*, esp. 170–205: a coalition is "a temporary alliance of distinct parties for a limited purpose," although they accumulate more tasks as time passes when not yet achieving that purpose (171).

12. I am grateful for the suggestion and example provided by Esler, *Galatians*.

Although Gagnon himself includes the modifying "*implied* audience" in the conclusion of this point (67), he does not appear to recognize what this implies: the make-up of the larger *actual* audience or situation within which the target audience is addressed may be very different from the rhetorically constructed target audience and situation. Gagnon also fails to recognize that Paul has revealed that his own perspective, indeed ministry as apostle to the gentiles, was inextricably tied up with his role as a representative (part of the remnant) on behalf of the interests of stumbling (that is, for my argument to be engaged: non-Christ-following) Jews (cf. 11:13–16, 26, 28–36).[13] In other words, Paul may have been concerned that his target recipients think about themselves in ways that involved them visualizing themselves impacting people and events that would not otherwise have occurred to them; awareness is relative, and there can be a calculated difference between the rhetorical concerns of the writer/speaker and the perceived or actual concerns of the recipients/hearers.

Paul writes specifically of his responsibility for non-Jews, but he frames his concerns, and what should now be theirs, in terms of Jewish conceptual and social perspectives on the pagan world of these non-Jews's past and present lives. This characteristic of the letter is especially strange if these non-Jews are members of communities already separated from contact with(in) Jewish communities. If the target non-Jews do not live out their identities in Jewish social space, why then is the clarification of their past, present, and future identity, as well as the call to behavioral conformity predicated upon and entirely concerned with all of this *Jewish* theological and social instead of relevant *pagan* stuff, especially since they are in Rome among Romans and others who would otherwise be expected to form a—if not *the*—primary reference group?

Gagnon argues that "there is no reason to construe the biblical quotations in Rom 15:9–12 in such a way that 'one another' in 15:7 means Jew and gentile," and he proposes instead an intra-gentile conflict (66–67). In general terms, that is a valid point, and Paul could be addressing conflicting groups of non-Jews. Yet the digression that follows this point indicates that Paul was addressing non-Jews about how to respond to the reactions of Jews to their thinking and behavior as well as to his own,[14] which the consensus views recognize, and Gagnon seems to recognize elsewhere too. Indeed, the context of this entire exhortation turns around the "reality"

---

13. See further my "Challenging the Limits That Continue to Define Paul's Perspective on Jews and Judaism."

14. Gagnon paradoxically observes: "Instead, the quotations document the assertion that God in Christ welcomed the Gentiles into the fold of Jewish believers (the remnant, not non-Christian Jews, contra Nanos)" (67).

to which Paul appeals in the verse that Gagnon seems to drop: "For I tell you that Christ became a servant of the *circumcision* to demonstrate God's truthfulness, in order to confirm the promises of the fathers, now that the *gentiles* glorify God for mercy. Just as it has been written..." (verses 8–9b; emphasis added). The several scriptures that Paul cited signaled the worship of God by non-Israelites within the midst of Israel, which, Paul reasons, will be recognized by his fellow Jews as evidence of the arrival of the awaited age to come, when such behavior would be expected to commence.

C. The Possibility That "Your Brother" Is a Reference to Non-Christian Jews[15]

I am perplexed by Gagnon's insistence that Paul does not and did not call or consider non-Christ-following Jews brothers and sisters of Christ-following non-Jews, or the differentiation he stresses on the basis of "ethnic" versus "spiritual" foundation (67–68).[16] Perhaps Gagnon means racial rather than ethnic, since any kind of perceived or real affiliation—including spiritual—that binds a group together as a social entity can signal an expression of ethnicity, including spiritual conviction or behavior.[17] Moreover, any kind of perception of differentiation between groups often gives rise to discrimination; this is characteristic of us-and-them language as well as actions that social identity theorists have amply demonstrated in modern individualistic cultures,[18] which would apply all the more to the more dyadic social world of the people and groupings under consideration.

I do not deny that there is a level of differentiation between those *to* whom Paul writes and those *about* whom he writes, or that this distinction has to do with the relative affiliation of either group with respect to trust in the gospel claims for Jesus as Christ; in fact, I argue that this differentiation is integral to Paul's authority to address those to whom he writes in Rome in the way in which he does, since he is an apostle of Christ (1:1–15; 15:1–33). But this does not mean that there are no circumstances under which he might also address non-Christ-following Jews as his brothers and sisters. In my view, he might address non-Christ-following non-Jews as his brothers and sisters apart from such qualification, and likewise address

---

15. As with point A above, I do not see how this issue conforms to Gagnon's definition of soft-evidence.

16. My response here applies also to the similar objections toward my view expressed by Reasoner, *The Strong and the Weak*, 135–36.

17. Cf. F. Barth, "Introduction"; Banks, *Ethnicity*.

18. See Hogg and Abrams, *Social Identifications*.

non-Christ-followers as the brothers and sisters of Christ-following non-Jews, since they are such, for example, in terms of Paul's belief in the One Creator God of all humankind. Moreover, it is a circular fallacy to argue that Paul did not indicate non-Christ-following Jews as brothers in many other cases (the interpretation of some of them can be contested too), so he cannot be doing so here, and thus that there is no evidence that he ever did so.

Fictive kinship does not consist of one tightly defined social-group affiliation to the exclusion of all others, but is dynamic, just as are familial aspects of identity (one can be a father, son, brother, husband, friend, and so on, without supposing that the others no longer exist when a new one is added). The nature of affiliation is multi-dimensional; depending upon the context of any person or persons, the salience of fictive kinship is ever changing (on whatever terms perceived by the parties in question, spiritual or material), as is a person's own identity. To give but one simple example, the salience of fictive kinship, like ethnicity, changes with proximity. For many North Americans, apart from biological, linguistic, or other constructions of group affiliation, the shift will be evident in terms of spatial location. When in his or her town, neighborhood affiliation might be of consequence for an intra-town ballgame. But town instead of neighborhood affiliation would be more salient for an inter-town game, whether merely one of the neighborhood teams, or made-up of all-stars from the various neighborhoods of the town. When flying from a town other than his or her own to another town within another state, then a shared home state may be sufficient to constitute fictive kinship. And if flying between two European cities, merely being from the U.S. may be the salient standard of "brother-and-sisterhood."

Fictive kinship can take many creative forms. Evidence of a poignant counterpoint to Gagnon's wooden kinship assumptions is found in the rabbinic commentary on the book of Genesis, Genesis Rabbah, as articulated by Jacob Neusner and Bruce Chilton. In the fourth century, when the Roman Empire was changing to Christian rule and repressive measures toward paganism began to include Judaism in reaction to the recently defeated pagan agenda of Julian, the rabbis identified Rome with Esau, the sibling rival of Jacob (i.e., Israel/Judaism), thus ingeniously finding the current crisis adumbrated in the lives of the patriarchs. Thus, in the Scriptures the enemy of the people of Jacob is ironically their brother as well. And how was this claim to common kinship conceived? "That concession—Rome is a sibling, a close relative of Israel—represents an implicit recognition of Christianity's claim to share the patrimony of Judaism, to be descended from Abraham and Isaac."[19]

19. Neusner and Chilton, *Jewish and Christian Doctrines*, 59–79, quotation from 62.

Paul does qualify his kinship reference to Jewish people who do not share his faith in Christ in Romans 9:3 as "brethren *according to the flesh.*" But the purpose of the reference is to communicate that the current standing of those Israelites is *not* what the gentiles to whom he writes might be beginning to resentfully suppose, that is, that they are no longer God's people, no longer brothers and sisters in the family created by the One God, no longer those for whom "the gifts and the call of God are irrevocable" (11:29). Quite the contrary, Paul insists that these Jews are the very ones for whom both the Christ-following Jewish remnant (among whom Paul counts himself; cf. 11:1–36) and the non-Jew target addressees are to be grateful, and to live with accordingly in faithful obedience (12:1—16:27). Therefore, Paul's qualifying comment about his Jewish kin by genealogical descent (flesh) here is an element of clarification, not a universal statement that limits him to only this point of reference in all rhetorical or social contexts. Paul uses this language to clarify that the standing before God of the non-Christ-following Jewish people, those empirical Israelites *about* whom he writes *to* these Christ-following non-Jews, is not as the target audience might suppose.

Has Gagnon missed the very purpose of Paul's conclusion by hanging so much on a qualification buried within one rhetorical point made in setting up the case? Do we have a letter from Paul by which to qualify, much less quantify, Gagnon's universal proposition that Paul *could not* consider non-Christ-following Jewish people the kin of Christ-following non-Jews? Does not the implied concern of the correspondence under consideration tell against any such proposal? There are several kinds of branches, but the tree has only one root by which they are made holy (11:16). Does not Paul logically include non-Christ-followers among those "for whom Christ died" (14:15),[20] whether the person in view believed that to be the case or not? Moreover, it seems that throughout 14:1—15:13 Paul has concern for non-Christ-following Jews specifically in view, since the disputable eating action of the strong/able "brother/sister" could "harm" the weak/stumbling (λυπεῖται) to the point of "destroying" him/her (ἀπόλλυε), leading this brother/sister to respond to the strong/able one's claim to good with "blasphemy."

Furthermore, along this line I challenge Gagnon's claim that "there is a theological reason for Paul's not calling unbelieving Jews brothers: in his mind, Israel (the Israel which is not a remnant) *at present* lies outside the sphere of salvation and inside the sphere of destruction" (67–68; emphasis his). Gagnon's list of citations includes 9:1–3, 22; 10:1; 11:17–24, but they

---

20. An inference also noted by Cranfield, *A Critical and Exegetical Commentary on The Epistle to the Romans*, 2.715–17, whom he refers to as "those outside the church" or "outsiders" (2.717).

must be torn out of their context to make such a point. Paul's argument of chapters 9–11 culminates in 11:25–31, wherein Paul contends that in spite of how things might appear to those to whom he writes presently, the stumbling of Israel are foremost in God's "present," albeit inscrutable, mind, and God is forever faithful to the covenant promises made. As the argument develops, before the verses of chapter 11 cited by Gagnon, Paul claims that his ministry to the nations seeks to bring about the successful alleviation of the suffering of the part of Israel that is presently stumbling (vv. 13–16). His ministry to the nations is in order to provoke to jealousy those Israelites he believes to be stumbling, by which he fulfills his role as one of the remnant, an image that only makes sense within the sphere of concern with the *whole* piece of cloth, which may be torn, but is *not* "presently" destroyed.

For Paul, some are stumbling, but in God's *present* plan they must not be considered to have fallen; rather, they are temporarily suffering "estrangement" (11:28) in the service of the very gentiles in Rome to whom Paul writes. Moreover, if he believed that his present ministry among the gentiles would be positively valued, as emulative jealousy implies, then this means that he believes that his actions will still be understood to represent Jewish communal values, and known among these Jewish people as expressions of their own Jewish expectations for a ministry among the nations when the awaited time has arrived. But how could this be conceivable if the addressees' groups were already perceived, in Jewish terms, as expressions of non-Jewish and thus pagan religious life, as would be the case for a new religious movement constructed apart from any Jewish communal life (or any Jewish people, per Gagnon), and how would they even be aware of the internal developments of such independent communities?[21]

In the years since I first responded with this essay, I have presented research on 1 Corinthians 8–10 that proves a challenge to the objections Gagnon raised by way of appeal to Paul's use of "brothers" and "weak" in that argument. Gagnon contends that "it is impossible that a 'brother' in 1 Cor 8:11–13, who is also a 'weak' person, can be a Jewish or Christian unbeliever," and that the "linguistic connections are simply too strong" to discount the parallels when deciding what Paul must mean by the use of these terms in Romans (68). I still maintain that each usage should be analyzed in its own context and that words and phrases can be used very differently, especially for different letters to different communities at different times to address different concerns, and that one cannot decide what either case must be because of the usage in the other; however, I have now argued for

---

21. For more detailed discussion of the implications of Paul's appeal to the jealousy motif in chapter 11, see my *Mystery of Romans*, 247–55; and "The Jewish Context of the Gentile Audience," 300–303.

the thesis (which I had not researched or published on at the time) that the "weak" in Corinth were most likely idolaters who were not Christ-followers, and that Paul both refers to them as "brothers" of the Christ-followers, and that it is for idolaters too "for whom Christ died," as he had for the Corinthians addressed. The interested reader can access my arguments in their original venues, and in volume 4 of this series.[22] If I am right, Gagnon's objections are now undermined, and I could, if I thought it was appropriate, make the same case that he has by appeal to parallels, although to the opposite conclusion: that is, that Paul used "brother and sister" as well as "weak" to refer specifically to those for whom Christ died who had not realized that (yet). Paul did this in order to call the Christ-followers to avoid behavior that would impede non-Christ-followers from doing so, and to instead undertake behavior that would help them recognize the changed lives that warranted a positive re-evaluation of the proposition.

D. The Monotheistic Character of the Appeal to the "Weak"

Gagnon agrees with me that "the 'weak' are acting with Jewish-based scruples," but prefers to understand that this does not indicate Jews, because non-Jews "can engage in 'Jewish practices'" (69). Indeed, and I argued that too, throughout the book, and in many ways since, so this observation hardly counts against my argument, although it is expressed as if it did so. But Gagnon finds little to agree with regarding Paul's use of "Lord," which, I submitted, need not signify Jesus, but also could do so without being conflated with Paul's references to God. Yet even if Lord did refer to Jesus in some of these verses (esp. 14:6–9), this could be applied rhetorically to the aims of the behavior of non-Christ-following Jews because, from Paul's vantage point as well as that of his target addressees, everything directed toward God could be understood to be directed to God's mediator (albeit unbeknownst to them by name), and this can also be understood in terms of the ideas related to mediator figures in Second Temple Judaism. Gagnon's own concessions in the midst of his argument are sufficient evidence, as far as I am concerned, to save the space for other topics. My argument does not hang on this point, and would not be impaired, as far as I see, if the case could be proven to be

---

22. Nanos, "The Polytheist Identity of the 'Weak,' and Paul's Strategy to 'Gain' Them: A New Reading of 1 Corinthians 8:1—11:1"; and "Why the 'Weak' in 1 Corinthians 8–10 Were Not Christ-believers." See too Land, "'We Put No Stumbling Block in Anyone's Path, So that Our Ministry Will Not be Discredited': Paul's Response to an Idol Food Inquiry in 1 Corinthians 8:1–13."

as Gagnon suggests. Paul's language does not depend upon the "intention of honoring Christ" by the weak/stumbling; that is the intention of Paul and his target audience, however, who believe in Jesus Christ as Lord, regardless of whether those about whom he writes do or not. They can attribute towards Christ the others' God-ward intentions and even interpret those of the weak/stumbling as *ultimately* Christ-ward from *their own Christ-following perspective*, certainly so in the midst of making a rhetorical point such as Paul is making about the importance of mutual respect for different convictions about how each should best serve God.

Gagnon offers several minor arguments at the end of this section, but they are not decisive, reflecting the variety of readings possible dependent upon an interpreter's working assumptions. His number 1 is a case in point. He appeals again to 1 Cor 8:11 to "delimit" what Paul writes in Rom 14:15 about the "weak" and "the one for whom Christ died" to "a fellow Christian" only, but I have already discussed why his interpretation of the evidence in 1 Corinthians is suspect, and why my reading of that language actually turns the point around in favor of my usage in Romans, but also why I don't think that kind of approach is methodologically sound (see C). His point number 2 suffers from circularity: just because Paul uses a word group one way in one letter does not mean he can only use it that way in another, and the usage to which Gagnon appeals is not as self-evident as he supposes, in addition to a very wooden approach to the terms themselves, and what they "can" mean. The objection in number 3 is to a supposed "close parallel" in Galatians, which bears no weight and can be disputed, and number 4 involves begging the question and circularity based upon Gagnon's premises rather than mine. The objections in numbers 5 and 6 are also examples of informal fallacies, being predicated upon the notion that Paul no longer regarded non-Christ-following Jews as a part of the community and thus could not address the Christ-followers by way of inclusive rhetorical arguments, when it is just such presuppositions about the make-up of the community and of Paul's viewpoints about his fellow Jews that are being challenged.

The evidence for what Paul "can" or "cannot" think is extremely limited. If Paul did not share Gagnon's ideological perspective that non-Christ-following Jews were not fictive kin within the people of God apart from trust in Christ and were not being protected in that standing among the righteous ones during this anomalous development until it was resolved (i.e., that "all Israel will be saved/kept safe"), then this objection to my reading is groundless.

E. Romans 14:22b–23 as Condemnation of the "Strong" for Eating in Doubt

Gagnon's opposition to my reading of 14:22b–23, which focused on the topic of the strong/able holding themselves back from any temptation to boastfully disregard the concerns of the weak/stumbling regarding (not) eating certain foods as expressions of faithfulness even though they are unable to believe (yet) in the gospel, is without much substance. In fact, returning to the text in view of Gagnon's argument has led me to recognize features that strengthen my proposal, as discussed below.

My initial objection is to the way that his criticism misrepresents what I had already argued, as if he is introducing elements that were not incorporated in my evaluations that ostensibly weaken my case. These informal fallacies include raising the topic that at issue is a judgment of conscience (preferably consciousness), as if my argument did not proceed similarly. Gagnon's appeal to 1 Cor 10:25–30 as a contrary indicator is gratuitous, since my argument works from the assumption that Paul assumed his target strong/able addressees in Rome knew that what they (ostensibly) proposed to eat publicly was questionable according to the convictions of the weak/stumbling, regardless of what may have been the case when he wrote to Corinth (which included a caveat about food not known to have been involved in idolatry, but was overall about food clearly known by all parties to be offered to other gods). I have challenged the presupposition that this language signifies the level of faith toward what is eaten rather than the level of trust in the propositional claim that Jesus is the Christ, so Gagnon's comments beg the question. I have argued my position on the basis of the context before and after this passage, not only Rom 11:20 or 14:2, to which he appeals, but the verses immediately preceding as well as following, although his presentation suggests that I had not done so. These criticisms may be calculated to persuade, but they do not represent legitimate representations of weaknesses in my arguments.

In *Mystery of Romans*, like Gagnon, I followed the prevailing translations for ὁ διακρινόμενος in 14:23: "to be at odds with oneself/doubt/waver." But on further inspection, after discussing this matter with Peter Spitaler, I realize that this was actually a questionable way to translate this participle. As already argued, *contra* Gagnon, if translated in this secondary way, this language does not "most naturally" refer to the weak/stumbling, but to the strong/able: in Paul's argument the appeal is to a higher value to substantiate the behavior Paul calls the strong to, one that challenges the temptation to behave otherwise by appeal to *their ostensible rights*. This approach renders the sentiment expressed in this verse arguably redundant, since that point is already expressed in verse 22. However, a new element is apparent if we interpret διακρίνω in the middle voice, which signifies "choosing to take issue with/dispute/criticize," rather than "doubting."[23]

Translating ὁ διακρινόμενος to refer to "the one choosing to dispute" the opinions of the other who is weak/stumbling in trust has the advantage of keeping in front of the reader the overarching concern of the argument since verse 1 not to do so: the addressees are instead to welcome the "weak/stumbling in trust," yet not "to disputes [διακρίσεις] over opinions [διακρίσεις]." The strong/able are to welcome the weak/stumbling without judging as wrong the behavioral practices that the weak/stumbling have calculated to be appropriate for themselves in the service of God.[24] This translation also works nicely for the usage of διεκρίθη in 4:20; that is, that Abraham did not take issue with or dispute with God about God's promise, but instead trusted God. I have argued that the relative faith/faithfulness of Abraham is paradigmatic for the constructing the distinction that Paul draws in Romans between the relative faith/faithfulness of the strong/able-to-trust and the weak/stumbling-in-trust, who are characterized in these terms because they dispute the "strong/able-to-trust ones's" claim that the promises of God to Abraham's seed are fulfilled in Jesus Christ, as well as the concomitant claim that these Christ-following non-Jews have been included in Abraham's family in Christ apart from proselyte conversion, that is, apart from becoming included in Israel.

If translated consistent with Paul's opening statement, it is the supposed strength/ability of the trust that the addressees have that is undermined by Paul's participial phrase in verse 23, "the ones choosing to take issue/dispute/criticize." Paul subverts the value of the strong/ables's theoretical rights regarding what they can eat when, as a result of disputing the value of the weak/stumblings's calculation of what is appropriate in the service of God, the strong/able choose to flaunt their rights with behavior known to offend

23. See διακρίνω in BAG, 185, 2.a. This is one of those interesting cases where the subsequent note 2.b observes that the meaning of doubt or wavering appears first in the NT, which raises a caution flag: Why does this unique meaning appear suddenly there? It is possible and arguably better to read the meaning of note a (to take issue, dispute) in 4:23, since disputing emphasizes that the nature of the tension is with another rather than within oneself alone; although self-doubt can be created by such tension, this remains a result and thus secondary consideration for translation. Likewise, the other NT verses listed read well with the meaning of dispute. Note also Louw and Nida, Lexicon, 33.412, to express disapproval, to criticize; see also 33.444. I am grateful to Peter Spitaler for bringing this matter to my attention; he was working on an essay, subsequently published: "James 1:5–8: A Dispute with God."

24. Διαλογισμός is related to the balancing or checking of accounts, and in general relates to one's opinion/scruples, that is, what one calculates/reasons/thinks/judges appropriate for oneself (cf. BAGD; Spicq, Lexicon, "Οἰκονομέω," and n. 13).

and cause further disrespect from the other "for whom Christ died." For Paul, this posture of disputing the sensibilities of the weak/stumbling-in-trust on these matters amounts to something worse than weakness/stumbling trust, for it is an act against faithfulness, being unfaithful, even sin, since it violates the essence of Godward trust/faithfulness.

Reading 14:23 in this way seamlessly links Paul's concern to challenge the addressees to serve Christ without asserting their rights in matters of food or drink or "anything that causes your brother to stumble," and instead to "pursue peace and the building up of one another" (14:19–22). The immediately following instructions of 15:1–3 build on this point: it is not self-pleasure according to one's perceived rights that are important in these matters, but rather, one's obligation, with Paul, "to bear-up the weakness/stumblingness of the not strong/able," that is, to follow the example of Christ to seek to "please" one's neighbor and "build them up." There is an edge to Paul's use of strength/ability. He challenges any temptation for these Christ-following non-Jews to grow arrogant toward the present stumbling fate of some Israelites, just as he did in chapter 11, for it is in service of the other and not of oneself that the strong/able faithfulness of a "renewed mind" is made manifest.

In summary, I have shown that Gagnon's assessment of at least two of these points as "soft evidence"—meaning that "if true, [they] apply equally to non-Christian Jews and to Christians" (65)—is mistaken. Moreover, no support was found for his conclusion that these points "are actually proof that the 'weak' are Gentile Christians" (81). Rather, each of my original points contribute to an internally consistent, logical, and probable interpretation of Paul's rhetoric. In addition, independent of challenging his assessment of my reading to make "the least sense" of the identity of the weak/stumbling where this supposed "soft evidence" is concerned, his response to these points does not warrant the remarkable claim to have also overturned the overwhelming majority view that the weak were Jewish people (including non-Jews who were behaving in Jewish ways), whether understood to be Christ-followers or not, or to have demonstrated that the situation indicated was "*intra-Gentile*" (66). Although not the focus of my rejoinder, his new proposition that the "most sense" is made "when they [the weak] are identified as [Noahide] *Gentile* Christians" (81; emphasis his) would require a much more substantial investigation than he has undertaken in his essay.

II. HARD EVIDENCE[25]

A. Internal Consistency with Romans 1–11

Although admitting some agreement, Gagnon challenges the value of the internal consistency between the arguments in chapters 1–11 and those in 14–15 (12–16, actually) that my reading ostensibly facilitates better than do the traditional approaches. He introduces this point with two observations that warrant comment. First, he claims that "one has to admit that chaps. 1–11 do not give us direct information about the 'weak'" (73). I admit no such thing, and neither does Gagnon's argument! He appeals to information in these chapters to establish who they are or are not, as have I, as have most interpreters of Romans (e.g., see his II.D).

Second, Gagnon grants that my reading makes chapters 2–4 and 9 "more directly pertinent to the situation in 14:1—15:13," yet suggests that it remains to be explained "why most of 14:1—15:13 is directed against the Gentile Christian 'strong' while most of chaps. 1–11 is directed against non-Christian Jews or has negative repercussions for them" (73). I do not agree with this later assertion, which begs the question rather than arguing the premise at dispute, and I have addressed his proposed challenge at length in the arguments to which he responded.[26] The criticism seems to turn on the idea that Paul is challenging Jews about their standing among the righteous ones, for example, from the traditional way of reading chapter 3 to be making the case that Jews are sinners, as if Jews did not know this well enough from the Tanak and temple rituals. This is not the place to take on this matter, but I find the traditional Christians assumptions from which that interpretation works, as well as many of the exegetical moves involved to sustain them, highly unlikely. Paul is not directing his arguments "against non-Christian Jews," but against misinformed or mistaken deductions made by Christ-following non-Jews about who they are and how they fit in alongside of Jews in the plans of God for all of humankind. I argued that Paul sought to inform the gentiles in Christ that their identification among the people of God was secure based on God's grace toward them, just like it is for Israelites, before he turned to articulating the concomitant obligations that come with that identification. Paul first explained how the non-Jew target addressees as well as Israelites fit into God's plan to date, then he censured any level of resentment toward those Israelites

---

25. I suggest that at least points A and C from his soft evidence belong with hard evidence too.

26. See also my discussion of the double character of the letter in "The Jewish Context of the Gentile Audience," 293–95.

who do not appear to share these Christ-followers present convictions. Paul criticized the failure of these gentiles to extend to the Jews in view the same lovingkindness that they are so grateful to have had extended toward themselves. Paul explained how God wishes to use these non-Jews in the plan to "protect all Israel," which involved articulating how the addressees' current miscalculation of the meaning of the present situation, and thus of the behavior that is appropriate, could inhibit such glorious results. Paul "expect[s] a direct correspondence between the two sections" at 12:1, for it is he who provides the conjunctions that bind together his "bold reminder" of "the obedience of faith" as the following chapters unfold—so rather than a failing, I see my argument helping to bring out the connections more clearly than have the prevailing views.

With respect to Gagnon's alternative reading, which posits uniquely that the "weak" are "Gentile Christians," his argument should actually engage the prevailing interpretations, although it is composed as though the problem is introduced by my reading. Unfortunately, each of the points that he offers as if they undermine my arguments represent the informal fallacies involved in misrepresentation, including appeal to premises other than mine (in this case, those of the traditional positions that I was also challenging), for there is nothing enumerated that actually challenges my own argumentation; overall, they are in fact elements of my case, *mutatis mutandis*. I argued 1) against Romans as "just a self-recommendation"; 2) that Paul was creating what Gagnon terms a "'debt theology' eliciting from the Gentile Christians a righteous conduct based on appeals for gratitude," although I did not use that phrase; 3) that this element was "made clear" in the transitions at 12:1 and 15:7; and 4) that in chapter 2 Paul developed a "layered trap" (I refer to a rhetorical gambit) by way of the imaginary Jewish (or, better, I suggest: non-Jew rhetorically asked to identify as a Jew to get the point: "if you call yourself") interlocutor that is sprung upon the unsuspecting target non-Jew addressees when they respond inappropriately to God's grace toward themselves or the Jewish other. Gagnon's summarizing point 5 admits that my reading recognizes the oblique relationship that also exists between these sections of the letter; what he fails to provide is an argument that this means the weak/stumbling "cannot" be as I have proposed on these grounds, not an uncontested point that these observations do not "require the 'weak' to be non-Christian Jews."

In addition, these five points do not "prove" the identity that Gagnon proposes, but of course that does not mean that such an identification "cannot" be made on other grounds. Gagnon simply does not provide them, so the reader is left only with his critique of the shortcomings of the traditional interpretations as if they represented shortcomings in mine, but is not provided with the argumentation for an alternative Gagnon proposal that is required to be able to engage it in detail.

B. The Incompatibility of Paul's Approval of the "Weak" and Their Observance of the Law

In this argument Gagnon seeks to undermine the basis of my criticism of the prevailing view that the weakness of the weak/stumbling is a result of the continued value they place upon observance of Jewish practices—what I called "Luther's trap"—which ranks the level of faith expressed in the actions of Christ-followers on the basis of a non-Jewish, Law-free evaluation of spirituality. Leaving aside that we are dealing with Paul's opinions as well as the limits of our own perspectives as we seek to understand him, and thus, *contra* Gagnon, *subjective* rather than "objective reality," it is Gagnon who concludes that the opinions of the weak about these dietary matters are "false" (75; "false scruples," 76). Paul instead tells the "strong/able" that they are not to proceed in their dealings with the weak/stumbling on any such dismissive basis, noting as well that what they believe and do is "for the Lord" (vv. 3–12). Is not judging the scruples of the weak/stumbling to be *false* precisely what Paul told his addressees not to indulge, but that Gagnon here, in keeping with the received view and as an example of "Luther's trap," confidently trips into?

I do not understand why Gagnon would claim that Paul merely *accommodates* instead of *commends* in these verses: Paul writes that what is being observed by the weak/stumbling is being done "in honor of the Lord" (vv. 6–7). And the line Gagnon seeks to draw between intention and action is almost certainly anachronistic as well as impossible for a later reader to deduce with any confidence. Paul does not make such a distinction explicit in this argument; instead, Paul states that the actions of the weak/stumbling-in-trust and the strong/able-to-trust both matter when they are done "for the Lord," and thus by definition should not be undertaken in a way that will harm the other, or judge them. Once again, Gagnon's appeal to Paul's use of the language of weakness in 1 Corinthians (in this case, to 9:19–23) is gratuitous; moreover, the argument as he poses it is misleading by way of begging the question, since it proceeds from his rather than my premises for how to read 1 Cor 9:19–23. It is Gagnon, not me, who argues that Paul's choice to become "weak to the weak" in 1 Cor 9:22 "meant that Paul became like someone who had faith in God but not in Christ" (76). In my view, even though some terms may be the same, the context of their usage is very different, and should be treated accordingly. In Rome, as I have argued the case, the strong/able-to-trust in Christ are to adjust their behavior in matters of diet as servants of "those for whom Christ died," whose opinions on such things, seemingly in keeping with prevailing Jewish norms, Paul (unlike Gagnon) commends to be appropriate for the weak/stumbling-about-trust in Christ. For 1 Cor 9:19–23, I have developed an interpretation in the years since Gagnon's essay that concluded Paul was not describing a change of lifestyle or behavioral adaptability to that of his various audiences (as if he would behave like the weak, in this case, or the lawless, etc., in how he ate or whether he observed Sabbath, e.g.), but rather how he adapted his rhetorical argumentation to the worldview of each kind of person he sought to win to his point of view (how he would argue from the premises of the weak, or the lawless, etc.).[27] In other words, however the weak are defined in 1 Cor 9:22, my argument there would not lead to the conclusion that what Paul is calling for the strong to *behave* like with respect to the weak is illogical, that by definition this would deny to Christ-followers their conviction of faith in Christ in order to do so.

Gagnon assumes, with the traditional views of Paul's language, that in verses such as 14:14, Paul is dismissing the relevance of Torah for Christ-followers when he states: "I know and am persuaded in the Lord Jesus that nothing is profane/common in itself; except [εἰ μή] for anyone who reckons it to be, for that one it is profane/common," not least because the latter part of Paul's statement is traditionally translated as if he wrote: "but it is unclean for anyone who thinks it unclean" (NRSV). Even if translated in the traditional way, one should be able to recognize that Paul grants that certain things are to be respected as profane to those who are convinced that is the case, and thus, given the argument, Paul is arguing that this conviction should be respected. What conviction? The conviction that certain food and drink must be avoided, such as Torah teaches Jews, for example. I have explained this position in *Mystery of Romans* (esp. 192–201), which Gagnon's argument does not engage, proceeding instead as if it had not been made, so I will not reiterate it here, except to remind the reader that Paul is arguing in a manner that draws from Scriptures and is taken up by the rabbis: All things are by nature created good; the categories of holy versus profane are not *intrinsic* to the animal or liquid but *imputed* to them by what the people of Israel understand to be the covenantal commandments of God. Paul reasons from his convictions about Jesus that, while the Christ-following non-Jews do not become Jews and thus are not put under these commandments technically (which Jews such as himself remain under, as members of

---

27. Nanos, "Paul's Relationship to Torah in Light of His Strategy 'to Become Everything to Everyone' (1 Corinthians 9:19–23)."

Israel), these non-Jews are to respect them, for the kinds of reasons that he provides throughout this letter. Paul is not arguing for "indifference" (*adiaphora*), but that difference between Jew and non-Jew is to be respected by those he addresses as followers of Christ!

Gagnon seems to think that by offering a new proposal that the "weak" are Christ-following Noahide gentiles he has escaped tripping into "Luther's trap," since the judgment has moved away from Jewish people. But has he done so? Apart from discussion of the problems of this identification in terms of the text, attributing to Paul the judgment of the opinions of the weak on diet as "false" still runs against what Paul allows for those to whom he writes. Furthermore, it is still the belief in the value and practice of Jewish life, now shifted to non-Jews, that Gagnon, in Paul's voice, dismisses as meaningful service of the Lord. I do not see any change of substance, but only towards which "Jewish" group the judgment is directed. It still constitutes a dismissal of the value of Jewish identity and behavior, supposedly now on the part of non-Jews who still claim to be identified in Jewish terms, as Noahide children of Abraham/righteousness.[28] Behaving in Jewish ways, the traditional judgment, remains the problem for Christ-followers in Gagnon's Paul too.

Gagnon offers three reasons why it seems to him "inescapable that Paul did indeed treat observance of the Mosaic Law by other Jews as *at best harmless and irrelevant, and for himself at best part of a pragmatic strategy for winning Jews to Christ*" (76; emphasis his). In doing so, Gagnon simply reiterates the traditional views, of which I was well aware and that I addressed already when writing the arguments he opposed, and his objection is not specific to my reading of Romans. Gagnon's case is against *any* interpretation of Paul that challenges the traditional way of reading Paul against Judaism and Torah. He warns to beware of interpretations that reflect the "contemporary models of pluralism," to which he seems to object (65), although he does not express similar suspicion about the contemporary models of contempt or misrepresentation of the other, or the legacies of harm arising from the traditional interpretations that he advocates. He also objects to the more respectful approach to Judaism that follows from the recognition of covenantal nomism as a grace-based system (to put the matter in traditional Christian terms) as argued by E. P. Sanders, and in the new-perspectives on Paul represented by Krister Stendahl and James D. G. Dunn.

28. For why posing the context as inter-Christian fails to escape the problem of promoting anti-Jewishness, see my "How Inter-Christian Approaches to Paul's Rhetoric Can Perpetuate Negative Valuations of Jewishness—Although Proposing to Avoid that Outcome."

Gagnon argues that the Law was regarded by Paul as universally problematic. He claims that it "excluded Gentiles from salvation and thereby undermined the confession of God's oneness" (76, a). But I read Paul very differently, and note below a few of his many positive affirmations of the Law and Jewish identity. For Paul, as for other Jewish people, the Law did not exclude *per se*, it defined how humankind *could be included* among the righteous ones of God in the age before the promise to Abraham on behalf of all the nations as well as Israel had arrived; i.e., by becoming Israelites (and Scripture includes accounts that do not conform strictly to this distinction either; e.g., Ruth, Naaman, those who responded to Jonah's preaching). Paul's conflict was with some other Jewish people and groups (in agreement with the other Christ-following Jewish apostles; cf. Gal 2:1–10) over the gospel's chronometrical claim that the awaited age had dawned, and thus that those from the other nations (non-Israelites) too could now be included among the righteous ones apart from becoming members of the nation Israel. Paul argued that it was the logical denial of this professed reality that compromised the oneness of God, should representatives of the nations that turned to God in Christ now be denied standing as children of Abraham apart from becoming children of the nation Israel.[29] When Paul in Rom 3:29–31 appeals to the inherent logic in the Jewish confession of the oneness of God in making a case for the equal inclusion of gentiles as gentiles, note that this very argument is based on the inherent value of the Torah (the confession of the *Shema* is Law-positive; cf. Deut 6!), and that Paul is quick to commend to these non-Jew addressees the continued positive role of the Torah in the midst of this rhetorical effort: "Do we then nullify the Law by this faith? May it never be! On the contrary, we uphold the Law." For Paul, Torah retains the value of that which it signifies in Hebrew, God's "guidance" or "teaching" for how to think and behave righteously.

Gagnon argues in his point (b) that "the Law was essentially 'undoable' for both Jew and Gentile" (76). Although framed differently than it has been in Christian polemic, the fact that Jews do not usually live their entire lives without ever transgressing the precepts of God's guidance was and is a view shared by most if not all Jewish people. But the Law provided for forgiveness as well, anticipating that humans will sin. So why the Law? Paul explains several purposes, as do other Jewish interpreters, but these do not include the traditional Christian straw man that it is to render sinful Israelites or anyone else righteous as if this was something inherently in contrast to trusting in God, from which Gagnon's (traditional Christian) logic works.

---

29. This was argued at length in chapter 4 of *Mystery of Romans*, and is argued more broadly in my later essay, "Paul and the Jewish Tradition: The Ideology of the *Shema*."

Paul can exclaim that he was blameless according to the righteousness of the Law (Phil 3:6), presumably not because he had never erred, but because the Law anticipates and provides for such, which renders, *contra* Gagnon, the Law essentially doable for those of the Law, Israelites.

Gagnon's claim (c), that "salvation through observance of the Torah made self-boasting (Rom 4:2) and the establishment of one's 'own righteousness' (10:3) possible . . ." also represents traditional Christian logic that has now been challenged not only by attending to Jewish reasoning taken on its own terms but also by some advocates of the New Perspective on Paul. Coupled with the last point, Gagnon's traditional Christian logic creates a damned-if-you-do/damned-if-you-don't outcome where any word from God is concerned. Would any Jews recognize their motivations to observe the Torah in such charges? To put the matter in Christian theological terms, the Law does not save anyway, *God* does; the Torah is a gift of God to the righteous as a result of God's grace: it is a privilege and responsibility to have and to obey (cf. Deuteronomy; so too Paul: Rom 3:1–2; 9:4–5; 11:28–29). And if Gagnon's view was right, so that the successful observance of the Law necessarily gave rise to "self-boasting," then how does the successful completion of any word from God not do the same, including the expression of faith or observance of the many instructions for living that come from the hand of Paul, not least the call to live according to "the Law of Christ"? The rabbis, recognizing the evil impulse present in humans along with the good, warn of the secondary possibility of self-congratulation; but this human conundrum does not negate the fact that the observance of the Law is the proper grateful response of a people whom God called and entrusted with this great gift. That it can be used wrongly, as can the confession of faith in Christ, does not speak against the Law, or Christ, but against those who do so.

And his point (d) similarly, like the above comments, construes the nature of the Law for Paul in a narrow way that has been effectively challenged by many Christian as well as Jewish scholars: the Mosaic covenant is not against the promise to Abraham, but follows from it as an additional expression of God's concern to communicate with sinful humankind in the present age, until the promises have been fulfilled. While the thrust of Paul's argument has in the past been construed by other interpreters in the same way, to mean that "the Law had become obsolete" (77), Paul declares emphatically, quite differently, "May it never be!" (3:31); indeed, the Law is for Paul "holy and just and good" (7:13), even "spiritual" (7:14), a special gift of God to Israel and not the nations (3:2; 9:4–5), and to faithful maintenance of such gifts God is forever committed (11:29).

Gagnon's second reason, the deduction that "the way in which Paul describes the Christian's relationship to the Law seems to preclude any possibility of Paul's thinking that the Law remained *binding* for himself and for other Jewish Christians" (77; emphasis his), is virtually indistinguishable from the first and third reasons, and consists of an assertion that he assumes to be self-evident from the stringing together of several verses. It is not evident to me, and the comments above as well as the arguments already offered in *Mystery of Romans* make that clear, as do now the many other arguments that I have published. Gagnon's traditional argument actually disregards the very point of my challenge that we need to read Paul's rhetoric *contextually*, that Romans is not Paul's view of the role of the Law for "every Christian," but addresses specific dilemmas that arise for Christ-following *non-Jews* seeking to live a way of life designed by and for Jews, especially when their claims for equality of standing apart from becoming Jews are in dispute. Paul does not address here any Christ-following *Jew's* relationship to Torah, including that of Paul himself; Paul's argument is specifically contextualized for *non-Jews*, the not-under-the-Mosaic-covenant-with-Israel people to whom he writes.

The third reason, that the Law did not continue to be valid for other than evangelistic (read: manipulative) reasons for Paul or any other Christ-following Jew, which is supposedly sustained by passages outside of Romans such as 1 Cor 9, Gal 2, or Phil 3 (77, esp. n 12), represents special pleading: one cannot expect every argument to engage every objection that arises from the traditional interpretations of every other text. In any event, Gagnon offers no new insights or arguments, but simply reiterates a construal of this language that has a long tradition, of which I was well aware when arguing the case that I did for Romans. Gagnon does not discuss how alternative interpretations of this passage mitigate the traditional line of argument, which stands as a critique in itself that what is self-evident to one interpreter may be anything but that to another. Appeal to longstanding interpretations of which all are aware as though beyond dispute may serve to harden ideologically constructed boundaries for perceiving reality, but it does not advance the discussion of new insights, and stands in the way of the historical-critical task.

In my view, none of the passages to which Gagnon appeals disqualify the conclusion that Paul was a Jew who faithfully observed Torah. In the years since Gagnon's article, I have engaged these texts in detail, demonstrating how each instead supports the interpretation of Paul as a Torah-observant Jew, so I will not undertake that very involved task here.[30]

---

30. Many of these are now available in these four volumes of my collected essays, as well as in other publications to which these refer.

Gagnon completes this argument with a warning: "In contemporary society, where it has become increasingly fashionable in scholarly circles to reshape Paul according to politically correct standards, historians need to be particularly sure that they are reconstructing accurately the 'historical Paul,' scandalous or not" (78). I commend the concern for proper practice of historiography, and thus all that claims to represent exegesis! I assume that Gagnon has not overlooked that pre-contemporary interpretations of Paul are also shaped by ideological values which privileged certain interpretations according to the standards of political correctness and the ruling elite of their time, and that the traditional interpretations to which he appeals are inherently anachronistic when measured against any concern to "reconstruct accurately the 'historical Paul,'" since they were developed to answer to the concerns of earlier interpreters, and not usually with much regard for what Paul might have meant in his own time. Further, these earlier constructions were the products of interpreters who generally dismissed or even abhorred the Jewish people and their religious practices, including those who, in the not-so-distant past, employed Paul's voice to support an incomprehensive level of crimes against humanity considered by some of them to be politically and legally compelling, as well as correct. No interpretation is value-free; but we are responsible for choices we make.[31] That the Paul I am constructing is scandalous to Gagnon and others who defend and promote traditional Christian (and for that matter, Jewish) constructions of the apostle should elicit similar self-reflection, not least if the impulse to defend and conquer is immediately aroused even by the very suggestion that Paul may have meant something other than the tradition to which one subscribes has upheld.

C. "Weak" Meaning "Stumbling"

The cases Gagnon offers against my proposal that ἀσθενέω is better rendered in this case as (being in a state of) stumbling, rather than weak, or that it refers to non-Christ-following Jewish people, are not compelling. Gagnon suggests some minor adjustments, such as that 14:4 indicates that the weak "are still standing upright through the Lord's (Christ's) help," and that this "affirms that they have not yet stumbled" (79). Regardless of the fact that Paul's statement in verse 4 can be read to imply that someone is already in need of the Lord's help in order to be upheld (ἀσθενέω is future passive), and the similar implication of 15:1, Paul's language by nature communicates an interested perspective; indeed, identity is itself a

---

31. Instructive is Elliott, *Liberating Paul*, 55–89.

social construction that is multifaceted, dependent upon the party and the point of view being expressed.[32] In other words, however translated or interpreted, this language is subjective as well as metaphorical. The fact that in 11:22 Paul can mix metaphors so that he uses "fallen" with respect to hypothetical branches after he has in the previous metaphor emphatically denied that those being described as stumbling while walking or running had "fallen" (11:11), tells against the kind of wooden use of language upon which Gagnon's criticism depends.[33]

It is doubtful whether those being discussed as "weak/stumbling" would have considered either their present situation or the outcome of their future response, if negative, to constitute weakness/stumbling; more likely, they would have understood their position on the matter to exemplify their strength, their steadfast faithfulness to God to confess and behave according to that of which they are convinced. This verse may in fact indicate what I have claimed apart from this verbal inference, that is, that in the opinion of Paul and the strong/able-to-trust-in-the-gospel-ones to whom he wrote, the stumbling (i.e., estrangement from the ideal of joining Paul in declaring the gospel to the nations) was already expressed in the life of those of Israel who did not share their trust in Christ or in the proposed incorporation of non-Jews as non-Jews among the righteous ones as though the end of the ages had already dawned. It is the meaning and outcome of this development that Paul interpreted differently than have those he addressed in Rome.

Moreover, I have answered the minor criticism raised already in *Mystery of Romans* by noting that this language for stumbling in chapters 14–15 is different from that of chapters 9–11, and that it brings to the fore an edge to Paul's employment of the terms.[34] Paul has moved from the figurative language of chapters 9–11, in which the current stumbling state of some Israelites is considered to be somehow according to God's inscrutable and to-date-unrecognized design, to articulating the subsequent issue of the attitude and behavior now incumbent upon these non-Jews in view of the mercy they have received. Paul discloses the knowledge of this mystery so that they will refrain from being the cause of stumbling, and to instead hold-up those suffering vicariously on their own behalf so that they do not fall.

This particular topic should be especially critical for Gagnon's claim that my interpretation of the language of the weakness/stumbling "cannot" be. Yet the reader finds instead the concession that my proposal is

32. See e.g., Jenkins, *Social Identity*, 19–28.

33. See now my "'Broken Branches': A Pauline Metaphor Gone Awry? (Romans 11:11–36)."

34. Nanos, *Mystery of Romans*, 119–24.

"intriguing," even the generous comment that "it receives additional support," although "there are some problems." He admits that "the connotation of 'stumbling' is possible," although the referent is "not necessarily" as I propose, even if my interpretation adopts the "basic sense" of the term, and in conclusion notes that "the context must be decisive." It is precisely the context, and thus the best way to interpret the usage of the words in this case, that is at dispute.

D. The Analogy of Abraham, Not Weak in Faith (Romans 4:19–21)

Gagnon agrees that the description of Abraham's faith in 4:19–21 is useful for interpreting chapter 14, even that "Nanos's interpretation is one plausible interpretation" (80). In other words, this "can" be. Abraham was not a "Christian," and Gagnon's effort to construe the identity of the weak/stumbling-in-faith to be Christian-yet-Torah-observing-*gentiles* seems strained throughout (80–81). Interestingly, where his own proposal is concerned, Gagnon asks the reader of his proposal to recognize that "the story of Abraham, as an analogy, does not have to fit in all its particulars" (80). Indeed, that is how we must approach analogies.

Why does Gagnon grant that weakness to regard Jewish diet as appropriate was still regarded by Paul to be a matter of *faith*, when Gagnon has concluded that Paul no longer considered the practice of Law an expression of faith, since it was now obsolete for the Christ-believer? Is continued Law-observance then not sin, since "whatever is not of faith is sin" (14:23)? If continued Law-observance is not commensurate with the practice of faith in Christ, one wonders in what way the weak/stumbling may be described by Gagnon as those who "have proven themselves 'strong' with respect to 'the promise of God' concerning Christ" (80). Why should such faith be esteemed strong/able by Gagnon's Paul if it remains Torah-observant, and thus opposed by Paul as not-faith?[35] They are then regarded as weak in *opinion* on what is dismissed by Paul, on Gagnon's terms, as a matter of "indifference" anyway (75, 81), but strong in faith in Christ where it is a matter of importance according to the measure of those who uphold the value of faith in Jesus Christ. One might wonder why Gagnon's indifferent Paul thought that this extensive instruction about respecting the sensibilities of the weak/ stumbling in faith, even if calculated by themselves to be in the service of the Lord, was warranted, instead of calling for the strong/able to teach the

---

35. A sympathetic critique of a similar failure of logic is expressed in Cranfield's response to an argument made by Barrett (*The Epistle to the Romans*, 2.690–91).

weak/stumbling to recognize, by word and example, that the Law is obsolete and opposed to God's purpose, since its continued practice weakened or sickened faith. That is the sentiment expressed in the tradition known as Paulinism, which Gagnon's arguments otherwise promote.

III. CONCLUSION

In his conclusion, Gagnon's argument implies that I have "alleged" Paul's "appeal" is to the weak/stumbling, but I have not done so: I *argued* that Paul's appeal is to the strong/able-to-trust-in-Christ, and he criticizes my not-position on the grounds that it is monotheistic in character rather than "a deeply christocentric appeal" (82). My case actually highlights the *christo*-centric matter of conviction that distinguishes these rhetorical groups more than the traditional readings, and Gagnon's, which make the matter revolve around a *nomos*-centric divide. I argue that the distinction revolves around their different convictions about the significance of Jesus as Christ. Gagnon's position (with most others) actually moves the issue to a judgment of faith in the value or not of Law-observance, so that it is not about the question of the meaning of Jesus Christ, or the admission of non-Jews as non-Jews, since both weak/stumbling and strong/able are taken to be Christ-followers. This results in devaluing of the christological basis of the group boundaries, for they do not provide the grounds for the controversy. Paul's argument leading up to the exhortations of chapters 12–16 were about whether one trusted the gospel proclamation or not, so it makes sense that Paul would then develop the implications for those who, like him, do so, and specifically with respect to behavior toward those who do not. The ability of this reading to hold together the overall argument of the letter versus the ability of the traditional view he defends to do so is more substantial than Gagnon's response admits.[36]

When Gagnon finally assesses the arguments against my view, so that it "cannot" be, one is confronted by a string of assertions that my interpretation is not "required." Indeed, it is not. I do not seek to claim otherwise. I argued at length in *The Mystery of Romans*, and in many cases since, for a historical-critical approach to a first-century Jewish document that offers a comprehensive reading of Paul's letter that is internally consistent while accounting for the available external evidence as well.

I am pleased to find that Gagnon grants the plausibility of many elements of my argumentation, what "can" be allowed, in the midst of an effort

---

36. Nanos, *Mystery of Romans*, 85–91, and the many arguments that turn on this issue in Donfried, ed., *The Romans Debate*.

to demonstrate that the situation and identification of the parties "cannot" be as I proposed; after working through the details and logical fallacies, I am all the more convinced of the probability of the case I argued.[37]

BIBLIOGRAPHY

Banks, Marcus. *Ethnicity: Anthropological Constructions*. London: Routledge, 1996.
Barrett, C. K. *The Epistle to the Romans*. 2nd ed. Peabody, MA: Hendrickson, 1991.
Barth, Fredrik. "Introduction." In *Ethnic Groups and Boundaries: The Social Organization of Culture Difference*, edited by Fredrik Barth, 9–38. Boston: Little Brown, 1969.
Boissevain, Jeremy. *Friends of Friends: Networks, Manipulators and Coalitions*. New York: St. Martin's, 1974.
Chilton, Bruce, and Jacob Neusner, eds. *Jewish and Christian Doctrines: The Classics Compared*. London: Routledge, 2000.
Cranfield, C. E. B. *A Critical and Exegetical Commentary on the Epistle to the Romans*. ICC. Edinburgh: T. & T. Clark, 1975.
Donfried, Karl P., ed. *The Romans Debate*. Rev. and exp. ed. Peabody, MA: Hendrickson, 1991.
Elliott, Neil. *Liberating Paul: The Justice of God and the Politics of the Apostle*. Maryknoll, NY: Orbis, 1994.
Esler, Philip Francis. *Galatians*. New Testament Readings. London: Routledge, 1998.
Gagnon, Robert A. "Why the 'Weak' at Rome Cannot Be Non-Christian Jews." *Catholic Biblical Quarterly* 62 (2000) 64–82.
Hogg, Michael A., and Dominic Abrams. *Social Identifications: A Social Psychology of Intergroup Relations and Group Processes*. London: Routledge, 1988.
Jenkins, Richard. *Social Identity*. Key Ideas. London: Routledge, 1996.
Land, Christopher D. "'We Put No Stumbling Block in Anyone's Path, So that Our Ministry Will Not be Discredited': Paul's Response to an Idol Food Inquiry in 1 Corinthians 8:1–13." In *Paul and His Social Relations*, edited by Stanley E. Porter and Christopher D. Land, 229–83. Leiden: Brill, 2013.
Nanos, Mark D. "'Broken Branches': A Pauline Metaphor Gone Awry? (Romans 11:11–36)." In *Between Gospel and Election: Explorations in the Interpretation of Romans 9–11*, edited by Florian Wilk and J. Ross Wagner, 339–76. Tübingen: Mohr Siebeck, 2010. (See chapter 6 in this volume of collected essays.)
———. "Challenging the Limits That Continue to Define Paul's Perspective on Jews and Judaism." In *Reading Israel in Romans: Legitimacy and Plausibility of Divergent Interpretations*, edited by Cristina Grenholm and Daniel Patte, 217–29. Romans through History and Culture Series. Harrisburg, PA: Trinity, 2000. (See chapter 11 in this volume of collected essays.)
———. "How Inter-Christian Approaches to Paul's Rhetoric Can Perpetuate Negative Valuations of Jewishness—Although Proposing to Avoid that Outcome." *Biblical Interpretation* 13 (2005) 255–69. (See volume 1, chapter 2, of this series of collected essays.)

---

37. Special thanks to Robert Brawley, William Campbell, Kevin Kiser, Mark Reasoner, and Peter Spitaler for commenting on an earlier draft of this rejoinder; of course, culpability for the views expressed herein falls entirely upon me.

———. "The Jewish Context of the Gentile Audience Addressed in Paul's Letter to the Romans." *Catholic Biblical Quarterly* 61 (1999) 283–304. (See chapter 3 in this volume of collected essays.)

———. *The Mystery of Romans: The Jewish Context of Paul's Letter.* Minneapolis: Fortress, 1996.

———. "Paul's Relationship to Torah in Light of His Strategy 'to Become Everything to Everyone' (1 Corinthians 9:19–23)." In *Paul and Judaism: Crosscurrents in Pauline Exegesis and the Study of Jewish-Christian Relations,* edited by Didier Pollefeyt and Reimund Bieringer, 106–40. LNTS 463. London: T. & T. Clark, 2012. (See volume 4, chapter 3, in this series of collected essays.)

———. "The Polytheist Identity of the 'Weak,' and Paul's Strategy to 'Gain' Them: A New Reading of 1 Corinthians 8:1—11:1." In *Paul: Jew, Greek, and Roman,* edited by Stanley E. Porter, 179–210. Pauline Studies 5. Leiden: Brill, 2008. (See volume 4, chapter 1, in this series of collected essays.)

———. "Some Problems with Reading Romans through the Lens of the Edict of Claudius." In *Mystery of Romans,* 372–87. Minneapolis: Fortress, 1996. (See chapter 2 in this volume of collected essays.)

———. "Why the 'Weak' in 1 Corinthians 8–10 Were Not Christ-Believers." In *Saint Paul and Corinth: 1950 Years Since the Writing of the Epistles to the Corinthians: International Scholarly Conference Proceedings (Corinth, 23–25 September 2007),* edited by Constantine J. Belezos, Sotirios Despotis and Christos Karakolis, 385–404. Athens, Greece: Psichogios, 2009. (See volume 4, chapter 2, in this series of collected essays.)

Reasoner, Mark. *The Strong and the Weak: Romans 14.1—15:13 in Context.* SNTSMS 103. New York: Cambridge University Press, 1999.

Spitaler, Peter. "James 1:5–8: A Dispute with God." *Catholic Biblical Quarterly* 71 (2009) 560–79.

Stuhlmacher, Peter. *Paul's Letter to the Romans: A Commentary.* Louisville: Westminster/John Knox, 1994.

Wilson, Bryan, "The Sociology of Sects." In *Religion in Sociological Perspective,* edited by Bryan Wilson, 89–120. Oxford: Oxford University Press, 1982.

PART III

A New Exegetical Approach to Romans 9–11 and Christian-Jewish Relations

5

Romans 9–11 from a Jewish Perspective on Christian-Jewish Relations[1]

PREVAILING INTERPRETATIONS OF PAUL'S arguments in Romans 9–11 send sharply conflicting signals about the fate of Jews who did not share his convictions about Jesus. These readings undermine efforts to challenge the largely negative, supersessionistic way that Christians have historically thought and talked about, as well as interacted with, Jews and Judaism. Romans 9 and the beginning of 10 are understood to criticize Jews for ostensible Jewish pride for celebrating being chosen by God, for seeking to observe Torah, and for supposing to have at any point faithfully observed that which God commanded; as punishment, Jews have been "replaced" as God's children by "Christians." But chapter 11 is often understood to mitigate the impact, at least to offer a positive future expectation for Jews, albeit one still shaped by the presupposition that they will ultimately *be saved*, *re*-joining the new family (which assumes the premise that they have been removed), when they ultimately recognize that Christians have been right all along about Jesus, and become Christians too.

I suggest that in spite of complicated twists and turns, if viewed from the first-century perspective of the apostle Paul—when Christ-followers were still practicing and promoting Judaism rather than a new, competitive alternative that became known as Christianity—each of the arguments in these chapters

---

1. This essay was originally written without annotations for translation into Italian for a non-specialist reader. In view of the inclusion of this essay in a volume where the arguments and sources are provided in detail in the other chapters, the original non-annotated style for non-specialists has been retained, although some of the arguments have been slightly updated to reflect subsequent research.

can be understood in much more promising—albeit for later readers, necessarily cross-cultural and thus not implicitly self-evident—ways. This follows from approaching Paul's arguments to originally reflect attitudes toward (other) Jews and (other ways of practicing and promoting) Judaism from an author who continued to identify as a Jew who practiced and promoted Torah-observant Judaism. For Jews of Paul's time, like for Paul, at issue was whether to change their convictions about the meaning of Jesus *within* Judaism, unlike has been the case for Jews after the movement became something other than Judaism (a Jewish way of living), which Jews had to convert *out of Judaism* into if they were persuaded of the gospel claims. When read within Judaism, his arguments do not support traditional Christian replacement-based theological reasoning, even though his deductions were beholden to the conviction that Jesus ushered in the messianic age, a propositional claim of which many Jews remain unconvinced, just as was the case then. In addition to proposing to advance more probable historical exegesis, these arguments can also be interpreted, *mutatis mutandis*, to express a level of generosity that offers more promising options for those concerned about the role of Paul's voice in Christian-Jewish relations today.

Paul introduces a progression of arguments in 9:1–5 by expressing great concern for his fellow Jews. He asserts, *in present tense*, their many gifts and callings as Israelites (which he similarly asserts to be *irrevocable* at the end of his arguments, in 11:28–29), regardless of whether they share his trust that Jesus is the Messiah, and thus in spite of not joining him in announcing that message (the gospel) to the nations. Paul thereafter, in 9:6, explains the troubling development of his and his addressees' time on which these chapters reflect: some of his fellow Jews are not (yet) able to share his perspective on Christ, while the non-Jews addressed are able to do so. The usual translations of verse 6 ("For not all Israelites truly belong to Israel" [NRSV]) express the idea that these Jews are no longer members of God's Israel, whether they recognize this to be the case or not, and Christian interpreters have usually concluded that those who believe in Jesus have become *true* Israel in their place. But Paul's language can be interpreted to indicate affirmation of their continued identity as Israelites, in keeping with what Paul has just argued in verses 1–5. In spite of the current disagreement about Jesus, verse 6 states that even those who are not (yet) joining Paul in the task of gospeling to the nations, who therefore are not acting like Israelites should when the time to herald the awaited day arrives ("For not all the ones from Israel [are presently bringing the message to the nations]"), nevertheless remain those God (and Paul) still calls Israel: "These ones are Israel [*houtoi Israêl*]"! (See chapter 10 in this volume.) That is what it means to have received the irrevocable calling and gifts God promised, regardless of how things might otherwise appear presently to Paul's addressees in Rome.

When translated as suggested, this language indicates that, for Paul, these Jews are still being used by God to carry out God's designs in an unexpected way, rather than, as traditionally interpreted, to conclude that these Jews have been removed from God's people and thus from God's service, albeit often presented with the caveat that they can be restored by becoming Christians, and will be upon the return of Christ. Paul's argument also can be read to signify that, unlike Paul, these Jews are not yet persuaded that they should be proclaiming Christ to the nations; however, this myopic state is being suffered by no fault of their own, and its purpose will be completed in due time. However inscrutable and even inconsistent with God's character that may seem, this is God's sovereign choice and will work out for good for all humankind, not least for "them." Paul returns to explaining this in more detail in chapter 11.

Paul also reveals that those Jews who are involved in proclaiming Christ, like himself, are also participating in this activity, not as variously surmised, because they had been more faithful or righteous or tried harder or been more humble, or trusted God rather than undertaking "works" to please God, or been less prone to "ethnocentric nationalism," but simply because God has chosen them from among the rest of the Israelites to initiate the process that is unfolding in real time before those whom Paul is addressing in Rome—that is, on the same terms that have always applied to Israel (and now to the non-Jews in Christ), by way of God's choice. Throughout this argument it remains important to Paul to maintain that even those Israelites who are not presently undertaking this task will eventually conclude to do so, but only when it is appropriate according to God's own timetable. He seeks to explain how it "is" rather than how it may "seem." The target audience of non-Jews—who are facing resistance to their claims to have become full members of the people of God through Christ apart from becoming Jews—must understand the difference, and this knowledge must shape their thoughts and actions in order for this "mystery" to now unfold as it should.

To illustrate this situation, in 9:30-33 Paul develops the idea that Israelites are to be the heralds of God's good news to the nations. He draws on imagery used by Isaiah, especially chapters 8 and 28:16. In view of the imminent attack of the Assyrians, the leaders of Israel were tempted to lead the people to take up arms to defend Jerusalem. Isaiah calls the Israelites to instead look to the cornerstone that has been set to serve as the basis for the tower that God will build to shelter them from the attack (pictured as flood waters pouring in around the base of the tower), and warns them against instead tripping over the very stone that foretells their safekeeping should they begin to prepare to fight rather than trust that God will provide the protection they need (by entering this tower). Paul argues that some Jews of his time are in a similar way stumbling over the cornerstone, which is the proclamation of Jesus as the awaited Christ who will rescue Israel from her enemies, and Savior of all of the rest of the nations too, which it is Israel's special privilege to announce to the nations. That this propositional claim is not yet self-evident, Paul is well aware, having himself required a personal revelation to become persuaded (Gal 1:13–16). But he proposes that the foundational event (stone) for initiating the awaited time has been recognized now by Jews such as himself, who must thus begin to proclaim this news to the nations. The Jews who have not yet been persuaded are characterized as presently stumbling over whether this news is to be announced to the nations *apart from* making those who respond members of the nation Israel. But Paul understands the gospel to teach that the age to come will be a time when God includes those from the other nations among the people of God apart from them becoming Israelites. Paul recognizes, by way of the gospel's propositional claims, that this is a stone that signals a future free of fear from the threats of the nations to the worship of Israel's God. However, he also sees that it can serve at the same time as a stone over which the very ones for whom it was designed to provide safety (Israel) stumble if they resist the entrance of those from the nations who have joined with those Israelites like Paul who are heralding the hope this event adumbrates for all humankind.

Paul maintains the proposition that those from the nations who respond to this message of good news in Christ remain members of the other nations thereafter, joining alongside of Israelites in the worship of the One God of *all* the nations. That is the "truth of the gospel." The non-Israelites thus cannot become Israelites, because then the proposition that the end of the ages has dawned, when all of the nations will recognize Israel's God as the one and only God, a propositional claim based in the confession of the *Shema' Israel*, will instead be undermined. If those from the nations become Israelites, which involves proselyte conversion (in the case of males, circumcision marks the completion of that rite), then God would still be only the God of Israel, of Israelites, and it would not be manifest that the awaited day has arrived. For, Paul maintains (borrowing again from the imagery of Isaiah's prophecies), when that day arrives, just as the wolf (those from the nations) will lay down alongside the lamb (those from Israel), so too those from the nations will join alongside of Israelites (Isa 65:25; see all of chapters 65–66, and 2:2–4). The wolves will not become lambs, but will no longer devour them. So too the members of the nations will not become Israelites, but will no longer harm them. Israel will no longer need Torah to protect herself from the nations (or be protected from them by a *pedagogos*, as Gal 3:24–25 puts the matter); instead Israel will continue to be guided by Torah, and will universalize this knowledge into first principles to guide those from the nations in the worship of the One God of all humankind (which we witness Paul doing in these letters, recognizable in his approach to why the Christ-following non-Jews cannot eat idol food in 1 Cor 8–10). For that is the day when *shalom* can be experienced by all of God's creation.

In the balance of Rom 10 and the beginning of chapter 11, Paul continues to explain that, although not all Israelites are presently undertaking to herald the good news to the nations, that there are some Israelites who are, such as Paul, and thus that Israel as a whole is fulfilling her role, albeit in an unexpected, divided, and divisive way. His readiness to do so is not because he has done better deeds, or the others worse ones; this reflects God's inscrutable design for how to achieve God's objective to show mercy to the nations, and thereafter, to show mercy to the rest of the Israelites on the same terms as has been shown to the nations.

Paul returns to the image of some Israelites metaphorically stumbling in 11:11, that is, not joining in the movement toward the nations with the proclamation of the good news of Christ for those from the other nations apart from becoming Israelites. The hypothetical question is whether the other Israelites have stumbled "so as to fall." The denial is swift and certain: "By no means!" Some are stumbling, but this misstep is ironically for the benefit of the nations, and it will not result in a fall for those Israelites either, for they will eventually regain their step, but only after some from the nations respond positively to those who do herald this message, such as Paul. This development is a mechanism by which God is accomplishing the unthinkable. For when these Israelites see Paul's successful ministry fulfilling the promised privilege of Israelites to bring the nations to the knowledge of God, they will be provoked to want to emulate Paul (i.e., to "jealousy of my ministry"), that is, to reconsider the claims of the good news of Christ for themselves, and thus for Paul's fellow Jews to join him in carrying this news to the nations, alongside Paul (vv. 13–15). In metaphorical terms, the rest of the heralds will find their footing again. Then all of the nations, Israel as well as the rest, will experience the fullness of the awaited day, a day that Paul believes has already dawned.

In the next few verses of chapter 11, it becomes evident that Paul's concern in writing this letter is significantly if not primarily to censure presumptuousness among these non-Jews toward those Jews who have not (yet, from Paul's perspective) joined Paul in proclaiming Christ, and the actions that follow from such prideful self-congratulation among these non-Jews. Jewish pride is not what Paul confronts, or the effort to fully observe Torah, or even the failure to have done so (i.e., as if Jews need to be told that they are sinners too), since no one can, as Jews know well, which is why Jewish Scriptures and traditions express dependence upon God's mercy in response to faith-based repentance, sacrifice, and prayer. What Paul directly confronts is any notion among Christ-following non-Jews that they have supplanted these presently not-persuaded Israelites, whom they have instead joined alongside of as fellow members of the household of God. In Paul's argument, the non-Jews addressed are additional, non-native members of the people of God, like a wild olive shoot placed among the natural olive branches of the cultivated tree. What they are to learn from these presently estranged Israelites is just how precarious is their own place in God's favor, and thus, just how important it is to live humbly and righteously, faithful to that which God has generously given to them. They are to learn from the example of what happens when some of God's own, which they are now too, suffer on behalf of the accomplishments of God's sovereign designs. In other words, like Jesus Christ, these Jews are suffering vicariously for the benefit of the nations. How then should their present role in God's plan be received? And how then should those characterized as a newly introduced limb that has benefited from their suffering think and behave toward them in the meantime?

Paul communicates this message first by way of an allegory of stumbling, which he uses to explain that the current situation is a temporary one that has allowed God to benefit these non-Israelites, but that will be incomparably better when the rest of the Israelites have regained their footing (vv. 11–15; cf. 9:30–33). Paul follows this with an allegory of an olive tree, as already noted, by which he directly confronts a wild olive branch grafted in among natural branches of the cultivated olive tree, in order to instruct it not to think that it is more favored by God than those natural branches presently suffering damage (vv. 17–24). In this extended metaphor, God tells this wild branch (and note, it is but one shoot among many natural branches), that, rather than presumptuousness toward some natural branches presently broken, it should fear all the more what may happen to itself if it should think or behave according to such an attitude, since it is not even natural to the tree. I write "broken," not "broken *off*," which is true to the Greek, since it allows for broken as in "bent" or "bent aside," or "sprained," while broken *off* implies *fallen*, because Paul emphatically *denies* they have fallen; rather, he insists, they are suffering estrangement as injured tree limbs (i.e., stumbling heralds). Paul goes so far as to state that the wild shoot should be in a state of fear. It should be concerned about the fate of the damaged branches, and recognize the favor it has enjoyed at their expense, for the wild shoot is to learn humbly from the natural branch. It must think and live graciously toward these branches.

Indeed, Paul concludes, the fate of all of these branches, natural and wild, are interrelated in God's design for how to reconcile all of the nations. Since God has shown such great mercy to even wild olive branches (idolaters previously not persuaded of the One God of Israel), which have actually suffered being cut off from a tree, and a wild one at that, now God can show mercy to the natural branches (worshippers of the One God who are not yet persuaded of Jesus Christ), who were not in need of similar mercy previously (vv. 30–32), but now have suffered like injured limbs. In the meantime, they have also been "callused" (v. 25, *pōrōsis*; usually translated "hardened") by God to protect them alive in the tree until the process has been completed. However limited by zero-sum thinking the premise for Paul's argument may be, Paul assures these non-Jews that although some Jews have been alienated from the gospel presently, this process is designed to offer mercy to the nations, and then, reciprocally, to these Israelites. For these Jews are "beloved for the sake of the fathers," to whom God made promises about the blessings they would enjoy; after all, "the gifts and calling of God are irrevocable" (vv. 28–29). Generosity, not begrudging envy or resentment at any slight they may be suffering, should guide their thinking, their intentions, and their actions.

Paul makes central to his message the affirmation that "all Israel will be protected [saved; i.e., kept/made safe!]" (11:26). This letter is not about challenging Jews (a) for misdirected faith, (b) for Torah-observance, (c) for (ethnocentrically) believing that Israel was chosen by God and must guard the Israelite identity from compromise by insisting that non-Jews become Jews to claim to be full members of this people, or even (d) for not believing in Jesus Christ. The basis of Paul's argument is not that Jews are in some way out of Israel or the people of God or the covenant, and need to get back in on the same terms as do non-Jews: they remain in, protected as God's people in a state of suffering on behalf of the salvation of the nations. They are suffering a state of discipline *for their lack of being persuaded to herald this news to the nations*. But this temporary estrangement is by God's design, as inscrutable as it may seem, after which they will be restored to their advantaged place. Naturally, this means that these Jews are not persuaded about Jesus as Christ, but that is not the problem Paul is articulating here, which is about the (in)ability of some (it turns out, most) Israelites *to undertake their assigned role* to take the word of God entrusted to them (3:1–2) to the nations *yet*, alongside of those Israelites like Paul who are already doing so.

In summary, Paul's message in Romans 9–11 is directed specifically to Christ-following non-Jews to help them understand the mysterious ways in which God is working among both Jews and non-Jews, including the present disagreement about the meaning of Christ. This present stage is a part of God's design. Although it might seem that all Israelites would be heralding this news to the nations, Paul argues that, by God's design, only some are now doing so (9:30–33; 11:1–5), but the rest will be restored to joining in and completing this task when the proper time has arrived. Paul does not return to the tower imagery from Isaiah, but to be consistent with the message he delivers by way of the stumbling and olive tree metaphors and the argument overall, he would have to insist that in spite of the threat of those who tripped being swept away in a flood, they were going to be protected by God, rescued by the faithfulness of those who awaited the building of the tower when they saw the cornerstone set in place, into which the rest would also ultimately climb.

Notably, nowhere does Paul call for these non-Jews to evangelize among Jews, or to imagine them to be in need of evangelization. Rather, in chapter 14, he warns his readers to welcome and avoid disputing viewpoints with these Jews, and calls for modification of behavior to accommodate their sensibilities about what is appropriate to eat if claiming to be children of righteous Abraham. Jews are to be encouraged by such behavior to respect the faith claims of these non-Jews. Indeed, throughout chapters 12 to 15, the major behavior Paul seeks to instill in these non-Jews is a commitment to living respectfully and graciously toward these Jews, and by extension, toward everyone. This is how Paul will provoke his kinspeople to emulate his ministry among the nations, and bring about "life from the dead" (11:13–15).

Most Jews today will not agree with Paul's way of seeing the situation, disagreeing with the claims made about Jesus as Christ (Messiah), and about whether they are in some state of discipline for not heralding the news of Christ to the nations. Naturally, Jews will find such notions offensive, and patronizing at best—Christians would too, if the terms were reversed. These ways of conceptualizing the world are not without implicit (when not explicit) criticism; they are not value free. Paul was a Jew, although a Christ-following Jew who was not in agreement on these matters with the majority of his fellow Jews. And the distance is far greater today between Jews and Christ-followers, who are generally not fellow-Jews involved in an in-house disagreement, as was the case for Paul. Today these represent two very different religions, and there is much history, including a legacy of harm toward Jews by Christians, often carried out in the name of Christ and Christian conceptualizations of Jews as the enemies of God (see still in the NRSV English translation of 11:28 that "enemies *of God*" is written, even though "of God" is *not* in the Greek manuscripts, and "enemies" is an adjective, i.e., "estranged"; that is, Paul refers to victims, not perpetrators). Reading Romans from the perspective suggested, within Judaism, can provide a more positive basis for relations between Christians and Jews in the future.

Paul sought to provoke respect for the Jewish "brother and sister" who did not agree about Christ when he wrote to these non-Jews in Rome. Would he not similarly challenge non-Jewish Christians about the development of their theology and policies, in Rome and throughout the world, in the twenty-first century? Indeed, it is a great pleasure to observe that this has been a corrective message of interest to the Catholic Church since Vatican II.

6

"Broken Branches"
A Pauline Metaphor Gone Awry?
(Romans 11:11–24)[1]

1. INTRODUCTION

[339] PAUL'S OLIVE TREE allegory is as puzzling as it is popular.[2] From country preachers to Oxford professors, many arguments and theological positions appeal to this figure to portray Paul's view of Israel and the church. To state but a few examples, elements of it are employed to proclaim the supplanting of Israel by the church,[3] the conflation of Israel with the church,[4] and especially that Christian gentiles are grafted into Israel, which the tree is understood to represent. This Israel is implicitly regarded as—and often

---

1. I want to thank Andy Johnson, Dieter Mitternacht, Daniel Stramara, and the conference members for helpful discussions of earlier versions.

2. I use allegory to refer to this imagery because this is an extended metaphor, following the lead of Esler, "Ancient Oleiculture and Ethnic Differentiation," esp. 106–7; Black, "Metaphor," esp. 275. By metaphor, I mean a figure of speech (trope) that communicates a thing, idea, or action by substituting a word or expression that denotes a different thing, idea, or action, often a word from a visual image or sound, suggesting a shared quality between the two words or expressions that remains at an imaginary level.

3. The history of this concept is traced in Simon, *Verus Israel*.

4. For the history of this concept, see Richardson, *Israel in the Apostolic Church*. The other text most often pressed into service to support this notion is Gal 6:16, where reference is made to "the Israel of God." That case is equally vague: the context fails to supply the referent, and the statement itself is further obscured by grammatical ambiguity, as Richardson has demonstrated. See further, Eastman, "Israel and Divine Mercy in Galatians and Romans."

explicitly renamed—"spiritual" or "true Israel," in contrast to the Israel that was and is composed of empirical descendants of Jacob as well as those who have become part of this lineage by way of proselyte [340] conversion. In essence, "Israel" in this sense functions as a metonym for "Christianity."

However, Paul draws none of these important connections explicitly. Bearing witness to this fact, interpreters often re-employ Paul's metaphorical language to assert significant theological propositions rather than re-stating them in non-metaphorical terms. Thus, when one wishes to argue that Christian gentiles are incorporated into Israel, the proposition is often expressed metaphorically: the gentiles have been "grafted into Israel." Yet people are not "grafted" into nations; Israel is not actually a "tree"; and Israelites and gentiles are not "branches." Likewise, when wishing to communicate that Israelites who are not Christians are no longer members of God's people, this too is expressed by means of a metaphor: they have been "broken off." Such metaphors are labeled "dead"; that is, they pass unnoticed as metaphors, common usage having made them so familiar that they appear to describe rather than allude to the things to which they refer. Consequently, such metaphors no longer function as tropes but rather appear to be plain speech.

For the first recipients of Romans, the imagery presented here offered a new way of interpreting reality. But in the history of the church's reading of Romans, this imagery has come to be understood as familiar and self-evident information that simply describes and confirms—rather than interprets reality. And often the particular aspect that was initially central to it has been lost from view: the confrontation of Christ-believing non-Israelites' pride toward those Israelites who do not share their convictions about the meaning of Christ. Rather than serving to reinterpret reality, this allegory has been reiterated as if it were a straightforward reflection of reality, as if the metaphorical language described what came to pass, what is, and what will be in terms of social reality, without regard for the limitations of metaphorical communication.[5]

Although it is regularly maintained that the broken branches refer to Israelites who have been removed from the tree that is Israel, Paul does not say that the tree is Israel. Moreover, he has just insisted, also in allegorical terms, that these Israelites have not "fallen," but merely "stumbled," missing a step (Rom 11:11). The allegorical imagery of walking or running that is implied by this notion of "stumbling" suggests that these Israelites have

---

5. The traditional role of this allegory to describe non-Christian Jews and Judaism being replaced by the church rather than to describe the precarious place and responsibility of non-Jewish Christians brings into question whether this allegory successfully communicated Paul's stated aims for it even for the original audience.

suffered impeded progress in their pursuit of a future goal, such as the hope of the age to come or of the rule and protection of God, or the role of proclaiming the gospel to the nations. It does not represent a [341] complete depiction of Israel as a whole nor offer an exhaustive account of Israel's story. Moreover, in both allegories it is only some Israelites Paul seeks to represent, making it unlikely that it is Israel *per se* that is in view. Rather, Paul speaks of some entity more all-encompassing than Israel alone. Paul's image includes not only the return of some of these Israelites to walking unimpeded or standing securely, but also refers to the tree or supporting branch in which the rest of the Israelites continue to partake as well as to the members from the rest of the nations who have joined them. Finally, the mystery revealed in the metaphorical language of verses 25–27 describes a process that will result in a future state of restoration. It emphatically denies that any kind of end point has already been reached in God's dealings with Israel, such as the image of broken-off branches seems to imply. When it comes to conceptualizing Paul's view of and expectations for Israel and its non-Christ-believing Israelites, has Paul's allegory of the olive tree obscured the interpretive tradition's view of the forest?

2. EXEGETICAL REFLECTIONS ON ROMANS 11:11–24

It is important to focus our attention on what Paul wants the members from the nations he addresses here in Romans to understand, and how he wants them to think and behave as a result. We will start our investigation with vv. 11–15, where an initial allegory of stumbling is introduced, and then move on to the tree allegory of vv. 16–24, discussing the language that follows in the rest of the chapter along the way. There are many interpretive decisions to be made among the available options, and the choices one makes have a profound impact upon one's understanding of the discourse and the consequences that follow from it, including—if not especially—Christian discourse about and relations with Jews and Judaism, indeed, with empirical Israel and Israelites today.

2.1 The Stumbling Allegory of Romans 11:11–16

2.1.1 Romans 11:11

Paul begins this section by introducing the first of three allegories, in which some have "stumbled" or "tripped": "they have not stumbled [ἔπταισαν] in order that they would fall [πέσωσιν], have they?" It seems that the tripping takes place while pursuing some course, either by walking or running. However, to the degree that Paul draws this imagery from Isaiah (which seems likely based on the sources he cites elsewhere in Rom 9–11), the allegory does not depict a competitive athletic event.

[342] The stumbling allegory follows vv. 9–10, where the language of tripping (σκάνδαλον) is used in a quotation of Ps 69:22–23, which Paul immediately prefaces with a citation of Isa 29:10 (v. 8; cf. Deut 29:4[3]). The imagery further recalls language introduced earlier in chapters 9–10.[6] In 9:30–33, Paul draws from Isa 28:16, which states that God will build in Zion upon a precious cornerstone a stone tower in which Israel is to take refuge. By doing so they demonstrate their trust in the Lord's provision to avoid the flooding that will engulf those who *stumble* in judgment (i.e., Judahites who seek to go to war in league with the Israelites, who are resisting the Assyrians), those who march but *fall* (πέσωσιν) backward, failing to listen to the word of the Lord (28:7, 12–13, 17). Paul couples this with a citation of Isa 8:14–15, a passage in which the Assyrians represent the flood waters (vv. 6–8), and the stone upon which the building for protection is founded becomes a stone over which some instead *stumble*. The issue appears to be whether the people of Judah will trust and thus take refuge in the promise of God to protect them from the threat of the Assyrians when the evidence of that protection presently consists only of the foundation stone, or whether they will instead consider that stone merely an obstacle in the way of their march to take matters into their own hands. When Paul takes up the imagery in Rom 9–11 (or in chapters 14–15), he does not explicitly identify the stone over which some trip; in the context, the stone could represent either trust in Jesus as the Messiah, or even more specifically, trust in Jesus as the Savior of the nations, whom Israel has the responsibility and privilege to proclaim as such.[7] This second dimension presumes trust in Christ as the one in whom to take refuge, but emphasizes, just as does Isa 40–66, the mission of proclamation by the heralds from

---

6. Paul appears to be reflecting on Isa 27–29, which is full of agricultural imagery, throughout Rom 9–11. In addition to the texts from Isa 28 mentioned below, he cites Isa 29:16 in Rom 9:20 concerning the clay having no right to question the potter. He draws on Isa 28:22 in Rom 9:28. In Rom 10:11 he again uses Isa 28:16, following right upon the heels of its appearance in Rom 9:33. Just before the start of the stumbling and tree allegories, Isa 29:10 is one of several verses cited to explain that God has caused some of Israel to be unable to see or hear (Rom 11:8). Paul uses Isa 27:9 coupled with Isa 59:20–21 (from another chapter full of agricultural metaphors) as proof for his argument that all Israel will be restored in 11:26–27.

7. Cf. Gaston, *Paul and the Torah*, 142–48.

Israel to the nations, a topic that Paul introduces in Rom 9[8] and discusses throughout Rom 10 and 11:1–10, right up to the stumbling allegory of vv. 11–15.[9] Indeed, [343] the question of whether these Israelites have "fallen" may well be traced as far back as the assertion in 9:6 that "it is not as though the word of God has *fallen* [ἐκπέπτωκεν]," a connection easily missed when πέπτωκεν is translated "failed," as it commonly is.[10] Paul's assertion that the word of God has not fallen follows Paul's expression of deep concern for the fate of his fellow Israelites and his cataloging of the privileges of these Israelites—including the fact that they are entrusted with God's "words/oracles," a motif already at work from 3:1–2. These privileges remain theirs regardless of their present standing concerning the proclamation of the Christ, who is also an Israelite.[11]

---

8. In 9:17, even Pharaoh's hardening is noted not to observe Pharaoh's fate or to discuss salvation but to highlight his role in God's plan to deliver Israel in such a way that God's name will be proclaimed to the nations.

9. The "works" at issue suddenly in 11:6 do not seem to refer to works-righteousness or to ethnic privilege but rather to the work of proclamation, Israel's special calling to the nations. The point is that God's choice of which Israelites are the faithful remnant now versus the unfaithful stumbling ones is not based upon whether these Israelites were more or less faithful previously, but on a prior choice of God ("favor"), so that it is not punishment, but fulfilling a plan of God's design that sets the remnant apart from the rest who are stumbling presently.

10. Most translations have *failed*, but the concept of *falling* is signified in this cognate of πίπτω.

11. Paul's next clause, in 9:6, has been the subject of much discussion, and it is especially important to replacement theology. The traditional translation is, "For not all Israelites truly belong to Israel [οὐ γάρ πάντες οἱ ἐξ Ἰσραὴλ]" (NRSV), but it seems that Paul should be asserting instead that even though some of his Israelite brothers and sisters are stumbling, to them belongs the title Israel and all the gifts that go with that calling—and irrevocably so, because of the promises made to their fathers—as he eventually affirms in 11:25 and 11:28–29. In other words, one would have expected him to argue here just what he does argue in 11:11, that some Israelites, even most, might be stumbling presently, but they have most certainly *not* fallen. It is possible to understand Paul in 11:11 as returning to his statement in 9:6 in order finally to undermine it, as if, for example, it represented the view of a dialogue partner rather than Paul's own. Alternatively, it is possible to punctuate 9:6 differently, as an assertion couched as a question: "But are not all these Israel, who are from Israel?" (cf. Klaus Wengst's translation, "Are not all out of Israel, 'Israel'?"). Such a question would follow naturally from the assertion in 9:2–5 of the continued gifts and calling of God to these Israelites regardless of their present problematic state. The answer would be, "Yes, they are; although they do not all properly represent Israel presently, in the end they will." Just as all of Abraham's seed are his children, yet there are distinctions among them (v. 7), so too all descendants of Israel are Israelites, but there are distinctions among them. The purpose of this line of argument would be to assure the non-Israelites addressed in Rome that they are not to develop their understanding of their identity as equal co-participants from the non-Christ-believing Israelites, whom Paul regards to be presently in error, but from those

[344] The imagery of stumbling appears again, following the allegories in Rom 11:11-16, in the argument of 11:25-27, where Isa 59:20-21[12] and 27:9[13] are cited, as well as in Rom 14:1—15:13, where Paul instructs the "strong"/"able" about the respect they should show to the "weak"/"stumbling."[14] Although the imagery is different and revolves around a vineyard rather than an olive tree, Isa 27:7 similarly asks whether the punishment of Israelites signals their destruction: "Has he struck them down as he struck down those who struck them? Or have they been killed as their killers were killed?" (NRSV). The answer given in Isa 27:9 ("Therefore by this the guilt of Jacob will be expiated, and this will be the full fruit of the removal of his sin"; NRSV) is cited by Paul in Rom 11:26-27 to prove that Israel's stumbling will not result in its fall; rather, all Israel will be restored once the time of the discipline of some Israelites—those who failed to take refuge from the coming storm (i.e., the attack of the nations)—is complete. Thus, although Paul develops the allegories from Isa 27 in different ways, he appears to get his inspiration for the stumbling motif from there. He draws inspiration as well from Isaiah's transition to a plant allegory in the argument that follows (an argument which is not confined to Isa 27, or even chapter 59, a text that Paul conflates with 27:9 in Rom 11:26-27).[15]

---

who, like Paul, are included in the Jewish communal subgroup of Christ-followers. See further Nanos, *The Mystery of Romans*, and Nanos, "The Jewish Context of the Gentile Audience Addressed in Paul's Letter to the Romans." (A detailed investigation with new conclusions about this argument is presented in chapter 10 of this volume.)

12. Note that Isa 59:8-10 depicts a person walking as if there is not sufficient light to guide one's steps, such as when the blind touch a wall in order to find their way. The context refers to the paths of righteousness on which the Lord will guide those who return from exile across the desert to Jerusalem, a theme that recurs throughout Isaiah (cf. 27:12-13; chs. 40-55, *passim*).

13. The announcement in Isa 27 appears to be for those from Israel who have been exiled by the Assyrians (vv. 12-13) and not simply for the members of the other nations per se. It is worth pondering whether Paul is similarly concerned in Rom 9-11 with the regathering of the dispersed of Israel among the nations (cf. 9:25-26, citing Hos 2:23; 1:10 LXX) and not simply with members from the other nations, with whom he also is concerned. From Paul's perspective, some of his fellow Israelites are tripping over this task. The idea that Paul is reaching out to his fellow Israelites first in each location as part of his strategy before turning to the gentiles is explored in the concept of Paul's "two-step" pattern in Nanos, *Mystery of Romans*, 239-88.

14. On the imagery of stumbling in Rom 14-15, see Nanos, *Mystery of Romans*, 119-65, which argues that in chs. 14-15 Paul addresses the same topic as in chs. 9-11, namely, the present "ability" to believe in the proclamation of Jesus Christ or the lack of such ability, which is portrayed as stumbling or growing weak in faith, but not as unfaith.

15. Note that it is the "fruit" of their sins that is at issue in 27:9, so that the imagery from trees/plants is invoked metaphorically. The fate that humans are described as

[345] In Rom 11:11, members of the other nations are declared to receive salvation as a result of some Israelites missing a step, tripping, or stumbling.[16] The outcome for these Israelites and that for the members of the other nations are inextricably linked. The Israelites who have missed a step have stumbled, but that they have fallen is unmistakably denied: *"May it never be!"* It is important to keep in focus that *Israel* is not presented as having stumbled. Rather, *some* Israelites have missed a step; other Israelites are still running or walking (i.e., successfully trusting God on the matter at hand). Central to this argument and to the following allegory and arguments is the existence of the remnant of Israel, a point that Paul has already established (cf. 11:1–2, 5, 7).

The misstep of some is said to be for the *gain* of the nations, resulting in their restoration (σωτηρία): "but their misstep is for the salvation of the nations." Paul asserts that these outcomes are related, but he does not explain why a negative development for one party is related to a positive development for the other. He likely draws on the idea of Israel as the servant who will bring restoration to all of humanity, even when some of her own children are being disciplined.

It is unclear to whom the pronoun in the next clause, "... to make *them* jealous," refers. In the majority of translations and commentaries, it is understood to refer to those missing a step; it signifies that the stumbling Israelites are being provoked in the sense of being made envious and, moreover, that they will conclude that these non-Israelites have something that they do not have. Thus, paradoxically, these Israelites (often termed "Israel," as if Paul has not just written that it is only *some* of Israel who are stumbling) benefit by being made jealous when salvation comes thereby to the nations.[17] However, since Paul writes of provoking these Israelites to jealousy/emulation (παραζηλῶσαι), the emphasis should be on these Israelites being provoked to reestablish their right relationship with God's purpose (as envisaged by Paul). His reference to their "jealousy" does not portray them seeking to deny entrance to non-Israelites, a motive that would be described instead as

---

suffering—being judged and disciplined, but not destroyed—aligns with the imagery of the tree as suffering damage and yet not being destroyed, a theme found throughout Isaiah (cf. Nielsen, *There is Hope for a Tree*, 71, *passim*; cf. Job 14:7).

16. Παραπτώματι is often translated "transgression" (NASB), but this obscures the metaphorical language of motion at play here and the idea the word carries in general of misstep (cf. *LSJ*, 1322), while the translation "fall" (KJV, ASV) completely undermines the point being made: the denial of just that outcome. See, Haacker, "Das Thema von Römer 9–11 als Problem der Auslegungsgeschichte."

17. No benefit to those Israelites not missing a step is noted.

envy or begrudging, φθόνος.¹⁸ The picture would thus be of some Israelites [346] stumbling and, while out of balance, watching others suddenly attaining righteousness (9:30), which makes these Israelites jealous.

In the traditional view, these Israelites are supposed to be jealous of the gentile Christ-believers. That would echo Rom 10:19, which draws from Deut 32:21, the song of Moses, wherein Israel is told that it is to be made jealous (παραζηλώσω) by those who are not a nation in retaliation for having made God jealous by way of idolatry. As stated in Deut 32, this provocation to jealousy has a negative valence. Yet it is not synonymous with begrudging, but rather with being provoked to get back on course, that is, to return to honoring Israel's God alone. However, it is not clear that it is jealousy of the *gentiles* to which Paul points. It may be that the stumbling Israelites will be provoked to jealousy by the other Israelites' success among the nations. If the Israelites in question see Paul and the remnant succeeding with the proclamation to the nations apart from themselves, it will make them want to emulate the remnant's behavior (see the discussion of v. 13 below). It will challenge them positively to want to regain their footing to complete the pursuit of God's righteousness, to which the Torah points, but now with the recognition that this is attained by way of faithfulness to the proclamation of Christ.

Not only is it not clear of whom the stumbling Israelites are to be jealous; it is also not clear that it is the stumbling Israelites themselves who will be provoked to jealousy in 11:11, as the traditional understanding of the verse would have it (although that is the topic of v. 13, discussed below).¹⁹ In v. 11, it would make sense to understand those being provoked to jealousy of Israel to be the non-Israelites, since it is they who are witnessing not only the stumbling of some Israelites but also God's continued extension of grace to these Israelites (cf. *T. Zeb.* 9.8).²⁰ When members of the nations see some Israelites stumbling, then some of these non-Israelites will recognize their chance to join those who are standing strong. Even though they had not previously been pursuing God's righteousness and justice for humankind, as the Israelites had been, they now have a chance to join in this pursuit, because they are now provoked to emulate those of Israel who are not stumbling (i.e., the remnant that has announced this good news to

---

18. Cf. Nanos, "'O Foolish Galatians, Who has Cast the Evil Eye [of Envy] Upon You?' (Gal 3:1a-b); cf. Stowers, *A Re-reading of Romans*, 305.

19. NRSV translates the last clause: "so as to make *Israel* jealous," but the Greek text only has the pronoun "αὐτούς," rightly translated "them" in KJV and NASB.

20. Although Paul mixes masculine αὐτούς and neuter ἔθνεσιν in ἡ σωτηρία τοις ἔθνεσιν εἰς τὸ παραζηλῶσαι αὐτούς, he similarly mixes these two genders when referring to gentiles in 2:14–15 (I am grateful to Andy Johnson for pointing out this parallel).

them). This interpretation of v. 11 offers some explanation for why Israel's stumbling is for the gain of the nations; [347] otherwise, the logic behind Paul's statement that the stumbling of some Israelites occurred in order for the non-Israelites to become co-participants is not provided.

Note that Paul's questions and answers are in the style of diatribe: he engages an imaginary interlocutor. The question that arises in v. 11 is a reaction to the argument preceding it (11:7–10), which cites several texts (Deut 29:4[3]; Isa 29:10, and Ps 68:23–24 LXX) to proclaim what appears to be a continuous state of insensitivity and alienation among these stumbling Israelites.[21] The answer unambiguously declares that this does *not* represent falling, as in being cut off, but rather a temporary state, tripping, from which one can recover one's footing. This rhetorical device can make it uncertain at points whether Paul is expressing his own viewpoint or one that he seeks to challenge. But it also suggests that a certain logical progression should be traceable in the argument.

2.1.2 Romans 11:12

The Christ-believing of the nations will receive all the more riches when the fullness (success) arrives for those (some) Israelites who are presently missing a step. The word ἥττημα carries more the sense of lack of comparative success (being less, weaker, inferior) and dishonor, rather than outright failure,[22] so it keeps the temporary state of those stumbling in view rather than alluding to them as having fallen. Paul asserts that the temporary stumbling of some will benefit the nations all the more when "their fullness" arrives, which signals their success, relative strength, or restored

---

21. Note that in Deut 29:4[3], the day is a sign of a changed fortune: the lack of heart and of seeing/hearing aright during the former events (capacities that God had not given to them) has now come to an end on "this day"; from now on they will perceive fully, if they but obey all the words of the covenant. Psalm 68 (LXX) is a plea for judgment against those persecuting the psalmist in his present suffering state, a state that is the result of God's wounding the psalmist (v. 27). In the passage cited, the psalmist explains that his enemies will be attracted to him like food on a table that is in reality bait in a trap (animal traps resembled tables that sprang up around the prey). Contrary to their expectation, therefore, they will be victims instead of victors when God comes to rescue the psalmist and to punish those whom God used temporarily to discipline him, but who themselves intended him harm. The psalm does not state that the enemies are Israelites. In fact, it may introduce here a criticism of non-Jews who would judge the Israelites who, according to Paul, are temporarily suffering by God's design—a topic that arises explicitly in Rom 11:18–24, where Paul confronts any incipient arrogance toward the branches of the olive tree that are presently suffering God's discipline.

22. Cf. Cranfield, *Epistle to the Romans*, 2:557, although he arrives at a different conclusion.

honor rating. Otherwise, one might logically conclude that their continued misfortune would be in the best interests of the nations, which is [348] at the heart of the presumption he will challenge in the tree allegory that follows. But Paul asserts that everyone—the whole *kosmos*—will benefit when this temporary state of suffering is over.

2.1.3 Romans 11:13-15

That Paul is specifically addressing Christ-believing non-Israelites in this argument, which is otherwise clear throughout this section in many turns of phrase and pronoun choices, is made explicit in v. 13: "Now I am speaking to you members of the nations." They are the encoded audience, regardless of whether there may be Israelites also among the audience (which seems highly likely, although how many and in what proportion remains anyone's guess).

It is imperative to Paul that these non-Israelites realize that Paul magnifies his service to the nations. He does this specifically "to provoke" the some missing a step "to jealousy," that is, to "emulation." As discussed above, this is different from "envy" or "begrudging." Furthermore, it is not about some Israelites being provoked by seeing the nations brought in, as if that signaled they themselves were being replaced. Indeed, it is precisely this kind of thinking that Paul will immediately challenge. Rather, it is about Paul's own ministry, to which the stumbling will be provoked to compare themselves.[23] Paul expects his fellow Israelites to recognize that their own privilege of declaring God's righteousness to the nations is being embodied successfully in Paul's ministry, not in their own. They will thus be stimulated to rethink Paul's message and then join him in declaring it to the nations. The theme of proclaiming the good news continues to be front and center in Paul's explanation of the present state of some of his fellow Israelites, those who have not yet been chosen to carry out this task, and in his description of the eventual state to which he seeks to restore them by leading them to recognize that their own aspirations are expressed in his success among the nations.

Although Paul's ministry may not appear to be directed to Israelites, he informs his non-Israelite audience that his service to the nations is not ultimately just for the benefit of the nations (i.e., themselves) but also for the benefit of the Israelites who have been stumbling. The nations are important, and Paul is their servant; yet their success is not his only aim but a part of a larger program aimed at bringing about the success of those who are stumbling.

---

23. Cf. Nanos, *Mystery of Romans*, 247–51; Nanos, "Jewish Context of the Gentile Audience," 300–304.

Based on the advantage that the members of the nations have received by way of the temporary stumbling of some Israelites, it may not be readily apparent or even logical that it is actually in [349] the best interests of the nations to seek the welfare of these Israelites rather than to wish for or perpetuate their disadvantaged condition. Paul argues that this will be all the better for the nations (i.e., for themselves)—as much better as "life from the dead" is compared to "reconciliation." Paul argues not from a negative outcome to a positive one, but from a positive outcome to an even better one.

Paul's approach here could be—and probably was—calculated to be insulting, for it implies, if it does not state outright, that the nations are being used in Paul's effort to achieve goals that are (at least significantly) beyond themselves and intended for the benefit of Paul's fellow Israelites, to whom they are tempted to see themselves as superior (see below). This concept and language echoes Isaiah's descriptions of God's using the nations to chastise Israel. However, their role must nevertheless not be mistaken for replacing Israel or even ultimately for attaining their own blessing. They are tools in God's hand to chastise Israel, but the remnant of Israel who have been scattered and exiled among the nations will one day be gathered and restored, and the nations (e.g., Assyria, Babylon) will be punished for their own mistaken presumptuousness toward God and Israel (e.g., Isa 10–11). Significantly, the arrogance of the nations is often defined similarly as "high" or "lofty" ideas about themselves [ὑψηλός; ὕβρις] and delivered in tree metaphors (e.g., 10:12, 33; counterpoint in 11:1, 10; cf. 2:12–13). The parallels are not precise, for these Christ-believers are now members of the people of God, but the allusion is apposite and the warning serious: in the allegory that follows, the Christ-believers from the nations face the threat of being "cut off" if they do not arrest their arrogance toward the Israelites suffering divine discipline.

In sharp contrast to the "New Perspective" proposition that Paul is against maintaining ethnic identity as meaningful,[24] Paul's continued ethnic identity is *played up* rather than devalued. Paul's identity as a Christ-believing *Israelite* separates him into a "we" group with these Israelites, in which the audience, members from the nations other than Israel, does not share. Paul pulls no punches on his ethnic identification with Israelites (cf. Rom 9:2–5; 11:1–2) and thus on his concomitant dissociation from those from other nations. He seeks to create a new sense of "we-ness" that encompasses non-Christ-believing Israelites within the "we" who stand in need of and can expect to receive the mercy that comes from being part

---

24. As exemplified repeatedly in comments on this section by Dunn, *Romans 9–16*, e.g., 684–85 and 693–96; Wright, "The Letter to the Romans," e.g., 681–82, 692.

of the family of the God of patient mildness as well as abrupt severity, [350] a shared identification that is larger than either Christ/not-Christ or the nations/Israel boundary lines. This implies that Paul regards these non-Christ-believing Israelites to be "brethren" in a significant way that even Christ-believing members from the other nations are not, including in terms of their ultimate shared fate.

A central element of this theme is that some Israelites are, according to Paul, more concerned with demonstrating the righteousness of Israel to the nations than they are with God using righteous Israel to gather in the nations as co-participants in the people of God, apart from becoming members of Israel (cf. chs. 9–10). Paul concludes this because, from his vantage point, all who are being faithful recognize that the goal of the righteousness upheld by Torah is Christ—and thus faith in Christ and making Christ known to all the nations.[25] Consequently, God will cause some Israelites to stumble over the proclamation of the meaning of Christ for the nations. Those non-Israelites who do respond to the message of Christ announced by some Israelites such as Paul will be the source of provoking the stumbling Israelites to jealousy of Paul's ministry, that is, to emulation of Paul's success at bringing these members of the nations to be zealous to uphold above all else the justice (righteousness) of God's plan for the reconciliation of the world.

The theme of the proclamation of the message of good, which is Israel's special privilege and responsibility, remains central. In Paul's argument, the remnant of Israel is faithfully carrying out this charge while the rest are stumbling over its execution because the proclamation of Christ to the nations is being undertaken apart from insisting that the members of the nations join Israel, the righteous nation. But the ultimate goal of this proclamation embraces the welfare of all Israel, as well as the welfare of the faithful from the nations.

---

25. In 10:4, Paul writes, "For Christ is the goal of Torah for righteousness/justice *for everyone who is being faithful* [παντί τω πιστεύοντι]." This statement arises in the context of explaining that some Israelites are not being obedient to the righteousness of God because they are seeking to establish their *own* righteousness or justice (i.e., for Israel, versus seeing themselves as chosen on behalf of the righteousness/justice of God for all humankind) (10:3). Thus, according to Paul, some Israelites are being jealous for God in the wrong way (10:2), in ignorance that the righteousness/justice of God is pointing to the inclusion in Christ of members from the other nations alongside Israelites without discrimination of status according to whether one is Israelite or non-Israelite. This equal access to the blessing of being declared among the righteous ones must now be recognized to be a present reality (10:8–12). It must not be overlooked that Paul's stated goal is to provoke such fellow Israelites to get back on track, that is, to be restored (10:1) to their rightful role as heralds to the nations (10:14—11:15).

2.1.4 Romans 11:16

[351] It is easy to overlook that between the stumbling allegory and the tree allegory, Paul briefly introduces yet another allegory that he does not develop. "If the first part (ἀπαρχή) is holy, also the lump of dough (φύραμα) [is holy]." In other words, if the initial portion of flour or starter dough was properly dedicated, then the lump of dough made from the rest of the flour is also dedicated. If Paul is drawing on Num 15:17–21, where a cake from the first of the dough is offered, the implication is that the rest can be served to others who are profane. Note that in Lev 23:14 offering the first of the dough makes holy the rest of the dough made from it. Yet Paul uses this metaphor differently, extending the holiness from the portion offered first to the entire entity.[26]

Whatever the precise imagery, the allegory suggests that Paul is communicating that the whole is identified with the parts. It is therefore likely that he is appealing to the role of the remnant of Christ-believing Israelites on behalf of those Israelites who are presently unfaithful to the task of announcing the gospel: just like the former, the latter are sanctified. Paul continues the thought of the previous verses, that the remnant of Israelites, among whom he counts himself, recognize that they are chosen at the expense of their brethren, and they are in anguish about the present suffering state of the rest. His ministry is on their behalf, and if successful among the nations, it will result in their restoration.

Paul is set apart for the good of the whole, for its protection, not its condemnation, a point he is about to emphasize with his non-Israelite target audience. Things are not as they appear; instead, even those presently missing a step have been set apart to God's purpose. One might be reminded here of Paul's earlier point, that even Pharaoh was set apart to be used by God specifically in order to further the proclamation of God's name (Rom 9:17, citing Exod 9:16); all the more so are all Israelites set apart to God's special purpose for Israel as promised to the fathers—as Paul will go on to argue emphatically in the rest of the chapter.

In this transitional verse, Paul also introduces the third allegory, which is of a vine or tree: "if the root is holy, even so are the branches (or shoots)" (Rom 11:16b). One important point for theological reflection is how one defines the root. Usually understood to be Israel, some early commentators point to Christ as the root, others to the remnant,[27] and [352] others to

---

26. Aune, "Distinct Lexical Meanings of ΑΠΑΡΧΗ in Hellenistic Judaism and Early Christianity," 121–22.

27. This was the position I took in *Mystery of Romans*, but I am reconsidering it in light of my present research.

the patriarchs.[28] Paul does not say. Perhaps an exact identification is not relevant to a proper interpretation of this allegory?

2.2 The Olive Tree Allegory of 11:17–24

Just as Paul's stumbling allegory probably draws upon imagery in Isaiah, so too Paul's olive tree allegory is likely derived from his extensive use of Isaiah throughout this section and the letter.[29] Isaiah 27:2–6 likely reflects the postexilic conflicts between Jews and Samaritans. It contains not only a promise of hope, but also a warning of judgment to those who grow up among his vines like thorns and briers, that is, a warning to the Samaritans, if they behave like enemies of God's purposes for his own Judahite children[30]—which is similar to the warning Paul seeks to deliver to the non-Israelites among his Jewish kinsmen in Rome! Note also in the introduction of Isa 27 (MT) that branches are presently being destroyed (27:10–11) and dried out branches gathered.[31] Although in Rom 11:27 Paul does not cite all of Isa 27:9, he does employ cognates of ἐκκόπτω. In other words, the "cutting down" imagery is explicit. In 27:6, Isaiah introduces the imagery of the Lord's plant filling the world with its shoots and fruit, although in the context the prophet more likely refers to a grape vine than to an olive tree.[32]

The imagery of trees and plants is of course not confined to Isaiah, but found throughout the Tanak, and it is a central theme developed in Second Temple Jewish literature, including the Dead Sea Scrolls.[33] Paul draws [353] from Hosea (1:10; 2:23 LXX) for several citations in Rom 9:25–27, and Hos 14:2–10 LXX refers to Israel as a fruitful olive tree (ἐλαία), refers to her "branches" (κλάδοι) spreading, and also speaks of her "being weak"

---

28. Fitzmyer, *Romans*, 614; Cranfield, *Romans*, 2:564–65; Bourke, *A Study of the Metaphor of the Olive Tree in Romans XI*, 65–111.

29. For fuller discussions of the intertextual elements, see Wilk, *Die Bedeutung des Jesajabuches für Paulus*; Wagner, *Heralds of the Good News*.

30. Cf. Nielsen, *There is Hope for a Tree*, 120–22.

31. There are significant differences between the MT and LXX descriptions here, with the MT developing the idea of the branches being stripped by cattle and gathered to burn by women, while the LXX refers to the cattle resting in the pastures after the trees used in idolatry have been cut down (v. 9).

32. Cf. Nielsen, *There is Hope for a Tree*, 119.

33. Swarup, *The Self-Understanding of the Dead Sea Scrolls Community*, traces many of these developments and demonstrates how the DSS community sees itself as the "eternal planting." This contains the idea of being the righteous remnant, one that lives on behalf of bringing righteousness to the nations. The imagery of plants is linked with the concept of Eden, the prototype of God's sanctuary, and with new creation.

or "stumbling" in terms that Paul uses in Rom 14:1—15:7 (ἀσθενέω). In Jer 11:16, Israel is called a beautiful, fruitful olive tree, but one whose branches will be damaged (ἠχρεώθησαν) for the evil it has done.[34] Job 14:7-9 is also suggestive, wherein the theme of hope for a tree arises: even after it has been cut down and dried out, when water is introduced it can sprout again. This theme of the vitality of the tree is evident throughout Isaiah.[35] In Isa 11:1, 10, which Paul cites in Rom 15:12, the shoot of Jesse sprouts from the stump; Isa 27:6 (Paul cites v. 9 in Rom 11:27) refers to a time when "Jacob shall take root, Israel shall blossom and put forth shoots and fill the whole world with fruit" (NRSV); and Isa 6:13 discloses that the "holy seed" will sprout from the stump of the tree after it is felled. Moreover, the gathering of olives from high limbs involves striking the tree, which makes it a suitable image for judgment, whether of Israel, some Israelites, or the nations (Isa 17:6; 24:13).

2.2.1 Romans 11:17

After relating that "some of the branches have been broken," Paul identifies the target audience as "you, being a wild olive which has been grafted in among them." Note the shift to singular, and the direct address to this wild olive (ἀγριέλαιος): "you [σύ]."[36] The rest of the allegory will develop around this feature of the diatribe.

The singularity of the you/wild olive is surprising in several ways, not least that it does not support—and likely intentionally undermines—the idea that there are many non-Israelites in this situation or that they are in the dominant position in Paul's communities.[37] He stereotypes them as one olive, denying to them as a group any variety. In social identity terms, Paul [354] arguably expresses the stereotyping perspective of an insider toward the outsider, one who lumps together the out-group (non-Israelites) but

---

34. Cf. *b. Men.* 53b, which offers a paraphrase of Jer 11:15-16, "Israel is like an olive tree: its product comes after pressure and crushing; even so will Israel's salvation come after its suffering" (Ginzberg, ed., *The Legends of the Jews*, 6:397-98).

35. Nielsen, *There is Hope for a Tree*, 76.

36. Cf. Tobin, *Paul's Rhetoric in Its Contexts*, 685.

37. This element arguably supports my thesis in *Mystery of Romans* that the Christ-believing gentiles are meeting in Jewish communities and thus represent a small audience being addressed directly in the midst of an Israelite synagogue subgroup of the larger Israelite community. In any case, it does not play into the usual later Christian perspective that there are many Christian gentiles (here, but a branch) and few to no representatives of Israel in the "church" (branches) after the supposed edict of Claudius.

recognizes among his own in-group (Israelites) rich diversity.[38] That is a long way from the eventual use of Paul's writings to stereotype Jews and Judaism in monolithic, negative terms.

Although normally translated "broken off," it is actually not clear that by using ἐξεκλάσθησαν to describe the state of some Israelites Paul has in view that they "have been broken *off*" or "pruned." The relatively rare verb ἐκκλάω can, and often does, signify breaking off. Yet in some cases ἐκκλάω indicates just broken, as in *dislocated*. Liddell and Scott's lexicon includes for ἐκκλάω in the passive "to grow weak" or "to be enfeebled," which could certainly be applied to the branches in question.[39] In Lev 1:17, a bird's wings for an offering are to be *"broken* [ἐκκλάσει]" but *"not* separated [οὐ διελεῖ]." Pausanias, *Graeciae descriptio* 8.40.2, describes a case when a fighter's toe was "broken" (ἐκκλᾷ), causing him to expire and lose the fight because "of the pain in his toe [ὑπὸ τοῦ δακτύλου τῆς ὀδύνης (LCL)]." It is not natural to read this as "broken off," since he is still feeling pain from the toe. Thus, ἐκκλάω is not always used synonymously with ἐκκόπτω ("to cut off"). Paul does not employ this latter word until the topic of severity and threat to the wild branch is raised in Rom 11:22 (ἐκκοπήσῃ); before that, in vv. 17, 19, and 20, Paul uses ἐκκλάω. Attention to these details brings up several matters to discuss.

When Paul turns in vv. 19–21 to challenging the wild olive's supposition that it has supplanted the broken branches in God's favor, he still describes the broken branches with ἐκκλάω. But in vv. 22–24, when he turns to threatening the wild olive directly that it will wind up broken off itself if it does not turn away from the presumptuousness it has expressed, the verb ἐκκόπτω is introduced. Here Paul begins to threaten his audience with the possible fate of being completely removed, "cut/chopped off," using a word that frequently communicates violent acts of smiting with weapons or striking a blow.

Unlike καλάω, cognates of κόπτω do arise in Theophrastus to describe the breaking or cutting off of branches, although it is not the term he employs for the technique of pruning related to grafting. Theophrastus (ca. 370–285 BCE) wrote two books describing plants, with many details about trees, grafting, and various injuries (like pruning). In *De causis plantarum* 1.20.3, the olive tree is described as a weak and delicate tree [355] that suffers from "cudgeling" and "breaking off" (κατακοπτομένη) of its "branches" (θαλλείας). In *Historia plantarum* 4.16.1, he observes that the

---

38. Hogg and Abrams, *Social Identifications*. See also the argument of Wagner, "'Not from the Jews Only, But Also from the Gentiles.'"

39. *LSJ*, 509.

olive tree becomes all the fairer after being cut all around (περικοπέντα). He differentiates between an almond tree that is cut back (ἐπικόπτωντα) and one that is pruned (διακαθαίρωνται) *(Caus. plant.* 2.15.3). *Historia plantarum* 4.16.1 refers to cutting off the crown of the tree as ἐπικοπη, which is also used in *Caus. plant.* 5.17.3 to describe "topping," a process that is said to kill many trees.[40]

However, when Theophrastus wants to describe proper pruning, especially when related to grafting, he usually uses διακάθαρσις and cognates (*Caus. plant.* 3.7.5–12; *Hist. plant.* 2.7.12). Olive trees are noted for requiring lots of pruning of dead wood and for being rapid sprouters. Proper husbandry provides for a healthy tree (*Caus. plant.* 16.1.2). Theophrastus notes that the smaller an olive tree is kept, the better the fruit it will bear (*Hist. plant.* 2.7.1).

I admit that it is possible that Paul's audience would have heard ἐκκλάω in the sense of "broken off" (the interpretive tradition certainly has). But the possibility should remain open that Paul was exploring a nuance in the construction of his allegory wherein the natural branches were damaged—akin to "stumbling" (Rom 11:11)—but not cut off—which would equate instead to "falling"—even if his readers have regularly missed this subtle point. That would be more consistent both with the running allegory's "stumbling" but not "falling" in v. 11 and with the language in vv. 25–32 concerning the process by which all Israel will be restored (discussed below).

Maybe Paul did not recognize this implication of his logic when it is reversed, since his focus is on making an *a fortiori* case that harm will happen all the more to the non-Israelites, if they should take a presumptuous posture, because their position is already more tenuous than that of the Israelites against whom they would be tempted to suppose such things. If nothing else, this nuance might help interpreters keep in view that it is the possible presumptuousness of the non-Israelites that Paul seeks to obviate in no uncertain terms, while presumptuousness is not identified here as the problem of the presently unfaithful Israelites or the reason why they are in this predicament. Presumption toward Israelites who are not Christ-believers is a special problem that Paul fears is present among the members of the nations in Christ in Rome.

Paul specifically calls the grafted-in olive, which signifies the non-Israelites, to be a wild olive (ἀγριέλαιος), whereas the natural branches, and thus even the ones broken or broken off, have grown on a cultivated [356]

---

40. "Cutting back" is also called κόλοθσις; see *Caus. plant.* 5.17.6 for ἐπιβόσκησις, "cropping," as in being eaten down by animals.

olive tree.⁴¹ It is quite unusual—if not unheard of—for wild olive branches or shoots or buds to be grafted into a cultivated olive tree. According to Theophrastus, *Caus. plant.* 1.6.10, a cultivated branch or shoot is grafted into a wild olive tree because the scion is better fed from the strong stock. The grafts hold better to the stronger tree, and this tree attracts more food, making it a finer producer. Its roots have adjusted to the climate and soil without assistance. If, conversely, wild scions are grafted on cultivated stock, the wild crop will improve, but "no fine fruit" will result.⁴² Such remains the case to this day. Theophrastus also explains that it is best to transplant the wild olive trees into the orchard first and then later plant the cultivated trees, from which the buds or twigs will be used for grafting. According to modern genetic research, the cultivated olive (*olea europaea*) and the wild olive (*olea oleaster*) of the Mediterranean basin have the same chromosome number and are interfertile; however, the wild differ in that they have smaller fruit, a thinner mesocarp, poorer oil content, and a long juvenile stage accompanied by the appearance of spinescent shoots.⁴³ In terms of productivity, one does not graft wild olive cuttings onto cultivated trees because the wild branches do not produce good fruit.

This oleicultural fact raises several questions about Paul's knowledge of the material around which his allegory turns, as well as about his intention for its message. Was Paul (and his secretary, Tertius) unfamiliar with the agricultural details, or was he intentionally turning the normal practice upside down in this metaphor in order to make or emphasize a point, one [357] that would have been all the more intelligible to the degree that his audience could have been presumed to know what he was doing? Was it already a rhetorical trope with which he was familiar and could expect his

---

41. Columella—roughly a contemporary of Paul, but from Spain and writing in Latin—refers to the wild olive as *oleaster* (or the diminutive *oleastellum* for small wild olive), and the cultivated olive as *olea* (Lucius Junius Moderatus Columella, *De re rustica* [*Rust.*]; idem, *De arboribus* [*Arb.*]). See Zohary and Hopf, *Domestication of Plants in the Old World*, 145-51; cf. Esler, "Ancient Oleiculture and Ethnic Differentiation," 112-13. I am grateful for a discussion of olive cultivation and grafting with Kjell Lundquist, Swedish University of Agricultural Sciences.

42. Theophrastus, *Caus. plant.* 1.15.3-4, explains that wild trees fail to ripen because their fruit is too abundant, denser, drier, and apt to draw the energy to the tree instead, so the stronger group is not always the better for fruit production. In *Hist. plant.* 2.3.1-2 it is noted that a cultivated olive may turn into a wild one, but a change in the other direction is rare, and the variation is usually in the fruit rather than the tree. Zohary and Hopf, *Domestication of Plants in the Old World*, 148, explain that some wild olive tree suckers or knobs were valued as stock material to plant in the orchards in order to graft cultivated scions to them. They further note that still in western Turkey some wild olive trees are protected in their natural state in order to graft cultivated scions onto them.

43. Zohary, "The Wild Genetic Resources of the Cultivated Olive."

audience to recognize, but of which later interpreters of this allegory have been and remain unaware? If intentional, it was likely calculated in keeping with the purpose of the passage we have been discussing all along, as several exegetes have noted: Paul seeks to put his non-Israelite target audience in their place so as to dissuade them from presumptuousness.[44]

44. Davies, *Jewish and Pauline Studies*, 153–63, notes that Paul uses the idea of descent from a wild tree to put these gentiles in their place and to communicate that Jews have advantages over them. I am less certain about Davies' argument that Paul chooses the wild olive tree to signify the gentiles because it implies the inferiority of the Hellenistic culture to the Jewish tradition or in order to confront anti-Jewishness in Greco-Roman society. I appreciate the insight in Baxter and Ziesler, "Paul and Arboriculture," that the metaphor is developed to stress God's intention to save Israel, which Paul discusses. But I do not agree that the purpose of the grafting here is to revive the tree. Columella, *Rust.* 5.9.16 (and Palladius, *De insitione* 53–54), mentions a technique used in the case where a cultivated olive tree is failing to produce fruit. A hole is drilled in the tree, and a green slip from a wild tree is placed into it in order to make the cultivated tree more productive (noted also by Cranfield, *Romans*, 2:565–66, who cites a discussion of this by W. M. Ramsay). Esler observes that this is not called grafting by Columella; it is not about growing a wild branch from a cultivated tree, and it is not mentioned by Greek authors or by later Latin authors, so it remains an obscure technique of which Paul was not likely aware (although something like this is mentioned in Philo, *Agriculture* 6, in more general plant terms); moreover, Paul's point turns on the role of the root as that which sanctifies and feeds the branch, and not the other way around (Esler, "Ancient Oleiculture and Ethnic Differentiation," 119–21). Paul does not make any point about the tree failing to produce good fruit; such a notion misses the point that Paul and other Christ-believing Jews represent a healthy fruit-bearing tree and that the holy root makes the branches holy (but with some branches in need of repair). It also mistakes the overall purpose of Paul's allegory, which is to put the gentiles in their place if they should regard the non-Christ-believing Jews with disdain. As noted, Theophrastus (*Hist. plant.* 4.16.1) observes that the olive tree becomes all the fairer after being cut all around (περικοπέντα), but he does not mention the idea that grafting helps the tree itself. Esler (ibid., 103–24) claims that Paul deliberately reverses the normal procedure of grafting cultivated olive branches onto wild olive trees in order to emphasize that these non-Israelites were innately non-productive and required grafting onto Israel. He does this in order to bring them down a notch, which is in keeping with Paul's explicit challenge to their entertaining haughty thoughts toward Jews. I am especially grateful for his essay, which prompted me to think about the arboricultural and oleicultural aspects of this allegory more deeply and to read Theophrastus and Columella in particular in order to do so. Among other things, he made me aware of why Theophrastus, from centuries before Paul, should be privileged over Columella, roughly Paul's contemporary: namely, because the characteristics of Greek olive tree grafting were different than for the Latin West, where olive trees were generally raised in nurseries from planting cuttings or seedlings rather than from grafting (ibid., 116–18, drawing on Foxhall, "Olive Cultivation within Greek and Roman Agriculture," 335–36). I do not agree with Esler, however, that this represents the expression of submerged aspects of Paul's ethnicity and kinship, which I believe Paul consciously and intentionally maintained, including the importance of Torah observance. Instead, I see Paul's argument here as based on just that ethnicity and kinship, which remain central to who he is and to what he understands his Jewish mission and groups to be:

[358] Common knowledge turned upside down within a metaphor or allegory is especially suited to communicating the unexpected. In this case, reversing the direction of the grafting is likely intended to reflect just how unusual present developments between Israelites and non-Israelites are and, again, just how tenuous is the place of non-Israelites among the righteous ones of God—like a wild olive grafted into a cultivated olive tree—and how quickly everything could change should they fail to keep up their part of the bargain.

Although the NRSV reflects traditional replacement theology, "and you ... were grafted *in their place*," the NASB and the KJV are closer to the Greek: "you ... were grafted in *among* them [σύ δέ ... ἐν αὐτοις]." This raises the next questions: among "what"/"whom" is the wild olive grafted and "where"?

Note that the wild olive shoot is feminine as well as singular, but this wild shoot is described as placed among "them [αὐτοις]," which is masculine (or neuter) and plural. The nearest antecedent for this pronoun is the broken branches (masculine and plural). If they had been broken off, this would be nonsense, since the grafting is not among branches no longer attached to the root; but if the branches have merely been broken, as suggested above, then these branches would be the natural referent of αὐτοις. The wild shoot would then be placed among the broken branches. Otherwise, the next antecedent would be the masculine and plural branches which are [359] made holy (Rom 11:16), thus signifying all the branches. In other words, the wild shoot is placed among the remaining branches as well as among the broken ones, which remain on the tree in an impaired state, for all of the branches have been declared sanctified by the holy root.[45]

---

expressions of Judaism as it should be and of God's faithfulness to the promises to Israel. He wants his audience to share that viewpoint. The main point, in agreement with Esler, is that the wild branches grafted into the tree sit in it more precariously than do the branches that have naturally grown on the tree. That point is made to confront any tendency among the gentiles to suppose that they are superior to those Jews who have not accepted their Christ-faith-based claims. Along a similar line, see Johnson Hodge, "Olive Trees and Ethnicities"; Johnson Hodge, *If Sons, Then Heirs*, 140–47. She helpfully highlights the use of tree analogies in antiquity to describe kinship lineage and ethnicity, and in this case to establish the hierarchical discrepancy between the Israelite over the non-Israelite branches. This discrepancy emphasizes the precarious situation of the gentiles Paul addresses, even though they are all related to Abrahamic descent by birth (Jews) or by adoption in Christ (non-Jews).

45. When discussing this phrase, Dunn notes a nuance that is supportive of the concern I seek to raise here: Paul's statement "must obviously mean 'among (the remaining) branches.' ... Paul's ambiguity on the point arises out of the fact that he still regards even the broken-off branches as still properly part of, or at least belonging to, the tree" (*Romans 9–16*, 661). Cranfield does not really discuss the options. He only says

Where was the graft made among these branches? Was the wild olive cutting grafted into the space left where a branch had been broken off? That is what the translation "in their place" certainly communicates. There are other ways to graft that do not include pruning branches in order to attach the graft in their place. Note that the wild olive is never explicitly called a branch, but simply a wild olive (ἀγριέλαιος); it could be a shoot, branch, or bud. And a new slit can be made in the supporting branch or trunk or root into which the shoot or branch or bud is inserted—it need not be made into the space left by a pruned branch.[46] But if Paul meant that the wild olive was actually grafted into a place made by breaking off one or more branches, this would raise significant problems.

First, branches that are used to attach a grafted shoot are not broken or broken off; they are carefully cut—pruned—in a specific way that prepares for the new shoot to be attached, generally along a diagonal slit made in a branch so that the shoot to be grafted, also cut along the same angle, can be aligned along the cut line, and then bound to the supporting branch. Paul does not employ any of several terms that refer to the kind of techniques used for pruning a branch in order to receive a graft. To this day, discussions in handbooks describing grafting techniques emphasize the quality of the blade and the exactness of the cut to be made, the type of which is determined by the kind of graft that will be implemented. However, breaking, as well as breaking off, branches is a normal, inadvertent by-product of harvesting olives, because the branches are shaken or raked or beaten to release the fruit, as well as picked (cf. Deut 24:20; Isa 17:6; 24:13). It is natural for some branches, especially twigs, to be broken or broken off as the picker moves within the tree. If one of these branches was then deemed to be appropriate for receiving a grafted shoot, it would require preparation with a specific cut; grafts are not made into merely broken branches.

[360] Second, it does not require cutting several branches to accommodate only one grafted-in shoot. Granted, the removal of branches might be done to make room for the graft or to eliminate competitors for the energy the root could provide or to clear out diseased or dead wood—or even because some branch was thriving better than the rest(!).[47] But it would seem a bit strange if many branches were pruned in order to make room for one wild olive cutting since the latter will, by definition, yield little to no usable fruit. This anomaly is perhaps overlooked in the interpretive tradition

---

that it must be the Jewish Christian branches that remain; consequently, the statement does not refer to the broken branches, although "the meaning is imprecisely expressed" (*Romans*, 2:567).

46. Theophrastus, *Caus. plant.* 1.6.1–10 (esp. 8); cf. Columella, *Rust.* 4.29.1–17; 5.11.1–15; 7.8.1–4; *Arb.* 26.1–9.

47. Theophrastus, *Hist. plant.* 2.7.2; *Caus. plant.* 15.1.1–3; 2.15.5–6; 3.7.5–12; 3.14.1–16.3; 5.17.5; cf. Columella, *Arb.* 17.3, for the "thriving" example.

because the singularity of the wild olive versus the plurality of the cultivated branches has not generally been discussed.

It should also be noted that Paul refers to κλάδος/οι (branch[es] or shoot[s]) and that Theophrastus generally uses κλάδος/οι to refer to branch(es) or twig(s), rather than the boughs or main branches (ἀκρεμών) from which they grow (*Hist. plant.* 1.1.9; 1.8.5; 1.10.7).[48] In other words, Paul does not seem to have in view here the main branches that grow directly from the trunk but rather the small branches or twigs which grow on the main branches. This contrasts with what seems to be the usual understanding of the figure, in which gentiles are thought to be grafted into Israel, which is represented by the main trunk or tree. But in Paul's image, the Israelites are also but small branches in the tree sustained by the main branches and trunk. The larger entity in view is more likely simply the people of God, the righteous ones, the descendants of Abraham according to promise—themes already taken up in the letter. Paul has nowhere stated that these gentiles have become members of Israel. Rather, his argument has specifically turned on the fact that they are not, and do not become, Jews, for it is by their acceptance precisely as members of the nations that the oneness of God for all the nations is made manifest (Rom 3:27–31).[49] The gentiles join Israelites in the worship of the One God (cf. 15:5–12), but they are not Israel, nor are they grafted into Israel.

2.2.2 *Romans 11:18*

[361] Paul confronts the wild olive directly, instructing it not to be arrogant toward the branches. If it is tempted to be arrogant, it must refrain and recognize that it draws its life from the thickness of the root of the cultivated olive tree, in which it has now become a co-participant (συγκοινωνός).[50] It is but another branch. It is not the source of its own sustenance but depends

---

48. *Hist. plant.* 1.1.9: "I call the 'twig' (κλάδος) the shoot coming as a single whole from these branches, as especially the annual shoot." *Caus. plant.* 5.1.3, refers to twigs/slips (κλωνες) or shoots/young branches/suckers (πτόρθοι) or boughs/main branches (ἀκρεμόνες) as various ways to name the extremities of trees that contain the starting points capable of sprouting.

49. Nanos, *Mystery of Romans*, 179–92; Nanos, "Paul and the Jewish Tradition: The Ideology of the Shema."

50. Theophrastus, *Caus. plant.* 6.8.7, uses λίπος for the fatty oil of olive trees rather than πιότης, which Paul uses here. But just a little later, in 6.11.6–7, he does employ πιότης several times for fattiness in the root of some fatty trees like the pine. Here he is talking about the problem of thickening in the root that does not let nutrients pass through to feed the part of the tree above ground, something that does not occur in trees with no "oiliness [λιπαρότης] or fattiness [πιότης]." So it is not quite the same as the oil itself, but rather the oil in the roots. He compares this fattiness to the fat in animals.

upon the same root upon which the natural branches (including the ones now broken) were already dependent. The inference Paul develops is that the wild olive does not stand alone now. A Christ-believing gentile has not supplanted Israelites or taken their place; at best, he or she has come in alongside Israelites who are faithful—a faithful Israel that existed already and that was thriving—and, implicitly, among all Israelites, for the graft is placed "among *them*" (11:17).

This feature of the allegory is interesting, not least because although Theophrastus regards the root to be the source of the sustenance of the tree branches and not the other way around (*Caus. plant.* 1.12.1–3), his view is more complicated than that.[51] He regards the twigs of trees to have the starting points of life in them, witnessed by their ability to sprout when cut off and planted (*Caus. plant.* 1.3–4), and he notes that the bud graft has a sticky fluid within it (the pure food that is also in the fruit) that contributes to its success in taking hold, like coalescing readily with like (*Caus. plant.* 1.6.1–4; 1.12.8–9).[52] Thus it may not have been so self-evident, in biological terms, that the wild olive shoot, newly grafted in, understood by definition that it was now dependent upon the root.

The distress that lies behind the directness of Paul's rebuke is palpable. However, the metaphor is ill-fitted to communicating that the broken [362] branches also benefit in the long run from things unfolding in this manner, a point that he has already asserted via the stumbling allegory and one that he will again insist upon in the verses following the olive tree allegory. Moreover, it is not self-evident why the grafted olive should not relish its gain at the expense of the branches.

2.2.3 Romans 11:19

The most probable intent of the tree allegory, and to a large degree of this entire section of Romans, becomes evident in the presumptive assertion Paul attributes to the wild olive: "Therefore, you will say: 'Branches were broken [ἐξεκλάσθησαν] in order that I might be grafted in.'" The wild olive offers this telling rejoinder to Paul's challenge to its potential arrogance: it supposes

---

51. Photosynthesis was not discovered until the eighteenth century.

52. See also *Caus. plant.* 5.1.3–4. *Hist. plant.* 2.1.4 states that olives grow in more ways than any other plant: from a piece of the trunk (στελέχοθς), from a cutting from the stock (πρέμνου), from the root (ῥίζης), from a twig/young shoot (ῥαβδου) and from a stake (χάρακος). This latter appears to be a stick that has been cut off, and sticks cut from olive wood are said to be able to sprout *(Caus. plant.* 5.1.4). Vegetative propagation of olives is primarily from the planting of knobs *(uovuli)* on the base of the trunk that root easily when cut off, but also from truncheons, cuttings, and grafting. Those planted from seed tend to resemble wild forms in their morphology and thus are useless for fruit (Zohary and Hopf, *Domestication of Plants in the Old World*, 146).

that God has made way for it by breaking the other branches.[53] The wild olive infers that God favors *it* more than the broken natural branches, for otherwise, why would they have been broken? This argument is based on zero-sum thinking, and Paul appears to be getting at a comparison in which the wild olive supposes its own gain is of greater concern to God than the loss of the others to whom God had previously been committed.

It is interesting that the wild shoot is given a voice here, admitting its presumptuousness but attempting to legitimate it. Isaiah 10:5–15 and 37:24–25 similarly give voice to the presumptuousness of the king of Assyria, which will be turned against him, and in both cases a tree metaphor is employed to communicate the reversal of fortunes (cf. 37:30–32).

The complexity of Paul's description of "some" Israelites who have "stumbled/been broken" has largely been missed in what has become in Christian theology a central description of "Israel" and "Judaism" as now "fallen/severed" instead of merely injured. In this line of interpretation, Paul is understood to be describing Israel *in toto* and not just *some* from Israel. Even when noted, this distinction is taken to signify that almost all Israelites are cut off or fallen and supplanted with non-Israelites, or that carnal Israel is replaced with spiritual Israel (i.e., the church), which happens to be made up almost entirely of non-Israelites. It is thus important to continue to draw attention both to the fact that it is *some* Israelites, not Israel as a whole, that is at issue, and also that it is the portrayal of the non-Israelites' presumptuousness around which the allegory turns and not an effort to describe Israel as a tree or to critique the viewpoint of the Israelites who are under discussion.

2.2.4 Romans 11:20–21

[363] Following a rhetorical gesture of *agreement* (καλῶς), Paul confronts the wild olive about its assertion in quite oppositional terms. Note, however, that this rhetorical approach by way of καλῶς ("well," "certainly"), unless it can be shown to be ironic, does not confront the zero-sum assumption at work in v. 19 or the assertion that the damage or removal of some branches was directly related to the insertion of the wild olive. It is, as observed above, common to prune (but not "break") in order to make space for new growth or grafts. Paul's approach misses an opportunity to confront the notion of supplanting present in the wild olive's assertion. He appears to be more concerned with another dimension of the wild olive's claim: what it mistakenly reflects about the nature of God and, specifically, God's commitment to his own, to empirical Israelites who are beloved for the sake of the fathers regardless of their present

---

53. Note that the branches are said by the wild shoot to be broken (ἐκκλάω), not cut off or pruned (ἐκκόπτω).

disciplinary state. What is specifically objectionable is presumptuousness at the expense of these Israelites. Although apart from the oral presentation experienced by the first audience it is not possible for later interpreters to be certain, I suggest that the message that follows Paul's expression of approval was intended to cut ironically. That is, Paul feigned to be impressed with the logic of the wild olive's rejoinder but proceeded to confront its statement as inappropriate and, in fact, dangerous.[54]

Paul's reproof separates the two actions of breaking and grafting and explains that they are not merely expressions of God's arbitrary favor and disfavor, as if God wanted to make room for the wild olive at the expense of the other, cultivated branches. Rather, it is the failed effort of the branches, their lack of faith, or more probably faithfulness, that led to their present plight of being broken. It is not simply the result of God's whim, as if God arbitrarily loved the new one more than the ones he had loved for a long time. God's favor as well as disfavor are expressions of God's justice. But God does love these branches nevertheless.

Israelites are in a covenant relationship with God, one made with their fathers, and God does not take kindly to the expression of arrogance or indifference, or even the harboring of harmful thoughts, toward these offspring. God is presented as a parent who has only with great pain disciplined a child (the "it hurts me more than it hurts you" sentiment), one who will not brook anyone making light of this development. Paul's language perhaps expresses a veiled threat: don't make God choose, or you will not like the outcome. And note that Paul does not make clear here what faith or faithfulness was so lacking in the natural branches to deserve this severe [364] reaction. If a non-Christ-believing Israelite were to read this, would he or she not wonder: is it absence of faith in the gospel for themselves or lack of faithfulness to the proclamation of the gospel to the nations, or is it something else? Note that in vv. 30–32, it is not-being-persuaded (ἀπειθέω) that is faulted. At the same time, however, this is all said to be part of God's plan; and note also that what it is they should be persuaded about is not stated. In v. 21, the broken branches are described as not having been spared. Does this imply that they could have been spared in spite of their unfaithfulness, except that it is not God's nature to allow that to happen, or does it suggest that this is a step in a larger plan?

God confronts presumptuousness by calling attention to the wild olive's precarious predicament: "Do not think highly, but fear, for if God did not spare the natural branches, neither will he spare you." The wild olive is to fear the same fate instead of delighting in the fact that the other

---

54. Cf. Quintilian, *Inst.* 8.6.54; Nanos, *The Irony of Galatians*, 34–39.

branches have suffered it. Why should the wild olive be fearful? Because of God's justice. If God does not spare natural branches when unfaithful, neither will he spare the wild olive branch (11:21; cf. 11:24: all the more will God graft the natural branches back in). At issue is not the pride of the creature toward the Creator per se, but pride in one's own good fortune at the expense of someone else. Instead, the proper response is empathy for the other and, in this case, understanding how one's own good fortune is tied to the present suffering of the other (cf. 11:28–32) as well as how one's role of continuing in that good fortune humbly and with correct behavior (yet to be explained, but chapters 12–15 will do so) is also a means to helping the other return to good fortune.

Just what fate one understands these Israelites not to have been spared is a significant issue. Throughout the discourse and at points along the way in this allegory, too, their fate seems to be harsh discipline, breaking/stumbling, yet not breaking off/falling. But here, when Paul finally discloses the severity of the threat facing the wild olive, he refers to being broken *off*. At this point, it does seem that the earlier argument of the grafted wild olive, and Paul's reply, both presume that the natural branches have been broken off rather than just damaged, even though the more severe and explicit description has not been employed until now. And it is natural for the reader aware of the language at this point in the allegory to supply it earlier. Moreover, it is natural to understand the analogy to be about being banished (cut off) rather than disciplined (dislocated). But was that the message Paul intended to communicate?

The wild olive is told that it "stands" or is "established" or "placed" (when translated "stands," ἕστηκας suggests a mixed metaphor looking back to the running allegory) "by its πίστις, faith," or probably better, "faithfulness." At issue for the wild olive (Christ-believing non-Israelites) [365] is not believing or trusting in Christ in the limited sense of confessing belief in Christ, for the wild olive believes and is confident of its faith in Christ and certain of God's grace. This forms, after all, the foundations of its presumption (cf. 1:8, 12). At issue is whether its reaction to Israelites presently suffering discipline reflects faithfulness to the implications of its own new place in God's family. The opposite of presumption here is not belief in Christ but the right attitude (and action) toward the non-Christ-believing Israelite neighbor. Hence, the point seems to be faithfulness to the covenant relationship with God in Christ. The mere confession of convictions can be self-serving, especially when intended to contrast oneself with another. In this case, Paul confronts his listeners for harboring a presumptuous attitude as well as demonstrating indifference to the suffering experience of the other who does not share their confession. These Israelites are also in covenant partnership with God, although they are presently suffering discipline, just as 11:28 affirms: presently "enemied (ἐχθροί)[55] for your sake, but beloved (ἀγαπητοί) for the sake of the fathers."

Paul's rhetorical strategy reveals no concern to confront either mistaken notions of works-righteousness or an over-emphasis on grace; moreover, it does not betray a concern to challenge any problem of ethnic superiority on the part of the broken branches. If anything, it promotes covenantal nomism. The people of God, regardless of their faithfulness to date, must remain faithful, rather than presuming favor, or they will experience disfavor instead.[56] That is how covenant partnerships work. I submit that Paul is enculturating non-Israelites into mainstream Israelite concepts of identity that Paul shares with his Israelite brethren, whether Christ-believing or not.[57] Contrary to the idea that Paul has abandoned

---

55. Note the adjectival usage here, in balance with ἀγαπητοί ("beloved"). A better translation might be "alienated," which captures the sense of the arguments for stumbling and broken for the benefit of the nations (see 5:10). Beck, "Translations of the New Testament for Our Time," 204–6.

56. The problem for the unfaithful Israelites is neither the traditional concern with works-righteousness nor the New Perspective focus on ethnic sense of priority, but the failure to see that non-Jews should now be brought into the community of righteous ones apart from becoming members of Israel, apart from becoming Jews, apart from undertaking the rite of proselyte conversion. When that proposition—which is central to the belief that in Christ this awaited day has dawned, with the result that the nations are to turn to Israel's God as the One God of all humankind—is resisted by some Jews, who demur from joining Paul to proclaim this good news, he regards that as a sign of unfaithfulness.

57. Note that by the usual logic (although this is apparently not recognized, since Israel or these Israelites are regularly criticized for lack of faith in God's grace), the Israelites in view presumably have faith in the covenant promises to themselves, in the pattern of God that was disclosed to Abraham, which included circumcision as a requirement for taking part in that covenant; at issue, then, is their desire to sustain proper covenant-defined identity as God disclosed it to be for all time, not their lack of faith. One might say these Israelites have great trust in God's grace. So in what respect is their faith/faithfulness said by Paul to be lacking? It seems logical to suppose that it is trust in the way God is working now toward the gentiles, which is the topic throughout this letter and in Galatians, where the truth of the gospel is defined as the equal inclusion of gentiles by faith in/of Christ apart from becoming Jews, members of Israel. The translation "faithfulness" would perhaps be better than "faith" since it keeps in view the idea that Paul believes these Jews are not being faithful to the proposition that they are to recognize the arrival of the awaited age and then declare the good news to the nations. Paul's analysis of their condition in these negative terms depends upon their being required to trust with him in the proposition, and thus, to accept his conclusion that it is faithful rather than unfaithful to God to announce this proposition as good news and not as an unproven rumor.

Israelite [366] priority or norms, Paul is assimilating non-Israelites into an Israelite cultural perspective.⁵⁸

It may be that Paul's choice of ὑψηλά to describe their pride or presumption in v. 20 (as also in 11:25; cf. 12:3), carries the nuance that the attitude of the non-Israelite Christ-believers has to do with thinking about themselves from an *elevated* view, as looking down upon lower branches, perhaps even branches now on the ground below.⁵⁹

Calvin's Olive Tree Imprint in *Commentary to Genesis*
(*RAMI VT EGO INSERERER[O]* = I shall be inserted as a branch;
DEFRACTI SUNT = They are broken off)

58. Nanos, "Paul and Judaism: Why Not Paul's Judaism?"; Nanos, "The Myth of the 'Law-Free' Paul."

59. Calvin regularly included a picture on the title page of his works that depicted an olive tree surrounded by branches on the ground, with several more in the act of falling. A human figure reaches up among the branches, and a banner in the tree states, *"noli altum sapere,"* "be not high-minded." This is the Vulgate translation of Rom 11:20, μὴ ὑψηλὰ φρόνει *(ne animo efferaris,* in Calvin, *Commentaries on the Epistle of Paul the Apostle to the Romans,* 425). I am grateful to Klaus Haacker for bringing this to my attention, and to Allen Mueller, Director of the Luhr Library, Eden Theological Seminary, for making a copy of the title page from Calvin's 1563 Catechism available to me.

In Isa 2:11, ὑψηλοί and ὕψος are used in a similar way, and then the imagery of the lofty tree's pride is invoked in v. 12. This word group has to do with height, and it is used negatively for high-mindedness in the sense of pride or presumption of a higher standing (cf. 2:17). In the introduction of Isaiah the metaphor of the tree is invoked to confront pride, and Paul explicitly cites from this introduction (Rom 9:29 cites Isa 1:9). Note also the rock that serves as a place of refuge (Isa 2:10), which seems to refer to the caves made in the rocks (caves and cliffs of rocks: 2:19, 21), which are mentioned alongside the tree language of 2:12. In 3:8, Jerusalem stumbles and Judah falls. Did this influence Paul in his choice and mixing of these two metaphors?

2.2.5 Romans 11:22–24

Paul continues by explaining that the faithfulness of God is just, as well as kind. He emphasizes the centrality of remaining faithful in order to enjoy God's favor instead of discipline—indeed, discipline even to the point of wrath. His scolding of the wild olive suggests that it is not just its intellectual presumptuousness that is at issue but also its lack of concerned behavior toward the suffering other that follows from such thinking. He does this in part by stating that God is quite naturally concerned even more for the suffering branches that are the target of its boast than for the wild olive. That is, if God does have favorites, it is not the wild olive but the natural branches, even the ones presently broken. They remain members of the Israel of God, beloved for the sake of the fathers, those for whom the gifts and the calling remain in the present tense (Rom 9:2–5; 11:28–29).[60]

The wild olive is told in 11:22, "Therefore, behold God's patient mildness (χρηστότητα) and yet abrupt severity (ἀποτομίαν)." The line of argument focuses on the character of God, who does not act arbitrarily. God is patient, but when pushed too far his punishment is severe. Ἀποτομία communicates a sense of abruptness or harshness; it is used as a substantive for "a split or hewn piece of wood," while the verbal form is used for cutting off a piece or segment. Thus, there may be a play on the theme that leads Paul to choose just this word (e.g., God's cutting action).[61] The point is not to push God too far but to behave so as to receive his mildness and generosity. Paul's choice of χρηστότητα may also be suggestive, playing off of the

---

60. See further, Soulen, "'They are Israelites': The Priority of the Present Tense for Jewish-Christian Relations."

61. *LSJ*, 223; K. Weiss, "χρηστός" *TDNT* 9:483–92, here 489–91, but not applied as proposed here; cf. Esth 8:12.

name Χριστός, alluding to God's mercy to Israel and the nations in Christ, if received faithfully (cf. Rom 9:22).[62]

The wild olive is told that those who have "fallen" (πεσόντας) have received God's abrupt severity (his cutting action). In contrast, it has received God's generous mildness, if it "remains" in that state; otherwise it "will be cut off" (ἐκκοπήσῃ) also. Paul's argument likely appeals to the notion of Israel's entitlement to be disciplined quickly for impiety so that the punishment will not be as severe as it would otherwise be (2 Macc 6:12–17; cf. Ps 94:12; Prov 3:11–12; Jer 30:11; Lam 3:31–33; Jdt 8:27; Wis 12:1–2, 26; *Pss. Sol.* 10.1; 13.7; 16.1–5). This also tells against the idea of these Israelites being broken off in Paul's mind; being wounded makes more sense of the nature of discipline for those who belong to the covenant made with the fathers.

[368] For the first time, we learn that the broken branches correspond to runners in the earlier allegory (Rom 11:11). Yet whereas they were earlier specifically said not to have "fallen" but to have "stumbled," here they are represented in this mixed metaphorical way as having fallen. Moreover, the first time we have a reference that makes clear that they are not merely "broken" but "cut off." Although the threat is specifically that the *wild olive* should fear being cut off, the "also" logically implies "cut off" to the present state of the broken branches too.

At this point, the olive tree allegory communicates a very different message concerning the state of some presently unfaithful Israelites. In the earlier stumbling allegory, these were said to have merely tripped; up this point in the tree allegory, they have been represented as merely injured (broken); and in the arguments following the tree allegory, they are shown to be suffering, but only until God restores them [or: but nevertheless being protected by God during this process]. In vv. 22–24, however, the stumbling Israelites are represented as having indeed fallen; they are not simply in a process that can be naturally stopped before stumbling results in a fall. They have already been cut off. They are portrayed as no longer part of the tree until they come back in, which will require a miraculous reversal of a previously unthinkable outcome, one that is treated now as both conceivable and suffered, at least metaphorically.

In the history of interpretation, it is the message derived from this part of the tree allegory that has superseded the stumbling allegory, providing the basis for presuming that a non-Israelite wild olive has supplanted cut-off Israelite cultivated olive branches. The consequences for describing the fate of Israel, or even just some Israelites, in terms that Paul has otherwise denied

---

62. Daniel Stramara brought this suggestion to my attention.

to his interlocutor until now even within this allegory, are undermined. The logic of the argument Paul wishes to make for eventual restoration has to be asserted by subverting the natural implications of the oleicultural metaphor with which he has been working: "for God is able graft them in again." A metaphor designed to threaten presumptuous non-Israelites with a horrible fate *they* might suffer but can avoid now becomes the headliner for a fate that *has been* suffered by some Israelites, or Israel—although that outcome is unreservedly denied in the earlier allegory, as well as in the argument for the restoration of "all Israel" that is to come (11:25–32).

Paul's argument for the temporarily disadvantaged state of these Israelites is not the only thing that goes awry here. The interpretive tradition, by emphasizing this to be a description of the state of some (or most) Israelites as fallen or broken off (and all the more so when they are referred to simply as "Israel" or said to be replaced by the church), instead of challenging this inference based upon the running allegory, has also contributed to this Pauline metaphor remaining out of step with the thrust [369] of Paul's argument. For at this point, Paul is not seeking to represent the fate of some of Israel, but to warn the wild olive of the fate *it* will meet, all the more, if it is unfaithful. An allegory intended to proscribe gentile presumption has become the source for descriptions of Israelite exclusion and replacement. Should this be so? Will it also require a miracle to be reversed?

Paul could arguably have made this point by staying with the idea that some of Israel are *broken*, yet the wild olive will experience an all-the-more-severe fate of being broken *off* if it is not faithful, because, as the next verse will state, it is not even a natural part of the tree. But Paul did not do this. Perhaps he was concerned to warn the wild olive in such terribly stark terms that he did not reflect on this implication of his argument. That even the word he put in the mouth of the wild branch was ἐκκλάω, not ἐκκόπτω, may suggest he did not imagine his allegory would be taken in the direction that it has been taken by later interpreters.

This is a place where interpreters must decide which allegory to choose to describe Israel, especially the condition of those of Israel who are being unfaithful, as well as just what it is to which they are being unfaithful. It is also where they must decide what it is that these Israelites (not Israel!) can be out of, or exist in a distressed state within. If out, does this mean "out of the covenant with the fathers"? "Out of Israel"? Such conclusions are hard to square with Paul's language elsewhere, such as in Rom 9:2–5, and in the verses following this allegory. Paul insists in 11:25 that some are temporarily "hardened," better "calloused" (πώρωσις, a process of protecting the body or plant while a wound heals), but nevertheless that "all Israel will be restored [σωθήσεται]," that is to say, healed (v. 26; see below). Moreover, the unfaithful of Israel are declared to be "beloved of God for the sake of the fathers," and for them "the gifts and calling of God are irrevocable [ἀμεταμέλητα: lit., without repentance]" (vv. 28-29).[63] I maintain that from Paul's perspective, these Israelites are not out of anything; rather, they are *in*, they are Israelites, a special identity that is different than being a member of the body of Christ (which includes Israelites and non-Israelites), but they are not presently functioning as they should be. In time they will "all" be restored. The tree allegory has proven unable to communicate this nuanced perspective effectively—it is itself broken.[64]

[370] In v. 23, the wild olive is told that if the broken natural branches do not remain unfaithful, they will be grafted back in, for "God is able" to such a thing.[65] God's power is magnified, but also highlighted is the role faithfulness for those with whom God interacts. God's generous mildness is not to be underestimated any more than his abrupt severity should be overestimated, especially in the case of Israelites. Perhaps Paul drew inspiration for this move from Isa 59, which portrays God in metaphorical terms (including images of plants and trees) as miraculously restoring Israel after no one else comes to her rescue.

Once again, Paul's language does not betray a concern with works-righteousness or overconfidence in God's calling, nor does he suggest that these Israelites were guilty of claiming ethnic superiority; they are simply accused of being unfaithful to their covenant calling. The continued ethnic identity and priority of the broken branches as Israelites, as distinguished from the Christ-believing encoded audience, who are members of the other nations, remains fundamental to the case Paul seeks to make and to way he makes it.

In Rom 11:24, the wild olive is told that if it, "being cut off (ἐξεκόπης) from an olive tree that is wild by nature," can be, "contrary to nature, grafted into a cultivated olive tree, how much more (*a fortiori; qal vaḥomer*) will the natural branches be grafted into their own olive tree." Note that the

---

63. Cf. Sievers, "'God's Gifts and Call Are Irrevocable.'"

64. Similarly assessing a problem with Paul's figure along these lines is Gaston, *Paul and the Torah*, 145-47.

65. Paul does not mention a similar special consideration of regrafting in the case of the wild olive shoot, were it to become unfaithful and be cut off. It is ironic to note, that, despite all of Wright's criticism of Israelites for supposedly appealing to a "favoured nation clause" (Wright, "Romans," 694, *passim*)—and as a result being cut off—he then consoles the Christian gentile that even if Christians fail to remain faithful, this will not result in their being cut off, but only temporarily disciplined (p. 686). Wright's consolation actually runs against the grain of Paul's argument here, which threatens the wild branch with being cut off while envisioning the restoration of the natural branches after a temporary time of discipline.

wild olive is referred to as "cut off" of its own "wild" tree, and the point is to put it in its inferior place according to nature. This point seems to be a very important element in the development of the metaphorical tension in the allegory. That Paul calls the procedure he has described "contrary to nature" may suggest that he knows he is reversing normal grafting practices in this allegory by depicting a wild scion grafted onto a cultivated tree. The contrast between "wild" and "cultivated" is made explicit, as is that between "grafting contrary to nature" and "grafting" to restore what is "natural." The cognitive difference between wild and cultivated is mixed with that between unnatural and natural, thereby magnifying the semantic tension. And the conceptual difference between these two kinds of olives, and thus between Israelites and members of the other nations, is framed in *a fortiori* terms. Gentile presumption [371] is thereby reproved "severely"; Paul wants to "cut off" any ideas that might be developing in that direction.

The wild olive remains identifiably different from, and by nature inferior to, the natural olives. This difference is integral to the imagery and the message.[66] The wild olive takes its precarious place alongside the natural branches, not in place of them; it is a part of the tree, but it can never be natural to the cultivated tree in the same way as the olives that grow from its own natural branches. In the *ekklēsia*, a Christ-believing non-Israelite is not "grafted into Israel." He or she does not become an Israelite, a member of Israel. Rather, he or she becomes a co-participant representing the other nations "grafted"—better, "adopted"—into the family of God.[67] Attention to the special, privileged yet humble place of Christ-believing non-Israelites is at the center of the Pauline message here.

Although twigs for grafting can be cut and saved in a dormant state for weeks or months,[68] it makes little sense to cut off branches from a tree that one intends to graft into that same tree in the future.[69] The image of cutting off communicates a final judgment that runs counter to the introductory guarantee of the holiness of the branches because of the holy root as well as to the claim of eventual restoration. Should Paul's idea of Israel be derived from such language? Or instead, should we recognize that the issue

---

66. Cf. Johnson Hodge, "Olive Trees," 84.

67. Ibid.

68. Lundquist, "Of Grafting," 84.

69. Marcus Aurelius, *Meditations* 11.8, mentions grafting back in cut-off branches in order to draw an analogy to those who cut themselves off from other men. He makes the point that if they are rejoined, just like a cut-off limb, they will not be quite the same as before, although he calls for them to rejoin nonetheless. This functions as a warning. He does not want them to separate themselves in the first place so that they will never suffer this disadvantage.

communicated here is about how non-Israelites fit into God's plan in an unexpected way for the purpose of severing at the source any presumptuous ideas among the non-Israelite Christ-believers in Rome toward those Israelites not accepting them as fellow members of the people of God according to the claims of the gospel of Christ? Developing resentment toward those who do not accept one on one's own terms may be natural, but Paul does not want such a "wild" attitude to arise or continue.

That Paul appeals to the miracle of the regrafting of the natural branches in order to show that it requires less of a miracle than does the grafting in of a wild olive bears witness to the inadequacy of the allegory to describe the temporary state of these Israelites or of Israel. But that was not its [372] purpose! It was developed to confront gentile presumptuousness with a message about their precarious state and to portray the temporary and vicarious suffering of these Israelites on their behalf. These concepts are essential to the warning he sounds for these non-Israelites, so that they will properly understand themselves precisely in positive rather than negative relation to the fate of all Israelites.[70] But in order to make the *a fortiori* comparison by which he aims to communicate the severity of the threat to their well-being, he portrays some Israelites *as if* they existed in a state that is naturally final: cut off. The unintended consequence of this approach is the subversion of his overall message. Rather than successfully confronting arrogance among Christ-believing gentiles toward those Jews of Rome who are not similarly persuaded about the meaning of Jesus Christ—and Christian arrogance toward Jews everywhere since—his allegory has been understood to support the notion that Israel has been cut out and replaced.

Paul's approach is not indifferent to ethnicity or ethnic priority. Rather, he appeals to them as the basis for confronting this wild olive cutting. If one is to extrapolate anything from this about Paul's view of the continued role of ethnic identity among Christ-believers, should it not be that Paul recognizes ethnic diversity in the *ekklēsia*? His argument does not function as if Christ-faith has eliminated either ethnicity or difference. He attributes to God ethnic discrimination, witnessed in the theme of "the Jew first, but also the Greek" that runs throughout the letter. The point is not to eliminate or deny ethnic identity, but to keep its relative valuation in proper perspective.[71]

---

70. As Soulen puts the matter: "Ultimately, Rom 9–11 is theologically significant because it propels Gentile Christians to recognize that affirmation of—and connection to—God's irrevocable calling of the Jewish people is an internal, essential, and perpetual dimension of their own identity as Christians" ("They are Israelites," 504).

71. This is also how I understand Gal 3:28, where it is clear that slaves and master, as well as men and women, continue to exist and be different. However, they are equal in status (this is also the implication of 1 Cor 7:17–24). For Paul, difference remains,

That perspective involves remaining faithful to that which God has shown to each group, remaining within God's patient generosity rather than provoking his abrupt severity. It seems a natural inference that Paul's listeners should also be concerned that God's favor be won for the other too. What they can do besides upholding the right, humble attitude is not articulated until 12:1, but it is the theme throughout the so-called paraenesis of the letter that follows in chapters 12–15. There Christ-believers learn not only how to behave rightly toward each other, but also toward their non-Christ-believing, "stumbling/weak" Jewish brothers and sisters.[72]

3. THE MYSTERY OF THE "HARDENING," "FULLNESS," AND "RESTORATION" OF "ALL ISRAEL"

There is not space to discuss the interpretation of 11:25–27 or the rest of the chapter in new ways in light of the preceding examination of vv. 11–24.[73] In the metaphorical word choices employed in 11:25–26a, Paul appears to draw from the tree allegory he has just completed, although he is no longer developing the allegory. The theme stays the same: Paul sets out an argument in order to censure presumptuousness among the Christ-believing non-Israelites in Rome, lest they become "high-minded in themselves" (ἑαυτοῖς φρόνιμοι). Like the tree allegory itself (including its uneven fit with the previous allegories of the stumbling and of the dough), this language can be as misleading as it can be enlightening. But it should at least be noted that three of the key terms, as well as the context of their usage, can be understood to represent plant or tree metaphors. They are found also in Theophrastus' descriptions of plant life: πώρωσις, the process of hardening a plant to protect it while healing from a wound; πλήρωμα, fullness or filling out of a plant; σωθήσεται, restoring or saving a plant. In addition, as already discussed, the contexts of the proof texts from Isa 59 and 27 cited by Paul in Rom 11:26–27 are full of the imagery of plants and trees.

4. CONCLUSION

The allegory of the olive tree does not sit well with the surrounding allegories and arguments. The problem includes not only elements internal to the allegory but also the manner in which certain elements of its message

---

but it must not legitimate discrimination in the present age among the Christ-believers.

72. Nanos, *Mystery of Romans*, 85–165.

73. See further Nanos, "'Callused,' Not 'Hardened.'"

contradict both the thrust of the allegory of stumbling that preceded it and the metaphor-laden argument for the restoration of "all Israel" that follows it. I submit that the tree allegory is the one Paul least intended to portray his conception of the unfaithful within Israel or his notion of Israel overall. Rather, it communicates his concern to confront the arrogance of the Christ-believing members of the nations in Rome toward non-Christ-believing Israelites, portraying the precariousness of their state by way of the figure of a wild olive cutting precariously grafted into a cultivated tree. In order to make his *a fortiori* case against these Christ-believing gentiles, he must portray the state of these Israelites in a [374] severe light. If they can be disciplined severely, *all the more* can the alien olive. Thus, these non-Jews are to recognize just how severe will be the consequences for failing to nip their presumptuousness in the bud.

However, the implications of Paul's portrayal of the olive tree—which is intended to make his case against the Christ-believers from the nations—led to a theological development that I believe Paul did not anticipate when he created it. For this allegory is used to describe Israel as if it were a tree and the state of non-Christ-believing Israelites (often simply: "Israel") as broken off, discarded, and dead branches on the ground below the tree, an image that clearly depicts them as having fallen. But in term of the stumbling metaphor, "fallen" is a condition Paul *emphatically insists* does *not* apply. Moreover, this conceptualization of Israel has been extended beyond the context of Romans to apply to Jews and Judaism ever since. That extension depends upon Paul's allegory remaining descriptive beyond its rhetorical and historical limitations, beyond its original prescriptive purpose to confront mistaken notions of self-importance among the early non-Israelite Christ-believers and to challenge their disregard for their non-Christ-believing Israelite neighbors, who are their brothers and sisters in the family of God. Ironically, an allegory written to *support* these Israelites has resulted in the theological legitimation of ideas and policies running in quite the opposite direction.

I believe that Paul would deny that these Israelites were broken off in the sense that this has been presented in the interpretive tradition and furthermore, that he would extend this denial to the present day if asked to describe the state of Jews and Judaism.[74] He would instead insist in the same unmistakable terms that he communicated in the stumbling allegory and throughout the letter when he perceived that such negative inferences might be drawn by his imaginary dialogue partner: "May it never be!" Rather, the

---

74. Cf. Nanos, "Challenging the Limits That Continue to Define Paul's Perspective on Jews and Judaism," esp. 217–18.

tree allegory was created with the special concern to describe the present state of the gentile believers in Christ, and the inferences about these Israelites are (il)logical byproducts of that explanation. What we have here is a Pauline metaphor gone awry.

If we approach the tree allegory as if it were designed not so much to represent the current state of these Israelites, or of Israel per se, but the present tenuous state of the gentiles in Christ, it will keep the focus on Paul's stated concern throughout this allegory and throughout this section of Romans. That concern is to change the minds of these gentiles towards the Israelites who do not share their faith in Christ from presumption to empathy. For Paul, theirs is not a final state of unfaithfulness, but a "not yet" [375] state that he expects to continue until he can get to Rome to complete his ministry among the synagogues there, followed by his turning fully to the members of the nations. The Christ-believing gentiles to whom he writes represent an anomaly. However glad he is for their faith, he remains concerned that their nascent resentment toward the Jews of Rome who do not accept their claims to equal standing, apart from proselyte conversion, based upon the proclamation of the message of Christ will prevent the successful completion of his ministry among them. That is why he writes this letter.[75]

At the root of many communication failures are different perceptions of reality along with different valuations of the options for comprehending it. Taking into account as well the generative dynamics of metaphor—and all the more of allegory—to constrain and mislead the imagination as well as to enlighten and correct,[76] we must be careful not to allow the possible interpretations of Paul's view of Israel or of the place of non-Israelites in the family of God to be limited by analogies, for example, to the realms of trees or stumbling or dough. This caution extends to rhetorical efforts to describe "reality" by way of illustration in general and to our lack of knowledge of the dynamics of the metaphorical or allegorical elements themselves. How much do we know about olive tree propagation in Paul's time and place, and how much did Paul, or his secretary, or his audience, or the earliest church interpreters, or the Reformers, or previous commentators? In addition, the gaps in the details of the allegory itself serve as a caution against pressing the metaphor too far, that is, against expecting the dynamics of trees and grafting to accurately or comprehensively describe the dynamics of people and

---

75. Cf. Nanos, *Mystery of Romans*, 3–40, *passim*.

76. Schön, "Generative Metaphor"; see also, in the same volume, Black, "More About Metaphor," esp. 36–41; Reddy, "The Conduit Metaphor."

kinship or to serve as perfect analogies from which to draw firm answers to our theological queries.[77]

It is likely the case that Paul's concern in Rom 11 is not one to which later interpreters of Romans have been attuned. It is inconsistent with their framework of consciousness or perception of reality, and all the more so now after thousands of years have passed without a reversal of opinion toward Jesus of Nazareth on the part of most Israelites. Moreover, to the degree that exegetes are unaware of just how unusual and unproductive it would be to graft wild olive cuttings onto cultivated trees (which is central [376] to detecting the analogy around which the allegory is constructed), the central message of the allegory goes unobserved altogether, or it is subordinated to other features that are more attractive and more conducive to enhancing self-esteem and group priority, which endeavors "naturally" involve devaluation of the other.[78]

The emphasis of the allegory for interpreters of Romans has often fallen on Israelites being cut off and gentiles being grafted on in their place, with the church now comprising the true or spiritual Israel, however phrased. Little attention has been given to the continuing relevance of ethnic identity or to the hierarchical values around which Paul worked. In the prevailing interpretations, neither the temporariness of this stage in Israel's history nor the precariousness of this development has been sufficiently sustained. The present investigation leads me to conclude that the primary controls to apply to every interpretive decision for this passage are along the following lines: Does it contribute to Paul's goal of making the members from the nations recognize their own humble place? Does it help turn presumptuous judgmentalism into empathetic generosity? Does it foster regard for the "other" as part of one's "self"? Does it focus on being only "a"—not "the"—member of God's larger family?

Paul sought to confront any temptation among his gentile listeners to be dismissive of or arrogant toward these Israelites, to suppose that God now loved the members from the nations other than Israel better than Israelites. He sought to communicate how their new membership in God's family and their concomitant responsibilities were intimately tied to the way that God would restore these Israelites in due time. That would be, in part, by way of God's activity among the gentile Christ-believers themselves, and

---

77. Black observes that the literal paraphrase of a metaphor can say too much and emphasize the wrong things and that it can be an inadequate translation because "it fails to give the *insight* that the metaphor did" ("Metaphor," 293, emphasis original).

78. That is, according to social identity theory: see Hogg and Abrams, *Social Identifications*; Tajfel, ed., *Differentiation Between Social Groups*. See also Rothgangel, "Christliche Identität ohne antijudische Kontrastfolie."

thus, by way of how they lived their lives among these Israelites, the subject to which Paul turns in chapters 12–15. I believe this was also the way that Paul understood his own service to these gentiles and, therefore, the way that he lived out his dedication to the restoration of his Israelite brothers and sisters. Attending to Paul's arguments from this perspective just might make his tree allegory more properly able to stand.

BIBLIOGRAPHY

Aune, David E. "Distinct Lexical Meanings of AITAPXH in Hellenistic Judaism and Early Christianity." In *Early Christianity and Classical Culture: Comparative Studies in Honor of Abraham J. Malherbe*, edited by John T. Fitzgerald et al., 119–25. NovTSup 110. Leiden: Brill, 2003.

Baxter, A. G., and J. A. Ziesler. "Paul and Arboriculture: Romans 11.17–24." *Journal for the Study of the New Testament* 24 (1985) 25–32.

Beck, Norman. "Translations of the New Testament for Our Time." In *Seeing Judaism Anew: Christianity's Sacred Obligation*, edited by Mary C. Boys, 200–210. Lanham, MD: Rowman & Littlefield, 2005.

Black, Max. "Metaphor." *Proceedings of the Aristotelian Society for the Systematic Study of Philosophy* 55 (1954) 273–94.

———. "More About Metaphor." In *Metaphor and Thought*, edited by Andrew Ortony, 19–43. Cambridge: Cambridge University Press, 1979.

Bourke, Myles M. *A Study of the Metaphor of the Olive Tree in Romans XI*. The Catholic University of America Studies in Sacred Theology, Second Series, 3. Washington, DC: The Catholic University of America Press, 1947.

Calvin, John. *Commentaries on the Epistle of Paul the Apostle to the Romans*. Edited and translated by John Owen. Grand Rapids: Eerdmans, 1947.

Cranfield, C. E. B. *A Critical and Exegetical Commentary on the Epistle to the Romans*. 2 vols. ICC. Edinburgh: T. & T. Clark, 1975.

Davies, W. D. *Jewish and Pauline Studies*. Philadelphia: Fortress, 1984.

Dunn, James D. G. *Romans 9–16*. WBC 388. Dallas: Word, 1988.

Eastman, Susan G. "Israel and Divine Mercy in Galatians and Romans." In *Between Gospel and Election: Explorations in the Interpretation of Romans 9–11*, edited by Florian Wilk and J. Ross Wagner, 147–70. Tübingen: Mohr Siebeck, 2010.

Esler, Philip F. "Ancient Oleiculture and Ethnic Differentiation: The Meaning of the Olive-Tree Image in Romans 11." *Journal for the Study of the New Testament* 26 (2003) 103–24.

Fitzmyer, Joseph A. *Romans*. AB 33. New York: Doubleday, 1993.

Foxhall, Lin. "Olive Cultivation within Greek and Roman Agriculture: The Ancient Economy Revisited." Ph.D. diss., University of Liverpool, 1990.

Gaston, Lloyd. *Paul and the Torah*. Vancouver: University of British Columbia Press, 1987.

Ginzberg, Louis, ed. *The Legends of the Jews*. Philadelphia: Johns Hopkins University Press, 1998.

Haacker, Klaus. "Das Thema von Römer 9–11 als Problem der Auslegungsgeschichte." In *Between Gospel and Election: Explorations in the Interpretation of Romans 9–11*, edited by Florian Wilk and J. Ross Wagner, 55–72. Tübingen: Mohr Siebeck, 2010.

Hogg, Michael A., and Dominic Abrams. *Social Identifications: A Social Psychology of Intergroup Relations and Group Processes*. London: Routledge, 1988.

Johnson Hodge, Caroline. *If Sons, Then Heirs: A Study of Kinship and Ethnicity in the Letters of Paul*. New York: Oxford University Press, 2007.

———. "Olive Trees and Ethnicities: Judeans and Gentiles in Romans 11:17-24." In *Christians as a Religious Minority in a Multicultural City: Modes of Interaction and Identity Formation in Early Imperial Rome*, edited by J. Zangenberg and M. Labahn, 77-89. London: T. & T. Clark, 2004.

Lundquist, Kjell. "Of Grafting." In *Le jardin de plaisir = Der Lust Gartten = Lustgard = The Garden of Pleasure: inledning. kommentarer: Introduction, Commentaries*, edited by A. Mollet, K. Tanner, and R. Tanner; translated by K. Tanner and R. Tanner, 81-85. Uppsala: Gyllene Snittet, 2007.

Nanos, Mark D. "'Callused,' Not 'Hardened': Paul's Revelation of Temporary Protection until All Israel Can Be Healed." In *Reading Paul in Context: Explorations in Identity Formation*, edited by Kathy Ehrensperger and J. Brian Tucker, 52-73. London: T. & T. Clark, 2010. (See chapter 7 in this volume of collected essays.)

———. "Challenging the Limits That Continue to Define Paul's Perspective on Jews and Judaism." In *Reading Israel in Romans*, edited by Cristina Grenholm and Daniel Patte, 217-29. Harrisburg, PA: Trinity, 2000. (See chapter 11 in this volume of collected essays.)

———. *The Irony of Galatians: Paul's Letter in First-Century Context*. Minneapolis: Fortress, 2002.

———. "The Jewish Context of the Gentile Audience Addressed in Paul's Letter to the Romans." *Catholic Biblical Quarterly* 61 (1999) 283-304. (See chapter 3 in this volume of collected essays.)

———. *The Mystery of Romans: The Jewish Context of Paul's Letter*. Minneapolis: Fortress, 1996.

———. "The Myth of the 'Law-Free' Paul Standing between Christians and Jews." *Studies in Christian-Jewish Relations* 4 (2009) 1-21. Online: http://escholarship.bc.edu/scjr/vol4/iss I /4/. (See volume 1, chapter 3, in this series of collected essays.)

———. "'O Foolish Galatians, Who has Cast the Evil Eye [of Envy] upon You?' (Gal 3:1a-b): The Belief System and Interpretive Implications of Paul's Accusation." Online: http://www.marknanos.com/projects.html.

———. "Paul and the Jewish Tradition: The Ideology of the Shema." In *Celebrating Paul: Festschrift in Honor of Joseph A. Fitzmyer and Jerome Murphy-O'Connor*, edited by Peter Spitaler, 62-80. CBQMS. Washington, DC: Catholic Biblical Association of America, 2012. (See volume 1, chapter 4, in this series of collected essays.)

———. "Paul and Judaism: Why Not Paul's Judaism?" In *Paul Unbound: Other Perspectives on the Apostle*, edited by Mark D. Given, 117-60. Peabody, MA: Hendrickson, 2010. (See volume 1, chapter 1, in this series of collected essays.)

Nielsen, Kirsten. *There Is Hope for a Tree: The Tree as Metaphor in Isaiah*. JSOTSup 65. Sheffield, UK: JSOT, 1989.

Reddy, Michael J. "The Conduit Metaphor—A Case of Frame Conflict in Our Language about Language." In *Metaphor and Thought*, edited by Andrew Ortony, 284-324. Cambridge: Cambridge University Press, 1979.

Richardson, Peter. *Israel in the Apostolic Church*. SNTSMS 10. London: Cambridge University Press, 1969.

Rothgangel, Martin. "Christliche Identität ohne antijüdische Kontrastfolie: Zur Bildungsrelevanz von Römer 9–11." In *Between Gospel and Election: Explorations in the Interpretation of Romans 9–11*, edited by Florian Wilk and J. Ross Wagner, 483–96. Tübingen: Mohr Siebeck, 2010.

Schön, Donald A. "Generative Metaphor: A Perspective on Problem-Setting in Social Policy." In *Metaphor and Thought*, edited by Andrew Ortony, 254–83. Cambridge: Cambridge University Press, 1979.

Sievers, Joseph. "'God's Gifts and Call Are Irrevocable': The Reception of Romans 11:29 through the Centuries and Christian-Jewish Relations." In *Reading Israel in Romans: Legitimacy and Plausibility of Divergent Interpretations*, edited by Cristina Grenholm and Daniel Patte, 127–73. Romans through History and Culture Series. Harrisburg, PA: Trinity, 2000.

Simon, Marcel. *Verus Israel: A Study of the Relations between Christians and Jews in the Roman Empire, 135–425*. Translated by H. McKeating. Oxford: Oxford University Press, 1986.

Soulen, R. Kendall. "'They are Israelites': The Priority of the Present Tense for Jewish-Christian Relations." In *Between Gospel and Election: Explorations in the Interpretation of Romans 9–11*, edited by Florian Wilk and J. Ross Wagner, 497–504. Tübingen: Mohr Siebeck, 2010.

Stowers, Stanley K. *A Re-reading of Romans: Justice, Jews, and Gentiles*. New Haven: Yale University Press, 1994.

Swarup, Paul. *The Self-Understanding of the Dead Sea Scrolls Community: An Eternal Planting, A House of Holiness*. Library of Second Temple Studies 59. London: T. & T. Clark, 2006.

Tajfel, Henri, ed. *Differentiation Between Social Groups: Studies in the Social Psychology of Intergroup Relations*. New York: Academic Press, 1978.

Tobin, Thomas H. *Paul's Rhetoric in Its Contexts: The Argument of Romans*. Peabody, MA: Hendrickson, 2004.

Wagner, J. Ross. *Heralds of the Good News: Isaiah and Paul "in Concert" in the Letter to the Romans*. NovTSup 101. Leiden: Brill, 2002.

———. "'Not from the Jews Only, But Also from the Gentiles': Mercy to the Nations in Romans 9–11." In *Between Gospel and Election: Explorations in the Interpretation of Romans 9–11*, edited by Florian Wilk and J. Ross Wagner, 417–31. Tübingen: Mohr Siebeck, 2010.

Wengst, Klaus. "Are Not All Out of Israel, 'Israel'?" In "First to the Jews and also to the Greeks": A Clearing through the Letter to the Romans." Online: http://www.jcrelations.net/First_to_the_Jews_and_also_to_the_Greeks___br___A_Clearing_through_the_Letter_to.3214.0.html?item=2906, accessed on 2 March 2018.

Wilk, Florian. *Die Bedeutung des Jesajabuches für Paulus*. FRLANT 179. Gottingen: Vandenhoeck & Ruprecht, 1998.

Wright, N. T. "The Letter to the Romans: Introduction, Commentary, and Reflections." In *The New Interpreter's Bible*, Vol. 10, 393–770. Nashville: Abingdon, 2002.

Zohary, Daniel. "The Wild Genetic Resources of the Cultivated Olive." *Acta horticulturae* 356 (1994) 62–65.

Zohary, Daniel, and Maria Hopf. *Domestication of Plants in the Old World: The Origin and Spread of Cultivated Plants in West Asia, Europe, and the Nile Valley*. 3rd ed. Oxford: Oxford University Press, 2000.

7

"Callused," Not "Hardened"
Paul's Revelation of Temporary Protection until All Israel Can Be Healed

[52] WILLIAM CAMPBELL IS keen to confront readings of Romans that idealize Christian superiority at the expense of Jews and Judaism. I hope this study can contribute to his lifetime effort to challenge the stubborn—perhaps one might even call it hardened—grip of that tradition by revisiting chapter 11, where the prevailing translations and interpretations of certain words and phrases continue to blunt the force of Paul's otherwise benevolent argument for the temporary, protected state of his fellow Jews, even though some (indeed, most) of them did not share Paul's point of view about the meaning of Jesus Christ.

In spite of Paul's explicit effort to check prideful attitudes toward Jews among the non-Jews to whom he writes in Rome, a negative characterization of Jews naturally arises from Paul's use of πώρωσις in Rom 11:25, which is typically translated "hardening," and thus, "a *hardening* has come upon part of Israel" (NRSV), or "that a partial *hardening* has happened to Israel" (NASB). Whether translated to indicate that only some Israelites have been hardened, as in the NRSV, or that Israel itself has been hardened to some degree, as in the NASB, commentators also regularly conflate this reference to hardness with God's hardening of the heart of Pharaoh—although Paul does not refer to the heart of Israelites being hardened. A negative judgment of the condition of the Jewish other is thereby perpetuated, however unwittingly, within an interpretive discourse surrounded by language designed to argue against just such hostile assessments of their condition.

This exegetical tradition makes it hard to ignore that, in spite of the uniquely positive role Romans 11 has played in the crafting of *Nostra Aetate* (No. 4) and other similarly sensitive Christian re-evaluations of Jews and Judaism since the Shoah, the discourse by which this generosity of spirit is expressed continues to be constrained contextually by the need to account for Paul's attribution of hardness to his fellow Jews. It can hardly avoid communicating negative assessments of the other to some degree regardless of the best of intentions, at least at the exegetical level.

[53] While I respectfully believe that Christians should hermeneutically distance themselves from such judgmental decisions about the motives of others or their standing before God if they arise in their sacred texts—which, after all, Paul instructs (2:1!)—in this case the challenge can be made at the exegetical level, for Paul's language in chapter 11 need not express such negative sentiments. By attending to this text's metaphorical attributes, including Paul's specific use here of πώρωσις rather than σκληρός, and its role in the larger context of his argument, the harsh visual representations that perpetuate this judgmental characterization, however unintentionally, can be revised—if not replaced.

1. ΠΩΡΩΣΙΣ VERSUS ΣΚΛΗΡΟΣ

Σκληρός is regularly applied to the hardening of the heart in the sense of being strengthened to express firm, stubborn resistance to God's will, or being insensitive to it. Paul uses the verbal form σκληρύνω, in 9:17–18, in keeping with the usage in Exod 9:12, 16, where it metaphorically describes God's hardening of Pharaoh's heart (LXX usually for Hebrew קשה, also חזק). The σκληρός word-group has to do with things hard or rough to touch, harsh sounds, or harsh or bitter tastes and smells. When used metaphorically, it generally connotes harsh or hard in the sense of austere, stern, insensitive, or stubborn.[1] Instead of eliminating Pharaoh, God is represented as making him stubbornly resistant to God's will so that the people of Israel would be freed. This hardening is undertaken in order to heighten the impact when Pharaoh is ultimately compelled to change his mind in the face of the inexorable suffering that his resistance provokes. In this way, God's power and thus name are made known among the nations.

But Paul does not use σκληρός or cognates to describe the state of Israelites; instead, he uses πώρωσις in 11.25 (and as a passive verb in v. 7: ἐπωρώθησαν) to describe the state of some (many) of his fellow Israelites.[2]

---

1. *LSJ*, 1612; K. L. and M. A. Schmidt, *TDNT* 5.1028–31.
2. It is also useful to note that interpreters often refer to Isa 6:10 as a cross reference

Πώρωσις (verb πωρόω) refers to a "callus" (verb: to callus) not to "hardness" or even "blindness" per se.

Πώρωσις is not a word common to the Tanakh. It is used once in verbal form in the Septuagint, Job 17:7, to refer to eyes "growing dim" from anger or grief (MT: כהה). As will be discussed, the context indicates that it is not "hardness," or even "blindness" per se, but "impairment" of sight that is at issue, which is better expressed by the Greek variant πεπήρωνται. Πώρωσις is not used in the Pseudepigrapha, Josephus, or Philo. It is common in medical discussions in antiquity. According to Hippocrates, *De alimento* 53, [54] it has to do with a process of healing following an injury: "Marrow nutriment of bone, and through this a *callus* forms [Μυελὸς τροφὴ ὀστέου, διὰ τοῦτο ἐπὶ πωροῦται]" (Loeb; trans. W. H. S. Jones).[3] In other words, the formation of a callus—which involves a process of hardening, to be sure—is to offer *protection* so that the injured area can sustain life. It promotes *healing* of broken bones or wounds, not harm or destruction, or metaphorical resistance. It creates an area less sensitive to touch, but that too is a positive feature versus the continuation of the sensation of pain where the injury occurred. There are several options worth exploring to translate and interpret πώρωσις in terms of the process Paul has been communicating throughout: some Israelites are temporarily stumbling or suffering an *injury* that can be and will be healed, witnessed in metaphorical terms by a *callus* on these broken branches.[4]

Given the negative valence of hardness in English combined with the derisive association to the disposition of Pharaoh's heart, hardening is not a helpful or an accurate translation choice for Paul's discussion of the condition

---

for Rom 11:7 and 25, but in Isaiah it is yet another different word, παχύνω (MT: וּמַן) to swell or thicken or make firm or fat; figuratively, to make impervious (to water), insensitive (Schmidt and Schmidt, *TDNT* 5.1025). The point is that Isaiah is to speak the word so that it will not penetrate the hearts of the target audience.

3. See also *De fractures* 23.10; *De articulis* 14.17, 24; 15.6; 49.18. Celsus, *De Medicina*. Aretaeus (trans. W. G. Spencer), 521, explains how to bind a broken bone tightly, "because in this position callus grows..."; see also pp. 527, 575. It is discussed several times in Galen, e.g., *Ars Medica* 1.387.18, and especially in his commentary (e.g., 18b.398-401, 412, 429, 505, 531, 541, 789) on Hippocrates' *De fractures*. Cf. *LSJ*, 1561; Schmidt and Schmidt, *TDNT* 5.1025-26; Thayer (ed.), *Greek-English Lexicon of the New Testament*, 559.

4. I want to thank Daniel Stramara for encouraging me to investigate the positive aspects of the translation "callus" here, which I raised in passing in *The Mystery of Romans*, 261-62, but did not pursue. Following more recent detailed work on the allegory of the olive tree and its branches, and thus the relevance of this translation choice in v. 25, I am now prepared to see the positive elements of this metaphorical tree terminology in the forest of the Romans 11 argument, one might say; cf. Nanos, "'Broken Branches': A Pauline Metaphor Gone Awry?"

of the Israelites he seeks to discuss. The difference implied can be profound; translating this as hardened in the sense of obdurate, stubborn, or insensitive hearts may obscure the very thrust of Paul's argument. This problem is evident in most discussions of this passage, for the prevailing approaches interpret hardness in a way that cannot avoid undermining the sympathetic force of Paul's argument, and thus the sympathetic interpreter, inadvertently but ineluctably, winds up expressing a negative judgment of intentions in the midst of seeking to communicate a message of goodwill.[5]

[55] Yet Paul does not mention the heart, and there is no evidence that πώρωσις was used to refer to the heart during Paul's time. Πώρωσις is attested later in Mark 3:5, John 12:40, and in the Pauline tradition responsible for Eph 4:18, and it became more common in commentaries and elsewhere in theological discussions after the second century CE, perhaps adumbrating the crossover that is common to English usage of hardness when translating πώρωσις as if synonymous with σκληρός.[6] We will return to discuss the case of 2 Cor 3:14, which refers to impaired vision.

---

5. Differently, but informatively, the opportunity to intentionally express criticism of Jews by way of this language is exemplified by Chrysostom: "'That blindness in part hath happened unto Israel.' Here again he levels a blow at the Jew, while seeming to take down the Gentile" ("Homily 19").

6. Cf. *Shep.* 30.1; 47.4; Pseudo-Clementina 158.8; Theophilus, *Ad Autolycum* 2.35.32; Clemens Alexandrinus, *Protrepticus* 9.83.3.6; *Stromata* 1.18.88.3.2; Origen, *Comm. in Evangelium Matthaei* 11.14.68. *1 Clem.* 51:3 still uses σκληρυνω with καρδία; as does also *Barn.* 9:5. I do not find grounds for the Schmidts's claim that "in the NT" it "is always fig., usually of the heart. It refers to hardening of the Jews in ... R. 11:7..." (*TDNT* 5.1026), or commentaries that refer to hardening of the heart similarly in discussions of Romans 11. For discussion of why in each of these later NT cases the meaning "hardened" is unlikely as well, and of the variants for each, see Robinson, *Epistle to the Ephesians*, 264–74. He concludes that in each case in the NT "obtuseness or intellectual blindness is the meaning indicated by the context" (273), not hardness, a finding that this study will challenge for blindness too, and he also shows that ancient translators and commentators approached πώρωσις and πήρωσις as interchangeable. Robinson, *Ephesians*, 274, does not like the choice of or description of callus for πώρωσις by Thayer (ed.), *Greek-English Lexicon*, or when callus is played off in the sense of "a covering has grown over the heart" by Sanday and Headlam, *Epistle to the Romans* (second edition [Robinson is responding to the first edition]), 314. Their comment is about Rom 11:7 (note that they read 11:25: "that hardening of heart which has come upon Israel"), but Robinson seeks to challenge the translation "harden" in particular, and does not approach Rom 11:7, 25 as representing the metaphorical imagery I suggest. Jewett, *Romans*, 694, 699–700, translates πώρωσις in v. 25 as "obtuseness," "as a failure to discern and to see what was simultaneously a willful act and divine punishment."

2. THE CONTEXT FOR PAUL'S USE OF ΠΩΡΩΣΙΣ IN ROMANS 11:25

Paul moves away from formal allegorical development of the olive tree allegory of vv. 17–24 when he begins v. 25. This change is evident in several ways, not least by moving from addressing a singular olive shoot in the allegory to "you gentiles" in the plural, whom he does not want to be ignorant of a mysterious process he seeks to reveal: "For I do not want you to be unperceptive regarding this mystery, brothers and sisters, so that you would not be mindful (only) for yourselves." It may be that, whereas the wild shoot stood implicitly for the non-Jews by way of a single cutting in the allegory in order to highlight the smallness and precariousness of their place among the people of God without suggesting that Paul has but one person in his sights, now Paul turns to addressing these non-Jews directly, and thus, in the plural.

[56] In contrast to Isaiah's prophetic speech to his fellow Israelites in a way designed to prevent understanding,[7] Paul declares that he seeks to make a mystery clear to his non-Israelite audience so that they will avoid the pitfalls of insensitive arrogance toward certain Israelites, and thus escape the disastrous consequences that follow from preoccupation with only their own wisdom and success. We might expect to find Paul thus employing simple, direct speech at this point to enhance clarity and avoid misunderstanding; but we do not. Instead, Paul continues to draw on metaphorical language in vv. 25–26a, and then on a conflation of the enigmatic texts of Isa 59:20–21 and 27:9 in the balance of vv. 26b–27. These ostensible proofs for his argument are also highly metaphorical, as is also their own context in Isaiah, which is itself full of inscrutable twists and turns; moreover, they do not easily align with what they are cited by Paul to prove.[8] One wonders if the mystery has become clearer or more confused, even if Paul's audience is now made keenly aware that there is something else going on that they should attend to seeing, something that should make them humble instead of filled with themselves.[9]

---

7. That Isaiah's prophetic language is itself that which causes misunderstanding is argued in B. R. Trick's 2009 SBL Annual Meeting paper, "Lest Their Hearts Understand," a copy of which he was kind enough to make available to me.

8. A reading of Isaiah 27 and 59 and the chapters and themes around them, including many allegories and metaphors from trees and plant life—which perhaps triggered as well as informed Paul's developments of these allegories and metaphors—cannot be taken up in detail here. Cf. Wilk, *Die Bedeutung des Jesajabuches für Paulus*; Wagner, *Heralds of the Good News*; Nielsen, *There is Hope for a Tree*; Hibbard, *Intertextuality in Isaiah 24–27*; Nanos, "'Broken Branches.'"

9. Cf. Patte, "A Post-Holocaust Biblical Critic Responds," esp. 231–32.

I propose that the metaphorical word choices employed in 11:25–26a are neither random, nor chosen to introduce a new set of visual representations around the theme of hard-heartedness, but continue to draw from the olive tree imagery that preceded them in vv. 17–24. Although Paul is not simply developing the allegory formally,[10] the theme stays the same: Paul sets out an argument in order to censure presumptuousness among the Christ-believing non-Israelites in Rome, lest they become "wise in themselves" (ἑαυτοῖς φρόνιμοι).[11] [57] yet, like the allegory itself, as well as its uneven fit with the previous allegories of the stumbling and of the dough, this metaphorical language can be as misleading as it can be enlightening.

Elsewhere I discussed why it is problematic to use such metaphorical language about grafting as if it is plain speech, and as if Paul had stated that it was Israel into which the graft was planted.[12] The tree and root should logically be some entity other than Israel, which remains unnamed. Thus the wild olive shoot has been grafted into a tree and partaken of the root alongside of the branches that remained (that is, among the Israelites ["among them" in v. 17]), but not into Israel. The grafted branch joins alongside of Israelite branches, the tree is some entity large enough to encompass members of Israel and of the other nations simultaneously, such as "the people of God" or "the righteous ones," but the tree does not appear to be "Israel" per se.

I have also discussed why it is lexically and exegetically preferable to translate Paul's reference to the broken branches as "broken," but not "broken *off*."[13] This allows the allegory of the olive tree in vv. 17–24 to correspond to the language on either side of it: beforehand, in vv. 11–15, with the allegory of stumbling but not fallen, through the portrayal of enhanced

---

10. Drawing on Black, "Metaphor," esp. 275. Metaphor refers to a figure of speech (trope) that communicates a thing, idea, or action by substituting a word or expression that denotes a different thing, idea, or action, often a word from a visual image or sound, suggesting a shared quality between the two words or expressions that remains at an imaginary level. An allegory is the development of an extended metaphor.

11. In addition to repeating the accusation of presumption (ὑψηλὰ φρόνει) in v. 20, note also the idea that in v. 18 the wild branch did not support the root, but the root the branch.

12. Nanos, "'Broken Branches.'"

13. Ibid., discusses how Paul moves from describing the plight of some of the natural branches by changing the verb from ἐκκλάω (broken as in dislocated) in vv. 17–21 to ἐκκόπτω (broken *off*) in vv. 22–24, when he seeks to describe the state that will result for the wild olive. This logical conundrum develops when he turns by way of diatribe to attributing to the wild olive shoot the claim to have supplanted the broken branches and thus gained advantage over them in v. 19, to which Paul responds with an *a fortiori* argument describing the all-the-more-severe state that the wild shoot should fear if it does not desist.

results for the non-Jews when these Israelites regain their step rather than confirming the zero-sum thinking that their absence increased the opportunities for the audience, and by the explanation that Paul's own ministry to the nations is for Israel's restoration rather than a testament to their failure or replacement, along with the theme of continuity expressed in the allegories of v. 16. This message of continuity rather than termination remains the theme after the olive tree allegory as well, with the assertion that "all Israel will be restored" (vv. 25-27), because these Israelites, while presently "alienated for your sake," are "beloved for the sake of the fathers," for "the gifts and calling of God are irrevocable" (vv. 28-29).[14] The proof-text Paul weaves together in vv. 26-27 [58] from Isa 59:20-21 and 27:9 attests to a time when "the Deliverer . . . will remove ungodliness from Jacob," and because of the covenant relationship will "take away their sins." Note, not remove the ungodly, or take away the sinners, but cleanse and restore Israel after a time of discipline has accomplished God's design.[15] And Paul wraps up his argument in vv. 30-32 by arguing that the present lack of "persuadedness" (to join Paul in declaring the gospel to the nations) by these Jews, and thus their need for mercy, follows after but is intimately linked to the former lack of "persuadedness" (of God alone versus idols) by these non-Jews, which led to their need for mercy. Thus, now all are equally "joined together" in the need for God's mercy, in view of which Paul calls for mercy toward rather than judgment of each other.[16]

14. The NRSV translation "they are enemies of God" is most disconcerting, not least because "of God" is not attested in any manuscripts. The contrast is between two adjectives, "enemied [ἐχθροί]" (better: "alienated") and "beloved [αγαπητοί]," the first "for your sake," and the second "for the sake of the fathers." See Beck, "Translations of the New Testament for Our Time," esp. 204-6; Sievers, "'God's Gifts and Call Are irrevocable.'"

15. It is possible that Paul is referring to the removal of sins from the nations with the citation of Isa 27:9, which uses a pronoun here ("their sins"), and is stitched into the place where continued citation of Isa 59:21 would be expected to appear. He thus weaves together a proof-text that explains the intertwined positive destinies of Israel and the nations, with the removal of ungodliness from Jacob (Israel) covered by the citation of 59:20. The balance of 59:21, which Paul does not cite, describes the continued role of Israel, but perhaps Paul wants to turn to the effects of that role for the nations ("until when the fullness of the nations commences") through the introduction of 27:9 instead. In this sense, Paul may see the forgiveness of the sins of the nations—for which he has argued throughout the letter and in v. 25 in particular—prefigured in the covenant made with Israel, yet unexpectedly not transpiring before the complete removal of the ungodliness from all Israel ("that a callus temporarily has formed for Israel . . . and thus all Israel will be restored"), these multiple aspects being simultaneously at work.

16. I see no reason to translate ἀπείθεια and cognates in these verses as "disobedience," when the idea of failure to be persuaded ("not-being-persuadedness") of that which Paul believes they should be persuaded makes sense of the context, even if

In each of these cases, Paul seeks to connect inextricably the favor that these non-Jews have received through the good news message with the present suffering of disfavor, of discipline being experienced by Israel through the some (many) Israelites who are not (yet) declaring this message to the nations alongside of Paul. This stage, he argues just as forcefully, is temporary, yet unquestionably to be followed by their rescue, not destruction.[17] All of these developments are, according to Paul, bound up in a mysterious, interlocking scheme of God's design. Thus, things are not as they might otherwise seem, for the present anomalous stage is required before the promised harmonious conclusion can materialize.

[59] Many of the current translation choices undermine Paul's argument that Israel is presently suffering a *temporary* divided *stage* involving the remnant and the rest in a larger plan God has designed in order to begin the process of gathering members from the other nations into the people of God (alongside Israelites, but not as Israelites) through the gospel. Once this gathering from the nations begins, it will be followed by the restoration of the rest of these Israelites, and thus of all Israel—but these Israelites are by no means to be regarded as having *already lost their standing* within God's covenant with Israel.[18] The usual choices of "broken *off*" (vv. 17–21),

---

English does not provide an exact equivalent. Not being persuaded of a propositional claim and disobeying what one knows to be a propositional truth are not the same thing. I also propose that God "(closely) joined together" (i.e., "has drawn together," "integrated") everyone rather than that God "confined" or "imprisoned" everyone in this state in order to demonstrate the equal need of his mercy for everyone, Jew and non-Jew, makes more sense of his use of συγκλείω in v. 32 (cf. Euripides, *Bacch.* 1300; Plato, *Tim.* 76a; *Crat.* 117e; Isocrates, *Or.*, 12[*Panath.*].24; 15[*Amtid.*].68; Xenophon, *Cyr.* 7.1.33; Thucydides 4.35.1; 5.72.1; see *LSJ*, 1665 [iii–iv]).

17. In some Jewish traditions, that Israel has a favored status is actually exemplified by God's discipline delivered quickly, even harshly, in order to bring it ultimately to faithfulness instead of destruction (2 Macc 6:12–17; cf. Ps 94:12; Prov 3:11–12; Jer 30:11; Lam 3:31–33; Jdt 8:27; Wis 12:1–2, 26; *Pss. Sol.* 10.1; 13.7; 16.1–5).

18. In traditional approaches, the premise is that these Israelites have been removed from their covenant standing and thus, like non-Israelites, need to be "saved" in the sense of being outsiders brought back into the people of God. But Paul's argument assumes they are still the people of God, albeit in a state of discipline (variously named and described, including alternately as a result of God's initiative or in response to their unfaithfulness or unresponsiveness) that results in the need to be restored to good standing. The so-called two-covenant approaches react to the traditional notion, yet also work from within its framework to the degree that they propose these Israelites are "saved" by Torah (thereby granting the need to find a way to describe an avenue for salvation); at the same time, this same framework remains in place in the arguments from which critics of the two-covenant approach work, however much I might agree with some of their criticisms of the two-covenant paradigm (e.g., Hvalvik, "A 'Sonderweg' for Israel"; Donaldson, "Jewish Christianity, Israel's Stumbling and the Sonderweg Reading of Paul"; Zoccali, "'And so all Israel will be saved,'" esp. 297–303. But Israelites

"hardened" (vv. 7, 25), "enemies [of God]" (v. 28), and "disobedient" (vv. 30–32), all work against Paul's otherwise generous thesis of vicarious and temporary suffering on the part of some Israelites and thereby Israel, and thus the present need for the Christ-following non-Israelites to regard them with respect and compassion. Moreover, beginning with the "therefore" of 12:1 through the end of the letter, Paul's audience is instructed to behave graciously toward these Israelites.

[60] Translation alternatives exist in each case that perpetuate Paul's sympathetic (if patronizing) message, and the spirit of the metaphor of "stumbling" but "*not* fallen" (v. 11). These include "callused" in the sense of "protected" rather than "hardened," which this chapter specifically addresses, but also "broken" rather than "broken *off*" in vv. 17–21, "alienated" rather than "enemies"—especially the unwarranted "enemies *of God*"—in v. 28, and "not-persuadedness" rather than "disobedience" in vv. 30–32.[19] In addition, as will be discussed, the preliminary and temporary nature of the present state of some Israelites and thus Israel in Paul's argument can be highlighted by translating the prepositional phrase ἀπό μέρους in v. 25 as "temporarily," rather than as if referring to "part" of Israel, or the whole of Israel "partially," even though each of these aspects remains relevant.

---

do not need to be "saved" in a way that parallels the needs of non-Israelites; some need to be saved from their errors (i.e., in the sense of having sinful acts forgiven, or periods of discipline lifted), but not in the sense of having become non-members of the people of God. Paul appears to be working from the notion that Israel is in a covenant based on promises to the fathers, into which Torah was introduced later for Israel in order that Israelites might live rightly and declare God's words to the nations, so that they too could enter into the covenant with the fathers for the blessing of the nations. But the nations do not enter into the covenant with Israel as if becoming Israelites, and thus not into a relationship with Torah on the same terms as Israelites. It is thus one covenant with different aspects for Israelites and for those from the other nations who turn to Israel's God as the one God of all humankind (both/and, rather than either/or). See Campbell, *Paul and the Creation of Christian Identity*, 33–53, *passim*; Nanos, "Paul and the Jewish Tradition: The Ideology of the Shema."

19. To name but two other translation choices that perpetuate this disconnect, in vv. 11–12, wherein Paul denies these Israelites have fallen but asserts that they have merely stumbled or tripped, παραπτώματι is often translated "transgression" ("by their transgression"; NASB), although this obscures the metaphorical language at play here, and the idea the word carries in general of "misstep" (NRSV: "through their stumbling"), and the translation "fall" in the KJV and ASV reverses the denial that they have fallen. In v. 17, the NRSV expresses replacement theology with "and you, a wild olive shoot, were grafted *in their place*," when the Greek expresses co-participation: "but you, a wild olive [shoot], were being grafted *among them* [σὺ δὲ ἀγριέλαιος ὢν ἐνεκεντρίσθης ἐν αὐτοῖς]" (as in NASB, KJV).

3. THE METAPHORS AND MESSAGES OF 11:25-27

In vv. 25-26, at least three of the key terms, and the context of their usage, can be understood to draw on tree metaphors: πώρωσις (callus), πλήρωμα (fullness),[20] and σωθήσεται (salvation/restoration/rescue/return to health).[21] The texts from Isaiah that Paul cites are not only set in metaphorical and [61] allegorical contexts, but largely turn around images of plants and trees.[22] Just before Isa 27.9, which Paul cites in 11.27, stands Isa 27.6 (LXX): "they that are coming are the children of Jacob. Israel shall bud and blossom, and the world shall be filled with his fruit."[23]

We must be careful not to expect that Paul's use of metaphor around a tree or plant theme functions as another fully developed allegory, or require it to comport too closely with what he has developed in the previous allegory; even the allegory of the broken branches did not correspond well to the allegory of the stumbling but not fallen Israelites that preceded it.[24] The limitations of metaphor, and of Paul's employment thereof, are evident to the degree that the branches are ultimately presented to be in need of (the miracle of) re-grafting. Paul got tangled up in the web of his own

---

20. In the case of πλήρωμα, this is common plant terminology. Theophrastus used this language regularly, e.g., in *Caus. plant.* 3.15.3 (line 10) he writes πληροῖ for how the fluid in vines "fills" them when dressed. In *Caus. plant.* 1.13.9 (line 6), he describes how a tree harvested early can "fill up" (ἀναπληροῦνται) again and become pregnant. In *Caus. plant.* 1.2.5 (line 10), συμπληροῦν refers to "fill out" as in the space around the tree, while 1.13.3 (line 3) describes how trees after sprouting and fruit production in spring are "replenished" (ἀντιπληροῦσθαι) with food again (πάλιν). *Hist. plant.* 3.17.1 (line 11), describes a tree coming back from deterioration as "renewed" (ἐξαναπληροῦται); in 5.6.7, a root will "fill out" (ἐκπληρόω) the whole space.

Besides the general sense of a plant or any part of a plant "coming in" or "beginning" to grow or bud or blossom fully at some point, in terms of grafting, fullness is envisaged to come in/commence (εἰσέλθῃ) when a grafted branch begins to draw life from the root of the tree. Theoph., *Caus. plant.* 1.6.3, discusses how a graft "takes root" (ῥιζοῦτια) and "seals over" (ἐπισμαίνε), after also discussing how bark grows over the graft and encloses it. See also *Hist. plant.* 5.2.

21. Theophrastus uses σώζω to signify the "preserving" or "saving" or "restoring" of a plant or tree, or the various parts of them, like the roots, stem, or branches; see *Caus. plant.* 1.4.5 (line 8); 1.7.2 (line 7); 1.19.5 (line 7); 1.22.2 (line 8); 2.16.5 (line 1); 2.17.5 (line 12); 5.16.2; 5.18.4 (line 3).

22. Isaiah 59-61 are full of plant metaphors, as are Isaiah 27-28. The context of Isaiah 59 is God coming to the rescue of Israel when no one else does. The context of Isaiah 27 is the gathering of Israelites from the dispersion (vv. 12-13 announce the regathering).

23. Brenton (trans.), *The Septuagint Version of the Old Testament*; NRSV, based on the MT: "in days to come Jacob shall take root, Israel shall blossom and put forth shoots, and fill the whole world with fruit."

24. A central topic of discussion in Nanos, "'Broken Branches.'"

rhetorical weaving while seeking to communicate the *a fortiori* severity that awaited the wild olive if it would presumptuously suppose that it had replaced these Israelites in God's favor. In this same vein, Isaiah's use of and mixing of allegories in the context of the language Paul cites in vv. 26–27 should not be expected to work seamlessly or comprehensively in Paul's argument, although we should try to make sense of the message they are enlisted to support.

It is unclear here if Paul envisages "all Israel" to be all of the branches that are Israelites, or the whole tree. The latter view informs the conflation of "the church is Israel" positions. That he does not name the tree or trunk or boughs but only branches may itself be instructive: creating a comprehensive picture of Israel or the church is not the point of the allegory. Rather, his goal is to explain the unusual and precarious place of the Christ-following non-Jews among the Israelites, so that they will humbly understand their own role is by God's design to live on behalf of all Israel's restoration, not to (mis)judge those Israelites in a temporary state of suffering. In vv. 25–26a, the Israelites are still identifiable, just as are the gentiles, so that the "all Israel" remains distinguishable from the implied "all the members of the nations,"[25] who are somehow an indication of the timing of this process. They are beneficiaries of the vicarious suffering of these Israelites, however difficult that may be to comprehend.

In other words, these groups, Israel and the nations, represent entities distinguishable from each other, different branches, while the implied tree is [62] a broader category into which they can both be incorporated, become one, such as the people of God, or the church, which will consist of "all Israel" and "all the other nations" too. In vv. 25–26, Paul discloses specifically the unexpected way that the "restoration" of "all Israel" is taking place ("and in this way"), which includes a temporary injury to, but also protection of, some Israelites and thus Israel ("a callus has formed temporarily for Israel"), a rescue involving discipline and forgiveness foretold in Isaiah, which Paul cites as proof, as well as the dawning of the "fullness" of the nations ("until when the fullness of the nations begins").

---

25. That this distinction remains important to Paul is a central thesis of all of William S. Campbell's work, as well as the work of Kathy Ehrensperger, a point with which I heartily agree.

3.1 That a callus ... has developed for Israel (ὅτι πώπωσις ... τῷ Ἰσραὴλ γέγονεν)

Paul represents the current state of Israel or of some Israelites (some natural branches) as that of having become πώρωσις (for the sake of simplicity, we will postpone translating ἀπὸ μέρους until after the other elements have been discussed). The problem with translating this state in terms of "hardened" has been discussed, and to this can be added the problem that the negative value judgment in the language of hardening in English would not contribute to communicating a mystery calculated to confront conceit toward these Jews from the non-Jews Paul addresses—which is the point of this disclosure.

Although Theophrastus (c. 370–285 BCE), who wrote two extensive treatments of plants, does not appear to use πωρόω, he discusses developments in plants in similar terms when writing of a growth or callus or knot (ὄζος, knot, corresponding to the eye of a vine, scion/offshoot from which a branch or leaf springs, but also used for unproductive knots), and he also refers to a "joint" [γόνυ] in olive trees that forms where a cut or injury has occurred (*Caus. plant.* 1.6.3; *Hist. plant.* 1.8.1–4;[26] 3.7.1; 5.2; see also Columella, *Rust.* 4.24.4–6). In trees and plants, it is derived from the sap (Theoph., *Caus. plant.* 5.16.4). This process closes the wound to protect the tree (*Caus. plant.* 3.7.5–12).[27] With fresh growth over the callused area, the callus becomes a knot within the trunk or branches. In modern plant terminology, that process is referred to explicitly as the forming of a callus.

---

26. Knotting, "as though one thing were made thereby into two and a fresh growing point produced, the cause being mutilation [πήρωσιν] or some other such reason ..." (1.8.4).

27. Theoph., *Caus. plant.* 5.16.4, observes that olive trees endure splitting because they quickly close their wounds with sap (which makes them hard to split). He says the olive tree is protected by a coating/bark (φολιός) that seals up/protects (ἀποστέγω) the piece cut from it to preserve/guard (τηρέω) its life (1.4.5). And for vines, he writes of a sap/juice (ὀπός)-like "tear of gum" or "exudation" (δάκρυοω) that collects at the cut, which must run off so the scion can be dry when the graft is made (1.6.8; 6.11.16).

"Callused," Not "Hardened" 165

[63] If Paul meant "callus," this need not carry the negative valence that "harden" does.[28] Instead, it would offer a more positive and arguably more salient choice that has to do with the healing and protecting process that takes place after an injury has occurred, such as after a branch has been broken or broken off.[29] The translation "that a callus *has happened* to Israel" expresses the perfect active verb γέγονεν ("has become") here. It allows the dative "to" or "for Israel" to be expressed. If discussing a callus in English,

---

28. Theophrastus uses σκληρός and cognates to describe the hard state of plants and trees and their various components, or parts derived from them, like wood (*Hist. plant.* 5.3.1).

29. Although interpreters do not develop this language in metaphorical terms here, or translate πώρωσις as callus, when the translation callus is discussed the negative aspects have generally been emphasized, e.g., that they are hardened and insensitive areas; cf. Robinson, *Ephesians*, 264.

we would express this as "has developed" or "has formed": "that a callus has developed/formed for Israel."[30] Either way, this also communicates the idea that the callus "has happened" for the benefit of some Israelites or Israel. (Of course, even the translation "callus" contains a value judgment that is at the very least patronizing, for Paul believes that his fellow Jews not joining him in declaring Christ to the nations have suffered a wound that elicits the need for this protective measure; but at the same time his point is that this is a part of the way God is working, using them, so that these Israelites are still a part of the way God is announcing the message to the nations.)

That Paul was describing a protective and healing callus rather than the idea of hardness as in stubborn, insensitive, or obdurate, is enhanced by attending to the manuscript variants for πώρωσις. Πωρόω and πήρωσις are regular variants for πωρόω and πώρωσις in the NT and other manuscripts. In their *TDNT* essay on the topic, the Schmidts conclude that switching between these terms was so common that it is not possible to determine the original, "the most one may deduce from it is that there was no longer any awareness of the difference in meaning between the two stems πωρ- and πηρ-."[31]

Although πήρωσις is not listed as a variant among Greek manuscripts for Rom 11:25,[32] Nestle-Aland (25th edition) does list the Latin variant *caecitus* (blindness/dullness) [64] in latt,[33] and syP also uses "blindness/dullness" (תוריוע),[34] which may indicate that these scribes worked from a Greek manuscript with πώρωσις, or that the two were used interchangeably. J. A. Robinson lists the translation choices in Latin as *obtusio* (dull/blunt/obtuse/blind) for Ambrosiaster and Hilary, and *caecitas* (obscure/blind) for

30. Louw and Nida, *Lexicon*, 13.80; 13.107.

31. Schmidt and Schmidt, *TDNT* 5.1027-28; cf. Robinson, *Ephesians*, 264-74. Theophrastus used πηρόω and πήρωσις, and cognates, to refer to the process of maiming or injuring trees or parts of trees, to their being thereafter maimed, wounded, harmed, injured, mutilated, disabled, or incapacitated (*Hist. plant.* 1.8.4; 2.4.3; 4.14.8; *Caus. plant.* 1.5.5). The variant πυρ- is attested for *Hist. plant.* 1.8.4 in U M Mon. γρ; Amigues (ed., trans.), *Théophraste. Recherches sur les Plantes*, 24.

32. Cf. Swanson (ed.), *New Testament Greek Manuscripts*, 181.

33. *Caecitās* and cognates not only refer to dullness/dimness of judgment, or making/being obscure, but also, interestingly, are used to refer to the removal of the eyes or buds from plants (Glare, *Oxford Latin Dictionary*).

34. Schmidt and Schmidt, *TDNT* 5.1027. I am grateful to D. Stramara for help with the Syriac variant for 11:25, which uses a verb and also introduces the heart (also added to v. 7). Lamsa's translation of the clause in v. 25 does not reflect the verbal change; it reads: "for blindness of heart has to some degree befallen Israel" (Lamsa, *Holy Bible from the Ancient Eastern Text*, 1132. Lamsa translates the verbal usage in v. 7 in a way that brings out the alternative aspect of dullness or darkness: "were dulled in their minds" (p. 1131; see also Payne Smith, *A Compendious Syriac Dictionary*, 407).

clar, vg, Ambrosiaster, and Augustine.³⁵ This variant tradition apparently accounts for Luther's German translation choice of "blindness" (*Blindheit*).³⁶ Also, for the earlier use of the verb ἐπωρώθησαν in v. 7, Swanson lists the variant ἐπωρώθησαν in the fifth-century uncial C.³⁷ Swanson also provides many Greek variants with an omicron rather than omega for the second letter, and a double ρρ in some cases, that is, with πόρωσις (including the case of P46) and πόρρωσις in v. 25, and ἐπορώθησαν, ἐπορρώθησαν, and ἐπορρόθησαν in v. 7.³⁸ These anomalies raise an interesting question when combined with the many cases of manuscript variation discussed in other NT texts by the Schmidts: why the consistent inconsistency in these vowels?

In the case of the switching between the omicron and omega in the second-letter position, the specialists surmise that this is due to the similar "o" sound of these vowels in πώρωσις and πόρωσις. But it may be that this anomaly bears witness to the earlier usage of πήρωσις in manuscripts no longer available to us. There is some reason to suppose that Paul may have been using cognates of πήρωσις, especially in 11:7, based on the kinds of disabilities that are described in the passages he cites from Isa 29:10 combined with some turns of phrase from Deut 29:3 in v. 8, and Ps 69:22–23 (LXX 68:22–23) in vv. 9–10, although neither πώρωσις nor πήρωσις are used in these texts.³⁹

Πήρωσις and πηρόω can denote being "wounded," "maimed," or "impaired" in some way, or being "blinded" (although cognates of τυφλός are used specifically for blindness, rather than merely obscured vision or generally damaged organs, including eyes). The only place where πωρόω is found [65] in the Septuagint, Job 17:7 (πεπώρωνται γὰρ ἀπὸ ὀργῆς οἱ ὀφθαλμοί μου), bears witness to a similar manuscript variation between πωρόω and πηρόω. This case refers to the eyes being disabled, but the eyes are not being callused; rather, vision is being impaired, as the manuscript variants from Codex Sinaiticus and Alexandrinus, among others, indicate by using πεπήρωνται, and in other manuscripts by the use of ἠμαυρωθησαν (μαυρόω: to darken, dim, make obscure).⁴⁰ The *Test. Levi* 13.7 uses πήρωσις in combination with τύφλωσις: εἰ μὴ τύφλωσις ἀσεβείας καὶ πήρωσις ἁμαρτίας;

---

35. Robinson, *Ephesians*, 267–69.
36. Schmidt and Schmidt, *TDNT* 5.1023, 1027.
37. Swanson, *New Testament Greek Manuscripts*, 170.
38. Ibid., 170, 181.
39. Paul did not include the first part of Deut 29:3, which refers to the heart, in his citation.
40. Rahlfs (ed.), *Septuaginta*, 299, lists AS^(s+); Robinson, *Ephesians*, 265, lists ℵ^(c a) A, and refers to the cases of ἠμαυρωθησαν.

"except the *blindness* of impiety and the *impairment* of sin."[41] This may well be a play on the synonymous usage of πήρωσις for effect; that is, it is a disability, an injury that inhibits proper function similar to what blindness (or better, "nearsightedness," since applied to impiety here) represents in terms of vision. The meaning "blindness of sin" misses the move between these two descriptive choices; the distinction as well as overlap between being impaired in the eyes and being similarly incapacitated elsewhere is at play.

Cognates of πήρωσις are found regularly in Philo (50+ times), but πώρωσις does not appear to be used at all.[42] Πήρωσις and cognates are translated throughout as impaired, disabled, or deprived, and refer to many different parts of the body (*Spec. Laws* 1.341). When πήρωσις is used with reference to the eyes or vision it describes a more general disability that can include the specific case of τυφλός (e.g., *Heir* 76; *Moses* 1.124; *Virtues* 7). In *Alleg. Interp.* 3.91, impaired is combined with blinded to describe the inferiority of recollection to memory (πηρόν καὶ τυφλόν πρᾶγμα); they are similar in valence here, but different qualities (cf. 3.231).[43] In *Flight* 121, Lot's wife's looking back is described as ἐπηρώθησαν, which would not refer to being blind exactly, but to being near-sighted. *Good Person* 55 refers to the failure to perceive the depths of the soul's suffering due to impaired reason (λογισμοῦ πήρωσιν; cf. *Providence* 2.20 [διάνοιαν]). This brings up the case of 2 Cor 3:14, where Paul states that "their thoughts (in the sense of what they perceived) [τὰ νοήματα αὐτῶν] were callused [ἐπωρώθη]," which seems to indicate that they were "obstructed." This is said to correspond to a "veil [κάλυμμα] laid over their hearts" in v. 15. The dynamic turns around perception or seeing, and this would suggest πήρωσις rather than πώρωσις, [66] or that πώρωσις can have a sense not so much of hardening, which does not describe sight or perception, but of covering up or obstructing the view of sight, understanding, perception, or thoughts; hence, covered by a callus. Moreover, Robinson shows that the early translators and commentators understood this in the sense of obstructed or blinded, and he concludes

---

41. Note that the context is the gaining of wisdom in the fear of God by the wise, which can protect them against all manner of loss, and cannot be taken away from them except when wisdom is coupled with impiety or sin.

42. No entries for πώρωσις as a variant are listed in Borgen, Fuglseth, and Skarsten (eds), *The Philo Index*.

43. In *Cherubim* 58, a mind that is blind (τυγλὸς) is compared and contrasted to being deprived (πηρωθέντα) of the external sight by the eyes. *Sacr.* 69, does refer to "the eyes/vision of the soul being maimed [τὰ ψυχῆς ὄμματα πεπηρωμένος]" (cf. *Worse* 22; *Posterity* 8; *Unchangeable* 93; *Spec. Laws* 3.6; *Contempl. Life* 10).

that this application of πώρωσις for the faculty of understanding is unparalleled if translated hardened.[44]

Likewise, πώρωσις is not used by Josephus, but he does use cognates of πήρωσις several times.[45] In *Ant.* 1.267, πήρωσις refers to Isaac's deficient eyesight when addressing Esau; in Gen 27:1, his eyes are described as "dim" or "dull" (ἀμβλύνω), but Isaac is not exactly blind. The general sense of maiming of any part of a person is evident in *Ant.* 4.280, when discussing the *Lex talionis* (Exod 21:24; Lev 24:19), and *War* 5.228, where it refers to any bodily defect on a priest, while in *Ag. Ap.* 2.15, πεπηρωμένους is used for those who have been maimed in contrast to the blind (τυφλούς) and leprous who came out of Egypt.

These cases suggest that interpreters unnecessarily refer to *blindness* rather than to *impairment* in a more general sense, for *dim* sight bespeaks impaired vision, lack of clarity, sometimes lack of far-sightedness as in myopic, but not exactly blindness.[46]

The passages Paul cites in Rom 11:8–10 do not refer simply to the eyes—although "eyes" provides the *gezerah shawah* linking his prooftexts—but they also refer to sluggish spirits, ears that do not hear, and backs that are bent, in addition to describing a temporary state of obscured vision rather than a permanent state indicated by blindness. Since πηρόω would make sense of this state if translated "injured" or "wounded" or "disabled," it may be suggested that Paul probably meant if not used πηρόω rather than πωρόω in v. 7 (cf. Philo, *Flight* 123; *Spec. Laws* 1.117). Since this cannot be proven, it can at least be suggested that the better translation of πωρόω here is in the sense of a temporary state likened to a protective callus that forms after an injury, rather than to a hardening in the sense of insensitivity, or stubbornness, or related to the heart, or alternatively, to blindness or obtuseness.

In the case of 11:25, the likelihood of πήρωσις originally written or intended rather than πώρωσις is neither as easy to infer, nor is it preferable. The proof-texts from Isa 59:20–21 and 27:9 do not suggest impairment any more than they suggest hardening; however, their metaphorical use of [67] plant language throughout supports the notion of callusing. Assuming that Paul

---

44. Robinson, *Ephesians*, pp. 265, 267; cf. Harris, *Second Epistle to the Corinthians*, 301: "the Israelites of Moses' day had calloused hearts that were insensitive to spiritual stimuli."

45. No variants or cases of πώρησις are listed in Rengstorf (ed.), *Complete Concordance to Flavius Josephus*.

46. Jerome's translation of Job 17:7 is *"obscurati"* (obscured, darkened) from the Hexaplar, and *"caligauit"* (misty, darkened) from the Hebrew (Robinson, *Ephesians*, 265, n. 1), so also not "blinded" per se, but "obscured."

was using this language metaphorically, it does follow that if there is a callus, there was an injury in need of such protection at the point of the wound until healed (i.e., saved, rescued, or restored). If Paul meant "that an injury (or a wound) has happened to/for Israel," the focus would be on the process of divine discipline, of the sustaining of an injury that is evident presently; it is not an indication of destruction, but of a temporary stage that makes necessary the future rescuing of the plant. If he meant "that a callus has developed for Israel," the focus would be on the process of being divinely *protected* after an injury has occurred, but all the more emphasizing that this development highlights a temporary stage in order to facilitate a healthy outcome; indeed, full recuperation according to God's design. That is consistent with the language of the texts from Isaiah in their contexts.

This association between the variant "injury/wound/impairment" and the translation suggestion "callus" works together; both keep the metaphorical quality of the language in view in a way that the usual translations "hard," "stubborn," "obdurate," "insensitive," "obtuse," and "blind" do not communicate, even, ironically, "obstruct."[47] Indeed, the suggested translations provide a positive and sympathetic instead of a judgmental—dare I suggest "insensitive"—valence to the images evoked.

3.2 The Issue of Translating ἀπὸ μέρους

Another translation and interpretation issue arises with Paul's usage of ἀπό μέρους in v. 25. As already discussed, this is usually translated either to refer to "part" of Israel, or Israel "partially." The latter can imply that it refers to all Israelites, but it need not, for it can refer to Israel in general because of the state of some Israelites, and thus in effect visualize the same idea as "part of Israel" translations (if "part" of the branches in a tree are callused or injured, "part" of the tree can also be described as callused or injured, or the tree "in part," or "partially," although this would still not indicate that all the branches are callused or hardened).[48] While the placement of the

---

47. I am thus in agreement with Robinson's conclusion that πώρωσις is not best translated "hardened," but in disagreement that it should be rendered "blinded," for it is not indicating that kind of permanent and completely damaged state, but an injury if pertaining to the eyes would better be translated in terms of obstructed vision, unable to see clearly, "partially blinded," "obstructed," "obscured," "blocked," "clouded," "darkened," "dimmed."

48. Jewett, *Romans*, 699–700, argues against taking this to apply to Israel as a whole, which was the position I maintained in *Mystery of Romans*, 263–64; Nanos, "'Broken Branches,'" but I now recognize how it could apply to Israel without meaning it applies to all Israelites, a distinction that keeping the tree metaphor in view in vv. 25–27 helps

prepositional phrase after "callus" could indicate a partial callus, that Paul [68] seeks to describe a partial callus rather than a full callus seems unlikely: a callus forms, or does not.[49] There are several other alternatives to explore.

Although rarely observed, this prepositional phrase can be translated "sort of,"[50] thereby signaling the metaphorical limitations of the image invoked: "that a callus, sort of, has happened to Israel . . . ."

The translation, ". . . in part," can be maintained, and refers to a process which "in part" consists of what is happening *preliminarily* in the service of a larger purpose or later goal; hence, *part of the reason* that a callus has formed for Israel is *because of the function it serves* until the fullness of the nations commences: "that a callus, in part (for a particular purpose), has formed for Israel, until . . . ." In addition to "in part," this sense can be communicated if translated "somewhat" or "to some degree";[51] that is, this has happened specifically in the service of the next development, or particularly until the next stage of the process has been reached. The translation could read, "that a callus, *to some degree*, has formed for Israel, until . . . ."

Another option arises from the fact that Paul seeks to describe a *temporary* state in the next clause, which is framed in time-sequential terms as "until . . . begins."[52] A translation capturing the partial time element would be true to the adverbial aspect normally indicated when this phrase is used, which some have argued is the grammatically proper way to read ἀπό μέρους here, so that this "has happened partially" to Israel.[53] As already

---

to visualize.

49. One could discuss specific stages in the process of callus development, but this does not appear to be the topic.

50. Stendahl, *Final Account*, 38.

51. Thayer, *Greek-English Lexicon*, 401. Chrysostom translated this as "in part," and the grammatical example he provides from 2 Cor 2:5 indicates a development partially applied to a group, but he nevertheless interprets it to indicate part of Israel: "But his meaning is nearly this, and he had said it before, that the unbelief is not universal, but only 'in part' . . . it is not the whole people . . ." ("Homily 19").

52. Sanday and Headlam, *Romans*, 335, note that the point is to indicate "that it is only temporary and that the limitation in time is 'until . . . .'"

53. Cranfield, *Epistle to the Romans*, 2.575, insists that it is adverbial, yet he concludes that it is "not all Jews" who are thereby indicated, which is however the same conclusion one would reach from taking this to be adjectival; moreover, an adverbial usage can indicate that it has happened partially to Israel, i.e., to all Jews, which Cranfield argues against. Although C. K. Barrett recognizes the phrase could be adverbial, he decides that it is used adjectivally here, and concludes, like Cranfield, ironically, that it is "*partial* in the sense that it was only a part (though the larger part) of Israel that was hardened" (*Epistle to the Romans*, 206). Dunn, *Romans 9–16*, 691, includes time, purpose, and people: "the blindness is partial as both temporary and as afflicting what Paul hopes will in the end be a relatively small proportion of his people . . . the

noted, when it [69] is recognized that Paul is dealing in plant metaphors, and something that happens to part of the tree also affects the whole tree partially as well, there is no reason to object to this translation on the basis that it is only some Israelites whom Paul appears to be describing as callused; however, there is another way to construe the message of this prepositional phrase that I have not seen explored.

One can translate ἀπό μέρους to highlight the time element of what is happening: it "has happened *for a while.*" Louw and Nida discuss how ἀπό μέρους can refer "to a relatively short period of time, with emphasis upon the temporary nature of the event or state—not long, temporary, for a little while, for a while."[54] In Rom 15:24, Paul writes of the fact that he will stay in Rome "for a while [ἀπό μέρους]" before he heads off to Spain. Thus, the phrase can be translated, "that a callus has formed for Israel *for a while*, until . . . begins," or, "that a *temporary* callus has formed for Israel, until . . . begins," or, "that a callus has formed for Israel *temporarily*, until . . . begins," or, in keeping with Paul's word order, "that a callus *temporarily* has formed for Israel."[55] These choices are fully compatible with the focus on a part of a process discussed immediately above, "for a while" emphasizes the time element over the developmental aspect. Both aspects are expressed by the adjective "temporary," or the adverb, "temporarily."

One of the strengths of developing the temporary time element in the translation is that it keeps the focus on Paul communicating a stage in a development that will come to a conclusion that may not be apparent to his audience at the time, which is the thrust of his argument throughout the larger sentence as well as the chapter overall. Another benefit is that it parallels the message of the proof-text Paul creates in vv. 26–27 to substantiate the mystery he seeks to disclose, which does not refer to part of Israel or Israel partially, but to a temporary stage in Israel's history, according to God's promise, when it will be delivered from ungodliness and sins. In the argument following these citations from Isaiah, Paul explains that while

---

harshness . . . against Israel is ameliorated by the setting of a time limit . . . is limited to a specific purpose and period." Fitzmyer, *Romans*, 621, observes that it is only part of Israel that is hardened, but includes that this hardening is "also temporary." Although Jewett argues against adverbial application to indicate hardening has happened partially to Israel as a whole, and against it meaning that the hardening itself is partial, but rather that it signifies that only part of Israel is experiencing this, he also implicitly recognizes the temporariness of this stage when he discusses the next phrase, for he understands "Israel's obtuseness lasting until the fulfilment of the predestined plan for Gentile conversion" (*Romans*, 700).

54. *Lexicon*, 67.109.

55. This time-element-oriented alternative works just as well if "injury" was indicated instead of "callus."

some Israelites are presently alienated, they are nevertheless beloved, and that at the end of this period they will be persuaded of Paul's message and join together with those from the rest of the nations similarly persuaded, Israel and the other nations together glorifying God for the receipt of mercy. I thus propose that Paul's effort to disclose this mystery as the present state of things *for a while*, as a *partial* and *preliminary* stage in a larger process that includes several stages leading to a previously unforeseen outcome, is visualized most usefully by the translation "temporarily."

3.3 PAUL'S MESSAGE

[70] Paul metaphorically describes an anomalous development in Rome that he does not want to be misunderstood. In Paul's view, his audience is witnessing a time when Israelites are divided in their response to the gospel message and thus some—a select few, such as Paul sees himself—are taking up the responsibility to proclaim this news to the nations, while others—indeed, the majority—are not.[56] This development is temporary, and Israel will be preserved throughout it. In due time, when the messengers such as Paul have turned fully to bringing this message to the nations; "in this way" or "then," those of his fellow Israelites who have not recognized *yet* that the age to come time has arrived—that it was thus time for bringing the message of good to those of the nations who will turn to the worship of the one God of Israel as the only God of all humankind (when "the fullness of the nations should commence")—will join him in this task. It has always been Israel's special privilege to bring the "words of God" to the nations (cf. 3:2); from Paul's vantage point, that time has arrived.

The purpose of describing this stage is to communicate a mystery to his non-Israelite audience about which they lack a proper understanding, for the Roman communities addressed have not experienced the way that Paul's ministry to the nations unfolds specifically in the context of his ministry to his fellow Israelites, and thus they fail to perceive how their destinies are inextricably combined. He cannot get to Rome yet, so he must write to explain that things are not as they may myopically appear to them to be: these members of Israel are not God's enemies, or theirs, but rather are suffering vicariously on the audience's behalf, however counterintuitive that may seem. "Therefore," in the chapters that follow (12–16), Paul instructs these non-Jews to regard these fellow members of Abraham's family with compassion instead of judgmentalism, and to seek to support them through

---

56. I have described this interpretation of Paul's message and ministry in detail in *Mystery of Romans*, 239–88.

this vulnerable time instead of insensitively dismissing them and their opinions, even though they do not share affiliation in Christ-faithfulness. They are to live righteously, which includes the demonstration of respect for Israelite covenant norms, for thereby they will avoid giving that push that might cause those stumbling to completely fall. In due time, upon Paul's arrival in Rome, and thus after the Jews there have the opportunity to witness Paul's success in bringing these members of the nations from idolatry and sin to the one God and righteousness through faithfulness to God in Christ, Paul predicts that his fellow Israelites will join him in turning fully to proclaim to the nations this message of the dawning of the long-awaited age of shalom. In other words, all Israel will be restored to her special task of proclaiming God's words of good news for and to the nations.[57]

4. CONCLUDING TRANSLATION OF ROMANS 11:7, 25-26

[71] The translation and interpretation of the aorist passive form πωρόω in 11:7 as "the rest *were callused*," is not as well suited to the context as would be "the rest *were wounded/disabled*," which implies that if πωρόω is original it could already be used in the direction of πηρόω. The allegory with broken branches and thus the protective need for a callus has not been introduced by v. 7; therefore, the reader is not prepared to infer the metaphorical quality of forming a protective callus, at least on the first reading. The message communicated in the proof-texts from Isaiah and the Psalms that Paul provides in vv. 8–10 speaks of a *temporary* period of time when God inflicts on some people spirits that are not alert (i.e., that slumber), eyes that do not see, ears that do not hear, and backs that are bent, in other words, a time of disability (not unlike the disabling he wants his audience to avoid allowing to develop among themselves through arrogant indifference to the plight of these Israelites!). In English, "the rest *were hardened*" does not successfully communicate temporariness; likewise, neither does "blinded." The negative valence of these choices does not signal that Paul is driving toward a favorable conclusion highlighting the eventual restoration of these Israelites. Furthermore, it fails to convey the generous spirit that one might expect to accompany Paul's earnest plea for his audience to live

---

57. I discuss the implications of this interpretation, and thus that history did not unfold as I understand Paul to have imagined that it would, as well as the hermeneutical opportunities that nevertheless arise from Paul's argument and doxology in vv. 33–36, in Nanos, "Challenging the Limits that Continue to Define Paul's Perspective on Jews and Judaism." Notably, this essay was developed in dialogue with the views William S. Campbell expressed in "Divergent Images of Paul and His Mission."

graciously toward these Israelites during this stage in God's design, just as these members from the other nations stand only because of the grace they have received and embraced.

The choice of the noun πώρωσις in 11:25, however, is warranted contextually, and can carry a positive meaning when translated metaphorically as "callus." Its potential for communicating in generous terms is enhanced when this language is understood to allude to the olive tree allegory it follows, combined with the metaphorical turns of phrase throughout vv. 25–27, which employ tree metaphors of "fullness" and "restoration," and reflect the metaphorical context of the passages in Isaiah from which Paul quotes.

When approached in metaphorical plant terms, the translation "callus" need not be understood in the sense of hardness or blindness, or be interpreted to signify insensitivity, or obduracy, or stubbornness toward God. Rather, the development of a callus envisages a protected state after the sustaining of an injury, and is thus intimately related to πήρωσις, the disability itself. The forming of a callus is a positive development undertaken by the tree to sustain the health of the injured part as well as the health of the overall plant, which is naturally affected by an injury to any part of it. Thus, [72] Paul may well be reaching back to the language introduced in vv. 7–10, but moving now to the next stage in the process, that of the *protected state* of the wounded part of Israel—until the final healing can be completed. The larger clause as well as the suggested translation of ἀπό μέρους as "temporarily" can emphasize the preliminary stage of protecting the injured area "until" the beginning of the next phase, when the grafted wild branch representing the nations is introduced, which must take hold "fully" to succeed, i.e., "come in" or "commence." That requires a healthy tree able to provide nourishment in a time of stress, if not yet a tree in which all of the natural branches have been restored to full health.

I therefore propose a translation that retains the character of metaphor drawing on an image of a tree following damage, such as would be the case for some broken branches in the allegory it follows: *that a callus temporarily has formed for (to protect) Israel*. This allegory also included the introduction of a wild shoot in need of recognizing its need "to take proper root" after being grafted among these branches, which includes its place among both the healthy ones and those presently undergoing the process of becoming callused to sustain life in their damaged condition. The tree Paul envisions includes not only all Israel, but also members from all of the nations alongside of the children of Jacob, all of God's created order coming into harmony, however different, as one people of God (cf. 15:5–13).

Hence, I suggest a translation of vv. 25-26 (with expanded explanations) in this direction [Note: see now the updated translation in the Appendix to this volume]:

> (25) **For I do not want you to be unperceptive regarding this mystery** (of the unexpected interdependence of the promised future for all Israelites with the beginning of the successful inclusion of those from the other nations among the people of God), **brothers and sisters, so that you would not be mindful (only) for yourselves** (as members from the other nations experiencing grace, and not graciously concerned about the welfare of those Israelites who do not share your convictions about the gospel), *that a callus temporarily has formed for Israel*, (to protect Israel) **until (the time) when the fullness of the nations should commence** (the successful introduction of a grafted shoot representing the nations, or the blossoming of that grafted shoot, representing when Paul turns fully to declaring the gospel to the nations following the divided response it receives when first proclaimed to his fellow Israelites), (26) **and in this way (or: and then)**[58] **all Israel will be restored** (that is, following the beginning of the positive response by some from the nations, witnessed by their turning from idolatry and sin to the one God and righteousness, Israel will be restored to full health instead of its divided state, for the production of abundant fruit from among the nations in response to Paul's declaration of the message to them triggers a process by which those Israelites not yet persuaded of the gospel will recognize what time it is, the awaited time to join Paul in proclaiming the good news to the rest of the nations), **just as it was written** (i.e., promised) . . . .

The suggested literal translation is:

> (25) **For I do not want you to be unperceptive regarding this mystery, brothers and sisters, so that you would not be mindful (only) for yourselves,** *that a callus temporarily has formed for Israel,* **until (the time) when the fullness of the nations should commence, (26) and in this way (or: and then) all Israel will be restored [or: made safe], just as it was written** . . . .

---

58. The issue of whether Paul's usage is modal ("in this way") or temporal ("then") cannot be resolved lexically. The interpreter must choose based on other contextual elements, the interpretation of which are of course also a matter of dispute. P. W. van der Horst, "'Only Then Will All Israel Be Saved,'" has made the case for the temporal, noting that the two options are not mutually exclusive (524), although the prevailing opinion is toward the modal, from which I argued in *Mystery of Romans* (cf. Jewett, *Romans*, 701); either one of these can express the interpretation proposed herein.

BIBLIOGRAPHY

Amigues, Suzanne, ed. and trans. *Théophraste. Recherches sur les Plantes. Tome I. Livres I–III*. Paris: Les Belles Lettres, 1988.
Barrett, C. K. *The Epistle to the Romans*. Rev. ed. Peabody, MA: Hendrickson, 1991.
Beck, Norman. "Translations of the New Testament for Our Time." In *Seeing Judaism Anew: Christianity's Sacred Obligation*, edited by Mary C. Boys, C. Lanham, et al., 200–210. Lanham, MD: Rowman and Littlefield, 2005.
Black, Max. "Metaphor." *Proceedings of the Aristotelian Society for the Systematic Study of Philosophy* 55 (1954) 273–94.
Borgen, Peder, Kåre Fuglseth and Roald Skarsten, eds. *The Philo Index: A Complete Greek Word Index to the Writings of Philo of Alexandria*. Leiden: Brill, 2000.
Brenton, Lancelot Charles Lee, trans. *The Septuagint Version of the Old Testament, with an English Translation; and with Various Readings and Critical Notes*. Grand Rapids: Zondervan, 1972.
Campbell, William S. "Divergent Images of Paul and His Mission." In *Reading Israel in Romans*, edited by Cristina Grenholm and Daniel Patte, 187–211. Harrisburg, PA: Trinity, 2000.
———. *Paul and the Creation of Christian Identity*. London: T. & T. Clark, 2006.
Celsus. *De Medicina. Aretaeus* Translated by W. G. Spencer. 1935. Reprint. Cambridge: Harvard University Press, 1971.
Chrysostom, John. "Homily 19." In *Homilies of St. John Chrysostom on the Epistle of St. Paul the Apostle to the Romans*, translated by J. B. Morris. Oxford: Parker, 1848.
Cranfield, C. E. B. *A Critical and Exegetical Commentary on the Epistle to the Romans*. 2 vols. Edinburgh: T. & T. Clark, 1975.
Donaldson, Terrance L. "Jewish Christianity, Israel's Stumbling and the Sonderweg Reading of Paul." *Journal for the Study of the New Testament* 29.1 (2006) 27–54.
Dunn, James D. G. *Romans 9–16*. WBC 38b. Dallas: Word, 1988.
Fitzmyer, Joseph A. *Romans: A New Translation with Introduction and Commentary*. New York: Doubleday, 1993.
Glare, P. G. W. *Oxford Latin Dictionary*. Oxford: Oxford University Press, 1996.
Harris, Murray J. *The Second Epistle to the Corinthians: A Commentary on the Greek Text*. NIGTC. Grand Rapids: Eerdmans, 2005.
Hibbard, James Todd. *Intertextuality in Isaiah 24–27: The Reuse and Evocation of Earlier Texts and Traditions*. Tübingen: Mohr Siebeck, 2006.
Hvalvik, Reidar. "A 'Sonderweg' for Israel: A Critical Examination of a Current Interpretation of Romans 11.25–27." *Journal for the Study of the New Testament* 38 (1990) 87–107.
Jewett, Robert K. *Romans*. Hermeneia. Minneapolis: Fortress, 2006.
Lamsa, George M. *Holy Bible from the Ancient Eastern Text: George M. Lamsa's Translations from the Aramaic of the Peshitta*. San Francisco: Harper & Row, 1968.
Nanos, Mark D. "'Broken Branches': A Pauline Metaphor Gone Awry? (Romans 11:11–36)." In *Between Gospel and Election: Explorations in the Interpretation of Romans 9–11*, edited by Florian Wilk and J. Ross Wagner, 339–76. Tübingen: Mohr Siebeck, 2010. (See chapter 6 in this volume of collected essays.)
———. "Challenging the Limits that Continue to Define Paul's Perspective on Jews and Judaism." In *Reading Israel in Romans*, edited by Cristina Grenholm and

Daniel Patte, 217–29. Harrisburg, PA: Trinity, 2000. (See chapter 11 in this volume of collected essays.)

———. *The Mystery of Romans: The Jewish Context of Paul's Letter.* Minneapolis: Fortress, 1996.

———. "Paul and the Jewish Tradition: The Ideology of the Shema." In *Celebrating Paul: Festschrift in Honor of Joseph A. Fitzmyer and Jerome Murphy-O'Connor*, edited by Peter Spitaler, 62–80. CBQMS. Washington, DC: Catholic Biblical Association of America, 2012. (See volume 1, chapter 4, in this series of collected essays.)

Nielsen, Kirsten. *There is Hope for a Tree: The Tree as Metaphor in Isaiah.* Sheffield, UK: JSOT, 1989.

Patte, Daniel. "A Post-Holocaust Biblical Critic Responds." In *Reading Israel in Romans*, edited by Cristina Grenholm and Daniel Patte, 225–45. Harrisburg, PA: Trinity, 2000.

Payne Smith, Jessie. *A Compendious Syriac Dictionary.* Reprint. Eugene, OR: Wipf & Stock, 1999.

Rahlfs, Alfred, ed. *Septuaginta.* 5th ed. Stuttgart: Württembergische Bibelanstalt, 1952.

Rengstorf, Karl Heinrich, ed. *A Complete Concordance to Flavius Josephus.* Study ed. Leiden: Brill, 2002.

Robinson, J. Armitage. *St. Paul's Epistle to the Ephesians: A Revised Text and Translation with Exposition and Notes.* London: Macmillan, 1903.

Sanday, William, and Arthur C. Headlam. *A Critical and Exegetical Commentary on The Epistle to the Romans.* 2nd ed. New York: Scribner's Sons, 1926.

Sievers, Joseph "'God's Gifts and Call Are Irrevocable': The Reception of Romans 11:29 through the Centuries and Christian-Jewish Relations." In *Reading Israel in Romans*, edited by Cristina Grenholm and Daniel Patte, 127–73. Harrisburg, PA: Trinity, 2000.

Stendahl, Krister. *Final Account: Paul's Letter to the Romans.* Minneapolis: Fortress, 1995.

Swanson, Reuben, ed. *New Testament Greek Manuscripts: Variant Readings Arranged in Horizontal Lines against Codex Vaticanus: Romans.* Wheaton: Tyndale, 2001.

Thayer, Joseph H., ed. *Greek-English Lexicon of the New Testament Being Grimm's Wilke's Clavis Novus Testamenti.* Chicago: American Book Company, 1889.

Trick, Bradley R. "'Lest Their Hearts Understand': Hardening Hearts through Misunderstanding in Isa 6:1—9:6." Paper from the SBL Annual Meeting, 2009.

van der Horst, Pieter W. "'Only Then Will All Israel Be Saved': A Short Note on the Meaning of καὶ οὕτος in Romans 11:26." *Journal of Biblical Literature* 119 (2000) 521–25.

Wagner, J. Ross. *Heralds of the Good News: Isaiah and Paul "in Concert" in the Letter to the Romans.* Leiden: Brill, 2002.

Wilk, Florian. *Die Bedeutung des Jesajabuches für Paulus.* Göttingen: Vandenhoeck & Ruprecht, 1998.

Zoccali, Christopher. "'And So All Israel Will Be Saved': Competing Interpretations of Romans 11.26 in Pauline Scholarship." *Journal for the Study of the New Testament* 30 (3) (2008) 289–318.

8

Romans 11 and Christian-Jewish Relations

Exegetical Options for Revisiting the Translation and Interpretation of This Central Text

I. INTRODUCTION

[3] IN ROMANS 11, Paul explicitly addressed Christ-following non-Jews about the standing of Jews who did not share their convictions about Jesus. Those interested in challenging the legacy of harmful teaching about and policies toward Jews and Judaism, such as those engaged in Christian-Jewish relations, widely recognize that this text offers hope for a different way forward.

This chapter informed the Vatican II's seminal reconsideration of the Jewish people and Judaism in the 1960s. It declared that, "the Jews remain very dear to God, for the sake of the patriarchs, since God does not take back the gifts he bestowed or the choice he made" (*Nostra Aetate* 4). Although this represented a radical position for the Catholic Church to uphold at the time, it is perhaps telling to note that this represents merely a restatement of the position the apostle articulated some 1,900 years earlier in Rom 11:28b–29 (NRSV): "but as regards election they are beloved, for the sake of their ancestors; for the gifts and the calling of God are irrevocable." Thus, while the theological viewpoint expressed in this foundational text was obviously not something new, the decision to [4] make it central for developing Catholic doctrine and policy represented a new development.

Pope John Paul II contributed in many ways to this spring-like renewal after centuries of chilling dismissals of the continued covenant standing of Jews and Judaism, which, ironically, had also appealed to statements made by Paul, including in Romans 11, even to these same verses. The Pope stayed very close to Scripture in his celebrations of this shared heritage. He stressed the contemporary implications derived from reading 9:4-5 and 11:28-29 in the present tense when Paul wrote these texts by declaring, "the people of God of the old covenant never revoked by God" includes "the present-day people of the covenant concluded with Moses," they are "partners in a covenant of eternal love which was never revoked."[1] When he visited the synagogue in Rome in 1986, the Pope pronounced the Jews his "dearly beloved brothers," even "elder brothers" in a special relationship based on "a living heritage."[2] In his "Homily at Mount Sinai," it is clear that John Paul II understood the covenant in view to include the Torah; drawing on Exod 31:18, he declared: "But now on the heights of Sinai this same God seals his love by making the covenant that he will never renounce."[3] Cardinal Walter Kasper, head of the Vatican's Commission for Religious Relations with the Jews, continued this trajectory: ". . . as Christians we know that God's covenant with Israel by God's faithfulness is not broken (Rom 11:29; 3:4) . . . ."[4]

Many Protestant and other Ecumenical organizations have made similar pronouncements also drawn largely from Romans 11. For example, the World Council of Churches declared in 1988 that the covenant with the Jewish people remains valid, and Judaism is a living tradition.[5] The United Church of Christ affirmed "its recognition that God's covenant with the Jewish people has not been rescinded or [5] abrogated by God, but remains in full force, inasmuch as 'the gifts and the promise of God are irrevocable' (Rom 11:29)."[6] In 1996, the United Methodist Church stated: "We believe that just as God is steadfastly faithful to the biblical covenant in Jesus Christ, likewise God is steadfastly faithful to the biblical covenant with the Jewish people. . . . Both Jews and Christians are bound to God in

---

1. The issue of the covenant and statements such as these by Pope John Paul II, and others, are surveyed by Henrix, "The Covenant Has Never Been Revoked: Basis of the Christian-Jewish Relationship."

2. "Address at the Great Synagogue of Rome," April 13, 1986.

3. February 26, 2000.

4. Kasper, "The Commission for Religious Relations with the Jews: A Crucial Endeavour of the Catholic Church," section III.

5. Sherman, "The Road to Reconciliation," 242.

6. Ibid., 245-46.

covenant, with no covenantal relationship invalidated by any other."[7] The Christian Scholars Group on Christian-Jewish Relations spelled out the issues and implications thus:

> For centuries Christians claimed that their covenant with God replaced or superseded the Jewish covenant. We renounce this claim. We believe that God does not revoke divine promises. We affirm that God is in covenant with both Jews and Christians. Tragically, the entrenched theology of supersessionism continues to influence Christian faith, worship, and practice, even though it has been repudiated by many Christian denominations and many Christians no longer accept it. Our recognition of the abiding validity of Judaism has implications for all aspects of Christian life.[8]

In spite of these appeals to Romans 11, and others like them, the language choices that continue to be made by the committees that translate this text, and by many in their interpretations of it, do not suggest a shared concern to reevaluate Paul's message here. Instead, they continue to express language choices that undermine this promising development at the source.[9] In the case of New Revised Standard Version (NRSV), which has become a standard choice for many academic audiences, it is disheartening to discover some decisions in chapter 11, vv. 17 and 28 in particular (which we will review), are more negative and introduce a greater degree of replacement theology than previous translations, including the King James Version (KJV). As a result, among English-only readers anyway, the best of intentions are undermined at the [6] very source to which they should be able to turn to understand and explain these reconsidered position statements on Jews and Judaism.

In addition to the direct language about Jews and Judaism this text provides for positive Christian assessments of Jews who do not share their faith in Jesus Christ, Romans 11 contains a great deal of metaphorical language that has had an equally profound influence upon Christian perceptions of Jews, both positive and negative. Moreover, the interpretation

---

7. Ibid., 245.

8. "A Sacred Obligation: Rethinking Christian Faith in Relation to Judaism and the Jewish People," xiv.

9. In addition, other texts (especially from Hebrews) have been understood to mitigate the otherwise seemingly clear message of these texts in Romans 11. Moreover, this trajectory has been challenged and altered by some Catholic interpreters in order to deny its otherwise seemingly clear reference to the endurance of the Mosaic covenant, although that continues to be adamantly maintained by others. See Cunningham, "Official Ecclesial Documents to Implement Vatican II on Relations with Jews."

of the message derived in this chapter influences decisions that are made throughout the letter, especially in the chapters that follow it. Once Paul has completed his argument, the "Therefore," of 12:1 announces how Christ-believing non-Jews are called to live in respectful relationships with each other and with all humankind, not least the Jews who were the topic in the chapters leading up to and through chapter 11, although, like the translation of chapter 11, that is not always readily apparent in the prevailing translations of chapter 12–16.[10]

While there are more topics and details than we can discuss here, we will survey several major ideas, word choices, and turns of phrase in Romans 11 that warrant reconsideration.[11] These include the two metaphors Paul develops: that of the stumbling while running to announce a message in vv. 11–15, and that of the olive tree in vv. 16–24, in which the language of "broken off" and "cut off" as well as "hardened" and "part of" or "partially" arise. Following these metaphors, we will consider a language choice arising in a direct statement that the Israelites in view are "enemies" in v. 28 (moreover, "of God," according to the NRSV).

Hopefully the following demonstration of alternatives to explore will offer future translators reason to alter their choices, even challenge, on the basis of historical probability, those who may not share these sensibilities.

II. SOME ARE "STUMBLING," BUT THEY HAVE "*NOT* FALLEN"

[7] In v. 11, Paul presents his viewpoint by way of a metaphor about some Israelites stumbling on a pathway. He portrays Israelites on the way toward a goal, drawing on an image of heralds bringing news to Israel and from Israel to the nations developed in Isaiah (see below). Within this imagery he insists emphatically that the Israelites in Rome to whom he is referring have merely *missed a step* and *stumbled*—but certainly *not fallen*.

Although conveying a judgment about these Israelites who do not share Paul and his audience's convictions about the meaning of Jesus for themselves, Paul employs an active image that bespeaks a temporary stage with a yet-to-be-realized positive outcome. The perspective expressed is condescending, to be sure, based on being correct and those in view being mistaken. But at the same time, Paul expresses a generous disposition, one that is based on the conviction that they are all involved in an ongoing

---

10. This topic is discussed in detail in my *The Mystery of Romans*.
11. For more detailed discussions see Nanos, "'Broken Branches'"; Nanos, "'Callused,' Not 'Hardened'"; Nanos, "Romans," 275–79 on Romans 11.

process in which their fates are inseparably linked. He also declares emphatically that things are not in a complete or final state from which conclusive judgments can or should be made.

Paul develops the image further in vv. 12–15, and in other images and statements throughout the balance of the chapter. He explains that this momentary misstep represents a stage in which non-Israelites can join in on the path alongside of those Israelites who are stumbling and those who have maintained their footing (like he views himself). He also insists that the non-Israelites' own ultimate aspirations will only be realized after those presently stumbling regain their stride. There are several dynamics central to the argument developed in this metaphorical language.

Paul insists that the non-Israelites who join the course do not replace those who are stumbling. He describes a road on which some Israelites are now stumbling while other Israelites continue on, with a gap opening between them into which others enter. The non-Israelites who thereby enter onto the pathway do not replace those who had been on it, but rather join along with those of Israel who are stumbling as well as those who are not. He emphatically asserts that the goal will be realized only when those temporarily stumbling have regained their stride and finished the course.

This resistance to the notion of replacement theology suggests that Paul anticipated that the image could be (mis)understood to express the zero-sum idea that there is only so much space available, that the elimination of those stumbling could logically be considered a desirable advantage for those who have just joined. Thus Paul resists anyone drawing that inference by declaring that those from the nations newly admitted to the path will only experience the ultimate goal when those of Israel temporarily stumbling regain their step, not by them stumbling "so as to fall." They are to see themselves as new, *additional* members of a subgroup within a larger group; moreover, they are co-dependent upon [8] the success of all the members thereof if they are to enjoy the ultimate goal—resurrection itself.[12]

Throughout Romans 9–11 Paul draws on the images in Isaiah of stumbling as well as heralds announcing news to communicate that some of the messengers of Israel have stumbled along the way and so are not yet announcing the message that has been entrusted to them to bring to the nations, the message of the arrival of the awaited day with the resurrection

---

12. Paul's use of this image to the end that he argues suggests that it is not a race with a prize for the winners (as individuals or as a group in competition with another group) that he envisions. Rather, it seems that he is describing the movement of a group of people who will only have successfully reached their destination when all of the slowest members have safely arrived too, invoking an in-group sense of concern about the welfare of everyone else on the journey.

of Christ.[13] From the opening of the letter to its conclusion, Paul presents his own apostleship to the nations to be based on scriptural expectations for that awaited event (cf. 1:1–15; 3:2; 10:14–16; 15). He draws upon this special role for Israel to herald God's word when he mentions that the inclusion (salvation) of these non-Israelites on the journey among the Israelites will serve to provoke the stumbling of some Israelites to jealousy (11:11–15). Paul explains that *his ministry* to the nations is calculated to provoke his fellow Israelites to *jealousy* (vv. 13–14). Likewise, in v. 11, the joining of these non-Israelites on the path while some Israelites are stumbling behind is described in terms of provoking jealousy.

In other words, Paul believes that when these Israelites see his success among the nations they will want to *emulate* him, to join him in completing this special task with which God has entrusted Israel, namely, to be the heralds of God's good news for the nations.[14] Paul's point is not that his fellow Israelites will begrudge the entrance of those from the nations, but that they will not want to miss out on playing their part in bringing this to pass. Seeing Paul's successful ministry among the nations will cause them to reconsider whether the promised and awaited age has begun.

In short, Paul envisions these non-Israelites joining in alongside of the heralds on the way to announce the news to the nations. Some Israelites are marching ahead, while other heralds have fallen behind. [9] They will witness the inclusion of those who have responded positively to the message announced by those ahead of them, such as Paul, and thus have to consider whether God is involved in this development.[15] Paul deduces that seeing this development will provoke those Israelites to feel jealousy, to want to take up this task too. Thus, these non-Israelites play a positive,

---

13. Isa 8:14–15 with chs. 27–29; see Nanos, "'Broken Branches,'" 341–50.

14. Cf. Nanos, *Mystery of Romans*, 247–55; Nanos, "The Jewish Context of the Gentile Audience Addressed in Paul's Letter to the Romans." Jealousy is not the same as envy in Greek. Jealousy, to which Paul refers, revolves around the idea that one wants something for themselves, often in the positive sense of wanting to emulate admirable behavior. Envy, on the other hand, is the begrudging of another, usually of their gaining or having something desirable, even if the one who begrudges the other also has that which is desirable.

15. A parallel to Paul's thinking is developed in Acts, which describes the reaction of Israelite Christ-followers to the unexpected receipt of the Holy Spirit by non-Israelites in ch. 10, and argues from the basis of this divine action to the conclusion reached in ch. 15; namely, that the developments among these non-Israelites bear witness to God's actions, which are interpreted, in conjunction with searching the Scriptures, as the arrival of the awaited age to come.

albeit provocative role in the restoration of his fellow Israelites to the course that God has set for them.[16]

Note that by Paul's logic he does not regard the Israelites who do not (yet) share his convictions about Christ to be (already) out of the covenants made with Abraham or Israel through Moses: their covenant standing remains "irreversible" (cf. 9:4–5; 11:1–2, 28–29). These Israelites are not in the same situation as non-Israelites. Rather, these fellow Israelites are judged by him to be "stumbling" *temporarily,* that is, slow to come to share his point of view on where Israel is, and thus the nations are, on God's timeline for reconciling all of the cosmos. They need their footing restored (i.e., saved, made safe/protected) so that they can complete the course, which he claims all Israel will experience (11:25–27).

It is a presupposition of Paul's argument that the Israelites he is discussing are already on the path, regardless of the less-than-desirable situation some of them are temporarily experiencing. They too have covenant standing by the calling and the faithfulness of the fathers, as well as a special gift to proclaim God's good news to the nations. Some (most) are not (yet) persuaded that the appropriate time has (yet) arrived to join Paul and other Christ-followers in making this announcement (see vv. 28–32, discussed below), because many are not (yet) convinced of the propositional claims Paul and other Christ-followers are making about [10] Jesus (and many are not even yet aware of such claims). Those from the other nations who are turning to God in Christ, such as the audience he addresses, have had to enter onto the path; that is, are being saved (rescued from worshipping other gods), brought into covenant standing from outside of it.[17]

16. The point here is missed when interpreted to suggest that Paul is signaling that these Israelites will react negatively to the entrance of those from the nations. That interpretation is a natural corollary of the usual understanding that what is portrayed is salvation or entrance into the covenant for non-Israelites as if that required the removal and thus replacement of Israelites, or at least that it signaled their removal from the covenant or salvation. However, it is not logical to assume that Paul would imagine that these Israelites would suppose that they have been replaced in the covenant if they have not been persuaded of the gospel proposition. Rather, they might be challenged to reconsider the message Paul proclaims if they witness Paul's success turning those from the nations to the worship of God, as expected of Israelite heralds upon the arrival of the age to come (v. 13), and all the more if those from the nations have joined alongside of Paul and some other Israelites on the way to announcing this news to others from the nations, when they themselves are not yet enjoying this awaited moment of vocational fulfillment (v. 11).

17. Paul maintains a distinction here between the identity of Israelites who have not confessed Jesus as Christ and those from the other nations, and thus what it is that each is expected to do. Israelites are to be faithful to the truth claims of the message that Jesus is the awaited Messiah (Christ) precisely because they are already in a covenant relationship, which involves declaring this message to the nations. Non-Israelites are to be faithful to this message by turning from other gods, and thus other ways of life, to the One God of Israel and all of the nations, thereby only now entering into a similar

Paul addresses the responsibility of these non-Israelite Christ-followers in terms of their *concepts* about and *attitude* toward those Israelites, which involves comprehending that their own standing among these Israelites is new, later, and co-dependent. In the next metaphor he will add to this the importance of *recognizing* their precarious place among these Israelites. In the chapters that follow Paul will address their *behavioral responsibility*, which is only at best implicit here: they are to avoid putting any obstruction in these Israelites' path that could cause them to fall, such as disrespecting Torah-derived Israelite norms for right behavior (see esp. ch. 14).[18] Until the resurrection arrives for which all await, they are to leave judging of the other to God and to instead be concerned with their own faithfulness, observed with generosity toward all fellow travelers (just as they depend upon God's generosity toward themselves), and regardless of any ill-will that they might suffer along the way (cf. 2; 12–15).

Nevertheless, even within this overall positive message in 11:11-15, of stumbling but not falling, and of complete success for the nations being dependent upon the eventual success of all of Israel, there are translation decisions that obscure the positive thrust, even reverse it.

III. "THROUGH THEIR FALL/TRANSGRESSION"? "FAILURE/DEFEAT"?

In v. 11, the KJV translates the second sentence in a way that immediately *reverses* Paul's denial that those presently stumbling have fallen: "I say then, Have they stumbled that they should *fall*? God forbid: but rather through their *fall* salvation is come unto the Gentiles, for to [11] provoke them to jealousy" (emphasis added). The English reader would suppose that Paul has simply repeated the Greek word translated "fall" (πέσωσιν, or "fall down," a subjunctive form of the verb πίπτω) in the first sentence, but that is not the case, and it would make little sense to have done so: Paul has just denied that they have fallen, so why represent them as having fallen to begin the next point? The NASB and NIV reinterpret and obscure the metaphorical color of the point by translating the phrase "But by their *transgression* . . ." (emphasis added). The NRSV retains the basic point: "But through their *stumbling*" (emphasis added). The Greek noun is παραπτώματι, which in this metaphorical context would be better translated "but by their *misstep*,"

---

covenant relationship with God and to the way of life that involves. Paul communicates this very message in a different way in vv. 30–32, although the point is obscured when the cognates of ἀπειθέω around which Paul works that argument are translated as "disobedience," as they usually are, instead of the logical alternative, "disbelief" or "non-persuadedness."

18. See Nanos, *Mystery of Romans*, 123-24.

which explains why they are "stumbling"; i.e., by their missing a step (and thus stumbling). An interesting alternative would be, "but by their *delay* [i.e., falling behind],"[19] which would instead suggest that as the result of their stumbling they are lagging behind. Either way, it would suggest that those Israelites who have stumbled have left a gap between themselves and those Israelites who have not stumbled on the course (such as Paul sees himself), a gap on the path into which some non-Israelites have now stepped in between these two groups of Israelites.

The problem of failing to maintain the argumentative point as well as to develop it within the metaphorical illustration continues in the translations of v. 12. The KJV translates v. 12 thus: "Now if the *fall* of them be the riches of the world, and the *diminishing* of them the riches of the Gentiles; how much more their fulness?" (emphasis added). Paul repeats the noun παραπτώματι from the second sentence of v. 11 in the first clause of v. 12, which the KJV repeats in its translation as "fall." Likewise, the NASB and NIV repeat the choice of "transgression," and the NRSV "stumbling." I suggest repeating "misstep" or "delay." In the next clause of v. 12, whereas the KJV translates ἥττημα as "*diminishing*," the NASB chooses "*failure*," the NIV "*loss*," and the NRSV "*defeat*." The latter choices maintain neither the point nor the metaphorical imagery; rather, they suggest that those who have stumbled have *failed*, suffered *defeat*; in short, that they indeed have *fallen*. Although "diminishing" (KJV) does not fit the metaphorical image, it is more in keeping with the spirit of the argument. The noun ἥττημα suggests that one is comparatively less successful ("lacking"):[20] "*lagging behind*" expresses the metaphorical idea.

These examples illustrate the kinds of historically viable translation alternatives that are available, offering both metaphorical continuity and argumentative consistency. In spite of being obstructed to some degree by [12] the prevailing translations, many have been able to stay the course in their interpretations. In the verses that follow, that course is harder to maintain.

IV. "BUT IF SOME OF THE BRANCHES WERE BROKEN *OFF*"?

The positive, temporary image maintained in the metaphor of walking and eventually arriving at the intended destination accompanied by more fellow travelers than originally set out, even if some trip along the way, is quickly undermined by the translation of the extended metaphor (allegory) that

---

19. Cf. *LSJ*, 1322.

20. *LSJ*, 780; Louw and Nida, *Lexicon*, 13.22; Cranfield, *Epistle to the Romans*, 2.557, although to a different conclusion.

follows it vv. 17–24. In this allegory, the olive tree is represented with some branches *removed*. Although Paul insisted that his fellow Israelites should *never* be described as "fallen," he now ostensibly portrays them—according to the prevailing translations—as already "broken *off*."

This allegory has generally been interpreted to indicate that Israelites who are not Christ-followers have been removed from covenant standing and must therefore join the people of God anew, just like non-Israelites, by turning to God through Christ. And that idea appears to be confirmed when Paul insists at the end of the allegory that "*God is able* to graft them in *again*" (vv. 23–24). That was certainly how Calvin understood this allegory.

Calvin's commentaries incorporated on the frontispiece an illustration of God pruning off branches from an olive tree, some in a state of falling and others already on the ground, while at the same time a few wild shoots were pictured grafted into the places from where these branches have been cut.[21]

Calvin's Olive Tree Imprint in *Commentary to Genesis*
(*RAMI VT EGO INSERERER[O]* = I shall be inserted as a branch;
DEFRACTI SUNT = They are broken off)

21. Cf. Calvin, *Commentaries on the Epistle of Paul the Apostle to the Romans*, 425.

That imagery strikingly contradicts the message and image of stumbling but not falling maintained in the previous metaphor. Does Paul mean to communicate that these Israelites have been already *removed*, when he has just insisted that they have *not fallen* in the previous metaphor, or that they stand in need of being grafted back in?

At the risk of being accused of trying to save Paul, I propose that the olive tree allegory has been misunderstood and mistranslated, in addition to being inadequate to the task to which Paul sought to put it. Allegories, like all analogies, are imperfect, and can be taken in various directions other than those the author developing them might have intended or anticipated.[22] I suggest that has been the case.

[13] The message of the olive tree allegory is a warning to the non-Israelites in Rome about their own precarious and potentially temporary place alongside of Israelites, including those who do not yet share Paul and the audience's convictions about Christ. *It was designed to warn them* not to become arrogant toward those Israelites or to suppose that they have replaced them, but instead to focus on their own faithfulness to the proposition to which they have professed allegiance. They are to be grateful for the grace received from God, and thus to think graciously toward the other, who likewise depends upon God's grace. They have joined alongside those already in a long-standing covenant relationship with God, albeit some in a temporary state of discipline within that relationship. They are to keep in mind that if some of those who are in a long-standing covenant relationship are (so far) slow to recognize the course that faithfulness calls them to take, how much more might it be expected to be a challenge for those who are not accustomed to the ways of God, and specifically, to being faithful to their calling within such a covenant, which involves the service of God and others, not themselves. Hence, the message overall is summed up in the warning to the wild shoot if it should suppose it has replaced some natural branches in God's tree, captured in the KJV translation: "Be not highminded, but fear!" (v. 20).[23]

The olive tree allegory can communicate this message, in continuity with the metaphor of stumbling, by focusing on its purpose to portray the precarious state of the non-Israelite among the people of God, and not the state of the Israelites, except as it serves the *a fortiori* ("all the more") case Paul otherwise seeks to make to curtail any temptation toward arrogance

---

22. Cf. Black, "More About Metaphor," 36–41; Reddy, "The Conduit Metaphor."

23. In keeping with the imagery, this might be expanded to read, "Do not think as if higher [than some of these natural branches], but be full of fear [humbly mindful of just how all the more tenuous is your own unnatural place in this tree]."

among his non-Israelite addressees.[24] Several translation alternatives can also help make this clear.[25]

[14] Since they are represented as "broken *off*" (ἐξεκλάσθησαν, from ἐκκλάω) in the prevailing English translations, one does not expect to immediately read that the wild shoot has been grafted "*among*" these branches. The NRSV inexplicably obscures the matter even more, even reverses the point, by introducing the replacement-theology idea that the wild shoot has been grafted "in their place," which represents a decision without any Greek manuscript evidence. But even if properly translated as grafted "among them" (ἐν αὐτοῖς), such as in the KJV and NASB (NIV: "among the others"), in order to maintain Greek gender consistency (masc.) this pronoun refers back to the wild shoot as grafted *among* the "branches [κλάδων]," the same branches traditionally presented as "broken *off*"! How is the reader to imagine a wild shoot grafted "among them" if the branches have been broken "off" from the tree? Here we confront an anomaly that should send translators searching for a logical solution. And there is one readily available.

The verb (ἐκκλάω) that Paul uses in vv. 17–21 can be translated "broken" as in "bent"![26] This was the choice made in the John Wycliffe English translation from the Latin Vulgate in the late fourteenth century, although not adapted thereafter.[27] That description would make sense of the image

---

24. In spite of the widely held view that Paul is describing non-Israelites being grafted into Israel, understood to mean becoming members of Israel, note that Paul does not describe the trunk or the tree or the roots as Israel; actually, he does not identify them at all. Israelites are natural branches. Note too that the branch from a wild olive tree is a single shoot grafted "among them." It is this shoot that Paul warns of its precarious position in the tree; thus the tree overall seems to represent a concept of the joint people of God, with members from the other nations alongside of Israel, but not thereby becoming members of Israel, but joint members of the one people of God drawn from all of the nations. For full discussion of Paul's theological view that non-Israelites remain non-Israelites and Israelites remain Israelites, see Nanos, "Paul and the Jewish Tradition: The Ideology of the Shema."

25. For details, see Nanos "'Broken Branches.'"

26. In Lev 1:17, a bird's wings for an offering are to be "broken [ἐκκλάσει]" but "not separated [οὐ διελεῖ]." Pausanias, *Graeciae descriptio* 8.40.2, describes a case when a fighter's toe was "broken" (ἐκκλᾷ), causing him to expire and lose the fight, because "of the pain in his toe [ὑπὸ τοῦ δακτύλου τῆς ὀδύνης]"; in other words, it was "bent," "dislocated," "broken," but not removed from his foot (Loeb; transl. W. H. S. Jones).

27. This is the only English translation of which I am aware that maintains "broken" but not "off" for ἐκκλάω in vv. 17–21. It was based on the Latin Vulgate (*Quod si aliqui ex ramis fracti ["broken," "fractured"] sunt, tu autem cum oleaster esses, insertus es in illis* [Clementine edition]): "What if ony of the braunchis ben brokun"; it also translates the wild branch "art graffid among hem," changing to "kit doun" for ἐκκόπτω vv. 22–24. The Catholic Douay-Rheims Bible is also based on the Vulgate, and the other exception I know of presently: it translates v. 17 as "broken" but not "off," however, in vv. 19 and

of a wild shoot planted among the branches of the tree, albeit in various states, some of them in some way suffering harm or damage. Broken limbs would also correspond to the idea of stumbling but not having fallen, upon which Paul insisted in the prior imagery, whereas "broken *off*" aligns with the notion of having *fallen*, in direct conflict with Paul's implicit and overall explicit argument. And it would make sense of Paul's grammar, which portrays the newly grafted single wild shoot *"among them."*

[15] The notion of branches being "cut off" does arise later in the allegory, however, in vv. 22-24. There Paul introduces the verb ἐκκόπτω, which does indicate being "cut off," in order to severely threaten the target of this allegory, the wild shoot. The wild shoot is warned that it will be "cut off" if it presumes to gloat about the present suffering of some of the natural branches, or to suppose that it has replaced them in God's favor. If natural branches can "fall" for unfaithfulness, then "all the more" can God "also cut off" a wild shoot, a turn of phrase that plays off of the fact that the wild shoot has already suffered the unnatural experience of being "cut off" from a wild tree in order to be grafted among the branches that have grown naturally on the cultivated tree.[28]

Although Paul does not actually state that the natural branches have been cut off, it is implied when warning the wild shoot to avoid being cut off *"also."* During this warning, he also mentions that some natural branches "fell [πεσόντας]" (v. 22) as the result of God's severe action toward those who were unfaithful, in order to call the wild shoot to remain faithful. But that the stumbling Israelites have fallen is precisely what Paul denied adamantly in the previous metaphor; declaring in v. 11, "May it never be!" Why Paul mixed his metaphors here (if that is what he did) is anything but clear, although it is a common problem when multiple metaphors are present, not least in Isaiah 27-29, from which Paul has drawn throughout chapter 9-11.

This choice of language suggesting the natural branches have already been severed has certainly shaped the prevailing translation and interpretive decisions throughout the allegory and the chapter. The conclusion is that Paul meant to communicate that some natural branches have been broken off; hence, fallen off of the tree. Need that remain the case?

---

20 it fails to maintain that distinction, writing "broken off" (from the 1899 American edition, which is based on the revisions made by Challoner in 1749-52; original version dates to 1582).

28. It is rightly often noted that in this allegory Paul reverses the normal oleicultural practice of cutting shoots from cultivated olive trees to graft onto wild olive trees, which will then bear eatable olives, while a wild shoot grafted onto a cultivated tree will not bear eatable olives. Cf. Theophrastus, *Caus. plant.* 1.6.10; Zohary and Hopf, *Domestication of Plants in the Old World*, 145-51.

The interpretive tradition has focused on the allegory as a description of the state of Israel (or some Israelites) rather than the state of the wild shoot (representing the non-Israelite addressees). It has also conflated the more severe "cut off" (ἐκκόπτω) introduced in vv. 22–24 to describe the hypothetical fate that the wild shoot must avoid with the "broken" (ἐκκλάω) state used to describe some of the natural branches in vv. 17–21. Although the inference from introducing the idea of the wild shoot being "cut off" complicates the picture, the translations "broken" or "bent" in vv. 17–21 would help the reader retain the distinction [16] between the present temporary state of some of the branches and the *a fortiori* inference that arises from the warning to the wild shoot about its own precarious state, since it would be "all the more" natural for it to be "cut off," being already "cut off" from another tree in order to be grafted in.

Paul seems to have sensed the problem introduced by the shift in his language when making his *a fortiori* case about the greater danger to themselves that the wild branch should recognize, rather than suppose its superiority. For he immediately insists that the Israelites branches would *also* be able to be grafted back in, all the more logically so, if branches not natural to the tree can be grafted into it. Ironically, it is at this point—when Paul seeks to save his allegory from a wrong inference about the state of the natural branches after making the case for the all the more logically dangerous state of the wild shoot—that his appeal to an unnatural interference in the process has decisively shaped the translation and interpretation of the allegory in precisely the *opposite* direction than he sought to communicate with respect to the *temporary* but *protected* (as we will see in the next section) state of the natural branches.

What Paul describes is not natural, but miraculous: one does not sever limbs from a tree with the intention of grafting them back into the same tree, and that does not seem to make sense of Paul's choice of metaphors here (or in those that precede and follow it). Does it not appear that Paul has gotten his allegory into a bit of a jam, and that he must appeal to a miracle in order to keep it from suggesting that the state of these Israelites is other than temporary—which is important to the message he wants the non-Israelites in Rome to draw from this chapter?

There are good lexical and grammatical reasons to revise the traditional translations as well as the interpretive implications that have generally been deduced to suggest that these Israelites have been cut off from God, or from their covenant standing. From Paul's point of view some have been unfaithful to their covenant responsibilities and are suffering the disciplinary results. But he wants to highlight that this state (or stage) is temporary, that he believes it will eventually result in their restoration. Therefore, he argues that while his non-Israelite audience has become aware of their own receipt of God's grace and at the same time become aware that some Israelites are suffering discipline from God, their own best interests will only be realized when this temporary, anomalous, disciplinary development has finished its course with the restoration of both Israel and the nations.

Although things have not turned out as Paul proposed that they would ("yet," many uphold), is it not time to make a change here in the way that this text is translated and interpreted? Would that not be faithful to Paul's historical purpose and better serve those who aspire to improve the options for Christian perceptions of and discussions about their Jewish neighbors? If not, why not?

V. "A HARDENING HAS COME UPON PART OF ISRAEL"?

[17] Paul turns to address his audience more directly in v. 25 as "brothers (and sisters)," instead of continuing in allegorical terms to discuss them indirectly as a wild shoot, yet he appears to continue to draw metaphorically upon the allegory he has just finished for his choice of expressions. One can hardly recognize this from the prevailing English translations. Moreover, the translation choices undermine the thrust of Paul's rather bluntly stated purpose to nip in the bud any incipient arrogance toward the Israelites under discussion: "So that you may not claim to be wiser than you are" (NRSV). Instead, they describe the state of Israel (or some Israelites) in language that suggests Paul is analogizing their state with the heart of Pharaoh, famously judged as "hardened." That hardly comports with the spirit of his argument, and this strikingly negative judgment of their state undermines the appeals often made to this passage to make otherwise positive statements about Paul's views of his fellow Israelites. Must it be so?

The connection with Pharaoh's heart and associated judgments of what is supposedly wrong with these Israelites are a regular feature of the interpretive tradition, but Paul does not use the Greek word used to describe Pharaoh's heart (σκληρός). Rather, he chooses a very different word (πώρωσις). English translations do not indicate this distinction at all, but it is telling. Πώρωσις (verb πωρόω) is usually used as a medical term to refer to a "callus" (verb: "to callus").[29] While a callus involves hardening, that is not a negative attribute for a damaged limb. Unlike the negative case of hardening of a heart, it is a positive one! A callus promotes healing,

29. Hippocrates, *De alimento* 53; *De fractures* 23.10; *De articulis* 14.17, 24; 15.6; 49.18. Celsus, *De Medicina*. Aretaeus; Galen, *Ars Medica* 1.387.18; *LSJ*, 1561.

protecting the injured area so that life can be conducted in and through it, thus serving the interests of the overall body (or plant), so that it can be restored (saved, healed, rescued).

There are several reasons to suggest translating Paul's language in v. 25 around "callus" rather than "harden." In addition to the imagery of a tree in the allegory just completed, it is supported by the metaphorical appeal to plant imagery detectable in Paul's use of other language throughout vv. 25-26a. He writes in the next clause of v. 25 about the time when the "fullness [πλήρωμα]" of the nations will arrive, which is just the way that full blooming or fruitfulness is described for plants.[30] In the clause after that, v. 26a, the ultimate goal is described as the "salvation [σωθήσεται]" of all Israel, in metaphorical [18] plant terms, its being "kept/made safe," "protected," "healed" or "restored."[31] Moreover, the passages of Isaiah 27 and 59 from which he draws to create the proofs of this process for Israel in vv. 26-27 are full of just this kind of plant imagery.[32]

Another reason to translate Paul's language here around the metaphorical appeal to a protective callus being formed to ensure the eventual restoration of the broken or bent branches and the tree overall, arises in the modifying phrase ἀπὸ μέρους, usually translated "part of" Israel, or Israel "partially." Traditionally, the prepositional phrase ἀπὸ μέρους is either translated to indicate that some Israelites have been hardened, as in the NRSV ("a hardening has come upon *part of* Israel"), or that Israel itself has been hardened to some degree, as in the NASB ("a *partial hardening* has happened to Israel") and NIV ("Israel has experienced a hardening *in part*").[33] But the phrase ἀπὸ μέρους can be translated to highlight the time element of what is happening: it "has happened *for a while*."[34] In Rom 15:24, Paul writes of the fact that he will stay in Rome "for a while [ἀπὸ μέρους]," that is, "temporarily," before he heads off to Spain.

This apparently overlooked option would keep the focus on the temporary nature of the anomalous events that Paul here discloses as a "mystery" to date in order to communicate that things will not turn out as they might appear presently to be, but very differently. The clause about the callus that has happened to or been formed for Israel is followed by two clauses having to do with stages in a process or developments over the course of time. This

30. Theophrastus, *Caus. plant.* 1.13.3 (line 3), 9 (line 6); 3.15.3 (line 10).

31. Theophrastus, *Caus. plant.* 1.4.5 (line 8); 1.7.2 (line 7); 1.19.5 (line 7); 1.22.2 (line 8); 2.16.5 (line 1); 2.17.5 (line 12); 5.16.2; 5.18.4 (line 3).

32. It is also found in many other places in Isaiah from which he draws elsewhere in Romans; see Nanos, "Callus."

33. Emphases added.

34. Cf. Louw and Nida, *Lexicon*, 67.109.

callus will last "*until* the fullness of the nations commences, and *then* (or: and *thus*) all Israel will be restored/protected."

Whether one prefers to emphasize the process or the element of time, there are several translation options to explore for this clause. "For a while" emphasizes the time element over the developmental aspect, but either or both aspects can be expressed by the adjective "temporary," or the adverb, "temporarily." We might translate the clause in any of the following ways: "that a callus has formed for Israel *for a while*," or, "that a *temporary* callus has formed for Israel," or, "that a callus has formed for Israel *temporarily*," or, in keeping with Paul's word order: "that a callus *temporarily* has formed for Israel." The purpose of this temporary development is on behalf of Israel, to protect Israel from harm until the promised restoration comes to pass: "a callus temporarily has formed for [the protection] of Israel."

All of these options still represent a value judgment on the part of Paul about those Israelites who do not share his convictions about Jesus [19] and thus about the appropriateness of announcing him as the Christ to the nations, which is integral to Paul's rhetorical purpose for engaging in this argument. Yet at the same time they represent a much more respectful view of his compatriots, are in keeping with the kind of judgments of the temporary state of many Israelites commonly made by Israelite prophets, and offer a much more promising translation for those engaged in rethinking Christian perceptions of and discussions about Jews who do not share their convictions about Jesus Christ.

It has always been strikingly discordant to encounter (and even to use!) "hardened" in descriptions of Paul's views of his fellow Israelites, whether in part or partially, in statements otherwise developed towards asserting that Paul held a positive view of his fellow Jews. Is there a good reason not to make this alternative, historically viable option available in the translations upon which those who can only read English depend (*mutatis mutandis*, in any other language translations for those readers), and to raise it within interpretive discussions of this text and these topics?

VI. "*ENEMIES* FOR YOUR SAKE? EVEN, "ENEMIES *OF GOD*"?

Following the appeal to proof texts in vv. 26–27 to demonstrate the certainty of "all" Israel's restoration, in vv. 28–29 Paul takes another pass at explaining why this outcome is beyond doubt, as well as why the unanticipated way in which it is unfolding ("a mystery") is to the benefit of his non-Israelite audience in the meantime, and thus, why they must not hold these Israelites in contempt. Yet once again current translation decisions, in addition to interpretive ones, mitigate if not entirely subvert the thrust of Paul's argument.[35] For example, the NRSV translates this two-verse sentence in the following manner: "As regards the gospel they are *enemies of God* for your sake; but as regards election they are beloved, for the sake of their ancestors; for the gifts and the calling of God are irrevocable" (emphasis added).

There is no manuscript evidence for the addition of the phrase "of God," *none*, and the prevailing translations avoid this egregious decision by usually writing: "enemies for your sake" (NASB, NIV, KJV ["sakes"]). Although the English reader can see that this representation of these Israelites as "enemies" is qualified with respect to the gospel, and although that can be understood in various ways, what the translations fail to help them recognize is that the Greek word ἐχθροί translated "enemies" [20] is an adjective. It mirrors the word ἀγαπητοί, translated properly in the next clause as an adjective, "beloved."[36]

In other words, Paul's point is not that they are enemies of God or that God is the enemy of them, or even that they are enemies of the non-Israelite addressees, but that they have been temporarily "enemied," that is, "alienated" or "estranged" by God for the sake of these non-Israelites. If they are suffering vicariously "for your sake," that ought to induce empathy—which is more in keeping with the point of Paul's argument here and throughout! This state is temporary, Paul insists, because they are beloved by God through their covenant standing as children of the fathers. Paul spelled out some of the irrevocable gifts to which he eludes in 9:4-5: "They are Israelites, and to them belong the adoption, the glory, the covenants, the giving of the law, the worship, and the promises; to them belong the patriarchs, and from them, according to the flesh, comes the Messiah . . ." (NRSV).

The translation *estranged* expresses the idea that has been central to Paul's assessment of some of his fellow Israelites throughout the chapter (such as "stumbling," "broken" or "bent"): they are suffering God's discipline temporarily, but will be restored, according to God's covenant promises to Israel. Of that eventual outcome Paul is certain—otherwise God would not be faithful to those *within* the covenant already made. It is in this light that he wraps up his argument to his non-Israelite audience about the need to focus on their own faithfulness, carried out with respect for the fact that God is dealing with Israel according to God's own designs for how all of humankind will be best served in the end, however inscrutable it may seem

---

35. Traced in Sievers, "A History of the Interpretation of Romans 11:29"; Sievers, "'God's Gifts and Call are Irrevocable.'"

36. Beck, "Translations of the New Testament for Our Time," 204-6.

to them along the way (vv. 30–36). According to Paul, the time for Christ-followers to judge the fate of Israelites, if there is even to be such a day, has certainly not yet arrived.

VII. CONCLUSION

There are undoubtedly many reasons that translation committees have not yet revised the translation of the language choices made in Romans 11. Why that might be is not the focus of the discussion offered here, but it is worth asking if it is not, at least in part, simply a matter of what John McWhorter labels "Path Dependence."[37] That is, what may seem normal and even self-evidently justified today can represent a choice made previously in a particular place and time that was shaped by very different factors. Once established and repeated, it tends to persist [21] and even discourage consideration of alternatives. And that continues, often without special concern expressed, even when other changes might suggest the need for reconsideration.

For example, keyboards for word processing continue to be designed according to the arrangement adapted for typewriters, which involved decisions to put certain letters where they would help avoid jams created when typing fast, and offer salespeople an easy way to type the word "typewriter" by using keys conveniently available in the top row. This keyboard arrangement, which came to be known as QWERTY, continues in spite of the fact that computer keyboards do not suffer from the problem of such mechanical jamming. McWhorter draws from this and other examples to point out the obvious: many present conditions are not the product of present day choices, but (and for any number of reasons) they often represent decisions made in the past under different conditions—even when those might be counterproductive to our best interests today.

It is not hard to recognize that those who translated and interpreted Romans in earlier periods, from Chrysostom to Augustine to Luther and Calvin to the English translation committees preceding Vatican II, were all interested in this passage for different reasons and with different sensibilities toward the topic of Paul's view of Jews and Judaism. It is harder to understand why the committees since then, which have almost certainly included some members who shared these new concerns and sentiments, have not done so in a more concerted way. Certainly some of the factors for any translation chosen include familiarity, tradition, the assumption that previous committees had investigated the options, that these choices

37. McWhorter, "Path Dependence."

are constrained by the meaning of the Greek words and grammar already thoroughly considered, and the force of habit. But theological disposition is a factor too, which has, at least for many on this matter, undergone substantial reconsideration.

In view of recent encouraging developments in Christian sensibilities and perceptions of, teachings about, and policies toward Jews and Judaism, combined with developments in historical research that offer the opportunity to present these texts in more historically probable ways, is it not time to challenge translation committees, commentators, and other interpreters of these texts, not least ourselves as interpreters of Paul—Christian, or not—to reexamine the alternatives and reconsider the choices made for English (and other language) translations and interpretations of this critically important text?

BIBLIOGRAPHY

Beck, Norman. "Translations of the New Testament for Our Time." In *Seeing Judaism Anew: Christianity's Sacred Obligation*, edited by Mary C. Boys, 200–210. Lanham, MD: Rowman and Littlefield, 2005.

Black, Max. "More about Metaphor." In *Metaphor and Thought*, edited by Andrew Ortony, 19–43. Cambridge: Cambridge University Press, 1979.

Calvin, John. *Commentaries on the Epistle of Paul the Apostle to the Romans*. Edited and translated by John Owen. Grand Rapids: Eerdmans, 1947.

Christian Scholars Group on Christian-Jewish Relations. "A Sacred Obligation: Rethinking Christian Faith in Relation to Judaism and the Jewish People: A Statement by the Christian Scholars Group on Christian-Jewish Relations." In *Seeing Judaism Anew: Christianity's Sacred Obligation*, edited by Mary C. Boys, xiv. Lanham, MD: Rowman and Littlefield, 2005.

Cranfield, C. E. B. *A Critical and Exegetical Commentary on the Epistle to the Romans*. ICC. Edinburgh: T. & T. Clark, 1975.

Cunningham, Philip A. "Official Ecclesial Documents to Implement Vatican II on Relations with Jews: Study Them, Become Immersed in Them, and Put Them into Practice." *Studies in Christian-Jewish Relations* 4 (2009) 1–36. Online: http://escholarship.bc.edu/scjr/vol4.

Henrix, Hans Hermann. "The Covenant Has Never Been Revoked: Basis of the Christian-Jewish Relationship." Accessed on Feb. 13, 2012: http://www.jcrelations.net/The_covenant_has_never_been_revoked.2250.0.html#27.

John Paul II. "Address at the Great Synagogue of Rome." April 13, 1986. Accessed Feb. 13, 2012: http://www.bc.edu/content/dam/files/research_sites/cjl/texts/cjrelations/resources/documents/catholic/johnpaulii/romesynagogue.htm.

———. "Homily at Mount Sinai." February 26, 2000. Accessed Feb. 13, 2012: http://www.ccjr.us/dialogika-resources/documents-and-statements/romancatholic/pope-john-paul-ii/332-jp2-00feb26.html.

Kasper, Walter. "The Commission for Religious Relations with the Jews: A Crucial Endeavour of the Catholic Church," section III. Accessed Feb. 13, 2012: http://

www.ccjr.us/dialogika-resources/documents-and-statements/roman-catholic/kasper/642-kasper02nov6.

McWhorter, John. "Path Dependence." Accessed Jan. 29, 2012: http://edge.org/response-detail/1515/what-scientific-concept-would-improve-everybodys-cognitive-toolkit.

Mark D. Nanos, "'Broken Branches': A Pauline Metaphor Gone Awry? (Romans 11:11–36)." In *Between Gospel and Election: Explorations in the Interpretation of Romans 9–11*, edited by Florian Wilk and J. Ross Wagner, 339–76. Tübingen: Mohr Siebeck, 2010. (See chapter 6 in this volume of collected essays.)

———. "'Callused,' Not 'Hardened': Paul's Revelation of Temporary Protection until All Israel Can Be Healed." In *Reading Paul in Context: Explorations in Identity Formation*, edited by Kathy Ehrensperger and J. Brian Tucker, 52–73. London: T. & T. Clark, 2010. (See chapter 7 in this volume of collected essays.)

———. "The Jewish Context of the Gentile Audience Addressed in Paul's Letter to the Romans." *Catholic Biblical Quarterly* 61 (1999) 283–304. (See chapter 3 in this volume of collected essays.)

———. *The Mystery of Romans: The Jewish Context of Paul's Letter*. Minneapolis: Fortress, 1996.

———. "Paul and the Jewish Tradition: The Ideology of the Shema." In *Celebrating Paul: Festschrift in Honor of Jerome Murphy-O'Connor, O.P., and Joseph A. Fitzmyer, S.J.*, edited by Peter Spitaler, 62–80. CBQMS. Washington, DC: Catholic Biblical Association of America, 2012. (See volume 1, chapter 4, in this series of collected essays.)

———. "Romans." In *The Jewish Annotated New Testament*, ed. Amy-Jill Levine and Marc Zvi Brettler, 253–86. New York: Oxford University Press, 2011.

Reddy, Michael J. "The Conduit Metaphor—A Case of Frame Conflict in Our Language about Language." In *Metaphor and Thought*, edited by Andrew Ortony, 284–324. Cambridge: Cambridge University Press, 1979.

Sherman, Franklin. "The Road to Reconciliation: Protestant Church Statements on Christian-Jewish Relations." In *Seeing Judaism Anew: Christianity's Sacred Obligation*, edited by Mary C. Boys, 241–51. Lanham, MD: Rowman and Littlefield, 2005.

Sievers, Joseph. "'God's Gifts and Call Are Irrevocable': The Reception of Romans 11:29 through the Centuries and Christian-Jewish Relations." In *Reading Israel in Romans: Legitimacy and Plausibility of Divergent Interpretations*, edited by Cristina Grenholm and Daniel Patte, 127–73. Harrisburg, PA: Trinity, 2000.

———. "A History of the Interpretation of Romans 11:29." *Annali di storia dell'esegesi* 14 (1997) 381–442;

Zohary, Daniel, and Maria Hopf. *Domestication of Plants in the Old World: The Origin and Spread of Cultivated Plants in West Asia, Europe, and the Nile Valley*. 3rd ed. Oxford: Oxford University Press, 2000.

9

The Translation of Romans 11 Since the Shoah

What's Different? What's Not? What Could Be?

[167] As DISCUSSED IN this morning's lecture,[1] Romans 11 provides graphic imagery by which to investigate the matters of Christian perceptions of and discourse about Jews and Judaism. Tellingly, it is the place where Paul expresses most explicitly his deep identification with and concern about the welfare of those among his fellow Jews who do not share his convictions about Jesus. He discloses these viewpoints specifically to elicit respectful empathy toward them by way of revealing a mystery: things will not turn out in the end as some non-Jews might suppose on the basis of how things presently appear, for "all Israel will be saved [= restored/rescued/made safe]." Moreover, he makes it clear that rather than judgmentalism or smug conceit, the proper recognition of their own precarious place and dependence upon God's grace bears witness to the fact that everyone, gentile as well as Jew, stands in need of God's mercy, and thus in need for merciful treatment by each other!

Chapter 11 completes an argument begun in chapter 9, which returns to themes foreshadowed in the first chapters that Paul is not ready to engage

---

1. The major details of the lecture this morning ("How Christians Talk about Jews: The Problems and Prospects of Paul's Message in Romans 11") reflects the exegetical and hermeneutical discussions available in Nanos, "Romans 11 and Christian and Jewish Relations."

until he has completed his arguments in chapters 5–8. Moreover, chapter 11 also sets up the "Therefore" of 12:1 and the chapters that follow. Therein, Paul exhorts the Christ-believing non-Jews of Rome to live in respectful relationships not only with each other, but with all humankind, and most relevantly, with Jews who do not share their convictions about Jesus. Paul explains to these non-Jews how they should imagine the present state of his fellow Jews as *also* their brothers and sisters in the family of God, as well as their own guest-like place among these Jews.[2]

It is readily apparent why Paul's statements in Romans 11 played a central role in Vatican II's document, *Nostra Aetate* 4, and other similar statements by Catholic and many Protestant organizations since, which draw explicitly on Paul's language in Romans 11 ("the Jews remain very dear to God, for the sake of the patriarchs, since God does not take back the gifts he bestowed or the choice he [168] made"; cf. Rom 11:28–29). Nevertheless, when we turn to current English language translations and interpretations of Romans 11 with this topic in mind, the very text from which the flowering of these respectful viewpoints on Jews and Judaism take root, we are confronted with language that would seem to cut off the emergence of these developments at their source. Ironically, translations have not caught up with sentiments that Paul's overall arguments are now understood to signify. Some important translations—including the RSV, NRSV, and several modern-language versions—represent choices that are more negative and replacement-theology-oriented than those in vogue earlier, not least when compared to the KJV and ASV, as well as other popular alternatives.[3]

This seminar offers us an opportunity to explore the translation alternatives I am suggesting, as well as some of the reasons these translations came to prevail in the first place, and why they have not already been changed in spite of very different sensibilities and even theological convictions by the denominations representing many if not most Christians, and what might be done to bring about changes that reflect these differences in future translations.

HISTORICAL FACTORS

The way that Romans has been translated into Latin and interpreted by Augustine and Luther, to name but two of the most famous Christian interpreters of Paul, and into many languages since, has had an immeasurable impact

2. Nanos, *The Mystery of Romans*.
3. Details were discussed in the earlier lecture; see Nanos, "Paul and the Jewish Tradition: The Ideology of the Shema."

on how Christians view Jews and Judaism—negative as well as positive. That influence is substantial not only within the churches, but in Western Society at large, and through missionary efforts and now globalization, in the perceptions of cultures around the world; hence, its direct relevance for today's lecture here in Hong Kong.

It is well known but perhaps not always attended to consistently in the framing of research approaches that neither Augustine nor Luther was really concerned with Jews or Judaism (contemporary or ancient) when they interpreted what Paul had to say in Romans. They were interested in how they could use Romans to develop and champion their views in contrast to those of their *Christian* rivals, whom they regarded as heretics. This polemical role for Romans continued, and continues, in various inter-sectarian battles waged within the Christian church.

In this role, Romans serves as a battleground for demonstrating one Christian group's claims to superior faithfulness to Paul's as well as Christ's teachings over a given rival Christian group's supposed inferior if not antithetical and thus heretical teachings. This dynamic is familiar to most people today in terms of the Reformation, which gave birth to Protestantism's protests of Roman Catholic policies and practices. Of course, there are no Roman Catholics mentioned in the texts of Paul's letters. But there are Jews mentioned there, and the policies and practices of Paul's fellow Jews [169] are central features of his arguments.

As a result, Christians and Christian groups have been waging battles against other Christians and Christian groups by turning the rivals into Jews, and their interpretations and behavior into Judaism. One strategy is to simply accuse them of "judaizing." The epithet generally remains undefined, and apparently need not be defined to be effective. It is applied as if it is self-evidently contrary to being a good Christian, with both the accuser and the accused convinced that Jewish values and ways of life are just plain wrong. To be so accused is to be judged to be in the wrong, for whatever reason, even if it has nothing to do with Jewish matters at all. Although no longer reminiscent of the original context of Paul's intra-Jewish polemic, but delivered from outside—as if Paul wrote of Judaism from outside of it, as if he did not still practice Judaism—it is Jews and Judaism that bear the brunt of criticism. Judaism serves only as the whipping boy en route to the real target, a rival Christian and their way of practicing Christianity. The implications for Jews extend much further; the horrors of the twentieth century have made this only too clear.

The negative role of the Jews in European society can be traced to the Revolt against Rome in the 60s CE, when the Judeans became anathematized as terrorists of the Roman empire, fit to be enslaved if not eliminated, commemorated in the Arch of Titus, where the victory over the Judeans is still portrayed to this day.

Relief, Arch of Titus in Rome, photo by Mark Nanos, 2009

The emperors Vespasian and his son Titus heralded this victory as the signifying [170] campaign of their reigns. They changed forever the ideal standing of Jews as upright subject people, however strange some of their beliefs and practices might have been regarded. It was from Jewish spoils, slave labor, and special taxation that the famous Colosseum was built, as well as the Temple to Jupiter, among other significant public works that commemorated forever, in stone, the conquest of the rebellious Jews.

When Paul wrote to Rome, which preceded these events by a decade or two, Jews were generally celebrated very differently, as strangers to be sure, just like Egyptians and Syrians. Nonetheless, they had been recognized and officially declared to be friends of Rome since the time of Julius Caesar, and granted special rights to practice their ancient customs, including permission to abstain from the civic cult to Caesar.[4] Romans could trust them to live according to the highest ideals, as outlined in their holy writings. Paul draws upon the widely respected reputation of Jews and Judaism in chapter 2 of Romans to argue from the well-known positive stereotype that anyone

---

4. Josephus, *Ant.* 14.185–89, the decrees are discussed from 185–267.

who would think to call themselves a Jew would be deeply opposed to doing other than what they said they would do, that is, Jews were widely known to avoid hypocrisy of any sort.[5] But many things changed for Jews and Judaism from the time of Vespasian, and later under Constantine. With the eventual Christianizing of the Roman Empire, the negative stereotype of the Jew and Judaism became part of the fabric of Christian rhetoric and policy.

The examples of inter-Christian polemicizing of Jews and Judaism can be multiplied endlessly. To name but one, consider how in the sixteenth century Luther finds fault with Jews in his particular interpretations of Romans, then segues into criticizing his various Christian rivals, whether Roman Catholic, Anabaptist, or others. Commenting on Rom 2:1, which refers to "whoever you are," a statement that is ambiguous and that at first sight would seem to be referring to anyone in general who would judge another rather than themselves, Luther instead concludes:

> This is indeed true of the heathen, yet *even in a greater measure of the Jews*. The Apostle therefore at the beginning of the chapter stresses the thought that in his accusation *he has in mind mainly the Jews*. To them we may compare, in a special degree, the heretics and hypocrites as also our modern jurists and priests, and lastly also those who quarrel among themselves and judge one another, while they do not regard themselves as offenders. Indeed they boast of their being right and even invoke God's wrath upon their adversaries; for certainly the Apostle here did not have in mind merely those who lived in Rome at that time.[6]

In other words, Paul had in mind those who lived in Rome during Luther's time, the Roman Catholic ecclesiastical hierarchy. Their fault in his view, judgmental hypocrisy, is attributed most especially to the Jews. Yet it should be noted here that as Paul's argument unfolds he makes the point that if one would call oneself a Jew he or she would be expected to be the most aware of and sensitive to avoiding hypocritical judgment (vv. 17ff.). A Jew would be well aware of his or her faults but also of being entrusted with God's words for the nations. It is just this Jewish self-perception of responsibility to be true to God's calling to which Paul appeals to instruct non-Jewish [171] Christ-believers in the way of faithfulness.

Several examples demonstrate the kind of judgments and judgmental language toward Jews and Judaism that is expressed in Luther's interpretation of chapter 11 of Romans, instead of the more positive evaluation of Jews and Judaism that one might expect to find there:

---

5. Cf. Epictetus, *Dissertation* 2.9.19–21.
6. Luther, *Commentary on the Epistle to the Romans*, 36–37 (emphasis added).

> 11:16: "By means of a twofold analogy the Apostle here supplies proof to magnify God's grace and destroy the arrogant (trans.: *Jewish*) boasting of righteousness."

The specific referent as "Jewish" is supplied by the translator, who understood it to represent Luther's intent, but that does not change the fact that it is suggested by those who represent Luther's interpretive trajectory. Yet Paul provides no such language here about Jews! Instead, Paul warns *non*-Jews in rather blunt, confrontational terms that they need to be careful of arrogance or they will be removed from their new place alongside of Jews as the people of God, who are the natural inhabitants of the metaphorical tree.

> 11:24: "The seed ... does not produce a good olive tree, illustrates ... that the Jews do not possess the glory—of the fathers simply because they were the seed of the fathers."

The inference Luther draws contradicts what Paul will write later in the chapter and that Luther will explicitly recognize in his comments there (vv. 28–29), as well as what Paul has written already in 9:1–5 about the continued, present gifts to and privileged identity of the Jews who do not share his convictions about Jesus. That is why Paul is engaged in an argument based on his conviction about the final outcome, that all Israel will be restored, from which he works backwards to disclose what this means presently, in spite of how things might otherwise appear.

> 11:26–27: "The purpose of the whole passage is to incite the people (trans.: *the Jews*) to repentance. Even if some among them are cast away, nevertheless, the lump must be honored because of the elect."

Again, the specific application to "the Jews" is inserted by the translator, but there is little reason to question that this is the intended referent for Luther. Nonetheless, it is hard to see how one could conclude that this passage is written to incite Jews to repentance! Instead, throughout Paul seeks to *incite non-Jews* to caution about the temptation toward arrogance lest these non-Jews be removed from God's grace. They can be part of the solution, but even if they fail to take Paul's warning to heart and thus to remain among the people of God, the final restoration of all Israel remains certain.

> 11:28: "The word 'enemies' must here be taken in a passive sense; that is, they deserve to be hated. God hates them, and so they are hated by the Apostles and all who are of God."

In the lecture I noted the problematic translation decision of the NRSV to add "of God," even though not attested in any Greek manuscripts, and thus to read "they are enemies *of God*," the implications of which Luther made clear long ago. Moreover, Paul's language suggests throughout these chapters that the present [172] situation is by God's design rather than earned, which Luther and many an interpreter is otherwise quick to supply when discussing what is "deserved." Nevertheless, how can Luther or any other interpreter conclude from Paul's argument here that God hates these Jews, or that they are hated by the Apostle Paul, or that Paul's instruction is meant to lead the non-Jews addressed (as those who now see themselves as "of God") to hate them?

TRANSLATION AND INTERPRETATION ALTERNATIVES

There are many translations alternative available to explore in chapter 11 (and throughout the letter). In the lecture I discussed several of them, especially the two metaphors Paul develops in this chapter: that of the stumbling while running to announce a message, and that of the olive tree. I showed how the Greek may be translated more in keeping with the metaphors around which Paul works his arguments as well as more consistently across the two metaphors and in support of the overall positive characterization of his fellow Jews as suffering a temporary setback but not an end point, as well as to emphasize the precarious place of the non-Jews directly addressed.[7]

First, I showed a number of problematic decisions in vv. 11–16, including the use of the language of "falling" and "failure" when Paul has already clarified that they have not "fallen" *down* but rather "lagged" *behind*, creating a gap into which some non-Jews can now join between them and those Jews (such as Paul) who have not experienced this "delay." Paul's point is that all will reach the destination, but because of this gap opening among Jews, non-Jews can also gain entry. Paul wants to confront any notion that the best interests of the non-Jews are ultimately served by the dismissal of these Jews, even though his positing of the opening for their entrance could have been taken to suggest such a limited good concept at work (someone must exit entirely for someone else to gain entry and attain the goal).

Then I explained why it is probably more accurate to translate the references in vv. 17–21 to the status of some of the Jews in terms of the natural branches not as "broken *off*" limbs, but as "broken" in the sense of

---

7. In addition to Nanos, "Romans 11 and Christian and Jewish Relations," already noted, extensive discussions of the translation and exegetical details are available in Nanos, "'Broken Branches'"; Nanos, "'Callused,' Not Hardened."

"bent." Although in a distressed state, these branches are still on the tree! Paul works around cognates of the Greek word *ekklaō* ("broken") in verses 17–21, which can express a temporary state of damage (as in "bent" limbs) that parallels his insistence in the previous metaphor of stumbling but not fallen, whereas "broken *off*," as usually translated, suggests instead fallen rather than merely temporarily stumbling, undermining his overall message. He does not introduce cognates of the Greek word *ekkoptō* ("cut off") until vv. 22–24, when he changes from describing the state of the non-Jews as a wild shoot among the Jews as the natural branches to the threat to the wild shoot of being [173] "cut off" yet again, this time from the tree into which they have been grafted. Paul threatens such a result for the wild shoot (non-Jews) if it (they) should suppose to have replaced the natural limbs, or to gloat or express indifference or judgmental arrogance toward their present plight instead of faithfulness, gratitude, and service (cf. 12:1ff.). When Paul's *a fortiori* inference arising from his stern warning to the non-Jews is read back into the earlier verses, it confuses the point he otherwise seems intent to make about the temporary stumbling or bending of some of his fellow Jews, that is, the anomalous lack of agreement that is presently being witnessed about the significance of Jesus, and thus whether Israel should be declaring him to the nations as the awaited one. He wants to make it clear that this unexpected development both serves the interests of these non-Jews for a time, and that it will eventually end with their agreement, but his introduction of this stern warning implies that the natural branches have been cut off rather than merely bent. He must then try to save the allegory (in vv. 23–24) by insisting that God can graft the natural branches back in again, that this would be more natural than grafting in a wild shoot in the first place, even though it is anything but natural to cut off branches only to seek to graft them back in again later, which Paul implicitly admits by appeal to God's omnipotence. To make his overall point against any incipient temptation to arrogance among the non-Jews specifically addressed, Paul compromises the allegorical clarity of his portrayal of the Jews temporarily suffering in order for these non-Jews to be incorporated "among them." Unfortunately, this has led, in my view, to a history of mistaken inferences about Paul's concept of the state of his fellow Jews and their replacement by non-Jews (hence, the NRSV translates *en autois* in v. 17 with "in their place" instead of the more natural, literal translation, "among them"). It also leads to the idea that non-Jews have been grafted into Israel, instead of among Israelites as fellow members of the people of God, but remaining distinct from Israel, as members of the other nations turning to Israel's God as the one and only God of all the nations too (cf. 3:29–31; 15:7–12).[8]

In vv. 25–27, I showed why "hardened" or "blinded" are not likely Paul's intended meaning, but "callused"—as in being protected in their presently harmed condition (resulting from stumbling or being bent)—and several other alternatives better capture Paul's message here. I also discussed problems and alternatives for several other specific language choices that follow after Paul's metaphor of stumbling and the allegory of the olive tree, including why "enemies"—and all the more of being "enemies *of God*"—are not warranted. Instead, the point is that some have been temporarily "estranged" (an adjective that parallels "beloved" in the next clause and alludes to the metaphorical descriptions as stumbling and bent). Moreover, the accusation that they are guilty of "disobedience" is more likely meant to communicate their present state of "not (yet) being persuaded." And they are probably not being presented as "imprisoned" or "shut up" in unpersuadedness (or disobedience), but rather the Jew and non-Jew have been "joined together" in this predicament, and thus together they are equally in need of God's grace, which is the theme of the final verses of the chapter (vv. 30–36).

I hope that we can discuss these in more detail during the time we have together [174] in this seminar, but first I would like to reflect on why these translations may have persisted in spite of changing sensibilities and methodologies.[9]

CONCLUSION, AND FURTHER REFLECTIONS

Why do we have this state of affairs? Beyond the many translation and interpretive issues that we could discuss together, and should, we could also discuss probable reasons for the translations and interpretations not changing yet to reflect these new sensibilities and interpretive insights. Below are some suggestions.

1. Translation Committees (and their Constituents)

- Are those who are chosen to serve on the committees likely to be conservative in approach, e.g., not likely to rock the boat with noticeable changes to long-repeated word choices? Do the people who want

---

8. Nanos, "Paul and the Jewish Tradition: The Ideology of the Shema."

9. During the discussion, it was made clear that current Chinese translations adopt choices that are equivalent to the traditional English translation choices that I am challenging.

The Translation of Romans 11 Since the Shoah 209

Bibles believe that the language itself is set, although the preferred sensibilities for how it is interpreted or applied may change? Is some combination of expectations of readers and anticipation of those expectations by committees and publishers at play?

- Do the committee members rely upon long repeated and well known glosses for the translations without supposing in many cases that there is the need to undertake new research, e.g., that there are reasons to question whether repeating previous translations represents the best alternatives?

- Do the translation and lexical traditions continue without challenge because the committee members are basically content with traditional conclusions?

- Or is repetition largely the result of "Path Dependence"? John McWhorter explains this dynamic by way of the following example:

    In an ideal world all people would spontaneously understand that what political scientists call path dependence explains much more of how the world works than is apparent. Path dependence refers to the fact that often, something that seems normal or inevitable today began with a choice that made sense at a particular time in the past, but survived despite the eclipse of the justification for that choice, because once established, external factors discouraged going into reverse to try other alternatives.

    The paradigm example is the seemingly illogical arrangement of letters on typewriter keyboards. Why not just have the letters in alphabetical order, or arrange them so that the most frequently occurring ones are under the strongest fingers? In fact, the first typewriter tended to jam when typed on too quickly, so its inventor deliberately concocted an arrangement that put A under the ungainly little finger. In addition, the first row was provided with all of the letters in the word typewriter so that salesmen, new to typing, could wangle typing the word using just one row.

    [175] Quickly, however, mechanical improvements made faster typing possible, and new keyboards placing letters according to frequency were presented. But it was too late: there was no going back. By the 1890s typists across America were used to QWERTY keyboards, having learned to zip away on new versions of them that did not stick so easily, and retraining them would have been expensive and, ultimately, unnecessary. So QWERTY was passed down the

generations, and even today we use the queer QWERTY configuration on computer keyboards where jamming is a mechanical impossibility.

The basic concept is simple, but in general estimation tends to be processed as the province of "cute" stories like the QWERTY one, rather than explaining a massive weight of scientific and historical processes. Instead, the natural tendency is to seek explanations for modern phenomena in present-day conditions . . . .[10]

This observation raises the prospect that many of the translation as well as interpretation matters continue to revolve around and reflect the theological concerns and battles of previous eras, most of them arising hundreds (as in the case of the quotes from Luther discussed) if not over fifteen hundred years ago, in cultural settings and social contexts not to mention languages very different from our own. Views of Jews, Judaism, and others were different among virtually all (widely known) Christian translators and interpreters in earlier generations, in general less generous. Yet their legacy persists when they are repeated as if assumed to be historically accurate for Paul for "present-time" exegetical and lexicographically driven reasons. Should they not be approached instead as (often mistaken) choices made at different, previous times for how to interpret Paul's language because of the "historical processes" at work in the lives of those earlier interpreters? Should they continue to be repeated without eliciting the recognition that there are other historically responsible exegetical alternatives to explore that would be more in keeping with the "present-time" sentiments of many Christians on these matters?

2. Motives

One can seldom know what motivates others. It is best to resist judging motives unless made explicit, but we should at least ask questions, for example, whether traditional sensibilities still characterize the views of the translation committee participants more than those involved in the council pronouncements on Jews and Judaism we surveyed. We might also ask:

- Does Christian self-identity still depend upon superiority to Jews and Judaism (supersessionism), as well as "in their place" (replacement) theology expressed in the unwarranted turn of phrase introduced in

10. http://www.edge.org/q2011/q11_9.html#mcwhorter

v. 17, instead of "among them," which is what the Greek contains? How does one account for the introduction of enemies "of God" in v. 28 late in the twentieth century?

- Are translators still primarily concerned about conforming their decisions to theological and ideological propositions already long held? For example, how open is a Protestant committee to making changes that would undermine traditional Protestant theological propositions, especially if the move might be construed to confirm more traditional Catholic positions—or even traditional Jewish ones?

- [176] Arguably things did not turn out as Paul presented them: is there a need to reduce dissonance, to save Paul, to rationalize away from the idea that he was mistaken?

- Is there resistance to the harshness of Paul's message that those who "believe" in Christ (i.e., Christians) can nevertheless "think" and "behave" in ways that "sever" their relationship to God, not least by the way that they treat those Jews in view in Paul's argument, i.e., those Jews who do not share their convictions about Jesus? Why is Paul's warning in v. 20 to the non-Jews about their attitude toward Jews who do not believe in Jesus translated in the NRSV as "stand in awe," when what is written is instead, "be afraid"(!)?

3. Historical-Critical Suspicion

Should translators and interpreters not take up the challenge of historical-critical suspicion, that is, willingness to find fault with and express distance from the views attributed to Paul? Some questions that arise include the following:

- In addition to questioning the alternatives available to Paul's interpreters, is it not also important to investigate Paul's own views with some distance, that is, apart from the assumption that whatever it was that he did mean to communicate is necessarily the way that things were, or are, or should continue to be conceptualized by those who do care about what Paul thought?

- Should not interpreters recognize that historical "reality" may have been different "in fact" and "interpreted" differently by other figures of Paul's time than his rhetorical approach to those people and events may suggest? Moreover, might not the motives of those figures he criticizes have been different than his aims and polemics claim and infer? Could they not have been perceived by themselves to be quite noble, and similarly have found Paul's actions and motives wanting? We do not have their point of view available to us; however, do we not owe it to them, and to his readers, to construct reasonable options for consideration?[11]

- If my reading of Romans 11 is correct, things did not happen in precisely the way Paul sought in this letter to communicate that they would turn out. Paul opened up that hermeneutical space at the end of chapter 11 by his appeal to God's sovereign designs being beyond complete comprehension by any human, and also beyond human imagination, if not also seemingly arbitrary and perhaps also self-congratulatory.[12] Is it then not time to seize this opportunity to rethink these translations and interpretations "with" Paul, to get our history right as far as possible, but at the same time also to reconsider the conclusions most rightly drawn for today, even when those might require some hermeneutical distance "from" him?

Thank you.

BIBLIOGRAPHY [177]

Luther, Martin. *Commentary on the Epistle to the Romans*. Translated by J. T. Mueller. Grand Rapids: Zondervan, 1954.

Mitternacht, Dieter. *Forum für Sprachlose: Eine kommunikations-psychologische und epistotar-rhetorische Untersuchung des Galaterbriefs*. CBNT 30. Stockholm: Almqvist & Wiksell, 1999.

Nanos, Mark D. "'Broken Branches': A Pauline Metaphor Gone Awry? (Romans 11:11–36)." In *Between Gospel and Election: Explorations in the Interpretation of Romans 9–11*, edited by Florian Wilk and J. Ross Wagner, 339–76. Tübingen: Mohr Siebeck, 2010. (See chapter 6 in this volume of collected essays.)

———. "'Callused,' Not 'Hardened': Paul's Revelation of Temporary Protection until All Israel Can Be Healed." In *Reading Paul in Context: Explorations in Identity Formation*, edited by Kathy Ehrensperger and J. Brian Tucker, 52–73. London: T. & T. Clark, 2010. (See chapter 7 in this volume of collected essays.)

———. "Challenging the Limits That Continue to Define Paul's Perspective on Jews and Judaism." In *Reading Israel in Romans: Legitimacy and Plausibility of Divergent Interpretations*, edited by Cristina Grenholm and Daniel Patte, 217–29. Harrisburg, PA: Trinity, 2000. (See chapter 11 in this volume of collected essays.)

---

11. I have argued for this reconsideration with respect to how to evaluate the identity of the "influencers" (often "opponents," etc.) of those Paul opposes in Galatians in Nanos, *The Irony of Galatians*; similarly, see Mitternacht, *Forum für Sprachlose*.

12. Nanos, "Challenging the Limits."

―――. *The Irony of Galatians: Paul's Letter in First-Century Context*. Minneapolis: Fortress, 2002.

―――. *The Mystery of Romans: The Jewish Context of Paul's Letter*. Minneapolis: Fortress, 1996.

―――. "Paul and the Jewish Tradition: The Ideology of the Shema." In *Celebrating Paul: Festschrift in Honor of Jerome Murphy-O'Connor, O.P., and Joseph A. Fitzmyer, S.J.*, edited by Peter Spitaler, 62–80. CBQMS 48. Washington, DC: Catholic Biblical Association of America, 2012. (See volume 1, chapter 4, in this series of collected essays.)

―――. "Romans 11 and Christian and Jewish Relations: Exegetical Options for Revisiting the Translation and Interpretation of this Central Text." *Criswell Theological Review* n.s. 9.2 (2012) 3–21. (See chapter 8 in this volume of collected essays.)

10

"The Gifts and the Calling of God are Irrevocable" (Romans 11:29)

If So, How Can Paul Declare that "Not All Israelites Truly Belong to Israel" (9:6)?[1]

[1] SINCE VATICAN II introduced *Nostra Aetate* 4 in 1965, it has become widely recognized "in our time" that Paul insisted God's choice of and promises to Israel were eternal, and that absolute affirmation of this continuity should shape Christian discourses about and relationships with Jews and Judaism. That document, and the many statements in this direction by other Christian organizations that followed it, appeal explicitly to Paul's statement that "the gifts and the calling of God are irrevocable" (Rom 11:29) as well as his exclamation that "all Israel will be saved" (11:26; both translations from NRSV).[2] Continued covenantal relationship between

---

1. This essay is a revision of a study originally written for translation into German for a Protestant liturgical pastoral guidebook for the reading of 9:1–8, 14–16: "'Gottes Gaben und Berufungen können Ihn nicht gereuen.'—Wie, also, sollten wir Römer 9,1–16 (insbesondere V. 6) übersetzen und verstehen?" in *"Die Gotteskindschaft des jüdischen Volkes (Röm 9,1–16)": Arbeitshilfe zum Israelsonntag 2016: 10. Sonntag nach Trinitatis*, edited by Volker Haarmann, Ursula Rudnick, and Axel Töllner, translated by V. Haarmann (Düsseldorf: Evangelische Kirche im Rheinland, Evangelisch-Lutherische Landeskirche Hannover, Begegnung von Christen und Juden Bayern, 2016), 14–23; <www.ekir.de/christen-juden>.

2. For some examples from Protestant churches, see Sherman, "The Road to Reconciliation," in *Seeing Judaism Anew*, edited by M. C. Boys; other essays in the volume discuss Catholic examples, and various other developments and statements.

God and all Israel is affirmed rather than denied on the basis that Israel remains "beloved because of the fathers" (11:28). That relationship is understood to operate presently—in various ways by various organizations—to some degree independent of whether Jewish people have become participants in the relationship that Christians celebrate with God through their faith in Jesus Christ,[3] [2] although traditionally it has been maintained that Jews will be convinced to share this conviction with Christians at some point in the future.[4]

Paul's argument begins in chapter 9 with the powerful promise of the continuity of his Israelite compatriots' identity as Israelites. Regardless of whether each Israelite already shared Paul's convictions about Jesus and thus presently undertook to proclaim God's good news to the nations alongside of himself, they all remain recipients of the gifts given to Israel (9:1–5). The argument ends in chapter 11 with the same message of God's continued commitment to the continuity of Israel, to which post-Shoah theologians appeal to shape new paradigms for the church going forward. However, the impact of these declarations of continuity is significantly mitigated when not entirely subverted by the way that the rest of the language in chapter 9 is translated and interpreted, and most significantly, in v. 6.[5]

The ostensibly contrasting idea is introduced dramatically in 9:6 to the reader of modern translations [*ou gar pantes hoi ex Israēl houtoi Israēl*]: "For not all Israelites truly belong to Israel" (NRSV).[6] Paul's language is presented as if designed to express that Israelites who do not believe in Jesus have already been excluded from identification as the Israel of God, although they can rectify that by becoming Christians (members of the church; or, less anachronistically, Christ-followers).[7] Translations commonly introduce

---

3. Cf. The Vatican's Commission for Religious Relations with Jews, "The Gifts and Calling of God are Irrevocable," marking the 50th anniversary of the ground-breaking declaration "Nostra Aetate."

4. The interpretation of the language in Paul on which these eschatological conversion scenarios are based is questioned by Nanos and Cunningham, "Implications of Paul's Hopes for the End of Days for Jews and Christians Today."

5. The tendency for Christian traditional interpreters prior to NA 4 to translate and interpret even 11:29 in ways that did not affirm eternal commitment to Jews who were not Christians is traced in Sievers, "'God's Gifts and Call Are Irrevocable.'"

6. KJV: "For they are not all Israel, which are of Israel"; NASB: "For they are not all Israel who are descended from Israel"; NIV: "For not all who are descended from Israel are Israel"; "Denn es sind nicht alle Israeliter, die von Israel sind" (Luther, 1912).

7. I want to bring particular attention to the earlier work of Lloyd Gaston on this tension, especially his essay "Israel's Enemies in Pauline Theology," and dedicate this essay to his memory. He highlighted Paul's concern that the role of Israel in bringing the gospel to the nations was central versus the usual emphasis on them becoming saved. Thank you, Lloyd; may your memory (continue to) be for a blessing.

the word "really" or "truly," which serves to help make this point, as if some current-day Israelites are not "really" members of Israel, not "truly" Israelites, although that qualification is not in the Greek manuscripts.

The verses that follow v. 6 continue to be understood to highlight this message of discontinuity, of Israel as an entity that is other than the one historically identified as the descendants of the tribes of Jacob/Israel. Instead, the church (the community of Christians) has taken their place and become Israel, variously worded (including such "supersessionist" terms as "replaced," "reconfigured," "redefined," "spiritual," "true," none of which were used by Paul to [3] describe Israel).[8] In this way, Paul's insistence that God's covenant promises to Israel are eternal and the church's traditional perspective that Paul could not have meant that Jews who did not believe in Jesus were still included in those promises, is supposedly resolved by redefining Israel so as to exclude those Jews while at the same time including any non-Jews who believe in Jesus Christ. But it is difficult to square that with Paul's opening and closing arguments: he was discussing Jews who did not agree with him about Jesus when he appealed to the certainty of their continued identity as Israel (9:1–5; 11:11–32).

Is there an alternative for those Christian interpreters (or anyone else) who wish to interpret Paul as accurately as possible and to avoid the legacy of this interpretive conundrum if not contradiction at the center of Paul's thinking about Israel, and the role these still play "in our time"? Yes, there is.

After all, logically, it makes good sense that Paul would design the arguments that follow his opening declarations in chapter 9 and precede his conclusions in chapter 11 to confirm rather than to contradict them. Before we focus on chapter 9, let us survey some of the conclusions

---

8. "On the part of many of the Church Fathers the so-called replacement theory or supersessionism steadily gained favor until in the Middle Ages it represented the standard theological foundation of the relationship with Judaism: the promises and commitments of God would no longer apply to Israel because it had not recognized Jesus as the Messiah and the Son of God, but had been transferred to the Church of Jesus Christ which was now the true 'new Israel,' the new chosen people of God. Arising from the same soil, Judaism and Christianity in the centuries after their separation became involved in a theological antagonism which was only to be defused at the Second Vatican Council. With its Declaration 'Nostra Aetate' (No.4) the Church unequivocally professes, within a new theological framework, the Jewish roots of Christianity. While affirming salvation through an explicit or even implicit faith in Christ, the Church does not question the continued love of God for the chosen people of Israel. A replacement or supersession theology which sets against one another two separate entities, a Church of the Gentiles and the rejected Synagogue whose place it takes, is deprived of its foundations. From an originally close relationship between Judaism and Christianity a long-term state of tension had developed, which has been gradually transformed after the Second Vatican Council into a constructive dialogue relationship." Commission for Religious Relations with the Jews: "The Gifts and the Calling of God are Irrevocable."

reached in chapter 11. This will help us develop working assumptions for re-reading vv. 6–16 of chapter 9, especially v. 6. Throughout, appeal will be made to more literal translations to re-evaluate the most probable meaning in its original context.

THE EXPECTATIONS CREATED BY THE CONCLUSIONS REACHED IN CHAPTER 11

It is widely recognized that Paul introduces a series of metaphors in chapter 11 to insist that those of his fellow Jews who have not joined him in his convictions about Jesus nevertheless remain members of Israel, and, as such, are ensured of receipt of God's promise of salvation, signified by his bold claim that "all Israel will be saved" (v. 26). Equally influential, indeed, the text around which *Nostra Aetate* 4 built, as already noted, is the related claim that while some [4] Israelites are presently considered "enemies [or: 'estranged' (discussed below)] for your sake," at the same time they remain "beloved for the sake of the fathers, for the gifts and the calling of God are irrevocable" (vv. 28–29). These statements can be made clearer and stronger, so too can be the messages in the metaphors preceding them.[9]

Although I have posed the tension between the positive message in 11:26, 28–29 and the negative one in 9:6 in traditional terms that raise the need to revisit the options for 9:6, the standard translation in chapter 11 ironically hides within it a supposition that should be noticed, and that I also want to challenge. The usual translation and interpretation of *sōzō* as "saved" is in a circular way supported by the way that 9:6 has been understood—that many Israelites are in some way already outside of covenantal standing as Israel, although they *will be returned* to that standing at some point in the future. However, the Greek verb translated "will be *saved*" in 11:26 is a future form of *sōzō*, which is not used to describe saving as in returning to life that which had died, so to speak, but to keeping alive—although the implications for the translation and interpretation of Paul's arguments seems to have gone unnoticed. In keeping with the usage of Paul's time, *sōzō* and cognates refer to "safekeeping," and in the future tense, as Paul used it here, to "will be *protected*" or "*preserved*," as in "*kept safe*," or "*delivered*" or "*rescued*" from danger, or for one who is ill (or, e.g., a branch

---

9. For more detail, see Nanos, "Romans 11 and Christian and Jewish Relations," and the several exegetical essays for the details referenced therein. Here and throughout this essay, readers might also want to consult the notes for Nanos, "Romans." For the German translation of reflections on Romans 11 when it arose in the reading cycle see Nanos, "Römer 11 und christlich-jüdische Beziehungen."

that is injured), to be "*healed*" (*LSJ*).[10] This applies to the other uses of cognates of *sōzō* in the immediate context: "for their protection" (10:1); and in 10:9-10 and v. 13, "protected." The context of the original texts in Deut 9:4-6 and 30:11-14 from which Paul draws are not about gaining entrance into standing as Israel, but about how to behave faithfully after they have entered the next phase of their covenantal relationship so that they will prosper and be protected in the land; these covenantal commandments and resultant blessings versus curses are based upon the covenantal descent standing that they *already* enjoy. While the traditional choice of "saved" can arguably communicate this idea, it should be [5] avoided in these cases because the translation "saved" has expressed the assumption that these Israelites already had lost their covenant standing for not believing in Jesus as Messiah (now challenged by *Nostra Aetate* 4), thus that they are in need of being "re-admitted" rather than "retained" in standing as the "true" or "spiritual Israel" of 9:6, the topic to which we will return.

There is good reason, then, in spite of the many positive uses to which this phrase has been put, to heretofore eschew translating this phrase as "all Israel will be *saved*," as well as the alternative I had adopted until recently recognizing this issue myself, "*restored*," since it arguably suffers from the same implication. The alternative, "all Israel will be *protected*," highlights the idea that these Israelites are being and will continue to be *preserved safely* in their already *preexisting* covenantal standing in spite of present circumstances that Paul's addressees might be tempted to interpret differently, such as in the direction of later Christian replacement theology. Following the olive tree allegory, the metaphorical implication is that "all the Israelite branches (i.e., the temporarily injured ones) will be *healed*." Perhaps to accentuate the defamiliarizing potential of this insight we should refer to all Israel being "made safe," or "*safed*."

Notice too that rather than "enemies" in 11:28, the Greek word *echthroi* should probably be translated "*estranged* (ones)," reflecting the parallel use of the widely recognized adjectival "*beloved* (ones) [*agapētoi*]," balancing the comparative contrast around which he is working.[11] This would represent another way of communicating Paul's judgment that these fellow Israelites are suffering what he has been describing metaphorically as "stumbling."

---

10. In English, we speak of the doctor "saving" the patient so that they "recover," by which we do not generally mean that the doctor brought them back after they were "lost" as in dead, but that they keep them from dying, healing or protecting them so that they recover instead of remaining sick or getting worse. These matters were the focus of my 2015 Society of Biblical Literature Annual Meeting paper: "Are Jews Outside of the Covenants If Not Confessing Jesus as Messiah?"

11. See Beck, "Translations of the New Testament for Our Time."

They are thus "lagging be-hind" as well as being "broken" (as in "bent" or "injured") branches to express his judgment that their not joining him in bringing the message of the gospel to the nations is a *failing*, but it is a *temporary* one in an ongoing process, and one in which God is complicit.

Yes, Paul's view does express a criticism of these other Jews based upon his convictions about Jesus; however, this alternative highlights that Paul regards this temporary state to represent vicarious suffering on behalf of the addressees without also suggesting that they are *enemies* of the addressees or, just as importantly, that they are "enemies *of God*" (an addition the NRSV makes without any manuscript evidence). At the same time, it captures the fact that Paul is seeking to describe the role of God's design and present appearances as different, and more promising, than the non-Jew addressees might otherwise suppose. They are witnesses of a point in an ongoing process, one that involves inscrutable elements being shaped by the divine in ways that defy even Paul's best efforts to unravel (cf. 11:33–36). Paul remains, nevertheless, certain of a positive end result for all of his fellow Israelites: eventually, this process will conclude with their *success*. He also argues in a way that should make the idea that he saw "Israel" per se as having *rejected* the gospel or *being rejected* by God impossible to suppose, for [6] Paul identifies his own activity to represent that *of Israel* (11:1–10). Even if the task as he understands it (bringing the gospel to the nations) is only faithfully being carried out presently by *some* Israelites, it is nevertheless being carried out *by Israel*! This point parallels closely the argument in 9:1–5, and should, I suggest, guide the interpretation of v. 6, to be discussed.

In the metaphors in 11:11–16, Paul insisted that while some Israelites have "stumbled," they have not "fallen," and that while this temporary development has created an opening for some non-Israelites *to join in alongside of them* on the course, the longed for culmination ("life from the dead" in v. 15) will only be achieved when those who have thus fallen behind for a while complete the course too. Although not always recognized, there is good reason to question whether this metaphor was designed to portray Israelites in terms of *salvation*, to state the issue in later Christian terms. Rather, Paul appears to be reflecting upon the prophetic notion that when the awaited day of good news arrives the *messengers* of Israel *will complete the task of running to announce this news* to fellow Israelites *and* to the nations;[12] nevertheless, some would-be messengers are stumbling presently rather than running; that is, they are presently not expressing faithfulness to complete this task. This fits: Paul has worked with the idea that Israel's chosen role was being entrusted with God's words or oracles since he introduced the concept in

12. See Isa 62:6–12.

3:2, and he will discuss whether or not Israel has been faithful to that trust at the end of chapter 9, and, it seems, throughout chapter 10 and into chapter 11, where he introduces the language we are discussing. Moreover, in chapter 11 (esp. vv. 20–22) he warns the Christ-following non-Jew addressees to remain faithful to their calling, to that which they believe to be true for themselves, rather than to consider it their task to judge these fellow Jews (so too in chapter 2, leading up to the declaration of 3:2).

For the sake of space, we will not discuss all of the translation choices in this metaphor of stumbling but not falling that can be improved to support rather than undermine a message of continuity (e.g., such as "misstep" rather than "transgression," "lagging behind" rather than "failure"), and move directly to the translation of the olive tree allegory that follows it in vv. 17–24.[13] The translations here can also be improved to support Paul's affirmations of Israel's protection.

The Greek word usually translated "broken *off*" (formed from *ekklaō*), can be translated very differently and thereby communicate very different implications both within the allegory of the olive tree and for the analogies drawn about Paul's view of his fellow Israelites. *Ekklaō* can be translated "broken," as in when a branch is "bent" so as to suffer a "break" or "crack" in it; although injured, it remains on the tree. Rather than contradict the prior metaphor, as if Paul had just stated rather than denied that these Israelites had indeed stumbled so as to "fall," which imagining limbs broken or cut *off* instead communicates(!), the allegory [7] can remain consistent, emphasizing a temporary problematic development, one that can be described as present alienation from faithfully accomplishing the assigned task rather than as abandoning it, and thereafter being abandoned by God.[14] I suggest translating *apistia* (11:23) in terms of the rest of the

13. Examples outside of the allegory are several as well, not least of which is that "disobedience" in vv. 30–32 can be understood instead as "unconvinced," which better represents the disposition of most Israelites, versus the idea of "rejecting," as if convinced but unwilling to humbly accept the truth.

14. The notion of the natural branches being broken "off" is an element in the replacement theological proposition that the wild shoot (note, singular for Paul, but almost always referred to by interpreters in the plural as shoots or branches) is grafted into the tree where the natural branches were pruned off (NRSV goes so far as to invent, "in their place," when Paul wrote "among them [*en autois*]") (v. 17). Problematic too is the notion that the shoot is grafted into "Israel," and thus the idea that the gentiles become members of Israel, when Paul does not identify the tree as Israel but Israelites as branches in the tree, the new shoot drawing from the same root (this is, notably, often the first basis for upholding the idea that the Christian non-Jew is now a part of Israel, however qualified, often as "true" or "spiritual," etc.). Along the same line, this metaphorical language is treated as if a literal theological statement and repeated endlessly without reflection on the fact that humans are not branches and are not grafted

Israelites' "lack of faithfulness" (at this point) to carry out Israel's calling to announce the message to the nations, not as if at issue in the metaphor is "unbelief" in Jesus as Messiah per se. "Unbelief" in Jesus would not make sense of the threat to the wild branch being rebuked, and thus to the corresponding comment about the broken Israelite branches: it is not failure to continue to believe in Jesus that would lead to the wild branch being cut out, but unfaithfulness to the responsibility it has toward the suffering branches, which is not to grow arrogant toward them and suppose it has replaced them as the recipients of God's gifts and calling. Moreover, following the allegory, the usual translation of v. 25 communicates that these Israelites have been "hardened," which has a negative valence and is often even analogized with the *hardening* of Pharaoh's heart, even though that is based upon a different Greek word (*sklērunō*; 9:18). Paul uses a form of the verb *pōroō* in 11:25. This is a medical term used to describe the temporary, positive process of a body or tree mending a broken element by creating a "callus."[15] A bent or cracked limb is "callused" to "protect" the injured area from further damage until it can be fully "healed"; in the meantime, it can continue to function within the tree toward its goal of producing fruit. "All Israel will be healed, protected, preserved, kept safe."

As we have surveyed, Paul concluded in chapter 11 that the present lack of participation by some (even many) Israelites (Jews) in the process of taking the message to the nations was part of a temporary stage in a larger design, one during which God was protecting these Israelites based upon the promises made to them through their ancestors, which was in keeping with the way that he began his argument in chapter 9. Now, let us see if we can read the verses in chapter 9 within the stream of this propositional logic, rather than as if it undermined it or set out an entirely different message.

THE AFFIRMATION OF THESE JEWS AS ISRAELITE "BROTHERS AND SISTERS" STILL IN COVENANTAL STANDING (9:1-5)

[8] Suddenly, at the marker we recognize as 9:1, Paul changes his topic from that of chapters 5 through 8.[16] He returns to the affirmation of the advantage

---

into trees (thus representing a dead metaphor). For the complete argument see Nanos, "'Broken Branches.'"

15. Nanos, "'Callused,' Not 'Hardened.'"

16. In view of the focus of this essay I am not engaging in detail with the various alternatives for who is asking or answering questions when diatribe is recognized to be at work here, but Paul introduces issues by way of one or more invented dialogue

of being a member of Israel—specifically, a Jew by genealogical descent—raised much earlier, at 3:2: Jews are "entrusted with the words/oracles of God"! The reason for suddenly addressing the implications of this topic is not self-evident.

The nature of the argument Paul commences may suggest that he wants to gainsay what might be inferred from the conclusion of the argument in chapter 8 about the certainty of God's commitment to those chosen in Christ, including those from the nations making up Paul's target audience. He seems to recognize they might reason that the corollary to their newfound assurance of God's commitment to their success, regardless of present appearances and troubles, can be calculated by them in zero-sum terms, whereby their good fortune is imagined to necessarily entail the replacement of the good fortune of someone else.[17] If so, Paul appears concerned that these non-Jews might infer what Christian theologians from the second century on in fact did advocate, that is, that Christ-following non-Jews (later: Christians) had become Israel, the *true* Israel of God, having replaced any Israelites not convinced that Jesus was the Christ—regarded as "rejecting the truth" and thereby being "rejected" by God.[18] Whatever the case, Paul launches into a spirited rebuttal of any such thinking in the first five verses of chapter 9.

Although Paul affirms the continuation of God's gifts and calling to his fellow Jews, he also expressed sadness and ongoing concern for their wellbeing. In language reminiscent of the prayer of Moses for solidarity with the fate of his fellow Israelites who were turning to other gods while he was receiving the commandments at Mt. Sinai (Exod 32:31–33), Paul asserts that he would vow to be accursed, cut off from Christ, for the sake of his kinsmen "according to the flesh," that is, by genealogical descent. He does not explain here what it is that leads to this display of empathy, but based on what follows, presumably it is on behalf of those of his fellow Jews who do not share his convictions about Jesus being the Messiah, perhaps more specifically their failure—from his perspective, yet, at this [9] time, anyway—to

---

partners. Judgments about which positions Paul upholds versus those to be attributed to his dialogue partner (and whether more than one partner or alternative positions), and who he (or they) represent(s) remains controversial, and the various implications are too many to discuss here.

17. This same concern surfaces in the argument of chapter 11, such as in the diatribe question in v. 19 attributed to the wild branch.

18. Richardson, *Israel in the Apostolic Church*. The discursive practice of describing Israel rejecting and being rejected by God continues to this day, which is readily witnessed by consulting the commentaries on this chapter.

join him in declaring the gospel to the nations.[19] Paul's qualification of kinship in terms of "flesh" is often turned into a binary contrast to suggest that his relationship to his fellow Jews is no longer one of "spirit." But the next statement undermines any such reasoning, or it should. Many of the elements listed are not only spiritual in nature, but affirm shared supernatural attributes as fellow Israelites and servants of God (e.g., to whom the practice of the cult, legislation, glory, etc., are entrusted, which are spiritual in nature, just as Paul declares *ho nomos* spiritual in 7:14).

Similarly, appeal to Paul's deep concern is regularly noted to argue that he must see his fellow Israelites as no longer Israel to make sense of it, or as those who are not the ideal, legitimate ("real") Jews. If that were so, Paul certainly confuses the point at the most basic level by continuing to refer to these others as "Jews" and "Israel" throughout the letter, and he does the same in his other letters too. Why not refer to the addressees directly as Israel and Jews and the others as formerly such, or as apostates, or something similar, if that is the way that he already sees the situation to have become, and presumes that his target audience does as well? Paul betrays the fact that he does not consider them to have lost their covenant standing and thus be in need of "being saved just like gentiles," to use the common phrasing. Just before v. 6, in v. 4, Paul declares unabashedly: "who are Israelites"! One might expect, based upon the long tradition of supersessionism and replacement theology—a tradition that appeals especially to vv. 6 and following—that Paul would have begun with: "who *were* Israelites"![20] But he does not.

Instead, Paul next launches into listing many specific elements of their continued identity as Israelites. Again, one might expect him to have qualified these as *former* if he saw his compatriots in later Christian terms, as having lost their standing in covenant as Israel unless they were re-admitted ("saved") following a change of confession about Jesus. But Paul describes the situation in terms of continuity, even if at the same time with serious concern. This suggests that Paul is expressing empathy based upon a potential future development, perhaps what they might suffer as Israelites for

19. Gaston, *Paul and the Torah*, 116–34, 135–50, raises the issue that Paul is discussing the declaration of the word to the nations by Israel, not its salvation, which I continue to find likely throughout Romans.

20. I have argued similar logic at work in 2:25–29, against the consensus readings, in Nanos, "Paul's Non-Jews Do Not Become 'Jews,' But Do They Become 'Jewish'?" Notice, too, the commentary habit to derive from Paul's affirmation of identity as Israelites that he was seeking to drive a wedge between that and their identity as Jews; cf. Dunn, *Romans 9–16*, 533: "The choice of title is obviously deliberate, 'Israelites' being preferred to 'Jew' (contrast 2:17, 28–29; 3:29)." In the direction I am arguing, see also Soulen, "They are Israelites': The Priority of the Present Tense for Jewish-Christian Relations."

failure to have that change of conviction. Logically, that would mean that he saw them as still Israel, remaining in covenantal standing but in need of "safe-keeping": if punished, however severely, this would [10] represent discipline according to covenantal (family) terms *as* Israel, which is not the same as being dismissed from standing as Israel.[21]

Consider the list of summary features Paul affirms to still apply to these "Israelites":

> ... and of whom are the sonship (i.e., adoption), and the glory (i.e., God's presence [Heb. *kovod*]), and the covenants (e.g., Abrahamic, Mosaic, Davidic, later prophetic, and these include the promise of the land, blessings, as well as discipline when warranted to allow to repent and retain covenant standing, etc.), and the giving of the legislation (to Moses, i.e., Torah guidance), and the cult (i.e., temple sacrificial system of worship [Heb. *avodah*]), and the promises (i.e., "to the fathers," like "the covenants," logically includes elements not mentioned explicitly, like "the land," and "the word entrusted," the theme around which he is working [see 3:2]; note the language in 11:29, "the gifts and the calling of God," to concisely cover this same ground), of whom (are) the patriarchs (i.e., the fathers: Abraham, Isaac, Jacob/Israel; hence, the affirmation that they are "the seed" in the argument to come, not merely of genealogical descent [flesh] but also of promise), and from whom is the Messiah (Christ, the Davidic covenant, see 1:1–5), who (is [an Israelite]) according to the flesh (i.e., by genealogical descent). May he who is God over all, be blessed forever. Amen ("it is so," "let it be so," indicating acceptance of what has been stated, although it might appear presently to the addressees to be otherwise).

There is not space here for further reflection on these many elements, but obviously there is much to explore for a full assessment of Paul's view of current covenantal standing of his fellow Jews, and thus, about what it was specifically that so deeply concerned him.

Largely missing in the conversation about this passage, too, is Paul's description of those about whom he is concerned as "brothers [and sisters]." Before we move to v. 6 and the problems that arise there, it is interesting to note that Paul uses many of the same terms to refer both to his fellow Israelites and to his fellow Christ-followers.[22]

---

21. See 2 Macc 6:12–17; cf. Ps 94:12; Prov 3:11–12; Jer 30:11; Lam 3:31–33; Jdt 8:27; Wis 12:1–2, 26; Pss. Sol. 10.1; 13.7; 16.1–5.

22. Many similar dynamics are covered in Nanos, *The Mystery of Romans*; this list is on p. 112.

Identification	for Christ-followers	for non-Christ-following Jews/Israelites
brethren	1:13; 8:29	9:3
adoption as sons	8:15	9:4
children of God	8:16–17	9:8
have the glory	8:18	9:4
Abraham as father	4:10–17	4:10–17
seed of Abraham	9:7–8; 4:13–18	9:7–8; 11:1
beloved of God	1:7	11:28
called	9:25; 8:28; 1:16	9:7, 24; 11:29
elect	8:28, 33	9:11
foreknown	8:29	11:2

[11] The idea that Paul sees these as two distinct identity groups, as former versus current family, so central to the idea of replacement theology, is not in keeping with the way that Paul's reasoning reveals itself on these matters—he argues for this *and* that, not this *or* that. These non-Jews (non-Israelites) who become members of the people of God through Jesus Christ join *together with* Jews (Israelites), who *remain* the people of God, whether Christ-followers or not; they *do not displace them*. The implications for reading Paul within Judaism are many, they guide the assumptions at work for the modern reader, starting from what one assumes were the assumptions at work for Paul and his original intended reader.

TRANSLATING AND INTERPRETING 9:6–16

Suddenly, the reader of this passage encounters a denial of a position that does not represent what he had been arguing for anyway, betraying that he assumes his audience may reason in a very different way than he does: (NRSV v. 6a): "It is not as though the word of God had failed." A more literal translation for "had failed" would be "has fallen [*ekpeptōken*]." The usual interpretation is based upon the idea that the Jews *rejected* the *gospel* and thus that they have been rejected by God, that they are not "saved." But Paul has not introduced the idea that the word had gone to Israel, so there is no basis for the addressees to suppose that the question concerns whether the word had failed to reach or convince these Israelites. Rather, he has written that the advantage of being a Jew and circumcised involved being entrusted with the special role of being the *messengers entrusted* to bring God's word *to the nations* (3:2; 10:15; cf. Isa 52:7–10). If those whom Paul has just insisted remain Israelites, with all that he lists still applying to them, but if they do not presently proclaim the words of God entrusted to them (that being the gospel, as understood by Paul and his addressees), this would logically raise an objection. If the plan for which Paul has argued is based upon Israel carrying out its trust to declare the word to the nations, then it is logical to ask how the nations will hear it, and whether their own fate can be tied to such a contingency. Put in these terms, Paul's language choice of "falling" appeals to the same metaphorical concern expressed in chapter 11 in terms of some stumbling, to which Paul also responds with the assurance that this is not the case (vv. 11–15). The issue is one of "faithfulness" to carry out the task "entrusted" to Israel (yet, or not), thus cognates of faithfulness or loyalty or trust are used for cognates of *pistis* throughout this essay, rather than faith or belief.

Then, in the rest of v. 6—as usually translated and understood, that is—Paul ostensibly introduces the (confusing if not entirely inscrutable) idea that these Israelites are not actually still members of Israel: "For not all Israelites truly belong to Israel" (NRSV). As already discussed, these translations not only introduce a major discontinuity into Paul's argument, but they have been used to communicate that Paul regards Israelite identity according to genealogical descent to be transcended now by a new concept of Israel, one consisting of Christians, primarily composed of non-Jews but including any Jews who have become Christians [12] (and, usually, certainly after a few centuries, if they have disavowed observance of Torah and the practice of Judaism, of Jewish communal life).[23]

Before we consider the literal translation and several alternative ways to understand Paul's statement, let us survey the case that he makes following this sentence, toward which we should expect him to be pointing.

The Message(s) of Verses 7–16:

A brief survey of these verses is all we have space to offer, but the message is relatively straightforward, even though elements of the traditional translation and interpretation are not. In vv. 7–9, Paul argues that although Abraham had children who were not through Sarah, those descended through her constituted the promised descendant line ("the seed"). Again, we have a similar appeal to the certainty that God's word will not be circumvented, in this case by the fact that Abraham had other children than those through Sarah. Rather than suggesting that Paul is opening up the description of

23. See Parkes, *The Conflict of the Church and the Synagogue*.

"Israel" in v. 6 to include children not of his genealogical descent, as the traditional view upholds it to be, the point Paul makes is that the line is narrowed down to only those born of Sarah's line, that is, through Isaac. That supports the idea he has asserted in vv. 4–5, that these descendants remain the seed to whom the promise was made even if some are not discharging (yet) the concomitant responsibility to declare the word. It also maintains the consideration that events may be unfolding in ways that seem random or even contrary to expectations, but that this all proceeds based upon God's timetable, "at the appointed time" (v. 9). Verses 10–13 form a unit that strengthens the point ("and again . . .").[24]

Is Paul driving a wedge between calling (grace and election/choice) and flesh (genealogical descent), or rather explaining that God chose a particular line of genealogical descendants to undertake a special task as "the seed"? I propose the latter. Notice that being chosen by grace and being genealogical descendants are not presented as binaries in this argument, although that is what one finds commonly asserted in the commentaries. The overall point is that the seed continues to be narrowed down through Abraham's genealogical descendants without regard for their activity, good or bad, and before any such activity has even taken place from which to influence God's choice: it is simply a result of God's sovereign choice that Isaac's wife Rebecca's younger son Jacob (Israel) rather than the [13] firstborn Esau will inherit the promise. When read together, vv. 10–13 confirm that *in spite of performance*, good or bad, God's word of promise to the specific descent line of Israelites—that they are entrusted with God's words—remains guaranteed. And those Israelites Paul has been defending as Israel (in spite of their present disagreement with him and his addressees about the meaning of Jesus) are included in this firm promise. And when read together, this leads to exactly what Paul will declare to be achieved by this argument in vv. 14–16!

Verse 14 poses the logical question that the argument preceding it has raised: *is God unjust* to choose whom God wills independent of

---

24. Interestingly, the German Protestant liturgical reading for which I initially researched this passage does not include vv. 11–13, skipping from vv. 1–10 to 14–16. That decision may contribute to, as well as reflect, the traditional interpretive judgment that the historically descended Israelites in question are not the promised seed on the basis of failure to *perform* correctly (in this case, the activity of believing in Jesus as Christ, or, alternatively, and contextually more likely, the task of carrying forth the gospel of Christ to the nations [has the word of God "fallen"?]). However, the traditional decision to attribute the identity of (true) Israel in v. 6 to those who are not of that genealogical descent line (i.e., Christ-following non-Israelites) does so at the expense of disregarding the text that Paul wrote to explain his position, in this case by deleting these passages from the reading!

behavior, whether good or bad, or even yet performed—specifically (although perhaps not as salient if the reader skips vv. 11–13), that only certain members of the line of Abraham through Jacob/Israel will inherit the promises made to Abraham, thus that these subsequent descendants and not others are the legitimate claimants to the promises made to the "seed"? In vv. 14–29, the answer is pronounced dramatically: God is sovereign and chooses accordingly.

There is one specific point in v. 16 that should not go unnoticed before we turn back to v. 6. The issue of God's sovereign choice is contextualized around the fact that it is independent of whether one wants God's mercy or pity or not, and, whether or not one is "running [*trechontos*]" (*"Laufen"*; Luther 1912). The usual English translations ("exertion"; NRSV) obscure the metaphorical nature of the comment, which does not help the reader recognize that Paul continues to work around the image of whether one is faithfully carrying out the entrusted task of bringing the word of God to the nations. The point is that God shows mercy to whom God wills, to whom the promises have been guaranteed by the line of genealogical descent (by flesh), in spite of whether any given Israelites have successfully been doing so, or not!

Paul's point is the opposite of the theological idea that has somehow emerged that he is removing the Israelites who do not believe in Jesus as Messiah and thus do not (yet) proclaim him to the nations from standing as (true) "Israel," based largely upon the message of v. 6 as usually translated and interpreted. Ironically, Paul's argument otherwise supports the commonly encountered theological impulse to highlight God's choice in spite of human effort.

No less ironic, Paul's focus is upon God's choice of Israelites as Israel on the terms of divine sovereign election, rather than their ability to perform adequately. His point is not that their supposed failure to *perform* adequately paves the way for their replacement by Christians—who by some unintelligible logic imagine themselves to take their own place as "Israel" independent of their own performance, good or bad, and on the basis of *grace and faith alone*![25] At the same time, the traditional views do

---

25. Pauck, ed., *Luther*, 265, translates Luther's comments on 9:6–9 as follows: "This word is spoken against the presumptuousness of the Jews and on behalf of grace, so that all proud confidence in righteousness and good works may be undone. For the Jews want to be regarded as the children of the Kingdom because they are the children of Abraham." Continuing on p. 266, after other comments: ". . . one does not become a son of God and an heir of the promise by descent but by the gracious election of God. Thus and only thus, the Spirit and the grace of God can arise as the pride of the flesh is put down. So then, why does man take pride in his merits and good works? They cannot in any way please God, because they are good and meritorious, but only because God

not attend to [14] the contextual argument that the choices of God here are related to those chosen for a special *task*, not about who is chosen to be saved, as usually described. This is highlighted in vv. 17–24, where the point made about God's choice of Pharaoh and other vessels (for wrath or mercy) concerns how God *uses* them, not whether God saves them.[26] These examples illustrate that the purpose of things—and thus determination of appropriate thinking and behavior—cannot be judged simply on the basis of how circumstances might presently appear, but must be based upon trust in God's ultimate promises; hence, any given events along the way may even be contrary indicators (as too might be birth order, against the prevailing normal expectations of who will inherit).

The Message(s) of Verse 6

Now that we have surveyed the context, let us return to v. 6. We have already discussed how the first sentence of the verse (6a), translated literally, suggests that Paul is referring metaphorically to whether the word of God has *fallen* in the sense that many of the Israelites have not joined Paul and other Christ-followers as messengers bringing the gospel—the news of good awaited—to the nations. No, he insisted, the word has not fallen, because it is going out through agents like Paul; thus, Israel *is* carrying out its trust, even if not every Israelite. I propose that the rest of the verse—which is a new sentence that consists of two clauses (6b-c)—is best understood in

---

has elected from eternity that they would please him. We do good only on the basis of gratitude, because our works do not make us good, but our goodness or, rather, the goodness of God makes us good and our actions as well."

Notice not only the introduction of pride in works here, but also the catch-22 that emerges for Jews, who are accused of trust that they have been freely chosen, witnessed by their genealogical descent to the line of fathers to whom the promises of their relationship were made, and simultaneously accused of seeking to earn God's favor. As members of this family line, in covenant with God, should they not be expected to seek to do what is right, or otherwise to be disciplined? So what is the problem with seeking to do good works if in a covenant relationship with one who instructs to do good works? It seems that, in addition to the need to introduce Jewish works-righteousness so as to argue against it, Luther's reasoning depends upon introducing the idea that a Jew must celebrate God's choice of themselves independent of Abrahamic descent; in other words, as if he or she is a gentile, and thus not already in a covenantal relationship that requires them to behave properly to continue that relationship in good terms. A similar logic appears to be at work in popular evangelical presentations of the gospel.

26. The issue in the discourse beginning at v. 16 revolves around defending God's justice, which includes references to Pharaoh and vessels of wrath and mercy as well as the Northern tribes verses Judahites, not to discuss who is "saved," but ways that God uses different people and means to achieve God's ends.

the context set up by the first sentence, even though that is not apparent in the interpretive tradition.

A more literal translation of the second sentence offers the opportunity to explore Paul's message in several directions. Literally, the sentence reads: "For not all the ones from Israel these ones Israel [*ou gar pantes oi ex Israēl houtoi Israēl*]." The grammatical construction and lack of specificity leave it to the interpreter to fill out the translation from working assumptions about Paul's intended message. In addition to recognizing that there would not have been [15] punctuation, that being a later interpretive addition, notice that Paul does not provide the verbs. That Paul is using Israel in two ways or dismissing some he has just described as Israelites in vv. 4–5 from identification as Israel is not as self-evident in the literal translation as it seems to be in prevailing translations. Rather, the basic idea seems to be that there are some who are not from Israel, or some who are not from the narrowed-down line of Israel, in a way that is analogous to there being some who are not of the line of Abraham's seed who will receive the promises, those not descended through Isaac and Jacob (Israel). As we reviewed, that is the argument that he makes after v. 6 (vv. 7–16).

It is not clear who are "not . . . from Israel" in 6b and who "[are] Israel" in 6c. I suggest that this convoluted language is linked to Paul's denial in the first clause of the idea that the word of God might have *fallen* (in 6a).

"These ones Israel" of the second clause (6c) seems most likely to refer to Paul's fellow Jews who have not joined him in declaring the conviction that Jesus is the Messiah, those whom he has just been describing in vv. 1–5 before the "For" introducing v. 6. It seems likely that the verb should be supplied to read as an affirmation, rather than a denial as traditionally presented: "these ones *are* Israel." Who then are the "all" who are "not . . . *from* [*ek*] Israel" in the first clause (6b)? And where shall we fill in the verbs for our native languages to translate these clauses, which will govern what is meant?

TWO ALTERNATIVE TRANSLATIONS FOR VERSE 6B-C

1) The first alternative to consider is to take the reference in the first clause to be to the *non-Jews* who are *followers of Jesus* about whose assurances he had been writing in chapter 8, all the ones who are in Christ Jesus but "not . . . from Israel."[27] In this sense, the word of God has not fallen, it has

---

27. Gaston, "Israel's Enemies," 94 n. 77, suggests "those outside Israel" in the sense of non-Jews who are Abraham's descendants also.

gone out into the world and been received by some from the nations, some who are not from Israel but who now have God's assurances of receiving the promises made to Abraham's seed as the ones anticipated in the idea of him being "a blessing to all of the nations" (4:16–18). If understood in this direction, then the literal translation would read: **"For all are not the ones from Israel[;] these ones are Israel."** An explanatory paraphrase might read: "**For all** [the ones God chooses who can rest assured of God's commitment to themselves, which includes non-Israelites who have become followers of Jesus Christ (i.e., the subject of chapter 8 that preceded his argument in chapters 9–11 to introduce his concern about those of Israel who were not helping to bring the gospel message to these non-Jews)] **are not the ones** [among the chosen of Israel presently bringing the message to the nations, such as is Paul, but who do constitute the ones just defended in vv. 4–5] **from Israel[;]** [on the other hand, however] **these ones** [the Israelites of vv. 4–5] **are** [legitimate members of] **Israel** [i.e., they are the ones chosen to bring the word]."

[16] Paul would be arguing that the word entrusted to Israel has not fallen, even if some Israelites are stumbling presently rather than carrying it successfully to the nations alongside of Paul. This affirmation and the argument he makes following it continue to affirm the "amen" at the end of v. 5, that what Paul has just asserted about these Israelites is true. It also accords with his insistence in vv. 1–3 that he is telling the truth when he expresses grave concern for their protection during this period, for, as he will express in chapter 11, he fears that these non-Jews might behave in such an arrogant manner so as to turn his fellow Jews away from considering to "emulate" him in this ministry to the nations (11:13–14). One advantage of making the distinction between non-Israelites and Israelites within the first clause is that it anticipates the argument to which Paul will turn after 9:16, after he has made the case for a narrowed down definition of who are the promised seed within the descent group. He introduces an analogy to the distinction between the northern tribes and Judah in order to explain how God can choose those from the nations as well as Israel. Another advantage is that it makes a definitive statement against the idea that non-Israelite Christ-followers are considered Israel here.

2) The second alternative is less complicated and follows Paul's word order exactly; I consider this the most probable reading. Both clauses could refer to those Israelites about whom he had been writing in the previous verses, all the ones who are not joining him in his convictions about Jesus. Again, the exact wording Paul uses is: **"For not all [are] the ones from Israel[;] these ones [are] Israel."** I suggest Paul meant: "**For not all** [the Israelites of vv. 4–5] **are the ones from Israel** [who are presently

bringing the message to the nations (although some, like Paul, are doing so successfully, so the word of God has not fallen even if some Israelites are presently stumbling rather than completing the task)][;] [nevertheless **these ones** [these Israelites who are stumbling, v. 4] **are** [legitimate members of] **Israel** [who should carry out this task, but failure to do so (yet) does not alter their legitimate standing as Israel, because they come through the line of the promised seed]."

Note that the contrast in the pronouns between the clauses (*oi* [the ones]/*houtos* [these ones]) is maintained in this translation (also in the first alternative), and that these pronouns link back nicely to the pronoun in v. 4: "*hoitines* [*which ones*] are Israelites." Together, these various ways of discussing the present anomalous situation communicate that the word *has not fallen* in spite of some Israelites presently tripping rather than successfully (i.e., faithfully) bringing it to the nations (as will be clarified further in chapter 11). The point is emphasized in the analogy drawn in vv. 7–16: neither is it the case that all the seed of Abraham are the ones who will inherit the promises as "the seed" through Isaac and Jacob—that is by God's choice, and remains the case in spite of any appearances to the contrary. The analogy should not be conflated; the argument it supports is not that some of these non-running Israelites are not Israel, but rather that there can be differences between legitimate Israelites, just as there are between those taking the message now and those who are not; nevertheless, they are all the Israelites promised those things listed in vv. 4–5, and again, differently [17] stated, in 11:25–32. Just as the prophets spoke to Israel, so now Paul writes: Things are not always as they appear to be—trusting God's eternal promises and patterns helps to avoid drawing the wrong conclusions and provides the basis for thinking and behaving appropriately instead, steadfastly anticipating what will take place "at the proper time."

CONCLUSION

The word entrusted to Israel has not fallen, even if some Israelites are presently stumbling rather than faithfully carrying it to the nations alongside of Paul. In time, Paul apparently expects them to regain their step and join him in the task, which is what he will argue in chapter 11 in more detail and by way of several metaphors.

Paul's appeal to the irrevocable covenant identity of his kinspeople need not ostensibly be revoked by the insertion of a replacement-theology translation choice. **These ones are Israel.** For Paul, these Israelites stand in need of protection during present circumstances, but they remain those whom God has chosen to carry out a task for which promises have been made, and for the completion of which gifts have been given. When translated in either of the alternative ways proposed, Rom 9:6 *supports* rather than sabotages the promises Paul affirmed in the preceding argument of vv. 1–5, and again in his subsequent arguments in chapter 11. Moreover, these alternatives corroborate rather than encumber appeals to these texts to substantiate calls for a new era of respectfulness in Christian concepts and discourses about as well as relations with Jews.

BIBLIOGRAPHY

Beck, Norman. "Translations of the New Testament for Our Time." In *Seeing Judaism Anew: Christianity's Sacred Obligation*, edited by Mary C. Boys, 200–210. Lanham, MD: Rowman & Littlefield, 2005.

Commission for Religious Relations with the Jews. "'The Gifts and the Calling of God are Irrevocable' (Rom 11:29): A Reflection on Theological Questions Pertaining to Catholic-Jewish Relations on the Occasion of the 50th Anniversary of 'Nostra Aetate' (No. 4)." Online: http://www.saeculumjournal.com/index.php/saeculum/article/view/27113.

Dunn, James D. G. *Romans 9–16*. WBC 388. Dallas: Word, 1988.

Gaston, Lloyd. "Israel's Enemies in Pauline Theology." In *Paul and the Torah*, 80–99. Vancouver: University of Columbia Press, 1987.

Nanos, Mark D. "Are Jews Outside of the Covenants If Not Confessing Jesus as Messiah? Questioning the Questions, the Options for the Answers Too." Paper presented at the Society of Biblical Literature Annual Meeting 2015.

———. "'Broken Branches': A Pauline Metaphor Gone Awry? (Romans 11:11–36)." In *Between Gospel and Election: Explorations in the Interpretation of Romans 9–11*, edited by Florian Wilk and J. Ross Wagner, 339–76. Tübingen: Mohr Siebeck, 2010. (See chapter 6 in this volume of collected essays.)

———. "'Callused,' Not 'Hardened': Paul's Revelation of Temporary Protection until All Israel Can Be Healed." In *Reading Paul in Context: Explorations in Identity Formation*, edited by Kathy Ehrensperger and J. Brian Tucker, 52–73. London: T. & T. Clark, 2010. (See chapter 7 in this volume of collected essays.)

———. *The Mystery of Romans: The Jewish Context of Paul's Letter*. Minneapolis: Fortress, 1996.

———. "Paul's Non-Jews Do Not Become 'Jews,' But Do They Become 'Jewish'?: Reading Romans 2:25–29 within Judaism, alongside Josephus." *Journal of the Jesus Movement in its Jewish Setting* 1.1 (2014) 26–53. Online: <http://www.jjmjs.org/uploads/1/1/9/0/11908749/nanos_pauls_non-jews.pdf>. (See volume 1, chapter 5, in this series of collected essays.)

———. "Romans." In *The Jewish Annotated New Testament*, edited by Amy-Jill Levine and Marc Zvi Brettler, 253–86. New York: Oxford University Press, 2011.

———. "Romans 11 and Christian and Jewish Relations: Exegetical Options for Revisiting the Translation and Interpretation of this Central Text." *Criswell Theological Review* N.S. 9.2 (2012) 3–21. (See chapter 8 in this volume of collected essays.)

———. "Römer 11 und christlich-jüdische Beziehungen: Exegetische Optionen für eine andere Übersetzung und Interpretation des Textes." In *"So wird ganz Israel gerettet werden": Arbeitshilfe zum Israelsonntag 2014: 10. Sonntag nach Trinitatis*, edited by Hanna Lehming, et al., translated by Volker Haarmann, 18–25. Düsseldorf: Evangelisch-Lutherische Landeskirche Hannover, Evangelische Kirche im Rheinland, Evangelisch-Lutherische Kirche in Norddeutschland, Begegnung von Christen und Juden Bayern, 2014.

Nanos, Mark D., and Philip A. Cunningham. "Implications of Paul's Hopes for the End of Days for Jews and Christians Today: A Critical Re-evaluation of the Evidence." *Studies in Christian-Jewish Relations* 9.1 (2014) 1–45. Online: <http://ejournals.bc.edu/ojs/index.php/scjr/article/view/5793>. (See chapter 12 in this volume of collected essays.)

Parkes, James. *The Conflict of the Church and the Synagogue: A Study in the Origins of Antisemitism.* New York: Atheneum, 1979.

Pauck, Wilhelm, ed. *Luther: Lectures on Romans.* Translated by Wilhelm Pauck. Philadelphia: Westminster, 1956.

Richardson, Peter. *Israel in the Apostolic Church.* London: Cambridge University Press, 1969.

Sherman, Franklin. "The Road to Reconciliation: Protestant Church Statements on Christian-Jewish Relations." In *Seeing Judaism Anew: Christianity's Sacred Obligation*, edited by Mary C. Boys, 241–51. Lanham, MD: Rowman and Littlefield, 2005.

Sievers, Joseph. "'God's Gifts and Call Are Irrevocable': The Reception of Romans 11:29 through the Centuries and Christian-Jewish Relations." In *Reading Israel in Romans: Legitimacy and Plausibility of Divergent Interpretations*, edited by Cristina Grenholm and Daniel Patte, 127–73. Harrisburg, PA: Trinity, 2000.

Soulen, R. Kendall. "'They are Israelites': The Priority of the Present Tense for Jewish-Christian Relations." In *Between Gospel and Election: Explorations in the Interpretation of Romans 9–11*, edited by Florian Wilk and J. Ross Wagner, 497–504. Tübingen: Mohr Siebeck, 2010.

PART IV

Special Occasions

11

Challenging the Limits That Continue to Define Paul's Perspective on Jews and Judaism

A RESPONSE TO GÜNTER WASSERBERG'S ESSAY

[212] IN HIS ESSAY in this volume, "Romans 9–11 and Jewish-Christian Dialogue: Prospects and Provisos," Günter Wasserberg has taken a contextual stance as a post-Holocaust German Lutheran to respect Jewish people and religion as equal before God independent of faith in Christ. Since his reading of Paul will not provide for a similar viewpoint, and since he is unconvinced by the attempts of others to modify Paul's voice in this direction (for example, in Romans 11)—especially those he calls "a two-scheme salvation"—he concludes that the Paul of the historical text must, for himself, be dismissed on this matter. He notes—rightly, on my understanding of the traditional reading too—that when taken to indicate the future conversion of all Jewish people, Romans 9–11 does not hold as much promise for mutual respect as many may think. I applaud and welcome this ideological decision, not least as a Jewish person. If I read Paul in the same way, I would likewise find it necessary to dismiss the voice of Paul on this and other matters. But I do not believe that one must read Paul as Wasserberg or those he cites have read him, and therefore I question the need for this conclusion.

Wasserberg's view of Paul is based upon at least two major premises: [213] (1) Paul believed in Christ as the Messiah of Israel and thus that other Jewish people must necessarily believe in Christ as well; (2) Paul believed and taught that Jewish identity and behavior were necessarily obsolete for himself and other Jewish believers in Christ and thus logically inferior for other Jewish people as well.

But I question whether the reading of Paul that has led to this conclusion is necessary, or the only alternative. First, in view of Wasserberg's commitment to the insights of the so-called New Perspective on Paul and Judaism, I find his argument internally inconsistent, being based upon traditional exegetical insights that must now be challenged. Second, in view of the historical contextual divide separating Paul and us, I suggest that setting Paul's language in his context as differentiated from ours offers more flexibility for incorporating Paul's voice than Wasserberg has considered.

I agree with the first premise of Wasserberg's view. Paul did believe in Christ and thought that all humankind, Jew and gentile, should do likewise. But I disagree with the conclusion that this means Paul would reject a Jewish (or other) position or person not sharing this faith. I believe that Paul's view may be contextualized differently than Wasserberg has done, and thus subordinated to Paul's larger understanding of the Creator God drawn from his confession of the *Shema,* that God is the One God of Jews (particularistic) and the One God of gentiles (universalistic).[1]

I disagree entirely with the second premise of Wasserberg's view. From my perspective and exegesis, Paul did not believe or teach that Jewish identity or behavior had been made obsolete for the Jewish people whether they believed in Jesus Christ or not. And this is the crux of the problem for recontextualizing Paul in regard to the first premise. Here I find Wasserberg's exegetical observations inconsistent with "New Perspective" observations and unnecessary as the grounds for the conclusions drawn.

I would like to elaborate briefly. Wasserberg admits that the traditional view of Paul has been undermined by the advances of the so-called New Perspective.[2] He observes that this view had relied upon material that in important ways has been discredited as eisegesis, with its worn-out assertion of Jewish legalism or works of self-righteousness as a foil for [214] the interpretation of Paul. One might expect, then, that his conclusions regarding Paul's usefulness would be rewoven not from these threadbare remnants,

---

1. Nanos, *Mystery of Romans;* "Why was Gentile Circumcision So Unacceptable to Paul?"

2. The phrase was coined by James D. G. Dunn in an article entitled "The New Perspective on Paul" now reprinted (Dunn, *Jesus, Paul, and the Law*), with reference to the groundbreaking work of E. P. Sanders (*Paul and Palestinian Judaism*). It should be noted that one of the features of this article was a challenge to the internal inconsistency in Sanders's argument that is not dissimilar to my challenge of Wasserberg herein, and such problems of internal inconsistency may also be observed among the many otherwise welcome advances made by "New Perspective" proponents, including Dunn; see, for example, discussion of "Luther's trap" (Nanos, *Mystery of Romans,* 88-95, 115-19).

but with the various new fabrics available to the exegete in view of recent insights into the period and Paul. But as I see it, this has not occurred. Take the unqualified appeal to the traditional interpretation of the Antioch meeting of Galatians 2 to establish the certainty of Paul's abandonment of Judaism. Yet this reading is no longer a given. I have argued, along with some other interpreters, that this example may be read in another way in which Paul is shown not to be against Jewish identity and behavior, but rather a champion thereof.[3]

To illustrate my concern, consider the exegetical limitations Wasserberg finds himself constrained by when deducing the possible value of Paul's voice. He resists the conclusion of interpreters where he believes that it necessitates the premise that Paul was schizophrenic in dividing his understanding of God's salvation into two parts.

This premise about Paul is based, as Wasserberg states it, upon the following logic: "To perceive Paul as, on the one hand, remaining a faithful Jew while, on the other hand, proclaiming Jesus as Messiah for the Gentiles without the law seems to posit a certain schizophrenia in Paul." This is, of course, based upon a premise unstated here, which may, however, be observed at work throughout his essay, and which is elsewhere made explicit. On one hand, Wasserberg asserts, "Paul was a Jew and continued to perceive himself as a Jew, one who believed in Christ." But on the other hand, he denies discussion of the problem that this logically adumbrates, as though unconnected: "Whether [Paul] was aware that his understanding of Judaism in light of the Christ event in effect abrogated Judaism by denying to the law the position it occupied in much of Judaism in his day is a different question." However, that this is not a different question may be observed in his own deduction when he states, "Paul's theology breaks with Torah Judaism inasmuch as he claims that the Torah has lost its binding authority."

It seems to me that this is the interpretive bedrock upon which Wasserberg rightly concludes the need to dismiss Paul, for this position attributes to Paul an ideological dismissal of Jewish identity or behavior that stands in the way of his post-Holocaust sensibilities and my own. Moreover, while it is an ideology of which he is willing to consider that Paul remains unaware, it is nevertheless one he appears to believe is logically [215] compelling for the Christ-believer on Paul's terms. The juxtaposition of statements illustrates how it is precisely the simultaneous retention of the traditional interpretive premise that prohibits Paul's participation in the dialogue, since "this Paul" does not share Wasserberg's sensibilities or respect for Jewish people and

---

3. Nanos, *Mystery of Romans*, 337–71.

behavior. I suggest that this is the matter that we should turn to in order to render a decision on the place of Paul.

A solution may be noted in the midst of Wasserberg's own argument, for he recognizes that among other Jewish believers in Jesus it is not apparently necessary to conclude that there can be no mixing of Jewish Torah observance and faith in Christ. Wasserberg grants that the Jerusalem Christ-believing communities remained "within the boundaries of Judaism"; therefore, they exist as an alternative Jewish coalition or Judaism, but not the only one. Thus, for these Jewish people faith in Christ did not go necessarily hand in hand with the rejection of Torah identity or behavior; they may remain faithful Jews yet proclaim faith in Jesus for gentiles without suffering a kind of schizophrenia. For them it is not an ideological necessity, and the kind of disrespect of Jewish identity and behavior that Wasserberg rejects is not inherent. Yet for Paul, somehow, his faith in Christ logically "marks a decisive break with Jewish self-identity and lifestyle," so that his Judaism is "a Gentile movement." (Admittedly, "Christianity," when *later* founded, did become one. But I believe this later development is *in spite of* Paul, not because of him, even if his writings were and continue to be construed in such a way that this may not appear to be the case.)

The view attributed to Paul cannot then be grounded on an ideological premise that is not necessarily deduced for other Jewish believers in Jesus without cause. For example, it would have to be grounded in Paul's own statements. That is, it would have to be based upon exegesis. And this Wasserberg recognizes as well. However, while in his essay Wasserberg grants that the traditional portrait of Paul is flawed on the matter of Paul's view of "Torah Judaism," he nevertheless draws deeply from this well for the exegetical basis of his argument. In this light, I submit that the prior logical and exegetical conclusions Wasserberg has accepted about Paul needlessly constrain the possibilities for Paul's voice.

I propose that Paul's historical framework may be contextualized in such a way that we find his even greater conviction, that the One God of Israel is the One God of all humankind, provides a guiding voice for [216] our own context today. To accomplish this, I suggest the following three steps.

First, we recognize that Paul's viewpoint was that of a Jewish reformer, so that his beliefs were framed within the Judaisms of his day. His beliefs represent a view of Jewish identity and behavior that was Torah-driven and observant, although informed by the "revelation" of Christ.

Second, we note that Paul's conviction in the One God of Jews and gentiles provides a framework for reconsideration of the context of his statements about, for example, Jewish identity or Torah observance, instead of universalizing them (i.e., applying statements in the same manner to Jews and gentiles both). For this Paul, the differences remained, but the discrimination did not. That is, his views of Torah for Jewish or gentile people were not the same. In this way, we keep in front of ourselves the view that Paul's writings represent his perspective on an inter- and intra-Jewish matter of his own time.[4] This offers a different way to cast the question Wasserberg asks today as a Christian, and a different premise for conceiving of Paul's response.

Third, we consider that Paul's plan for mission and his statements about the restoration of Israel or of all humankind are limited to their historical context, that is, within the framework of his own ministry. Developments since then would need to be reconsidered in later times for appropriate application—for example, of principles and patterns of thought. When considered in this way, the cross is no longer only a symbol of a Jewish martyr of the Roman Empire, but also of harmful Christian policies toward Jewish people. So, too, the context of arguments against the adoption of Jewish identity by gentile believers in Christ is worlds apart. This has so changed that the priority of the concern and even the grounds of the argument are obscured if not entirely lost on the modern gentile Christian reader of Paul. Most would hardly consider such a course of interest to be a logical extension of their faith in this Jewish person, Jesus Christ; however, in the context of Paul's life and message, this was sensible and desired. One need but consider the context of Galatians! In fact, recognizing this lack of resonance with the historical situation may go a long way toward explaining the common interpretive recontextualization so that it appears to be Jewish identity and behavior for Jewish people as well as gentile people in view in these Pauline texts. Perhaps it is inconceivable for the later interpreter that [217] Pauline law-free gospel-believing gentile people could be so engaged by the desire for Jewish identity and behavior that after their faith in Christ these people could really imagine becoming Jewish proselytes was an advantage for themselves.

These considerations will permit us to reframe the question. We may seek to understand how Paul's larger view of God's intentions for his creatures, because of his conviction of God's oneness, would impact what might be said in our context now. In other words, that Wasserberg has chosen to let an ideological conviction shape the context of his faith in Christ in view of historical developments since Paul's time, need not require a conclusion that Paul would not share this sensibility. Rather, I imagine that Paul would. I believe that since Paul's faith in Christ was set within a particular historical

---

4. Nanos, "Inter- and Intra-Jewish Political Contexts of Paul and the Galatians"; Nanos, "The Jewish Context of the Gentile Audience in Paul's Letter to the Romans."

context shaped by an understanding of who God is and what God is doing that was driven, for example, by the Scriptures of Israel, the confession of the *Shema*, and trust in the irrevocable calling and gifts of God, we might responsibly undertake the task of reassessing his voice guided by a hermeneutic rooted in his respect for the convictions of Jewish people who did not share his belief in Christ. But this is a perspective that can arise only in a time after Paul, a time after this Jewish coalition and the other Judaisms took different directions than he had foreseen, a time after the foundation of Christianity and its history checkered with the failure to respect Jewish people and behavior, or worse.

In Romans 11, Paul was occupied with challenging the growing arrogance among gentiles toward Jewish people who did not share their faith in Christ. He reveals a surprising mystery of God's present dealings with an unforeseen outcome for Israel: although there is vicarious suffering on behalf of these gentiles now, ultimate restoration is certain.[5] I do not read this as an outline for some distant triumphalism, when all Jews will be converted to Christianity, which would be against the rhetorical intent to confront Christian gentile conceit. Nor do I read it as the "two-scheme salvation" that Wasserberg finds too modern for Paul.

Rather, I read this as an expression of the process Paul expects to unfold as he proclaims the gospel: when he turns successfully to the [218] gentiles with the message of Israel's Lord as the One God of humankind, it will provoke other Jewish people to emulative jealousy "of his ministry."[6] They too will want to participate in the ministry that Israel has long awaited, once they see the gentiles coming in, turning to the worship of the One God with renewed minds. He hopes that they will recognize that this means Israel's restoration has begun in Jesus Christ, and thus those who have not yet believed will reconsider. But Paul's conception of how things would turn out has not come to pass. And so his view must be read within its historical context, and not directly transferred to our own.

Paul's recognition of this as a mystery only now revealed, that is, as a process unrealized before in the contexts of his own time, implicitly admits of the limits of human understanding, without revelation, to distinguish the way things are from how they may appear. Paul provides a context for this mystery resonating with echoes of the *Shema*. For Paul explicitly admits that there is much he still does not comprehend, an insight that may point the way toward a mutually respectful hermeneutic for those who seek to bring

---

5. Nanos, *Mystery of Romans*, 239–88.
6. Nanos, "The Jewish Context of the Gentile Audience Addressed in Paul's Letter to the Romans."

Paul's voice to bear upon the topic of Jewish-Christian relations in the later context of our own time:

> O he depth of the riches and wisdom and knowledge of God! How unsearchable are his judgments and how inscrutable his ways! "For who has known the mind of the Lord, or who has been his counselor?" "Or who has given a gift to him that he might be repaid?" For from him and through him and to him are all things. To him be the glory for ever. Amen. (Rom. 11:33–36)

A RESPONSE TO WILLIAM S. CAMPBELL'S ESSAY

William S. Campbell's essay, "Divergent Images of Paul and His Mission," highlights the tension perceived in the received view of Paul between Romans 11 and elsewhere, including a text as close as chapter 9. Campbell discusses the various solutions in modern scholarship, which suggest that Paul was going one way in his earlier work, and in this letter too, but then changed course suddenly in chapter 11. This is seen as inconsistent, an anomaly that needs to be set in its subordinate role and explained on the basis of some flaw on Paul's part, or at least in his argument. In [219] the various proposals considered, the priority given to Israel in chapter 11 is regarded as a compromise of Paul's principal new insight of God's impartiality argued in chapter 9, which is due to his failure to divest himself fully of his former ideological particularism as a Jewish person. The critique of such positions and their presuppositions is excellent.

But Campbell accepts the appearance of Paul's inconsistency, and thus advances another way to reduce the resulting dissonance this creates for the interpreter seeking coherence. He proposes that the most powerful case against Paul's consistency may come from Paul's own three different voices: one found in his other letters, one from his missionary activity to the gentiles, and the third, which seems to arise suddenly in chapter 11 in contrast to the preceding chapters. Thus, Campbell divides the possible approaches along the line of, Was "the apostle facing a changed situation, or the outcome of a development in his thought"?[7] This may prove helpful for

---

7. It may be noted that both are, of course, natural, but I think that "changed situation" may imply that it is a continuum in a location, rather than emphasizing the case that it is a *different* situation in each location, although each situation certainly changes as well. This distinction can be important in that we ought not to look for the kind of development likely to be explainable within an evolving situation when we are dealing with an entirely different one, with different people, set in a different location, as is obviously the case, for example, between Galatians and Romans.

the traditional exegete, but I suggest that the problem really vexing a "New Perspective" interpreter like Campbell, or a Jewish interpreter like myself, lies elsewhere, namely, in the portrait of Paul that sets up this inconsistency.

In other words, I question whether Paul's approach in Romans 11 needs to show him to be inconsistent in any of the ways suggested. Ironically, I find the foundational conviction that Campbell shares with these other interpreters of Paul to be inconsistent with the spectrum of Paul's voices as I hear them. Consider briefly each of the three discussed from another perspective.

First, in a (presumably) earlier letter such as Galatians, for example, Paul's mission to the gentiles is set within a prophetic call by the God of Israel, and his letter ends with a blessing upon the Israel of God. The struggle may be interpreted *within Israel* regarding the proper means for including gentiles as full children of Abraham since the coming of Christ. That is, the struggle is between the former conclusion maintained by the guardians of the traditions of the fathers (i.e., proselyte conversion) and a new development (claiming to be consistent with the Scriptures) that has now been revealed by Israel's God in Christ to Paul and the other apostles of this movement. Thus, Paul understands the tension created by the good news of Christ (which now includes gentiles without proselyte conversion as equal participants among the people of God with Jewish people) to set this Judaism apart from the other Judaisms, including those of which he had been formerly a most zealous and outstanding member.

Second, as I read Galatians 2, this mission is in unity with that of the Jerusalem apostles.[8] When we look for evidence from outside of Paul, the only picture [220] available with any time proximity is that of Luke, with which this would agree. This suggests that Paul's mission to the nations has always been set within the framework of Israel's restoration.

And third, the letter to the Romans is full of positive comments about Jewish identity and the value of Torah *prior* to arriving at chapter 11:

- Paul opens by locating his good news of Christ within Israel's history ("the good news of God, which he promised beforehand through his prophets in the holy scriptures ... concerning his Son, who was descended from David according to the flesh" [1:1–3]);
- he continues with such affirmations as Jewish diachronical priority ("to the Jew first" [1:16; 2:10]);

---

8. Nanos, *Mystery of Romans*, 337–71; "Intruding 'Spies' and 'Pseudo' Brethren"; so too Koptak, "Rhetorical Identification in Paul's Autobiographical Narrative."

- and notes the advantage of Jewish identity demonstrated in the possession of "the oracles of God" (3:1–2);
- he explains the powerful unification derived from exegesis of the *Shema*, along with the confirmation of the Torah by faith (3:29–31);
- and clarifies the fatherhood of Abraham, who "received circumcision as a sign or seal of the righteousness that he had by faith" (4:11);
- he emphasizes the positive nature of Torah as "holy and just and good" (7:12), not to mention "spiritual" (7:14), while the very aim of walking in the Spirit is the fulfillment of "the just requirement of the Torah" (8:4);
- moreover, he powerfully affirms the eternal value of Jewish identity and privilege at the beginning of chapter 9 (9:4–5).

In sum, I do not find Paul's "other voices" raised against the pro-Jewish Paul of Romans 11, but rather consistent with it, and, interestingly enough, Campbell goes on to point out some of these references as well. For example, it seems that Campbell's recognition of the role of Abraham as father equally and inclusively of Jews and gentiles in the argument of chapter 4 is consistent with the "earlier Paul," if you will. It is certainly central in Galatians, and to the same purpose: non-Jewish people may step up to equal status with Jewish people as children of Abraham and thus of God, a step that had usually been understood to be reserved for gentiles who became Jewish proselytes. In fact, Paul begins chapter 9 with the assertion of Israel's special and eternal place and his own willingness to suffer vicariously for Israel, noting that "God who is over *all* be blessed forever" (9:5). And this is echoed in the final verse of chapter 11, from which the "therefore" of 12:1, which sets up the balance of the letter's message, [221] emanates: "For from him and through him and to him are *all* things. To him be the glory forever" (11:36).

This dynamic may be helpfully clarified in terms of social identity theory.[9] The way in which we understand ourselves to be identified socially, for example, within group A rather than group B, is instrumental in our self- as well as group-identity and differentiation, and thus, discrimination. Social identity theorists have demonstrated that it does not take a value judgment beyond group identification to account for discrimination: group A people

---

9. This school of social psychology traces many of its fundamental insights to the work of Henri Tajfel (e.g., *Differentiation between Social Groups*; see also Hogg and Abrams, *Social Identifications*; Robinson, *Social Groups and Identities*). Groundbreaking application of this theory to Pauline material is available in Esler, *Galatians*; and also for Matthew in Saldarini, *Matthew's Christian-Jewish Community*.

will discriminate against group B people (and vice versa) merely by the fact of group membership.

As long as the choice for the interpreter is to understand Paul socially defined as pro-Jewish *or* pro-gentile, he or she must locate Paul along only one side of the spectrum of social self-interest (within either group A or group B). It seems that interpreters draw the line between Jews and Christ-believers, or more recently, Jewish Christ-believers and gentile ones. But I suggest that another way to read the text indicates that Paul has drawn the line in keeping with the understanding often expressed in the Scriptures of Israel, that is, around all of the created order, with Israel in service of the other nations. In this sense, Abraham is the father of *all* who trust in the One Creator God, who is Lord of Israel *and* the nations. Paul understands even what might be regarded as socially embedded self-interest as an Israelite (group A) to be in the service of God when the focus is on reaching out to the gentiles (group B), and thus in no way associated with turning away from Israel. They all are his children (group C), all one family. The social identity is inclusive of both people equally, of all of creation (A plus B within C).[10]

At points, Campbell avoids the usual category bifurcation, noting that the argument of Romans is pro-Jewish *and* pro-gentile, because it is set within the particular role of Israel on behalf of the universal good of all humankind. Building on the suggestion of Fitzmyer and others regarding Paul's usage of Hosea and Isaiah in Rom 9:24–29, he observes that the topic under discussion is God's activity with relation to Israel, and not a switch to the gentiles. Rather, Israel will be restored and the gentiles' blessing, which is the minor focus of the section, develops in this light. In this way, a foreshadowing of the discussion of Israel's hardening and restoration in chapter 11 is provided, and the element of "surprise" exclaimed by many commentators is instead anticipated.

Campbell notes that what Paul "intends to argue for is an extension of Israel's privileges to Gentiles (rather than a transfer of them away [222] from Israel)." I would qualify this slightly. It is not that gentiles get Israel's privileges, but that Israel's privileges and those now available to the nations by the service of Israel are equal, as they were given equally to all of creation, to all of Abraham's children, even if by necessity to one of the children (that is, Israel) first, it then being that child's privileged responsibility to bring this news to all of the other nations. It is not a zero-sum situation of the present evil age, but a conviction that the awaited one has dawned. This

---

10. I take this formation of a unified community to be the principle expressed in Paul's "new creation" language (e.g., Gal 6:15; 2 Cor 5:16–19; cf. Rom 12:1–5; 1 Cor 7:17–24; Gal 3:28).

would help Campbell to avoid the trap he seeks to overcome because of his sensitivities toward Jewish people, but that logically follows in the received view: the notion of a transfer from Israel to the gentiles, meaning in effect the gentile church; moreover, it avoids the problem of considering gentiles who believe in Jesus as thereby becoming Jewish people or members of a "spiritual Israel" or "true Israel." Thus, Campbell's notice of distinction is maintained, that Jews in Christ remain Jews, while gentiles remain gentiles. I have tried to put this simply, in stating that the difference (A or B) remains, but the discrimination does not (all are C).[11]

In further discussion of Romans 9, Campbell notes that the consensus has largely moved away from the earlier systematic treatments of predestination toward a recognition that the intention is to show how God has maintained his purpose for his people, even through unexpected figures such as a Pharaoh. I think that this can be pushed further in the light of the foreshadowing Campbell has recognized, so that the real surprise is that God may be up to something with Israel and the gentiles that is different than it may appear presently to the addressees in Rome—Paul's message meaning, "Do not be fooled, God is faithful to Israel and all who call upon him, and faithful too to prevent Israel harm, such as may result from gentile conceit against Israel."

I understand the mystery in Romans 11 to set out Paul's view that in some unexpected way the pro-gentile aspects of the development, and the current lack of participation in this scheme by some Israelites, is not to be taken to mean that the line has been redrawn so as to exclude these Jewish people. But they are rather "surprisingly" served by these fortunate gentiles. And this is to confront a social identity boundary among the Roman gentiles that is beginning to be drawn mistakenly, so as to preclude the continued participation of Jewish people who were not part of this coalition. Paul's message undermines this gentile-centric viewpoint by asserting this to the gentiles: the Jewish people's good has been on behalf of you, so now your good as gentiles is on behalf of [223] them (ch. 11); "therefore," have your viewpoint altered (to see things from God's vantage point) so that you are dedicated to their service, not destruction (chs. 12–16). It is in this light that the jealousy motif may be taken to redirect the gentiles' misunderstanding of their current role, for even Paul's mission to the gentiles is in the service of Israel first (11:11–15). And it is arguably the purpose of the remaining chapters, wherein the appropriate halakhic behavior for the Roman gentiles in Christ is spelled out.

11. Nanos, *Mystery of Romans*; Nanos, "Why Was Gentile Circumcision So Unacceptable to Paul?"

In the end, I do not see that the proposed different voices of Paul demonstrate inconsistency within or between the Paul(s) of Romans 11 and elsewhere. That is, the problem of Pauline inconsistency—to the degree that one considers this a problem—appears to lie with the interpreter's fashioning of a Paul and Paulinism that bifurcates his pro-gentile and pro-Jewish stances. I suggest that these texts may be read so that Paul's pro-gentile concern derives from a corresponding, indeed, a prior one that is pro-Jewish. I submit that this comes from his guiding Israelite conviction: God is One.

BIBLIOGRAPHY [224]

Dunn, James D. G. "The New Perspective on Paul." In *Jesus, Paul and the Law: Studies in Mark and Galatians*, 183–214. Louisville: Westminster/John Knox, 1990.

Esler, Philip F. *Galatians*. New Testament Readings. London: Routledge, 1998.

Hogg, Michael A., and Dominic Abrams. *Social Identifications: A Social Psychology of Intergroup Relations and Group Processes*. London: Routledge, 1988.

Kotpak, Paul E. "Rhetorical Identification in Paul's Autobiographical Narrative: Galatians 1:13—2:14." *Journal for the Study of the New Testament* 40 (1990) 97–115.

Nanos, Mark D. *The Mystery of Romans: The Jewish Context of Paul's Letter*. Minneapolis: Fortress, 1996.

———. "Why Was Gentile Circumcision So Unacceptable to Paul? The Role of the *Shema* in Paul's Gospel." Paper presented at the Central States regional meeting of the Society of Biblical Literature, St. Louis, March 23–24, 1996. (See volume 1, chapter 4, in this series of collected essays for a later, published version of the arguments in this paper.)

———. "Intruding 'Spies' and 'Pseudo' Brethren: The Intra-Jewish Context of 'Those of Repute' in Jerusalem (Gal. 2:1–10)." In *Paul and His Opponents*, edited by Stanley E. Porter, 59–97. Pauline Studies 2. Leiden: Brill, 2005. (See volume 3 in this series of collected essays.)

———. "The Inter- and Intra-Jewish Political Contexts of Paul and the Galatians." In *Paul and Politics: Ekklesia, Israel, Imperium, Interpretation*, edited by Richard Horsley, 146–59 Harrisburg, PA: Trinity, 2000. (See volume 3 in this series of collected essays.)

———. "The Jewish Context of the Gentile Audience Addressed in Paul's Letter to the Romans." *Catholic Biblical Quarterly* 61 (1999) 283–304. (See chapter 3 in this volume of collected essays.)

Robinson, W. Peter, ed. *Social Groups and Identities: Developing the Legacy of Henri Tajfel*. Oxford: Butterworth-Heinemann, 1996.

Saldarini, Anthony J. *Matthew's Christian-Jewish Community*. Chicago: University of Chicago Press, 1994.

Sanders, E. P. *Paul and Palestinian Judaism: A Comparison of Patterns of Religion*. Philadelphia: Fortress, 1977.

Tajfel, Henri, ed. *Differentiation between Social Groups: Studies in the Social Psychology of Intergroup Relations*. New York: Academic, 1978.

12

Implications of Paul's Hopes for the End of Days for Jews and Christians Today

A Critical Re-evaluation of the Evidence

1. RECENT CATHOLIC INTEREST IN PAUL'S ESCHATOLOGY

[1] IT IS WELL known that the groundbreaking 1965 Second Vatican Council declaration, *Nostra Aetate*, relied heavily upon Paul's Letter to the Romans to state that the Jewish people remain "most dear" to God (Rom 11:28), and, to them belong "the glory and the covenants and the law" (Rom 9:4). As a recent study of the post–World War II revolution in Catholic theology about Jews and Judaism explains: "Without Romans and its confirmation of God's promises to the Jews as well as the eschatological hope for unity in an unspecified future, the church would not have had language to talk about the Jews after the Holocaust."[1] In addition to the major changes that followed from this new focus on past promises and their relationship to the ultimate future, the eschaton, *Nostra Aetate* also recommended that research and discourse be undertaken in a new spirit: "this sacred synod wants to foster and recommend that mutual understanding and respect which is the fruit, above all, of biblical and theological studies as well as of fraternal dialogues."[2] It

---

1. Connelly, *From Enemy to Brother*, 256. This important volume provides a vivid narrative of how Christians who sought to combat the appeal that Nazi antisemitism had for Christians, turned to Romans and over the 1940s–1960s and gradually came to read it with new eyes.

2. Second Vatican Council, *Nostra Aetate*, §4.

thus seems very fitting to us that, as its fiftieth anniversary approaches, this consideration of that [2] declaration's roots in Paul's eschatological expectations—which flowed from God's irrevocable covenantal promises—is the combined work of a Jewish exegete (Mark Nanos) and a Catholic biblical theologian (Philip Cunningham). Both authors will speak to the issues raised, but in general Nanos will focus on insights into the translation and interpretation of Paul's language approached from within the late Second Temple Jewish thought-world in which it was written with some attention to the reception history of Paul's language, while Cunningham will focus on how Paul's language can—and just as importantly, cannot, apart from significant qualifications—be usefully employed to address Christian theological concerns today.

Our effort is not without precedent. For many decades now, both Catholic and Protestant ecclesial statements have appealed to Romans to foster a positive relationship between Christians and Jews. Jews have likewise appealed to Romans in efforts to improve dialogue and relations going forward. On the one hand, this development represents the historical-exegetical rediscovery of long-overlooked positive sentiments toward those of his kinspeople who did not share Paul's newfound conviction that Jesus was raised. For Paul and likeminded associates (see Acts 3:20–21), this marked Jesus as the awaited messianic figure, and led them to conclude that the end of the ages had thus been initiated. On the other hand, the modern recourse to Romans arguably arose from the ethical need that Christians felt, and some Jews welcomed, to find a new way to read Paul's representations of Jews and Judaism following the horrendous sufferings of Jews in cultures that were partially shaped by long-lived, anti-Jewish readings of Paul, including Romans 11.

In a pivotal passage in that chapter wherein Paul describes the restoration of Israel as well as the reconciliation of the rest of creation, he reveals his conviction that this process was going to reach its next stage through the completion of his ministry to the nations. He confidently describes the inevitable destiny of the Jewish people in positive terms (albeit somewhat [3] less obviously in the currently prevailing construals, a topic that will be discussed more fully below). The NRSV translates Paul's insight thus: "I want you to understand this mystery, a hardening has come upon part of Israel, *until the full number of the Gentiles has come in*. And so *all Israel will be saved; as it is written* . . ." (Rom 11:25–26; italics added; see too vv. 11–15).[3]

---

3. NRSV translation. A different, more promising translation of this verse will be discussed below. [See too now the Appendix in this volume.]

In the past decade or so, these words have been the subject of a lively conversation within the Catholic community. The interpretation of Paul's ideas about the eschaton framed the discussion of why the Catholic Church today does not organize campaigns to convert Jews to Christianity, as some other Christian groups do. This topic had also been a pivotal one during the deliberations at the Second Vatican Council in 1964 over the draft of what would become *Nostra Aetate*. Language that suggested an interest in promoting a contemporary Christian "mission to Jews" was replaced by an eschatological phrase: "the Church awaits the day, known to God alone, when all people will call upon the Lord with one voice and 'serve him shoulder to shoulder' (Zeph. 3:9)."[4]

These topics again came to the forefront in February of 2008 when Pope Benedict XVI composed a new prayer for Jews in the Good Friday services of the small number of Catholics who utilize the pre-Second Vatican Council Tridentine liturgical rite. The revised intercession asked God to "illuminate their [Jews'] hearts so that they may recognize Jesus Christ as savior of all men."[5] Since this revised prayer was issued without explanation and published as *pro conversione* [4] *Iudeaorum*, many observers concluded that the prayer was meant to encourage the proselytization of Jews by Catholics.

To counter this understandable impression, Cardinal Walter Kasper, the president of the Pontifical Commission for Religious Relations with the Jews, composed an important essay that was printed in the Vatican newspaper at the pope's request. He argued that the prayer was not promoting the missionizing of Jews, but rather drew upon the eschatological perspective of Romans 11:

> The salvation of the Jews is, for St. Paul, a profound mystery of election through divine grace ([Rom] 9:14–29). God's gifts are irrevocable and God's promises to his people have not been revoked by him in spite of their disobedience (9:6; 11:1, 29). The hardening of Israel becomes a boon for the salvation of the Gentiles.... When the *full number of the Gentiles has entered into salvation*, the whole of Israel will be saved (11:25ff.).... So one can say: God will bring about the salvation of Israel in the end, not on the basis of a mission to the Jews but on the basis of the mission to the Gentiles, when *the fullness of the Gentiles* has entered.... In this prayer the Church does not take it upon herself to orchestrate the realization of the unfathomable mystery.

---

4. For full details on this internal Catholic exchange, see Cunningham, "'God Holds the Jews Most Dear': Learning to Respect Jewish Self-Understanding."

5. John Paul II, *Pro conversion Iudeaorum*.

She cannot do so. Instead, she lays the *when* and the *how* entirely in God's hands. God alone can bring about the Kingdom of God in which the whole of Israel is saved and eschatological peace is bestowed on the world.[6]

Pope Benedict himself followed this logic in a book published a few years later:

> [5] Here I should like to recall the advice given by Bernard of Clairvaux to his pupil Pope Eugene III on this matter. He reminds the Pope that his duty of care extends not only to Christians, but: "You also have obligations toward unbelievers, whether Jew, Greek, or Gentile" (*De Consideratione* III/i, 2). Then he immediately corrects himself and observes more accurately: "Granted, with regard to the Jews, time excuses you; for them a determined point in time has been fixed, which cannot be anticipated. The *full number of the Gentiles must come in first*. ..." (*De Consideratione* III/i, 3).

Hildegard Brem comments on this biblical passage as follows:

> In the light of Romans 11:25, the Church must not concern herself with the conversion of the Jews, since she must wait for the time fixed for this by God, "until *the full number of the Gentiles come in*" (Rom 11:25). ... In the meantime, Israel retains its own mission. Israel is in the hands of God, who will save it "as a whole" at the proper time, when *the number of the Gentiles is complete*.[7]

Pope Benedict and those he cites, Bernard of Clairvaux and Hildegard Brem, all adduce Paul's phrase about the "full number of the gentiles coming in" to argue that the salvation of Jews is divinely guaranteed and will be God's doing. Benedict made the same point elsewhere when he said that the new prayer: "shifts the focus from a direct petition for the conversion of the Jews in a missionary sense to a plea that the Lord might bring about the hour of history when we may all be united."[8] Therefore, since it is not a responsibility of Christians to "convert" Jews, the Catholic Church does not support any missionary campaigns toward Jews.

[6] But one could ask, did Paul mean the same things by "full number of the gentiles coming in" (as typically translated) as do these current

---

6. Kasper, "Striving for Mutual Respect in Modes of Prayer." Italics added to the "full number" phrase, others are original.

7. Ibid., 44–45, 47. Italics added.

8. Benedict XVI, *Light of the World*, 107.

applications or actualizations of his words? From the point of view of Catholic theology, do these current applications mean to say that once the quota of gentiles has been reached at the End of Days Jews will simply fulfill their divine destiny by becoming Christians? Or that the entire post-New Testament Jewish people, including those who have practiced the rabbinic tradition for as long as Christianity has been practiced, will simply collapse—in a zero-sum fashion—in the face of a divinely inspired recognition that Christian expectations about Christ's "second coming" or return (*parousia*) have proven correct after all?

Furthermore, do such formulations pay any heed to Jewish self-understanding, as required by the Vatican's 1974 Guidelines to Implement *Nostra Aetate*?[9] The texts mentioned above apparently proceed from the assumption that Jews need salvation in the way Christians have traditionally conceptualized the Jewish need for it—by coming to have faith in Jesus Christ. Jews cannot be expected to recognize themselves in descriptions that do not acknowledge that their own beliefs and convictions are the product of covenantal fidelity to God. Rather, they must remain faithful to what are clearly believed to be the calling and gifts of God. This problem is perhaps especially apparent in a paragraph of the 1994 *Catechism of the Catholic Church*, which also appealed to Romans 11:

> The glorious Messiah's coming is suspended at every moment of history until his recognition by "all Israel," for "a hardening has come upon part of Israel" in their "unbelief" toward Jesus [Rom 11:20–26; cf. Mt 23:39]. St. Peter says to the Jews of Jerusalem after Pentecost: [7] "Repent, therefore, and turn again, that your sins may be blotted out, that times of refreshing may come from the presence of the Lord, and that he may send the Christ appointed for you, Jesus, whom heaven must receive until the time for establishing all that God spoke by the mouth of his holy prophets from of old" [Acts 3:19–21]. St. Paul echoes him, "For if their rejection means the reconciliation of the world, what will their acceptance mean but life from the dead" [Rom 11:15]? The "full inclusion" of the Jews in the Messiah's salvation, in the wake of "the full number of the Gentiles" [Rom 11:12, 25; cf. Lk 21:24], will enable the People of God to achieve "the measure of

---

9. Commission of the Holy See for Religious Relations with the Jews, "Guidelines and Suggestions for Implementing the Conciliar Declaration, *Nostra Aetate*, No. 4," Preamble: "[Christians] must strive to learn by what essential traits Jews define themselves in the light of their own religious experience."

the stature of the fullness of Christ," in which "God may be all in all" [Eph 4:13; 1 Cor 15:28].[10]

While alleviating Jewish concerns about active Christian proselytizing in historic time, does not the "eschatological postponement" approach conveyed by the above quotations nevertheless perpetuate the judgment, albeit more benignly phrased, that the church is the community that has "gotten it right," which Jews will eventually come to recognize too? Does it not imply that Jews who have not believed in Christ have compromised their covenantal standing, that they lack "faith" and or have acted unfaithfully (hard-heartedly) in response to the gospel's claims, as if these claims were known to be true [8] but rejected? Does not an "eschatological postponement" model work from the notion that these Jews remain in an incomplete relationship with God from which they need to be "saved"? Although different from traditional "replacement theology" or "supersessionism," recognition of these kinds of implications have led some scholars to identify this approach as retaining aspects of traditional triumphalism, a kind of "eschatological supersessionism."[11] Jesper Svartvik has insightfully framed this matter as follows:

> To put it bluntly, Jews are [thus] tolerated because of a Messianic theology which proclaims that in days to come Jews will become Christians. . . . But a Christian theology of Judaism cannot be based on such a narrow understanding of eschatology. This line of thought does not allow the others to define themselves, something which must be the starting-point in interreligious dialogue. Simply put, it does not allow Jews to be Jews as the vast majority of Jews define themselves.[12]

In this essay we hope to address this concern directly, by exploring both exegetical as well as theological aspects. We ask: Do the Apostle Paul's

---

10. *Catechism of the Catholic Church*, §674. Scriptural citations presented as footnotes in the Catechism are included in square brackets above. The concatenation of Pauline, deutero-Pauline, Matthean, and Lucan perspectives in this paragraph raises the question as to whether all these New Testament texts really share the common viewpoint expressed here. More specifically to Romans, the Catechism quote fails to convey all of Paul's thought here. His reasoning is that God has caused those Jews who have thus far not responded positively to the gospel to be in some way connected to its spread among the gentiles. If it desired to cite Paul literally, the Catechism should have more accurately reflected Pauline thought here by saying, "The glorious Messiah's coming is suspended at every moment of history until the 'full number' of the gentiles have heard the gospel." See further below.

11. Korn, "The Man of Faith and Religious Dialogue."

12. Svartvik, "Geschwisterlichkeit: Realizing That We are Siblings," 320.

letters—upon which this eschatological scenario relies—require, or even support as most appropriate today, a Christian expectation that envisions that the fate of Judaism will be fulfilled when the distinctive identity of Jews as Jews dissolves in the face of the glorious return of Christ Jesus in messianic splendor? Can Christians theologize about this as if certain that this is what Paul meant, let alone that he accurately glimpsed the eschatological future? Could [9] Paul have possibly been thinking in such binary terms about "Judaism" and "Christianity," when the only church he knew was a subgroup within Judaism, when faith in Jesus as Messiah was an option conceptualized within Judaism, not by conversion from it to a different religious affiliation?

2. PAUL: JEWISH APOSTLE OR JEWISH APOSTATE?

To address these questions, it must be realized that in the almost fifty years since the promulgation of *Nostra Aetate*, there have been sweeping developments in Pauline studies that could rightly be called paradigm shifts. We argue that these shifts provide a credible, even compelling, way of actualizing Pauline eschatology in a post-*Nostra Aetate* church that does not lead inevitably to the scenario of Christianity triumphing over a mistaken Judaism at the End of Days. To show this, it is necessary to survey the development of new perspectives in Pauline scholarship.[13]

The dominant reading of Paul for centuries, heavily influenced by Reformation-era debates, saw him as the wedge that split apart the new grace-filled Christian church from Judaism and its "Law."[14] According to this ubiquitous Christian view, which naturally also shaped Jewish perceptions of Paul's attitudes toward Jews and their religious sensibilities, Paul declared the end of the "Law" as a futile effort by the Jewish people to earn God's favor. He is imagined to have proclaimed the "Law-free gospel" because he discovered that one [10] could not become "righteous"

---

13. It is not our purpose in this essay to exegete every Pauline passage that bears on new understandings of Paul. Readers are advised to consult the works cited in the notes for treatments of Pauline rhetoric in such passages as 1 Cor 9:19–23; Gal 3:23; Phil 3:7; or 1 Thess 2:14–16, for example.

14. We put "Law" in quotation marks to denote that the word *nomos* in Greek (Paul's native language) has different cadences from the Hebrew word *Tôrâ*. The latter is better rendered in English as "Teaching" or "Guidance," thus signifying "God's Guidance for Israel," a positive connotation as well as a contextually specific one that is obscured if not altered beyond recognition when translated "Law" and especially when put in contrast to "grace" or "love," as it has been so often in Christian theological representations.

by doing good works since no one was without sin. We want to stress that Judaism never upheld this straw man of perfectionism. The temple and its sacrificial system by definition gave witness to a relationship based upon God's grace toward those who acknowledged themselves to be sinners. Nevertheless, the subsequent prevailing Christian view proceeded from the conviction that a new universal community that realized its total dependence on God's merciful grace, which Jews ostensibly had not realized, or, alternatively, arrogantly rejected, had now come into being because of Jesus Christ and the birth of Christianity.

Assuming that Paul had forsaken Judaism after experiencing Christ, the Reformers likened the Jewish way of life to Roman Catholicism as both being, in their outlook, religions based on the futile effort to earn God's favor. Reformed Christianity, on the other hand, was thought to be similar to Paul in perceiving the need to depend only on God's mercy. Paul became the champion of "justification by faith" against all the rituals and practices of Roman Catholicism. In this perspective, what Paul wrote was interpreted to be in opposition to Judaism, by way of which the Reformers projected what they found objectionable within Roman Catholicism onto Judaism: e.g., that it was "works"-based, legalistic, loveless, filled with empty ritual, arrogant, and corrupt. The "Paul" that Christians thereby constructed was not only the founder of Christianity, but his calling to do so was intimately tied to negative portrayals and valuations of Jewish identity, beliefs, and behavior from which he supposedly found freedom. This is why he was thought to have desired the "conversion" of Jews as well as non-Jews. In response to this caricature that Christians presented as admirable and desirable in sharp contrast to that which Judaism ostensibly offered, Jews naturally approached Paul with the widespread presupposition that he was a renegade, and worse than that, that he was anti-Jewish in a way that [11] directly contributed to the harm the Jewish people have experienced over the centuries at the hands of Christians.[15]

This way of constructing Paul (as well as the negative Christian foil, Judaism), although representing what became the dominant view (and arguably still is, especially at the level of popular culture), has suffered a significant challenge in recent years. Many present-day New Testament and Pauline scholars (which includes some Jews) have become much more aware of the danger of anachronistically reading Paul's writings through the lenses of later Christian polemics and have also moved away from the previously presumed, fundamental dichotomy between Judaism and Christianity. They

---

15. Langton, *The Apostle Paul in the Jewish Imagination*, esp. chs. 1–4; Nanos, "A Jewish View," 159–65.

have begun to reconsider Paul as standing *within* the Jewish world of the late Second Temple Period—not apart from it.[16] A particularly significant turning point occurred with the widespread realization among Christian scholars that the preponderance of late Second Temple Jewish texts understood the Torah as God's gracious gift to Israel.[17] It was a Christian distortion to imagine Judaism as a legalistic religion of "works righteousness" that [12] sought to earn God's approval through the ritual performance of commands. Rather, late Second Temple Jewish texts understood Torah-observance as an act of gratitude for having already been divinely favored by God's decision to initiate a covenant with Israel. With this understanding of Judaism, important aspects of the conventional contrast between Paul and "law-bound" Judaism could not be easily sustained.

As Magnus Zetterholm neatly summarizes:

> [M]any of the established truths about Paul have thus been challenged, for instance, the idea that Paul ceased observing the Torah[18] or that he created a new religion based on universalism instead of Jewish particularism. If the old caricature of Judaism can be proven false and it can be assumed that first-century Judaism was not characterized by legalism and works-righteousness, it seems quite unlikely that Paul found reason to leave Judaism for Christianity. If the Torah was given by grace and contains a sacrificial system that makes it possible for the individual to atone for his or her own sins, it seems, on the contrary, likely that Paul continued to express his relation to the God of Israel through the Torah, God's most precious gift to the Jewish people. From this point of departure, other factors must

---

16. The history of this paradigm shift has been superbly charted in Zetterholm, *Approaches to Paul*, and it is the focus of Nanos and Zetterholm, eds., *Paul within Judaism*.

17. This development is traceable to the influential papers and essays by Krister Stendahl, including "The Apostle Paul and the Introspective Conscience of the West" and Sanders, *Paul and Palestinian Judaism*. This trajectory is now called "the New Perspective on Paul" (NPP), which brings a more accurate understanding of late Second Temple Judaism to the task of interpreting Paul. However, the NPP did not locate Paul himself and his own theologizing within the Judaism it now constructed in terms of "covenantal nomism." See note 23 below.

18. 1 Cor 9:19–23 is a key text on the question of whether Paul relaxed his personal Torah practices when pastorally appropriate. Mark D. Nanos argues that in this passage Paul explains his strategy of "rhetorical adaptability" rather than the adjusting of his behavior, as traditionally imagined. Paul was actually "Torah-observant as a matter of covenant fidelity, and known to be halakhically faithful by the audience to which he addressed this text"; hence, they understood that he was not writing of adjusting, for example, his dietary behavior, but how he adapted his arguments for the gospel to the argumentative premises of his various audiences ("Paul's Relationship to Torah in Light of His Strategy 'To Become Everything to Everyone,'" 139).

have led to the distressing conflicts within the early [13] Jesus movement. This insight has led scholars to emphasize ... the relationship between Jews and non-Jews within the Jesus movement....[19]

Another way to get to the heart of the paradigm shifts in recent Pauline scholarship is to ask the question: "Was Paul Jewish or Christian?" The question is not as straightforward as it might appear. Upon reflection it becomes clear that it cannot be answered without considering the operative definitions of both "Jewish" and "Christian." This in turn leads to a greater awareness of the risks of anachronism.

It is crucial to recall that Paul proclaimed his good news to the nations while the temple in Jerusalem still stood. At least seven of the letters attributed to him in the New Testament may well be the only New Testament books written prior to the temple's destruction by Roman legions in 70 C.E. The temple served as a central locus of a wide variety of Jewish subgroups, including Greek-speaking Jews in the diaspora. With its annihilation, a centuries-long process of reorienting Jewish life began, eventually resulting in normative rabbinic Judaism.

Notably, the Greek word for "Christian" does not appear in any of Paul's letters. Its absence is instructive. Certainly, Paul became convinced that Christ Jesus had been "established as Son of God in power according to the spirit of holiness through resurrection from the dead" (Rom 1:4 NRSV). He could thus be well described as messianically or eschatologically enthusiastic about Jesus and the imminence of a new creation. But "Christian" has come to convey a discrete religious group identifiably separate from Jewish communities. This distinction simply did not yet exist during Paul's life-time.[20] It is more accurate to think of believers in the [14] Crucified-and-Raised-One as a particular Jewish subgroup. Pamela Eisenbaum puts it this way:

> Paul believed that the recognition of the one God by Gentiles was necessary so that they might have a share in the world to come. Thus, Paul was not a *Christian*—a word that was in any case completely unknown to him because it had not yet been invented. He was a Jew who understood himself to be on a divine

---

19. Zetterholm, *Approaches to Paul*, 229–30.

20. A similar dynamic holds true for another New Testament book, the Letter to the Hebrews. If readers come to that text assuming that a distinct "Christianity" existed when the letter was written, they will likely read passages such as 8:13 as ascribing obsolescence to "Judaism." Jesper Svartvik has convincingly shown how anachronistic and self-serving such a reading is. See his "Reading the Epistle to the Hebrews without Presupposing Supersessionism."

mission. As a Jew, Paul believed himself to be entrusted with the special knowledge God had given only to Jews. However, Paul also believed the resurrection of Jesus signaled that the world to come was already in the process of arriving and that it was time to reconcile non-Jews to Jews, not because they were necessarily hostile to each other but because, if all people were potentially children of God, Jews and Gentiles must now be considered part of the same family; this entailed a new level of interaction and intimacy.[21]

Moreover, Paul's self-descriptions as a "member of the people of Israel, . . . a Pharisee" and as an "apostle to the gentiles" (Rom 11:13), challenge the persistent notion that Paul changed "religions." Yet that way of conceptualizing Paul and his "mission" of founding "churches" (usually "Gentile Christian churches") remains an underlying premise even when interpreters point out that there was not yet such a thing as "Christian" or "Christianity" into which to "convert." Many read Gal 1:13, for instance, to mean that he formerly lived in a Jewish way (practiced Judaism) but no longer does so (presuming he is now a Christian, thus converting to and [15] practicing Christianity). However, without the presupposition that Paul must have "switched religions," his language more likely means that he no longer practices Judaism in quite the *same way* that he did before ("my former way of living in Judaism as compared to the way that I live in Judaism now"), that is, he was now practicing Judaism shaped by the conviction that the messianic age has dawned, which he did not believe to be the case before.[22]

Since many people still think of Paul as no longer having upheld, practiced, or promoted Torah, or as not beholden to the God-given Mosaic covenantal stipulations to which Jews held themselves in response to God's gifts and calling (this in spite of Paul's own comments, e.g., Rom 9:4–5 and 11:28–29), it is hard to avoid the conceptual implications as well as the discursive practices associated with the long-lived anti-Jewish reading of Paul. When readers imagine that Paul sees Judaism as the "other," it is probably inevitable that they will negatively contrast Judaism with "Christianity" as they understand it. "Christian" virtues of faith, faithfulness, grace, forgiveness, love, freedom, universalism, inclusivism, or non-discrimination tend to be denied to the "othered" tradition of Judaism.

---

21. Eisenbaum, *Paul Was Not a Christian*, 3–4.

22. Just as a Catholic might discuss the way that he or she formerly practiced versus how they now practice, without suggesting that they are no longer a Catholic. On this passage and this topic of Paul's self-understanding within instead of from outside of Judaism, see Nanos, "Paul and Judaism: Why Not Paul's Judaism?"

This traditional way of proceeding is generally coupled with the widely held Christian notion that Jews are thus out of the covenant with God if they do not become Christians, that "Jews need to be saved just as do gentiles," and, ironically, drawing on Romans 11, that they "have been cut off" yet "can be grafted back in" "by faith." If one presents Paul as discovering God's grace appropriately only by faith, that naturally suggests—when compared to the Judaism he supposedly left [16] behind—that Judaism is not based on grace or faith; thus, some other (negative) explanation of the way that Jews think and live must be supplied.

This kind of reasoning is manifest in many readings and translations of Romans 11. That is not to say that Paul's positions cannot be contrasted with his former way of perceiving and practicing the same things, but that the terms for drawing the contrast should not continue to be essentialized and retrojected into a supposed contrast between (first-century) Judaism and (Pauline) Christianity. Rather, the contrast has to be historically contextualized, which involves recognizing that what changed for Paul was his perception of *the meaning of Jesus—within Judaism*.

This very brief sketch of a vast and complex body of contemporary research is intended to lead to this observation about current Pauline studies: Paul is more properly envisioned not as having forsaken Judaism to champion a new universal religion (a Jewish apostate), but as one feeling called within Judaism to proclaim to the nations a Jewish message about the God of Israel's acts through Christ (a Jewish apostle). Although intermediate positions are possible between these basic models, we suggest that there are good historical and exegetical reasons for today's readers to favor the latter approach to Paul's letters.[23]

[17] In addition, the zero-sum eschatological scenarios that see Christianity "winning" and Rabbinic Judaism "losing" at the End of Days are based upon translations of Romans 11 that were themselves shaped by the binary understanding that Paul had forsaken "Judaism" and converted to "Christianity." By its very nature, the act of translation often requires

---

23. While tangential to this essay, we want to observe that the "New Perspective on Paul" (see note 17 above) did not deal with several elements of the traditional negative Christian perception of Judaism. Thus Judaism could continue to serve as a foil for articulating what made Pauline Christianity unique and attractive versus Judaism, which Paul still is understood to have left behind as his "former" religion. There linger also key contrasts, including attributing to Judaism the essentialized traits of arrogance, self-righteousness (including reliance upon badges of identity), judgmentalism, particularism (also referred to as nationalism, ethnocentrism), exclusivism, selfishness, and even works-righteousness. Such alleged features of late Second Temple Judaism are contrasted unfavorably with Pauline "Christianity" (which we would suggest might with greater historical accuracy be called "Pauline Judaism" or "Apostolic Judaism").

translators to shape the language of reception so that it makes sense of words and ideas and even metaphorical or ironic elements that the language of origin presupposes. Those translational word choices are significantly governed by whether the translators conceive of Paul as a Jewish apostle or apostate. *We hope to demonstrate below that very different actualizations of Romans 11 ensue when theologians work from translations based upon the paradigm of Paul within Judaism.*

Furthermore, besides recognizing the very different nature of the Christ-assemblies of Paul's day, today's readers also must reckon with his very different vision for the ultimate destiny of all things, his eschatology. Twenty-first-century readers of his letters almost certainly engage Paul's letters with the presupposition that the "End of Days" is sometime in the far-off, indefinite future. But that most likely was not Paul's perspective. For him the expected future was beginning now, albeit awaiting significant future developments, some of which were intimately tied to his own ministry among the nations.[24] The raising of the Crucified One to the life of the age to come had triggered the birth pangs of the new creation. The time had come for the rest of the nations to know the God of Israel.

3. READING PAUL AND HIS ESCHATOLOGICAL HOPE FROM "WITHIN JUDAISM"

Reading Paul as within Second Temple Judaism requires careful attention to the historical context of Paul's language. This exegetically-grounded effort offers new and [18] significant hermeneutical advantages, not least with respect to Christian-Jewish relations today. Many of the most relevant passages relating to the matter of Paul's relationship to Judaism are being exegetically argued, and there is a growing list of participants in this venture.[25]

The basic insight proceeds from some simple perspectives noted above, although generally their implications have not been fully integrated into the way that Paul and his communities are conceptualized or discussed. If we take fuller consideration of insights such as Krister Stendahl's, that Paul was called rather than converted, that his concern with justification by faith was primarily focused on legitimating the inclusion of non-Jews within God's family rather than on individual salvation, and that fighting

---

24. Nanos, *The Mystery of Romans*, 239–88; see discussion below.

25. Leading voices have been participating in the Paul and Judaism Consultation of the Society of Biblical Literature Consultation for several years. See Nanos and Zetterholm, eds., *Paul within Judaism*

works-righteousness was not his life's work,[26] and combine them with the now widely recognized historical insight that there was not yet any such thing as or named Christianity into which to be converted or into which to seek to convert others,[27] it logically follows that Paul would have continued to practice and promote Judaism, albeit in an eschatologically enthusiastic form, centered on Christ. If one assumes that his audiences knew this about him (or in the case of Rome, had heard this about him), then they would have read him very differently than those Christians who since the time of the church fathers have generally assumed that they knew him to have abandoned Judaism for a supposedly "Law-free" Christianity.

[19] Eschatological elements are woven throughout the central features of this re-reading. When Paul became convinced that Jesus was raised from the grave, this signaled for him the beginning of the awaited age to come within the midst of the present age. This was the message that he was called to announce to the nations, including those children of Israel scattered among them. This is eschatological reasoning by definition.[28] Obviously, for himself and other Jews similarly convinced of these propositional truth claims, the most appropriate interpretation of the Torah had then required reevaluation in the light of the change of eons in which they now believed.

Paul's perspective was thus "chronometrical": it was "time-conditioned" by his sense that the awaited eschatological time was now breaking into the midst of present historical time as God's plans for a new creation approached their imminent culmination. His driving concern was the question of what was appropriate "now" in the light of the beginning of the age to come among those who followed the Jesus who had been raised from the dead. The full "day of the Lord" had not yet arrived, and thus the

---

26. Stendahl, *Paul Among Jews and Gentiles*.

27. It has become common to see this stated in introductions to Pauline studies, followed by beginning to write about Paul's Christian views, Christian mission, Christian churches, and so on, as if the insight had not been stated. Paradigms do not change easily, and terminological traditions can be an important deterrent to that process, in this case, perhaps, disclosing that Pauline scholars among others, are not quite ready to embrace the logical implication that Paul was thus still practicing and promoting Judaism, even if that of representing a (small) subgroup of Jews.

28. Although sometimes noted by New Perspective interpreters, it should be stressed that Paul's impulse to take the message to the nations was already an Israelite/Jewish ideal present in, e.g., Isaiah's prophecies of the future role of Israel. This shows another value in reading Paul from within Judaism. In Rom 3:1-2, Paul boldly claims that the role of the Jews and circumcision is important because they were "entrusted with God's words/oracles," and throughout he imagines himself as a servant of Israel bringing the good news to the nations. He sees some of his Jewish kin stumbling and falling behind himself (in their role as Israel) to be faithful to joining him as heralds of this news, at least presently (cf. 9-11).

time-claims of Paul and his group could be readily disputed at the empirical level. But for those who "experienced" the revelation of this "new creation," there was a need to reinterpret how to live Torah now, in the "time-in-between-times," we might say.

The most prominent theme in Paul's writing about the Torah concerns the needs of non-Jews. For the emerging "Paul within Judaism" interpreters, it is a focal point for how [20] to best contextualize the nature of his rhetorical comments, and thereby to avoid globalizing what Paul writes about non-Jews and the Torah onto all Jews by supposing he is addressing "everyman" in every argument. This contextualization includes attending to whether any given statement is descriptive or prescriptive.

The non-Jews "in Christ" were not to become Jews in order to demonstrate the truth that the end of the ages had arrived. The time had come for the nations to join alongside of Israel in worshiping the One Creator God of all humankind. By its nature, this truth claim demands that gentiles remain non-Jews, members of the rest of the nations.[29] Paul had come to recognize that the prophets could be read to announce this otherwise unexpected turning of those of the nations from idols to the One God as a signal of the arrival of the time when the wolf (nations) will lie down and dine alongside the lamb (Israel), as Isaiah related the metaphor (Isa 11:6; 65:25). Thus Israel and the nations together must practice an egalitarian way of life in their gatherings (*ekklēsia*). To live this way, different yet equal, will, Paul argues, require the enabling of God's Spirit (which can be understood to represent the end-of-the-ages or eschatological way of living) to guide and empower their lives. What is important to note but so often overlooked is that this is nothing other than a *Jewish* aspiration, one grounded in Jewish Scriptures and teachings, especially Isaiah, whom Paul quotes and echoes throughout his letters, Romans in particular.

The difference between this Jewish group and others is the chronometrical claim that this is the appropriate way to live faithfully to Torah now, that something has changed among humankind and thus that Israelites/Jews must develop a new relationship with those from the nations who turn to her [21] God through faithfulness to Jesus Christ. The difference is thus not between Judaism and Christianity. It is not even between the essential ideas, motivations, and impulses among different Jewish groups' beliefs and practices; it is the result of different conclusions about *what time it is* and thus about which interpretation of God's "Teaching" for Israel (=Torah) is now the most appropriate or faithful to Israel's covenantal responsibilities.

---

29. For fuller discussion, see Nanos, "Paul and the Jewish Tradition: The Ideology of the Shema."

In addition, just as those Jews who have received the Spirit of God—the Spirit of the age to come, the Spirit that raised Jesus from death (Rom 1:4)—have to live out the Torah differently in the emerging new epoch, these Jews also have to develop ways to teach those from the nations how to live righteously as non-Jews. But non-Jews, who have received the same Spirit, are not taking on Torah observance formally, precisely because Torah was given to guide Israel, not the rest of the nations, except in the general sense of guidance in living rightly toward God and neighbor. That is why we can call Paul's propositional claims for the gospel "chronometrical": the dynamic from which Paul's (and his fellow Jesus-followers') reasoning is distinguishable from that of other Jews and Jewish groups is based on a different understanding of what the current time represents. This conditions their ideas about the most appropriate way to think and behave, including, of course, how to interpret and apply Torah (but not in any way to dismiss Torah). Other Jews might well agree that such a position will be appropriate "on that day," but, because they don't share Paul's conviction that the Crucified One has been raised, for them that day has not yet dawned.

From Paul's perspective, non-Jews needed to learn how to consult Tanakh and Torah and other teachings and customs without being technically bound to all of them in the same way as Jews. But these former pagans in Paul's assemblies were obligated to turn from being slaves to sin and worshipers of other gods to being servants of righteousness and the One True God. Moreover, they were initially doing so [22] by joining Jewish subgroups of followers of Jesus; hence, Torah behavior was normative for communal life.[30]

This raises a question we seek to explore: What might Paul's first-century eschatological expectations in the Letter to the Romans mean for Christians regarding how to best conceptualize theologically and morally their discussions about and relations to Jews and Judaism today?

---

30. By way of analogy, when a non-Catholic attends a Mass, he or she will be expected to behave according to basic cultural norms. This does not require that they become Catholics, that is, formally bound to behave outside of these communal gatherings in the same way as are Catholics. Such behavior when among Catholics also does not make them Catholics, but their behavior is Catholic-like when attending Mass, even though guests. The context for the non-Jews turning to God through Christ was more complicated, because they were becoming full members of the people of God without also becoming members of Israel, which was now recognized within these groups as one of the people of God with people from other nations being reconciled to the One God of all humankind. Thus, while Torah-derived behavior was customary in these groups because they were founded by Jews, they did not regard the non-Jews as merely guests, making for the kind of complications that Paul's letters were written to seek to resolve.

4. ROMANS 11: LEAVE ALL JUDGMENTS TO GOD

Unlike, say, Thessalonica and Corinth, the assembly (or assemblies) of Christ-followers in Rome were not founded by Paul, but by other apostles who may have traveled directly from Judea. Although it seems likely that there were Christ-following Jews among the assemblies, Paul's argument targets non-Jews among them who have turned to Christ. Sometimes these non-Jews are specifically singled out [e.g., "Now I am speaking to you gentiles" (11:5–6, 13; 11:13–32; 15:15–16)], but in many other cases Paul's focus on the non-Jews is evident in various ways, for example, by his choice of pronouns (e.g., "they" in 3:1–3; cf. 9:1–5; 10:1–2; 11:1, 11–32; 15:25–32).[31] One [23] of the important implications of attending to this focus on instructing the non-Jews is the logical challenge it poses to the traditional assumption that Paul is in some way trying to make Jews realize that they too are sinners or hypocrites and related suppositions. Instead, the later reader can now recognize that Paul writes from positive understandings of Jewish traditions, including the principle that one must "practice what one preaches" or be guilty of hypocrisy (ch. 2). He writes to the Romans in order to help non-Jews learn to think and live similarly.[32]

A. Unity among Jews and Gentiles in Christ

As with his earlier letters, Paul seeks to promote oneness between the Jews and gentiles in Christ. He challenges any nascent indifference or resentment that might be arising. Such reactions must not guide the behavior of the non-Jews who now believe in Jesus as Christ toward Jews who do not share this conviction (Rom 3:1–2; 9–11). This concern is later presented in cryptic terms directed to the "strong" (or: "able" to believe Jesus is Christ) to censure

---

31. Many exegetes representing different views of the implications recognize the make-up of the target audience is non-Jews who believe in Jesus; cf. Stowers, *A Rereading of Romans*; Das, *Solving the Romans Debate*. In addition, Nanos argues that the assemblies in Rome were likely still subgroups of the larger Jewish communities, creating the confusing situation for these non-Jews that Paul's message targets: Nanos, *Mystery of Romans*; Nanos, "The Jewish Context of the Gentile Audience Addressed in Paul's Letter to the Romans"; Nanos, "To the Churches within the Synagogues of Rome." Agreement with that proposed scenario is not necessary to our argument, but it helps to make sense of the widely recognized implication that Paul is targeting non-Jews in this letter about their attitudes toward and confusion about Jews as well as righteous standing and behavior. Paul is addressing non-Jews confused by their recent entry into a new Jewish social world centered on the Raised One.

32. See Nanos, "Romans," *JANT*; Nanos, "Paul's Non-Jews Do Not Become 'Jews,' But Do They Become 'Jewish'?"

their behavior so that it does not cause the "weak" or "stumbling" over the gospel's chronometrical assertions about Jesus and the standing of [24] these non-Jews to trip over these claims; Rom. 14:1—15:13).[33] Boasting of one's status with God without complete dedication to living according to such a relationship with God, which includes living in ways that show compassion toward others, especially others (i.e., the "stumbling") who may not be treating one well perhaps because of disagreements about these truth claims, functions as a sign of failure to realize one's dependence on God's mercy (see also, e.g., 3:9, 27; 5–6). It also shows a lack of concern that the "Body of Christ" must be united in order to serve the well-being of all of humankind (12:1–21).[34] Boasting in what one has received as a gift from God instead of focusing on how accordingly to give to others signifies, for Paul, an inadequate or immature understanding of faithfulness.

Paul objects to news he has evidently received about the non-Jews being tempted to contrast their newly realized righteous standing with God through Christ Jesus with that of Jews who do not share this perception (11:11–32). In order to prevent these non-Jews from acting out of resentment, Paul explains the status of Jews who do not share their convictions about Jesus in very positive covenantal terms that appeal to God's faithfulness never to fail to uphold promises that God has made. As mentioned earlier, Paul's eschatologically framed instructions to remain faithful in the present rely both upon God's faithfulness to keep the covenantal promises made in the past as well as the hoped-for future of which the [25] prophets often spoke—even when things do not appear to be following along according to the prevailing interpretations of that script.

Paul emphatically insists that these other Jews have not lost their covenantal standing, but are in a temporary state of being "unconvinced" (11:30–32),[35] in order for God to begin the stage of bringing those from the

33. Nanos, *Mystery of Romans*, 144–65.

34. Although not highlighted in the commentary tradition, the "therefore" at 12:1 following the argument for living graciously instead of judgmentally or indifferently toward those Jews who do not share these non-Jews, convictions opens Paul's instructions through the rest of the letter, suggesting not just the internal concerns among Christ-followers, but also the way that these Christ-followers think about and live among those who do not share their faith in Jesus. This perspectives helps to explain the presence of instructions about seeking respect and avoiding vengeance in 12:9–21, the otherwise enigmatic appearance of the call to subordination and paying of taxes in 13:1–7, the instructions about how to live respectfully toward the "weak"/"stumbling" in chapters 14 and 15, as well as the concern with the success of Paul's collection upon arrival in Judea.

35. In view of the argument Paul is making about the present state of many of his fellow Jews, appealing to the guarantee of God's faithfulness to restore all Israel in vv. 25–32, and that God is using this present anomalous situation as a way to include non-Jews among the people of God, the more common meaning of *peithō* as persuade

nations—who themselves had been characterized by being "unconvinced" of the One God (as seen in their polytheism) until now—into favored standing alongside of Israel. Paul wants both Jews and gentiles "in Christ" to recognize that they have equally been beneficiaries of God's grace and so seek to live with each other in equality and unity (15:7–13).

B. A Temporary Development That Paul's Ministry Will Address

It is in this context that we turn to examine more closely the language Paul uses to disclose the mystery of how God is presently working among Israelites and non-Israelites in 11:25–26. The NRSV translates the passage as follows:

> So that you may not claim to be wiser than you are, brothers and sisters, I want you to understand this mystery: a hardening has come upon part of Israel, until the full number of the Gentiles has come in. And so all Israel will be saved . . . .

[26] As usually translated and interpreted, Paul is understood to be envisioning a time when Jesus will return, the *parousia* or second coming of Jesus. The full number of the gentiles is understood to indicate the time when all those from among the nations destined to turn to God through Christ have done so. This is next to be followed by the arrival of Jesus in glory, and then that the rest of the Jews will realize that he is the Christ and so believe in him, in effect becoming Christians. This way of understanding Paul's message in these verses is a central element in the current Catholic eschatological reasoning we mentioned at the outset.

We propose that it is unlikely that Paul is trying to sketch out for a countless succession of Christian generations a time that remains still in the indefinite future for us today. Rather, he describes an era he believed would take place *during his lifetime and ministry*, even though he saw that this process was not turning out precisely as he imagined it would. His confession that God's plans are a mystery he cannot even begin to grasp (11:33–36) provides the warrant for later readers to seek not only to understand Paul's language in its original context, but also to begin to rethink what Paul might say to us today, after a history he couldn't imagine and when things did not turn out as he had hoped—yet. Would he not still be convinced that God's

---

or be persuaded/convinced (see *LSJ* 1353–54) in vv. 30–32, around which Paul's point works, seems warranted, rather than the prevailing translations that introduce the notion of "disobedience." See Nanos, "Romans," *JANT*, notes to vv. 30–32 on p. 278.

promises were certain but that it was his own understanding that needed adjustment? Wouldn't he then begin to rethink how to understand not only the present but also the future?

If Paul is explaining in vv. 25-26 the role that he sees his own ministry playing in the mystery of God's work among Jews and non-Jews, then the element of time is accentuated in a different way than has usually been highlighted. This can be demonstrated from the prevailing translations, and even more when we show an alternative translation to make better sense of his positive treatment of Israel's present, temporary state, one that is clearly central to the message he seeks to deliver to the non-Jews in Rome.

[27] In his explanation, Paul employs two metaphors: that of messengers proceeding along an assigned route, some of whom stumble on the way and thus open gaps for others to enter into the event as well (vv. 11-15); and that of an olive tree with bent branches, opening spaces into which foreign branches can be grafted (vv. 17-24). The runners symbolize the God-given mission of Jews to be "lights to the nations," a task which Paul believes must now be vigorously pursued since the End of Days has commenced with the raising of Jesus (ch. 10). Those running to announce this news to the nations most enthusiastically and faithfully are, for Paul, Jewish followers of Christ such as himself, while those who are stumbling (but not falling) are unconvinced Jews who do not realize what is happening.

The pattern that Paul has experienced in his ministry, but which the Christ-following gentiles in Rome will not experience until Paul's planned arrival, involves him, as a representative and messenger of the unfolding restoration of Israel, delivering the gospel message first to the synagogues of Rome.[36] He cites Isa 59:20-21 to this effect in v. 26: "The Deliverer will come from Zion." Paul combines this language with that of Isa 27:9. These passages have to do with God coming to the rescue of Israel, gathering Israelites from among the nations, where her fruit has filled the whole world. Some

36. In *Mystery of Romans*, 239-88, Nanos explains in detail how the concerns Paul expresses in Romans, indeed, the exigency that provokes him to write this letter, arise from fear that the growing resentment among these non-Jews will lead to events that close off willingness to welcome him to share his views in the synagogues of Rome upon his planned arrival. Paul's ministry follows a two-step pattern of preaching first to Israelites scattered among the nations, which provokes a divided response. This event signals the time to turn fully to the nations, which in turn provokes his fellow Jews to reconsider whether the end of the ages expectations for Israel to enlighten the nations has indeed begun, as Paul claims, when they witness members from the nations turning from their gods to the One God through faith in Jesus. This interpretation of Paul's strategy is compatible with the pattern traced in Acts (see, e.g., 13:13–14:7), in sharp contrast to the traditional readings of Paul, which find the (very Jewish and synagogue oriented) Paul of Acts to be very different than the Paul traditionally constructed from his letters.

[28] of his fellow Jews will be convinced when he preaches in Rome; some will not; then he will turn fully to the non-Israelites there, and their positive response will provoke his fellow Jews to reconsider whether the age to come has indeed arrived, and thus, whether it is time to proclaim the gospel to the nations alongside of Paul.[37]

This scenario is what Paul tried to communicate throughout chapter 11, especially in vv. 11–32. He developed a series of metaphors and explanations, albeit cryptic, to this end. One metaphor, drawing upon Paul's insistence that Israel's special trust is God's words/oracles (3:2), functions by picturing some of his fellow Israelites stumbling instead of continuing, with him and other Christ-following Jews, to bring the news to the nations (vv. 11–16). He insists that the gap that has opened among these Israelites, because some have stumbled instead of carrying out this task, has benefited the non-Israelites. *This is a temporary development*; in time those who have stumbled will catch back up. This will result in a situation far superior to the present anomalous condition, which Paul likens to the superiority of the resurrected life of the new creation to normal, mortal history.

In another metaphor, that of the olive tree, Paul pictures some branches as being broken (as in bent, to be discussed below), while others remain in good health, such as he sees himself representing (vv. 17–24). In the argument following these metaphors, Paul seeks to explain these developments as a mystery involving the intertwined fates of Israelites and members from the nations in codependence [29] upon the mercy of God, leading in time to the reconciliation of those from the nations and the restoration of "all Israel."[38]

In vv. 25–26, Paul provides a kind of timeline. The NRSV translates the passage thus: "So that you may not claim to be wiser than you are, brothers and sisters, I want you to understand this mystery: a hardening has come upon part of Israel, until the full number of the Gentiles has come in. And so all Israel will be saved; as it is written . . . ." In spite of translation choices that we believe can be greatly improved, the idea that Paul is engaged in disclosing a series of events comes through, and that he sees the end result

---

37. Paul calls this provoking his kinsmen to "jealousy of his ministry" in vv. 13–14. Paul uses jealous here in the positive sense of "emulation" to make the point that he expects his fellow Jews to see in the success of his ministry among the non-Israelites the fulfillment of their own expectation, as Israelites, to share in the privilege of bringing the message of God's reconciliation to the nations, which will provoke them to reconsider whether the chronometric claims of the gospel are being confirmed. See Nanos, *Mystery of Romans*, 283–85; Nanos, "Jewish Context," 300–304.

38. The brief discussion of passages from Romans 11 draws upon a series of published works noted below at certain points, and in a more summary fashion, in Nanos, "Romans 11 and Christian and Jewish Relations"; Nanos, "Romans," *JANT*, 275–78.

for Israel in positive terms. This passage is also central to the prevailing Christian position that Paul foresees a time when the Jewish people will believe in Jesus Christ. We too see a timeline, but differently, and we suggest a translation that retains both the metaphorical elements that follow from the olive tree allegory just completed in the previous verses, as well as one that better captures the positive valence of Paul's comments about the present condition of his fellow Jews.

We propose that Paul is explaining how his ministry is unfolding among Jews and non-Jews, following a pattern that will also take place when he is able to reach Rome. It is not likely a scenario in the distant future involving the *parousia*, after Paul's lifetime, but his expectations about what will happen as a direct result of his ministry when he arrives in Rome in the near future. The situation in Rome had not developed according to (Paul's) plan, because, well, Paul has not yet been able to get there to carry out this strategic program for reaching Israel and the nations in what he considers to be the proper order. The anomalous situation of tensions between Jews and non-Jews in the assembly or assemblies in Rome is a [30] direct result, but one he hopes to rectify soon. As we will discuss, things did not turn out quite as he imagined that they would, and he allowed for that too, in vv. 33–36, wherein he describes God working in human history beyond the ways that we can imagine, even if the ends are guaranteed by promise.

Paul refers to the state of Israel, or some Israelites, as *pōrōsis*, which has traditionally been translated as "hardened" or "blinded," and often compared to the hardened heart of Pharaoh. Yet Paul does not use *sklēros* here, which is the term used to describe Pharaoh's heart. The word he uses, *pōrōsis*, is a medical term referring to the formation of a "callus" to protect a wounded limb. It is a positive development, a temporary way for the body (or plant) to preserve the health of the limb and thus "all" of the body.[39] It makes little sense to characterize his fellow Jews as "hardened," in the usual negative sense that is likened to that of Pharaoh's heart, in an argument in which he seeks to provoke these non-Jews to be charitable, whereas to characterize them as in a state of repair, while still a value judgment, is at least generous. Moreover, the adverbial phrase *apo merous*, usually translated as if adjectival, *"part of* Israel" or "Israel *partially,"* can be translated as "for a while" or "temporarily,"[40] preserving its function to modify the verb "has happened." We thus have the translation: "that a callus has temporarily happened for Israel," signifying that God is protecting these Israelites in spite

---

39. Nanos, "'Callused,' Not 'Hardened.'"

40. Cf. Rom 15:24, where Paul writes of his plan, before heading off to Spain, to stay in Rome "for a while" or "temporarily" (*apo merous*)!

of present appearances of their state from the viewpoint of the non-Jews addressed. We suggest that Paul is referring to the initial divided state of Israel that results from his proclamation of the gospel in the synagogues, with some Israelites accepting the chronometric claims and joining Paul, and others rejecting—"unconvinced" by these claims. The next phrase is likewise of interest.

[31] The temporary protection will function "until" a certain point in time. That point seems to draw, as does the callus imagery, from the tree allegory, by referring to "fullness" (*plērōma*). This might be when the graft takes, or when it bears fruit. If metaphorical, it is unlikely to refer here to "the full number," as often translated. This callus will protect Israel *"until* the fullness of the nations *begins/commences* (*eiselthē*),"* in other words, when the fullness of the nations is addressed by the fullness of *Israel*, i.e., by the stumbling messengers who get with the program and the bent or injured branches after their wounds are healed under the protection of a callus. With both the messengers on the road and the olive tree metaphor, Paul is referring to the positive response to his preaching when he and all Israel turn "fully" to those of the nations following his initial preaching aimed at his fellow Israelites. In terms of the metaphor of some stumbling, this represents those from the nations who step into the temporary gap that has opened up between those who are still walking in full step and those temporarily falling a bit behind because of tripping over whether the end of the ages has really begun with Jesus, who thus doubt whether it is appropriate at this time to bring this message to the nations (vv. 11–15). Paul argues that the message of the gospel will be fully effective only when the gap among the messengers has been closed back up, and not by the falling aside of those (Jews) who have tripped. Non-Jews in the Jesus assemblies must not think in zero-sum terms and boast over those Jews who are unconvinced that the day of the Lord is imminent, as Paul makes clear in the words that follow.

Paul completes his sentence by asserting the prophetic promise: "and then (or, and thus), all Israel will be restored (or, saved/rescued)," followed by the cobbling together of passages from Isaiah discussed above that affirm God's benevolent intention toward Israel in the end, following the disciplining of some who are presently unfaithful. This affirmation of God's promises for Israel's restoration continues in the balance of the chapter, including the exclamation that [32] Israel is "beloved for the sake of the fathers," and that "the gifts and calling of God are irrevocable" (vv. 28–29).

The time element is central throughout the disclosure of this mystery, but is it not built around events Paul anticipated to take place in his own lifetime as a direct result of his ministry among Israelites of the diaspora and those from the other nations whom he sought to reach, "to the Jew first, and also to the Greek," as he puts it several times in Romans? We will return to this matter, but first a few more elements in Romans 11 deserve further consideration.

C. A Slip into but Then a Recoiling from Binary Thinking

Let us turn for a moment back to Paul's allegory of the olive tree. There Paul added a further twist to his argument of some stumbling temporarily by drawing on imagery from an olive tree, to which the prophets also appealed in their arguments about the future in contrast to the present state of things (e.g., Isa 27–29). The message is similar, supporting the basic lines of argument against drawing mistaken conclusions from the present appearance that many of Paul's fellow Jews are not joining him to announce the gospel to the nations ("yet," as Paul sees things). But Paul develops the point in several new directions, some of which on the surface, especially as commonly translated, can be understood to undermine rather than enhance the logic of his argument thus far. This seems to arise from his move into a diatribal conversation with the wild shoot from a wild olive tree that has been grafted in among the natural branches of a cultivated olive tree.

As Paul develops the allegory, God is seen as poised to engage the wild shoot's mistaken notion of divine favor at the ultimate expense of some natural branches now described as broken (vv. 20–24). Paul labors to clarify that this is only a temporary state, as he did in the previous metaphor. But perhaps because he addresses a wild shoot that has been cut off from a wild tree, he changes his language from what he introduced when depicting some of the natural branches as [33] "broken" as in "bent" by way of verbal forms of *ekklaō* (in vv. 17–21), to terms revolving around "cut off" as in "pruned" by way of verbal forms of *ekkoptō* in vv. 22–24.[41] This has led interpreters to choose to translate Paul's allegory throughout the whole olive tree passage as if the natural branches had been cut off of the tree rather than remaining on the tree, albeit bent, and thus protected by the formation of a callus until eventually restored to good health. But the point to which Paul directs attention is any nascent tendency for the wild shoot to proudly celebrate its new place at the expense of some natural branches that have suffered temporary impairment. His metaphorical language, easily missed in the translation, takes aim at any temptation for the shoot to suppose it is now superior to the natural branches that are suffering from being bent: "Do not think of yourself as above (the other branches), but be afraid."

---

41. For a fuller explanation of the translation decisions to which we are appealing, see Nanos, "'Broken Branches': A Pauline Metaphor Gone Awry?"

Paul's switch from *ekklaō* to *ekkoptō* raises a zero-sum implication (they lose, you win) that Paul then tries to overcome by claiming that God can graft back in natural branches that have been cut off more easily than God can graft in a shoot cut off of a wild tree, which is, from a strictly horticultural perspective, not reasonable. But it should be noted that when he described the state of some of these natural branches at the beginning of the allegory, before having God address the wild shoot's presumptuousness directly in a diatribe, he had described them simply as broken/bent (*ekklaō*), not cut off (*ekkoptō*).

In the olive tree imagery, the wild shoot that is grafted among the branches is used to represent the precarious place of the non-Jews among the Jews even though some (many) of the Jews do not (yet) share their faithfulness to Christ and the declaration of the gospel to the nations (notice, there is but [34] one single branch placed "among" the branches natural to the tree). In both of these metaphors, as in the somewhat more direct comments in vv. 25–26 and the citations in 26–27 (conflating parts of Isa 27:9 and 59:20–21) as well as the conclusions drawn in vv. 28–31, the *temporariness* of the present situation is emphasized. There are some Jews who are convinced of this unfolding process, such as Paul, and there are some who are not. Paul explains that this divided state is actually a part of God's plan to spark the proclamation of the gospel to those of the nations, such as the addressees of Paul's instructions here. But that is not the end goal. Rather, Paul understands God to be using the commencement of this activity among the nations to provoke his fellow Jews to question—when they see these non-Jews turning from idols to the worship of the One God, turning from slavery to sin to slavery to righteousness (cf. ch. 6)—whether indeed the end of the ages has commenced, that time when Israel will be restored and the nations reconciled. He seeks to provoke his fellow Jews to jealousy of his "ministry," that is, to want to become fellow-participants in what Paul is experiencing, the fulfillment of Israel's entrustment with God's words/oracles (11:13–14; cf. 3:2).

The unexpected turning to the nations after the divided response to the gospel among Jews will, Paul believes, provoke the reconsideration of this message by the rest of the Jews. He argues that when his kinspeople see those from the other nations turning to the One God through Paul as messenger (= apostle) of Israel, that they will recognize he is fulfilling their own aspirations to be the light to the nations when the awaited age arrives. They will thus conclude that the age to come must have begun and reconsider the message about Jesus. They will conclude with Paul that it is their calling to now proclaim this message to their fellow Jews among the nations as well as to the rest of humankind. In time, not only will all Israel be rescued from the suffering of the present age, but the reconciliation of the world will finally arrive (11:12, 15). In terms of Paul's metaphors, the stumbling messengers will resume their commanded course and the callus-protected [35] branches will be fully healed on the tree, but now with those of the nations walking alongside or grafted among them.

Paul uses this argument to address directly any nascent ideas stemming from zero-sum thinking among the non-Jews in Rome that their gain has come at the expense of Israelites—as if having replaced them, as if there is room for only so many. It would be natural enough to conclude that if somehow the present level of being unconvinced of the gospel claims among many Jews had opened a gate for the admission of non-Jews among the people of God, then all the more benefit would it be for these non-Jews if those Jews remained unconvinced: would these non-Jews not have replaced those Jews as the people of God? Wouldn't it be better for more non-Jews to "get in" if fewer Jews remained unconvinced? Paul rejects this potential reasoning and confronts it head on: some Israelites, to be sure, have stumbled over his taking the message to the nations that the birth pangs of the new age had begun with the raising of the Crucified One. But they have not fallen, only temporarily tripped so as to open a gap into which some non-Jews can step alongside them. That analogy nevertheless suggests a zero-sum or limited good reality, that someone had to suffer some kind of loss for another to enjoy some kind of gain.

The idea that there are only so many good resources and thus that for one to gain more requires another to lose something is still common today, arguably a part of the theological reasoning we seek to dispute, and it was all the more common for Greco-Romans of Paul's time, where the idea of envy and thus the evil eye was an accepted explanation of the leveling affects one should fear with the gaining of additional goods or fortune.[42] Paul tries to correct this impression, but [36] analogies are always problematic in some way. So he argues in *a fortiori* style that as great as this development of a gap among Israelites has been for inviting the non-Jews who turn to God through Christ into sharing the space with them as God's people, the fullness of the opportunity it provides will only be realized when those Israelites who are temporarily falling a bit behind regain their step when they recognize the in-breaking of God's reign. More Jews will bring light to the nations: it will be like "life from the dead!" (11:11–15).

This provides an interesting case where we can see Paul arguing against the zero-sum logic that his own arguments and analogies otherwise

---

42. Cf. Gouldner, *Enter Plato*; Walcot, *Envy and the Greeks*. Nanos has applied this element to the interpretation of Galatians; see *The Irony of Galatians*, 184–91, 279–80.

implicitly encourage, and doing so by appeal to an eschatological reality that can be more readily recognized by avoiding the impulse to suppose there are a limited number of people who can gain "at that time." God is therein recognized to be powerful enough to work independently of the limited resources that restrict human perceptions shaped by limited realities, including human frailties, failings, and the self-focused and fatalistic suppositions that characterize the thinking and life of the present age.

The point of Paul's allegories, censuring any suggestion that a non-Jew will ultimately gain the most by the loss of the Jew who does not share his new-found faithfulness to Christ, much less to have replaced the Jew, has unfortunately been undermined both by translations and interpretive discussions. The most obvious case is the decision to translate *ekklaō* as "broken off" or "cut off," but perhaps the most egregious case is to translate *en autois* as "in their place" (v. 17), explicitly expressing that Christ-following non-Jews have replaced Jews who have not become Christ-followers, when it instead means engrafted "among them."[43] When translated "among them," [37] the reader remains aware that it is among the branches referred to as broken that the shoot has been grafted, which retains the salience that the branch must still be on the tree, although bent, rather than, as commonly conceptualized, as totally severed from the tree. The allegory can advance the temporary condition central to the previous metaphor of stumbling but not fallen, but it works directly against that if the natural branches, representing Jews who do not believe Jesus is the Christ and thus do not join Paul to declare this among the nations, have been cut off. They would have actually fallen, despite Paul's emphatic rejection of this in v. 11.

Again, we see Paul appeal to eschatological reasoning to undermine perceptions based upon appearances in the present time and age. His arguments proceed from the conviction that the end of the ages has dawned, but that this is not yet apparent to everyone, not least to many of his fellow Jews, and that is cause for great concern and grieving on his part, and, he argues, it should be also for the non-Jews who have turned to God through Christ.

For Paul, the present non-persuaded state of many Israelites about the gospel is inextricably tied to the non-persuaded state of many of those from the nations until that time. God is using this temporary stage, which is a part

---

43. Another inexplicable NRSV translation decision is writing "they are enemies *of God* for your sake" in 11:28, when there is no manuscript evidence for "of God." Furthermore, the word translated enemies is an adjective (*exthroi*), better rendered something like "estranged for your sake," paralleling the adjectival "beloved [*agapēthoi*] for the sake of the fathers" with which it is balanced, and referring to the state of impairment that Paul has just appealed to in various metaphorical ways as stumbling and bent, temporarily, and for your benefit. See Beck, "Translations of the New Testament for Our Time," 204–6.

of Paul's own strategy for how to declare the gospel among Jews and non-Jews, to reach all of humankind in order to bring about the next stage, the awaited inexorable reign of God. In the meantime, the message is that these non-Jews must remain faithful to what they have received and leave the judgment of others to God—a message that remains pertinent today.

Paul is certain that "all Israel will be saved" or "rescued" from the present, temporary stage of God's mysterious [38] way of reconciling all of humankind, of bringing about the day when the wolves will lie down with the lambs and not devour them. The gifts and the calling of God are certain and irrevocable, which means that God is beholden to all Israelites in covenantal terms stretching back to promises made to Abraham, just as parents are beholden to their children. There are many stages in a relationship, but the bond is not broken. What Paul insists upon is not judging the final outcome by present appearances. He even tries to explain current events in terms that might help one understand the anomalies that present circumstances present to one who is convinced that the outcome will be other than it may seem today.

If Paul believed that his own ministry among the nations, turning to them fully with the gospel, would provoke his fellow Jews to reconsider the message that with Jesus the new creation was dawning and that they therefore had a responsibility to announce to this to the nations, this did not play out as he envisaged it in the Letter to Romans—certainly not yet. We propose that an awareness of the ad hoc nature of Paul's arguments in Romans 11 invites Christians to consider how best to actualize Paul's eschatological reasoning today.

Central to his argument is the ideal of taking account of one's own responsibility to be faithful in view of the gifts received, and to leave to God the judging of whether another is being responsible to their covenanting with God. God has promised the restoration of Israel; how that is to take place, what events it will involve, is not ours to decide or even to know.

Although Paul would almost certainly still believe that it will involve his fellow Jews recognizing Jesus to be the appointed Messiah whose work remained uncompleted, it must be remembered that for him that was still an option *within* Judaism. It was not a decision to turn *from* Judaism and to convert to a new religion. It is consonant with Paul's own reasoning to stress that God is bigger than any boxes—even the ones he could draw, not to mention those that have emerged [39] over history—and to focus on living graciously toward each other in the temporariness of our own time, according to what each believes to represent faithfulness. We argue that it does violence to basic Pauline convictions for readers today to simply echo his first-century imminent eschatological speculations as if not reshaped by their own, later interpretive concerns and perspectives. A messianically-enthusiastic Pharisee within late Second Temple Judaism almost certainly imagined the eschaton from within a very different thought-world than have most Christians in later gentile churches. These differences—and the implications of the intervening millennia—must be respected.

5. CONCLUSION: PAUL'S ESCHATOLOGICAL SPECULATIONS AND ZERO-SUM ESCHATOLOGIES

In this essay, we have envisioned Paul as working from within Judaism, shaped by his eschatological convictions about the meaning of Jesus for Israel and the nations. Convinced that he was living in the throes of the birth of the new creation, this messianically-oriented Pharisee adapted and applied existing Jewish apocalyptic imagery to address the pastoral needs and questions of the nascent assemblies of the Crucified, Raised, and Coming One. Most specifically, he addressed what he saw as an unhealthy attitude arising among some non-Jews in the Roman Christ-assemblies.

Christians who actualize Paul's reflections in today's ecclesial context are, in a sense, imitating Paul, the other apostles, the evangelists, the authors of the later books of the Tanakh/Old Testament, and the rabbis in bringing earlier traditions to bear on their own particular circumstances. For the Catholic Church today, this includes actualizing Pauline writings in the context of a community that doesn't share his perspective on what the evangelizing of the nations signified within Judaism, or the immediacy of a mission driven by the imminence of the eschatological events he expected but that did not occur in his lifetime. Since—unlike Paul and his communities—the church has come to represent a non-Jewish [40] entity, and is thus compelled to consider how its relationship to Israel as the "other," its commitment to "genuine brotherhood with the people of the Covenant"[44±]—rather than to their replacement or conversion to Christianity—must shape how it actualizes Paul's words today because it does not share his first-century vantage point on how this "chronometrical" timetable would play out within Judaism.

Two additional points should be made about drawing upon Paul's eschatological writings today. The first results from a tendency to reify what Paul himself admits are faltering human efforts to grasp divine Providence in

---

44. John Paul II, "Prayer at the Western Wall" (March 26, 2000); Benedict XVI, "Address at the Great Synagogue of Rome" (January 17, 2010); Benedict XVI, "Address to Delegates of the Conference of Presidents of Major American Jewish Organizations" (February 12, 2009).

its ultimacy. It is simply not possible to actualize these texts as if they provide consistent and detailed eschatological timetables and sequences, or at least, to do so without the exegetical imperative to read these texts across the cultural and temporal divide between Paul's time and our own.[45] Paul speculated on the basis of foundational convictions, adapting contemporary concepts in an ad hoc fashion—sometimes persuading his audience (as well as later readers), sometimes failing to do so—in response to pastoral issues in the earliest assemblies.[46] Additionally, we [41] might note that hesitancy about end-times details is expressed elsewhere in the New Testament.[47]

A second concern we've stressed is the deep-seated habit of thinking about eschatology in tendentious, zero-sum ways. Paul himself resisted such approaches, and even he could slip into that way of thinking in his ad hoc way of arguing, focused on whatever pastoral matter he sought to address rather than the writing of theological treatises per se. Today, there are many Jews and Christians who imagine that at the dawning of the messianic age one tradition will finally learn that it was wrong and that the other was right. Some Christians envision that Jews will finally recognize their error in failing to acknowledge Jesus Christ as the Messiah and Son of God. On the other hand, some Jews "believe that the worship of Jesus as God is a serious

---

45. For Catholics, this dialogue across the centuries is required. See the Pontifical Biblical Commission, *The Interpretation of the Bible in the Church* (1994), III.

46. Without adding another major section to this paper, we note that Paul elsewhere also speculated eschatologically in order to address pastoral needs. In 1 Thessalonians, Paul had to respond to unexpected deaths in the assembly: were the dead unworthy of seeing the imminent day of the Lord? He answered with a reassuring eschatological vision founded on the conviction that just as Jesus was raised, so, too, those who have died "in Christ" will also be raised (4:13–18). In 1 Corinthians Paul disagreed with those who, apparently finding corporeality distasteful, rejected the idea that the physical body of Jesus was raised after his death. Paul argued that eschatologically the flesh of sinful humanity will be replaced by the spiritual flesh of the new humanity (15:12–58). He depicts Christ's eschatological deeds in very physical terms: he will hand over the kingdom to God the Father, after he has destroyed every ruler and every authority and power. Then "when all things are subjected to him, then the Son himself will also be subjected to the one who put all things in subjection under him, so that God may be all in all" (15:28). Once more, Paul has responded to a pastoral situation in one of the assemblies he had founded by drawing upon existing tropes to produce an eschatological scenario that affirms teachings he believes to be defining, in this case that Christ physically died and was physically as the "first fruits" of what will happen eschatologically.

47. This is true elsewhere in Paul (Rom 11:33–36; 1 Cor 15:50), and also in the later Synoptic tradition, most pointedly in Mark 13:32//Matt 24:36. If not even the Son knows "the day and the hour," then presumably his followers cannot presume to know how or when the eschaton will unfold. Indeed, such presumption would disrespect divine freedom to act in surprising ways that elude human prognostication.

religious error displeasing to God even if the worshipper is a non-Jew, and that at the end of days Christians will come to recognize this."[48]

Such binary thinking, which basically casts Jews and Christians in the role of either winners or losers, seems so self-serving as to be unworthy of association today with the covenanting God of Israel or the church. Surely, Christian theologians who are committed to overcoming supersessionism [42] toward the Jewish people and tradition can be more creative than uncritically reiterating polemics from the church's anti-Jewish past. Fortunately, the Pontifical Biblical Commission has offered an intriguing perspective on this issue:

> What has already been accomplished in Christ must yet be accomplished in us and in the world. The definitive fulfillment will be at the end with the resurrection of the dead, a new heaven and a new earth. Jewish messianic expectation is not in vain. It can become for us Christians a powerful stimulus to keep alive the eschatological dimension of our faith. Like them, we too live in expectation. The difference is that for us the One who is to come will have the traits of the Jesus who has already come and is already present and active among us.[49]

The use of such expressions as "we, too, live in expectation" and "the eschatological dimension of our faith," remind readers that both Judaism and the church will, in a sense, be superseded in the reign of God. In particular, the formulation that the eschatological Messiah will possess "the traits of Jesus," which will be recognized as such by Christians, is very notable. A similar expression was used by Cardinal Walter Kasper, past president of the Pontifical Commission for Religious Relations with Jews, when he said, "But whilst Jews expect the coming of the Messiah, who is still unknown, Christians believe that he has already *shown his face* in Jesus of Nazareth whom we as Christians therefore confess as the Christ, he who at the end of time will be revealed as the Messiah for Jews and for all nations."[50] Although the PBC was referring to the traits of an eschatological Messiah being [43] recognizable by Christians as belonging to Jesus, Cardinal Kasper was speaking

---

48. Berger, "On *Dominus Iesus* and the Jews."

49. Pontifical Biblical Commission, *The Jewish People and Their Sacred Scriptures in the Christian Bible* (2001), §21.

50. Kasper, "The Commission for Religious Relations with the Jews: A Crucial Endeavour of the Catholic Church."

of Jesus of Nazareth as having proleptically[51] manifested and as continuing to manifest the eschatological Messiah to the church.[52]

While one quotation looks forward to the future eschaton and the other looks to the past as manifesting the eschaton, they both use metaphoric speech to address the as-yet-unrealized expectations of many Christians and Jews. In each case, the practices of both traditions will be altered in the age to come, e.g., Catholic sacramental life will be rendered obsolete by life in God's direct presence and will Jews continue to study Torah in the divine presence?

Furthermore, Jewish recognition of the eschatological "One who is to come," since their "messianic expectation is not in vain," according to this phrasing, logically depends upon Jews perceiving some identifiable messianic "traits" communicated by the Jewish tradition. One way of conceiving of these messianic matters, although there are diverse ideas both among and between Jews and Christians, is that the eschatological Messiah will therefore be recognizable by both Jews and Christians on the basis of different legitimate but converging "traits." This is the "both/and" option.

It follows that each community, by seeing the other's recognition, would fully understand for the first time the "rightness" of not only its own point of view, but of the other's as well. What had been opaque about the other in historic time would become transparent in eschatological "time."

This all suggests that eschatological scenarios have greater complexity than simple zero-sum phrases like "a [44] Jewish turn to Christ" or "Christians will see their error." If, as Christians would certainly posit, the birth of the church was part of the divine plan, then Christians must also contemplate the possibility that the development of the post-temple rabbinic heritage was also part of the divine plan. Likewise, Jews must grapple with whether or not the birth of the church reflected God's will for Israel as light to the nations.[53]

We suggest that this was, in fact, what Paul was up to in Romans 11: seeing the advent of Christ in terms of Israel's universal mission as presented in the Tanakh. Today's readers should recognize that his effort to combat nascent ideas of zero-sum replacement involved different pairings

---

51. A prolepsis is a premature or anticipatory eruption of eschatological realities into historic time.

52. A relevant quote from an earlier PBC document also speaks of the resurrection as a proleptic witness: "The resurrection of Christ . . . by its very nature cannot be proved in an empirical way. For by it Jesus was introduced into 'the world to come'" [PBC, 1984, 1.2.6].

53. For more on this point, see Cunningham, "Reflections from a Roman Catholic on a Reform Theology of Christianity."

(non-Jews as well as Jews as still salient categories) in Christ vs. those not yet persuaded of Jesus as Christ, rather than Christians vs. Jews in today's categories.[54] Ironically, the ways in which Paul's words were later translated and interpreted fostered the very kind of binary thinking he was seeking to counter (which was, as discussed, incongruously also present in the images with which he sought to counter it).

If, then, as an exercise of divine freedom, God now works on behalf of our two related covenanting communities so that we learn to walk through historical time together, it may be that the eschaton will indeed bring about our absolute reconciliation, not in the sense of one ceding itself to the other, but rather in the sense of both joining in yielding themselves to the ultimate Reality.

[45] Perhaps in the PBC study's eschatological allusions we can discern a resonance with the humble doxology penned two millennia ago by the apostle as he pondered the relationship resulting from Israel's initially divided response to the non-Israelites who were turning to Israel's God through faith in Jesus. Following his assertion that everyone has at times misunderstood the Holy One, Paul appeals to the criterion of humility that everyone should thereafter embrace, both for themselves, and in their refraining from judging others:

> O the depth of the riches and wisdom and knowledge of God! How unsearchable God's judgments and how enigmatic God's ways! "For who has known the mind of the Lord? Or who has been his counselor?" "Or who has given a gift to him, to receive a gift in return?" For from him and through him and to him are all things. To him be the glory forever. Amen. I appeal to you therefore, brothers and sisters, by the mercies of God, to present your bodies as a living sacrifice, holy and acceptable to God, which is your spiritual worship. Do not be conformed to this world, but be transformed by the renewing of your minds, so that you may discern what is the will of God—what is good and acceptable and perfect. For by the grace given to me I say to everyone among you not to think of yourself more highly than you ought to think, but to think with sober judgment,

---

54. We would observe, too, that the fact that we have presented a hopefully defensible reconstruction of Paul's logic in Romans 11 (based on understanding him as a Jewish apostle within Judaism) is itself sufficient reason to doubt facile binary readings (based on the highly questionable view of Paul as Jewish apostate outside Judaism). To the degree that current Christian "eschatological postponement" approaches are themselves predicated on Paul as standing outside Second Temple Judaism, then they are also questionable.

each according to the measure of faith that God has assigned (11:33—12:3; NRSV).

Humility is a virtue that is perhaps insufficiently valued in academia. There is much more that we don't "know" than what we suppose we do. Perhaps it is time to theologize accordingly, especially when it impacts our views of the other who claims to seek to do God's will also, according to what is "believed" by them, like ourselves, to be most appropriate for "now."

BIBLIOGRAPHY

Beck, Norman. "Translations of the New Testament for Our Time." In *Seeing Judaism Anew: Christianity's Sacred Obligation*, edited by Mary C. Boys, 200–210. Lanham, MD: Sheed and Ward, 2005.

Benedict XVI. *Light of the World. The Pope, the Church, and the Signs of the Times. A Conversation with Peter Seewald*. San Francisco: Ignatius, 2010.

Berger, David. "On *Dominus Iesus* and the Jews." Paper delivered at the 17th meeting of the International Catholic-Jewish Liaison Committee, New York, May 1, 2001. Online: http://www.ccjr.us/dialogika-resources/documents-and-statements/analysis/498-berger01may1.

Catechism of the Catholic Church. Washington, DC: United States Catholic Conference, 1994.

Commission of the Holy See for Religious Relations with the Jews. "Guidelines and Suggestions for Implementing the Conciliar Declaration, *Nostra Aetate*, No. 4." Online: http://www.vatican.va/roman_curia/pontifical_councils/chrstuni/relations-jews-docs/rc_pc_chrstuni_doc_19741201_nostra-aetate_en.html

Connelly, John. *From Enemy to Brother: The Revolution in Catholic Teaching on the Jews, 1933–1965*. Cambridge: Harvard University Press, 2011.

Cunningham, Philip A. "'God Holds the Jews Most Dear': Learning to Respect Jewish Self-Understanding." In *A Jubilee for All Time: The Copernican Revolution in Jewish-Christian Relations*, edited by Gilbert Rosenthal, 44–58. Eugene, OR: Pickwick, 2014.

———. "Reflections from a Roman Catholic on a Reform Theology of Christianity." *CCAR Journal* (Spring 2005) 61–73.

Das, A. Andrew. *Solving the Romans Debate*. Minneapolis: Fortress, 2007.

Eisenbaum, Pamela. *Paul Was Not a Christian: The Original Message of a Misunderstood Apostle*. New York: HarperCollins, 2009.

Gouldner, Alvin Ward. *Enter Plato: Classical Greece and the Origins of Social Theory*. New York: Basic, 1965.

John Paul II. *Pro conversion Iudeaorum*. Online: http://www.ccjr.us/dialogika-resources/documents-and-statements/roman-catholic/pope-benedict-xvi/425-b1608feb5

Kasper, Walter Cardinal. "The Commission for Religious Relations with the Jews: A Crucial Endeavour of the Catholic Church." Paper given at Boston College, November 6, 2002. Online: http://www.ccjr.us/dialogika-resources/documents-and-statements/roman-catholic/kasper/642-kasper02nov6-2

———. "Striving for Mutual Respect in Modes of Prayer." *L'Osservatore Romano* (April 16, 2008) 8–9. Online: http://www.ccjr.us/dialogika-resources/documents-and-statements/roman-catholic/kasper/651-kasper08apr16.

Korn, Eugene. "The Man of Faith and Religious Dialogue: Revisiting 'Confrontation' After Forty Years." Paper delivered at the conference, "Rabbi Joseph Soloveitchik on Interreligious Dialogue: Forty Years Later," Boston College, November 23, 2003. Online: http://www.bc.edu/content/dam/files/research_sites/cjl/texts/center/conferences/soloveitchik/Korn_23Nov03.htm

Langton, Daniel R. *The Apostle Paul in the Jewish Imagination: A Study in Modern Jewish-Christian Relations*. New York: Cambridge University Press, 2010.

Nanos, Mark D. "'Broken Branches': A Pauline Metaphor Gone Awry? (Romans 11:11–36)." In *Between Gospel and Election: Explorations in the Interpretation of Romans 9–11*, edited by Florian Wilk and J. Ross Wagner, 339–76. Tübingen: Mohr Siebeck, 2010. (See chapter 6 in this volume of collected essays.)

———. "'Callused,' Not 'Hardened': Paul's Revelation of Temporary Protection until All Israel Can Be Healed." In *Reading Paul in Context: Explorations in Identity Formation*, edited by Kathy Ehrensperger and J. Brian Tucker, 52–73. London: T & T Clark, 2010. (See chapter 7 in this volume of collected essays.)

———. *The Irony of Galatians: Paul's Letter in First-Century Context*. Minneapolis: Fortress, 2002.

———. "The Jewish Context of the Gentile Audience Addressed in Paul's Letter to the Romans." *Catholic Biblical Quarterly* 61 (1999) 283–304. (See chapter 3 in this volume of collected essays.)

———. "A Jewish View." In *Four Views on the Apostle Paul*, edited by Michael F. Bird, 159–93. Grand Rapids: Zondervan, 2012.

———. *The Mystery of Romans: The Jewish Context of Paul's Letter*. Minneapolis: Fortress, 1996.

———. "Paul and the Jewish Tradition: The Ideology of the Shema." In *Celebrating Paul. Festschrift in Honor of Jerome Murphy-O'Connor, O.P., and Joseph A. Fitzmyer, S.J.*, edited by Peter Spitaler, 62–80. Washington, DC: Catholic Biblical Association of America, 2012. (See volume 1, chapter 4 in this series of collected essays.)

———. "Paul and Judaism: Why Not Paul's Judaism?" In *Paul Unbound: Other Perspectives on the Apostle*, edited by Mark Douglas Given, 117–60. Peabody, MA: Hendrickson, 2010. (See volume 1, chapter 1 in this series of collected essays.)

———. "Paul's Non-Jews Do Not Become 'Jews,' But Do They Become 'Jewish'?" *Journal of the Jesus Movement in its Jewish Setting* 1.1 (2015) 26–53. Online: <http://www.jjmjs.org/uploads/1/1/9/0/11908749/nanos_pauls_non-jews.pdf>. (See volume 1, chapter 5 in this series of collected essays.)

———. "Paul's Relationship to Torah in Light of His Strategy 'To Become Everything to Everyone' (1 Corinthians 9.19–23)." In *Paul and Judaism: Crosscurrents in Pauline Exegesis and the Study of Jewish-Christian Relations*, edited by Reimund Bieringer and Didier Pollefeyt, 106–40. London: T. & T. Clark, 2012. (See volume 4, chapter 3 in this series of collected essays.)

———. "Romans." In *The Jewish Annotated New Testament*, edited by Amy-Jill Levine and Marc Zvi Brettler, 253–86. New York: Oxford University Press, 2011.

———. "Romans 11 and Christian and Jewish Relations: Exegetical Options for Revisiting the Translation and Interpretation of this Central Text." *Criswell*

Theological Review N.S. 9.2 (2012) 3–21. (See chapter 8 in this volume of collected essays.)

———. "To the Churches within the Synagogues of Rome." In *Reading Paul's Letter to the Romans*, edited by Jerry L. Sumney, 11–28. Atlanta: Society of Biblical Literature, 2012. (See chapter 1 in this volume of collected essays.)

Nanos, Mark D., and Magnus Zetterholm, eds. *Paul within Judaism: Restoring the First-Century Context to the Apostle*. Minneapolis: Fortress, 2015.

Pontifical Biblical Commission. *The Interpretation of the Bible in the Church*. (1994). Online: http://www.piercedhearts.org/scriptures/interpretation_bible_church_summary_presentation.pdf

———. *The Jewish People and Their Sacred Scriptures in the Christian Bible* (2001). Online: http://www.vatican.va/roman_curia/congregations/cfaith/pcb_documents/rc_con_cfaith_doc_20020212_popolo-ebraico_en.html

Sanders, E. P. *Paul and Palestinian Judaism: A Comparison of Patterns of Religion*. Philadelphia: Fortress, 1977.

Stendahl, Krister. "The Apostle Paul and the Introspective Conscience of the West." *Harvard Theological Review* 56 (1963) 199–215.

Stowers, Stanley Kent. *A Rereading of Romans: Justice, Jews, and Gentiles*. New Haven: Yale University Press, 1994.

Svartvik, Jesper. "Geschwisterlichkeit: Realizing That We Are Siblings." In *Kirche und Synagoge: Ein lutherisches Votum*, edited by Folker Siegert, 315–27. Göttingen: Vandernhoeck & Ruprecht, 2012.

———. "Reading the Epistle to the Hebrews without Presupposing Supersessionism." In *Christ Jesus and the Jewish People Today: New Explorations of Theological Interrelationships*, edited by Philip A. Cunningham, Joseph Sievers, Mary C. Boys, Hans Hermann Henrix, and Jesper Svartvik, 77–91. Grand Rapids: Eerdmans, 2011.

Walcot, Peter. *Envy and the Greeks: A Study of Human Behaviour*. Warminster, UK: Aris & Phillips, 1978.

Zetterholm, Magnus. *Approaches to Paul: A Student's Guide to Recent Scholarship*. Minneapolis: Fortress, 2009.

Appendix
Translating Romans 11:11—12:1a within Judaism: Literal-Oriented and Expanded Versions

This appendix offers a literal-oriented translation first, followed by an expanded one; both are based on the research undertaken to date, much of which is discussed in these essays.

The translation offered attempts to follow the Greek literally, which includes an effort to make choices that express the metaphorical elements.

Brackets [] indicate notes, literal translation alternatives, and implied grammatical elements. In the case of the expanded translation, my explanations and suggested paraphrases, as well as the passages from which Paul cites, are also in brackets. The translation proper is offered in **bold** to help to distinguish it from the bracketed information, and the **brackets in bold** supply words (usually verbs) to make sense of Greek in English.

LITERAL-ORIENTED TRANSLATION

11:11 **So I ask, have they not stumbled so they might fall? Not at all! Rather, deliverance for the nations [arrives] by their misstep, which [is] in order to vex them** [to emulate me].

11:11 Λέγω οὖν, μὴ ἔπταισαν ἵνα πέσωσιν; μὴ γένοιτο· ἀλλὰ τῷ αὐτῶν παραπτώματι ἡ σωτηρία τοῖς ἔθνεσιν εἰς τὸ παραζηλῶσαι αὐτούς.

¹² **Now if their misstep [tripping over this stone on the path] [achieves] enrichment for [the] kosmos, and their lagging behind [achieves] enrichment for [all the] nations, how much more [enrichment will be achieved by] their complete complement!**

¹³ **But I am speaking to you members of the nations; indeed, therefore, inasmuch then as I am an emissary to** [lit., of; i.e., those from the] **nations, I consider** [how to best carry out] **my service,**

¹⁴ **if somehow I might vex my flesh** [i.e., my kin, fellow Israelites] **to emulate me** [i.e., of my service to the nations]**, and thus I might protect some of** [lit., from/out of] **them.**

¹⁵ **For if their delay [achieves] reconciliation of [the] kosmos, what [will] the acceptance** [of your inclusion achieve] **except life from the dead!**

¹⁶ **Now if the starter-dough [is] holy, the entire batch [is] also; and if the root [is] holy, the branches [are] too.**

¹⁷ **And if some of the branches were bent (aside)** [or: broken]**, but you, a** [single] **wild olive shoot was grafted in among them, even partaking jointly** [with them] **of the nourishment of the olive tree:**

¹⁸ **Do not boast against the branches! Now if you are tempted to boast against them,** [take note:] **you do not nourish** [lit.: enable] **the root; rather, the root** [nourishes] **you!**

¹⁹ **You will** [be tempted perhaps to] **plead then, "Branches were bent (aside)** [or: broken] **so that I might be grafted in!"**

²⁰ **Well** [you have a point, but take note]**; they were being bent (aside)** [or: broken] **to [represent] unfaithfulness, but you were established** [i.e., grafted] **to [represent] faithfulness. Do not think proudly, but be afraid!**

¹² εἰ δὲ τὸ παράπτωμα αὐτῶν πλοῦτος κόσμου καὶ τὸ ἥττημα αὐτῶν πλοῦτος ἐθνῶν, πόσῳ μᾶλλον τὸ πλήρωμα αὐτῶν.

¹³ Ὑμῖν δὲ λέγω τοῖς ἔθνεσιν· ἐφ᾽ ὅσον μὲν οὖν εἰμι ἐγὼ ἐθνῶν ἀπόστολος, τὴν διακονίαν μου δοξάζω,

¹⁴ εἴ πως παραζηλώσω μου τὴν σάρκα καὶ σώσω τινὰς ἐξ αὐτῶν.

¹⁵ εἰ γὰρ ἡ ἀποβολὴ αὐτῶν καταλλαγὴ κόσμου, τίς ἡ πρόσλημψις εἰ μὴ ζωὴ ἐκ νεκρῶν;

¹⁶ εἰ δὲ ἡ ἀπαρχὴ ἁγία, καὶ τὸ φύραμα· καὶ εἰ ἡ ῥίζα ἁγία, καὶ οἱ κλάδοι.

¹⁷ Εἰ δέ τινες τῶν κλάδων ἐξεκλάσθησαν, σὺ δὲ ἀγριέλαιος ὢν ἐνεκεντρίσθης ἐν αὐτοῖς καὶ συγκοινωνὸς τῆς ῥίζης τῆς πιότητος τῆς ἐλαίας ἐγένου,

¹⁸ μὴ κατακαυχῶ τῶν κλάδων· εἰ δὲ κατακαυχᾶσαι οὐ σὺ τὴν ῥίζαν βαστάζεις ἀλλ᾽ ἡ ῥίζα σέ.

¹⁹ ἐρεῖς οὖν· ἐξεκλάσθησαν κλάδοι ἵνα ἐγὼ ἐγκεντρισθῶ.

²⁰ καλῶς· τῇ ἀπιστίᾳ ἐξεκλάσθησαν, σὺ δὲ τῇ πίστει ἕστηκας. μὴ ὑψηλὰ φρόνει ἀλλὰ φοβοῦ·

²¹ For if God did not spare the natural branches, [all the more] [God] will not spare you.

²² Therefore, witness God's patient mildness and yet abrupt severity [like an olive tree's caretaker]: **simultaneously** [proceeding with] **severity for the ones falling, but** [with] **God's patient mildness for you, as long as you continue to** [warrant] **that patient mildness; otherwise, you even will be pruned off.**

²³ Now, these [branches] too—unless they continue in that unfaithful state—will be invigorated, for God is able [all the more] to invigorate them again.

²⁴ For if you have been pruned off from what is a naturally wild olive tree, and, contrary to nature, been grafted into a cultivated olive tree, how much more will this one be invigorated, which is natural to its own tree.

²⁵ **For I do not want you to be unperceptive, brothers** [and sisters], [about] **this mystery, so that you would not be mindful** [only] **for yourselves, because for a while a callus has formed for** [the protection of the injured branches of] **Israel, until the fullness of the nations shall commence,**

²⁶ **And in this way** [or: and then] **all Israel will be made safe;**

as it is written,

"The Deliverer will come out of Zion; he will bend back [or: take away] ungodliness from Jacob."

²⁷ "And this is my covenant with them, when[ever] I take away their sins."

²⁸ **Sure, regarding the gospel,** [they are (presently)] **estranged on your behalf, but regarding election** [they are (still)] **beloved on account of the fathers,**

²¹ εἰ γὰρ ὁ θεὸς τῶν κατὰ φύσιν κλάδων οὐκ ἐφείσατο, [μή πως] οὐδὲ σοῦ φείσεται.

²² ἴδε οὖν χρηστότητα καὶ ἀποτομίαν θεοῦ· ἐπὶ μὲν τοὺς πεσόντας ἀποτομία, ἐπὶ δὲ σὲ χρηστότης θεοῦ, ἐὰν ἐπιμένῃς τῇ χρηστότητι, ἐπεὶ καὶ σὺ ἐκκοπήσῃ.

²³ κἀκεῖνοι δέ, ἐὰν μὴ ἐπιμένωσιν τῇ ἀπιστίᾳ, ἐγκεντρισθήσονται· δυνατὸς γάρ ἐστιν ὁ θεὸς πάλιν ἐγκεντρίσαι αὐτούς.

²⁴ εἰ γὰρ σὺ ἐκ τῆς κατὰ φύσιν ἐξεκόπης ἀγριελαίου καὶ παρὰ φύσιν ἐνεκεντρίσθης εἰς καλλιέλαιον, πόσῳ μᾶλλον οὗτοι οἱ κατὰ φύσιν ἐγκεντρισθήσονται τῇ ἰδίᾳ ἐλαίᾳ.

²⁵ Οὐ γὰρ θέλω ὑμᾶς ἀγνοεῖν, ἀδελφοί, τὸ μυστήριον τοῦτο, ἵνα μὴ ἦτε [παρ'] ἑαυτοῖς φρόνιμοι, ὅτι πώρωσις ἀπὸ μέρους τῷ Ἰσραὴλ γέγονεν ἄχρι οὗ τὸ πλήρωμα τῶν ἐθνῶν εἰσέλθῃ

²⁶ καὶ οὕτως πᾶς Ἰσραὴλ σωθήσεται,

καθὼς γέγραπται·

ἥξει ἐκ Σιὼν ὁ ῥυόμενος,
ἀποστρέψει ἀσεβείας ἀπὸ Ἰακώβ.

²⁷ καὶ αὕτη αὐτοῖς ἡ παρ' ἐμοῦ διαθήκη, ὅταν ἀφέλωμαι τὰς ἁμαρτίας αὐτῶν.

²⁸ κατὰ μὲν τὸ εὐαγγέλιον ἐχθροὶ δι' ὑμᾶς, κατὰ δὲ τὴν ἐκλογὴν ἀγαπητοὶ διὰ τοὺς πατέρας·

²⁹ because the gifts and the calling of God are irrevocable.	²⁹ ἀμεταμέλητα γὰρ τὰ χαρίσματα καὶ ἡ κλῆσις τοῦ θεοῦ.
³⁰ For just as you formerly doubted God, but now received mercy [despite] your doubt,	³⁰ ὥσπερ γὰρ ὑμεῖς ποτε ἠπειθήσατε τῷ θεῷ, νῦν δὲ ἠλεήθητε τῇ τούτων ἀπειθείᾳ,
³¹ similarly, now they doubt your [receipt of] mercy, so that they too [now] may be shown mercy;	³¹ οὕτως καὶ οὗτοι νῦν ἠπείθησαν τῷ ὑμετέρῳ ἐλέει, ἵνα καὶ αὐτοὶ [νῦν] ἐλεηθῶσιν.
³² For God joined together everyone into a state of doubt, so that [God] might show everyone mercy.	³² συνέκλεισεν γὰρ ὁ θεὸς τοὺς πάντας εἰς ἀπείθειαν, ἵνα τοὺς πάντας ἐλεήσῃ.
³³ O the depth of God's riches and wisdom and knowledge! How unsearchable are his decisions and how inscrutable his ways!	³³ Ὦ βάθος πλούτου καὶ σοφίας καὶ γνώσεως θεοῦ· ὡς ἀνεξεραύνητα τὰ κρίματα αὐτοῦ καὶ ἀνεξιχνίαστοι αἱ ὁδοὶ αὐτοῦ·
³⁴ "For who has known the mind of the Lord?	³⁴ τίς γὰρ ἔγνω νοῦν κυρίου;
Or who has become his counselor?"	ἢ τίς σύμβουλος αὐτοῦ ἐγένετο;
³⁵ Or who has delivered up [advice] to him,	³⁵ ἢ τίς προέδωκεν αὐτῷ,
and will be giving [advice] back to him?	καὶ ἀνταποδοθήσεται αὐτῷ;
³⁶ For from him and through him and to him are all things. To him be the glory forever. Amen.	³⁶ ὅτι ἐξ αὐτοῦ καὶ δι᾽ αὐτοῦ καὶ εἰς αὐτὸν τὰ πάντα· αὐτῷ ἡ δόξα εἰς τοὺς αἰῶνας, ἀμήν.
¹²:¹ I therefore beg of you, brothers [and sisters], through the compassion of God...	¹²:¹ Παρακαλῶ οὖν ὑμᾶς, ἀδελφοί, διὰ τῶν οἰκτιρμῶν τοῦ θεοῦ....

LITERAL-ORIENTED TRANSLATION WITH EXPANSIONS

¹¹:¹¹ So I ask [i.e., rhetorically], **have they** [Israelites who are not announcing Jesus as Messiah to the nations because not persuaded that he is risen and thus that the end of the ages has dawned, when the role entrusted to all Israelites to complete as God's messengers begins; see Rom 3:1–2; 9:30–33; Isa 8; 28] **not stumbled so that they might fall? Not at all! Rather, the deliverance for the nations** [arrives] **by their misstep, which** [is] **in order**

to vex them [to emulation, to want to reconsider to take up the entrusted task when they see my success at carrying out Israel's role; cf. vv. 13–14].

¹² **Now if their misstep** [tripping over this stone on the path; cf. 9:30–33] **[achieves] enrichment for [the] kosmos, and their lagging behind [achieves] enrichment for [all the] nations, how much more [enrichment will be achieved by] their complete complement!**

¹³ **But I am speaking** [i.e., targeting my comments here] **to you members of the nations; indeed, therefore, inasmuch then as I am an emissary to** [lit., of; i.e., to those from the] **nations, I consider** [how to best carry out] **my service** [my calling to the nations (cf. Gal 1:16; 2:8–9), which it is important for you to understand],

¹⁴ **if somehow** [by the way I carry out my service] **I might vex my flesh** [i.e., my kin, fellow Israelites] **to emulation of me** [having witnessed the success of my service to the nations, they will conclude that the awaited time has arrived, and will want to join me in announcing this news to the nations; and Paul may be signaling a competitive element, as in, to want to catch up to my success]**, and thereby I** [by the way I conduct my service] **will protect some of** [lit., from/out of] **them** [from stumbling until at the risk of falling, or perhaps, protect them from the impact of the non-Jews's temptation to arrogance, which is what the following arguments seek to stop].

¹⁵ **For if their delay [achieves] reconciliation of [the] kosmos, what [will] the acceptance** [of your inclusion; i.e., their acceptance of you non-Jew Christ-followers as joint-members of the people of God from the other nations representing the dawning of the awaited age, as declared by the gospel; see v. 31: "now they doubt your [receipt of] mercy"]**[achieve] except life from the dead!**

¹⁶ **Now if the starter-dough [is] holy, the entire batch [is] also** [cf. Lev 23:14; Num 15:17–18]**; and if the root [is] holy, the branches [are] too** [i.e., those from Israel taking up this sacred task, like Paul, bear witness to the dedication of the rest of Israel to the task too, even if not yet self-evident].

¹⁷ **And if** [extending this metaphor into an allegory] **some of the branches were bent (aside)** [or: broken]**, but you, a** [single] **wild olive shoot was grafted in among them** [Note: not "grafted into Israel" but among them; i.e, among the branches, which signifies joining alongside of Israelites but remaining distinct as a branch that is not representing Israel but those from the other nations; also note that this means that those that have been injured

are still on the tree; hence, they were not "broken *off*"], **even partaking jointly [with them] of the nourishment** [lit., fattiness] **of the olive tree:**

[18] **Do not boast against the branches! Now if you are tempted to boast against them,** [take note:] **you do not nourish** [lit.: enable; bring the nutrients to] **the root; rather, the root [nourishes**; i.e., brings the nutrients up to] **you!**

[19] **You will** [be tempted perhaps to] **plead then** [i.e., rejoinder], **"[But these] Branches were bent (aside)** [or: broken] **so that I might be grafted in!"** [i.e., we are now the object of God's primary concern, not them; they were moved aside so God can focus on us; we have replaced them in God's favor!]

[20] **Well** [you have a point, but take note]; **they were being bent (aside)** [or: broken] **to [represent**; this is an allegory: branches can hardly be unfaithful or without faith, after all] **unfaithfulness** [to your inclusion apart from becoming Israelites, per the gospel of Christ], **but you were established** [i.e., grafted into the tree among them] **to [represent] faithfulness** [to that gospel-based inclusion as those from the nations]. **Do not think proudly** [as if loftier branches, or as if the only branches with which the caretaker is still concerned], **but be afraid!**

[21] **For if God did not spare the natural branches,** [all the more] **[God] will not spare you** [i.e., logically, your placement in the tree is even more precarious than is theirs, should you become unfaithful to that which is expected of you].

[22] **Therefore, witness God's patient mildness and yet abrupt severity** [like we observe in an olive tree's caretaker]: **simultaneously** [proceeding with] **severity for the ones falling** [on the severe side in this analogy; or, for the branches falling to the side to present a space for you to be placed among them], **but** [with] **God's patient mildness for you, as long as you continue** [to warrant] **that patient mildness; otherwise, you even will be pruned off** [entirely, that is: a fate worse than being bent aside temporarily to graft in a shoot!].

[23] **Now, these** [bent (aside) **branches] too—unless they continue in that unfaithful state—will be invigorated** [like a new shoot (such as yourself) grafted in experiences invigoration so that it might bear fruit, but in their case as a branch completing the healing cycle; non-metaphorically: like Paul, they will become messengers who bring this message to the nations too], **for God is able** [all the more] **to invigorate them again.**

²⁴ **For if you have been pruned off from what is a naturally wild olive tree, and, contrary to nature, been grafted into a cultivated olive tree, how much more will this one be invigorated, which is natural to its own tree.**

²⁵ **For I do not want you to be unperceptive, brothers** [and sisters], **[about] this mystery** [of how God is working among Israelites in an anomalous way], **so that you would not be mindful** [only] **for yourselves** [the members of the nations presently benefiting from the display of God's patient mildness towards you], **because for a while a callus has formed for** [the protection of the injured branches of] **Israel, until the fullness of the nations shall commence** [i.e., which occurs when some from Israel (like Paul) can travel to each place to carry out Israel's entrusted ministry to bring the words of God to the nations, which temporarily involves this divided response among Israelites, followed by the inclusion of some from the nations, and then the experience of the rest of the Israelites witnessing this success and joining the remnant in this task thereafter],

²⁶ **And in this way** [or: and then] **all Israel will be made safe** [i.e., protected through divine promise (vv. 28–29) during this anomalous process (vv. 26b–27; 33–36) of temporary estrangement (v. 28) until Israel is able to humbly (vv. 30–32) complete this special calling];

> **as it is written** [prophesied in Scripture],
>
> **"The Deliverer will come out of Zion; he will bend back** [or: take away] **ungodliness from Jacob."** [citation from Isa 59:20; cf. Isa 40:6–11]
>
> ²⁷ **"And this is my covenant with them** [citation from Isa 59:21a], **when[ever] I take away their sins** [or: failings, such as not (yet) bringing the message to the nations alongside of Paul; citation from Isa 27:9b]." [i.e., do not mistake the process of God's temporary disciplinary action toward some Israelites, who are God's own—which is undertaken for their good, as prophesied—as if this represented final judgment]

²⁸ **Sure, regarding the gospel, [they are** (presently)] **estranged** [i.e., as the metaphors of stumbling and bent (aside) signify] **on your behalf** [i.e., metaphorically creating a gap or space for you who are from the nations to join among them because the end of the ages has begun], **but regarding election** [God's choice] **[they are** (still)] **beloved on account of the fathers** [to whom promises about their descendants were made],

²⁹ **because the gifts and the calling of God are irrevocable** [cf. 9:4–5].

³⁰ **For just as you formerly doubted God** [i.e., that Israel's god is the One and Only God], **but now received mercy** [as those representing the nations who had worshipped other gods] **[despite] your doubt** [toward the One God],

³¹ **similarly, now they** [these particular members of Israel] **doubt your [receipt of] mercy** [by God to have become already members of the people of God apart from becoming members of Israel, because they are not persuaded that the end of the ages—when this kind of worship together with those from all the other nations would be warranted—has arrived, and thus they are not (yet) joining those of us announcing this news], **so that they too [now] may be shown mercy;**

³² **For God joined together everyone into a state of doubt, so that [God] might show everyone mercy** [i.e., both Israelites and those from the other nations had the similar experience of failing to be convinced to be faithful to God in some way and at some time, even if the particulars of which each of them should have been persuaded were not precisely the same and did not take place at the same time; the logic that follows, that each should thus show mercy toward the other, is the topic of the instructions that begin in 12:1 and extend through the rest of the letter].

³³ **O the depth of God's riches and wisdom and knowledge! How unsearchable are his decisions and how inscrutable his ways!**

³⁴ **"For who has known the mind of the Lord?**

> **Or who has become his counselor?"** [cf. Isa 40:13LXX; Paul evokes here the storyline of Israel's restoration presented variously in Deutero-Isaiah, which follows the anomaly of discipline by exile, often presented in metaphorical terms, including by way of trees]

³⁵ **Or who has delivered up** [advice] **to him,**

> **and will be giving** [advice] **back to him?** [cf. Job 41.3 (MT); 42:1–6; also 35:7; the point seems to echo the previous verse's statement, expressing the conclusion to which Job eventually arrives, even though the wording is not a direct quote of the extant manuscript traditions for Job.]

³⁶ **For from him and through him and to him are all things. To him be the glory forever. Amen.** [cf. 1 Enoch 84.2–4; 93:11–14; 1 QH 7.26–32]

¹²:¹ **I therefore beg of you, brothers** [and sisters], **through the compassion of God…**

Index of Ancient Sources

TANAKH/HEBREW BIBLE

Genesis

27:1	169

Exodus

9:12	154
9:16	124, 154
21:24	169
31:18	180
32:31–33	222

Leviticus

1:17	127, 190
23:14	124, 289
24:19	169

Numbers

15:17–24	124
15:17–18	289

Deuteronomy

6	92
9:4–6	218
24:20	132
29:3	120, 167
29:4	120
30:11–14	218
32	57, 119
32:21	119

Esther

8:12	140

Job

14:7–9	126
14:7	118
17:7	155, 167, 169
35:7	292
41:3	292
42:1–6	292

Psalms

68	120
68:23–24 LXX	120, 167
68:27 LXX	120
69:22–23	167
94:12	141, 160, 224

Proverbs

3:11–12	141, 160, 224

Isaiah

118, 183, 262

1:9	140
2:2–4	106
2:10	140
2:11	140
2:12–13	122
2:12	140
2:17	140
2:19	140
2:21	140
3:8	140
6:10	154
6:12	126
8	105, 288
8:6–8	115
8:14–15	115
10–11	122
10:5–15	135
10:12	122
10:33	122
11:1	122, 126
11:6	263
11:10	122, 126
17:6	126, 132
24:13	126, 132
27–29	115, 191, 272
27–28	162
27	117, 125, 146, 157, 162, 194
27:2–6	125
27:6	125–26, 162
27:7	117
27:9	115, 117, 125, 157, 159, 162, 169, 268, 273
27:9b	291
27:10–11	125
27:12–13	117, 162
28	115, 288
28:7	115
28:12–13	115, 117
28:16	105, 115
28:17	115
28:22	115
29:10	115, 120, 167
29:16	115
37:24–25	135
37:30–32	135
40–66	115
40–55	117
40:6–11	291
40:13 LXX	292
52:7–10	226
59–61	162
59	117, 143, 146, 157, 162, 194
59:8–10	117
59:20–21	115, 117, 157, 159, 169, 268, 273
59:20	159, 291
59:21	159
59:21a	291
62:6–12	219
65–66	106
65:25	18, 106, 263

Jeremiah

11:15–16	126
11:16	126
30:11	141, 160, 224

Lamentations

3:31–33	141, 160, 224

Hosea

1:10	117, 125
2:23	117, 125
14:2–10	125

Zephaniah

3:9	251

Index of Ancient Sources

APOCRYPHA

Judith

8:27	141, 160, 224

Wisdom of Solomon

12:1–2	141, 160, 224
12.26	160, 224

2 Maccabees

6:12–17	141, 160, 224

PSEUDEPIGRAPHA

1 Enoch

84.2–4	292
93.11–14	292

Psalms of Solomon

10.1	141, 160, 224
13.7	141, 160, 224
16.1–5	141, 160, 224

Testament of Levi

13.7	167

NEW TESTAMENT

Matthew

23:29	253
24:36	278

Mark

3:5	156
13:32	278

Luke

4:16–22	12
21:24	253

John

12:40	156

Acts

3:19–21	253
3:20–21	250
10	184
13:13—14:7	268
13:14–15	12
15	184
15:21	12
18:1–4	10
18:2	9–10, 25, 27, 29–30
18:3	27
18:4	27
18:12–17	29
23—26	29
24:5	29
28	29–30
28:17–22	23
28:21–22	23
28:22	27

Romans

1–11	51, 55, 87
1	14, 45
1:1–15	78, 184
1:1–7	46
1:1–5	224
1:1–3	244
1:3–4	46
1:4	258, 264
1:5–6	13, 45
1:7	74, 225
1:8–15	46
1:8	36, 137
1:9–13	46
1:12	137
1:13	13, 45, 47, 59, 225
1:16–17	46
1:16	60, 225, 244
1:18—2:29	48
2–4	87
2	55, 88, 186, 220, 265

Romans (continued)

2:1	154, 204
2:9	46
2:10	244
2:14–15	119
2:17–29	56
2:17	223
2:17ff.	204
2:25–29	223
2:28–29	223
3	55
3:1–3	14, 265
3:1–2	16, 56, 93, 109, 116, 245, 262, 265, 288
3:2	93, 173, 184, 220, 222, 224, 226, 269, 273
3:4	180
3:9	266
3:21–26	48
3:27–31	133
3:27–29	48
3:27	266
3:29–31	92, 208, 245
3:29a	48
3:29b–30	48
3:29	223
3:31	48, 56, 93
4	55, 245
4:2	93
4:10–17	225
4:11	245
4:13–18	225, 278
4:16–18	231
4:19–21	97
5–11	49
5–8	201
5–6	266
5:10	138
6	45, 273
6:16–23	56
7:1	45
7:7—8:4	56
7:12	56, 245
7:13	93, 245
7:14	55, 93, 223
7:16	56
8	230–31
8:4	245
8:15	225
8:16–17	225
8:18	225
8:28	225
8:29	225
8:33	225
9–13	69
9–11	xxi, xxvii–xxviii, 45, 49–51, 81, 96, 109, 115, 117, 145, 183, 191, 231, 237, 262, 265
9–10	115, 123
9	xxiii, 87, 200, 215–16, 220–21, 243, 245, 247
9:1–16	xxvi, 214
9:1–10	227
9:1–8	214
9:1–5	14, 48, 56, 104, 205, 215–16, 219, 221–22, 230, 233, 265
9:1–3	80, 231
9:1	221
9:2–5	116, 122, 140, 142
9:3	80, 225
9:4–5	93, 180, 185, 196, 223–24, 227, 230–32, 245, 259, 291
9:4	223, 225, 232, 249
9:5	231, 245
9:6–16	225
9:6–9	228
9:6	xv, xxiii, 104, 116, 214–19, 223–24, 226–33, 251
9:6a	225, 229–30
9:6b	230
9:6b-c	229–30
9:6c	230
9:7–16	226, 230, 232
9:7–9	226
9:7–8	225

9:7	116, 225		231–33, 237, 242–47,
9:8	225		250–51, 253, 260–61,
9:9	227		265, 269, 272, 280–81
9:10–13	227	11:1–36	80
9:11–13	227–28	11:1–10	116, 219
9:11	225	11:1–6	55
9:12	115	11:1–5	110
9:14–29	228, 251	11:1–2	118, 122, 185
9:14–16	214, 227	11:1	14, 32, 225, 251,
9:14	227		265
9:16	228–29	11:2	225
9:17–24	229	11:5–6	265
9:17–18	154, 270	11:5	118
9:17	116, 124	11:6	116
9:18	221	11:7–10	120, 175
9:22	80, 141	11:7	118, 154–56, 161,
9:24–29	246		166–67, 174
9:24	225	11:8–10	169, 174
9:25–27	125	11:8	115, 167
9:25–26	117	11:9–10	115, 167
9:25	225	11:11—12:3	32
9:28	115	11:11—12:1a	xvi, 285
9:29	140	11:11–32	46, 56, 216,
9:30–33	105, 108, 110,		265–66, 269
	115, 288–89	11:11–27	73
9:33	115	11:11–24	112, 114, 146, 272
10	xxiii, 107, 116,	11:11–17	289
	268	11:11–16	114, 117, 206,
10:1–2	14, 265		219, 269
10:1	80, 123, 218	11:11–15	108, 114, 116,
10:2	123		158, 182, 184,
10:3	93, 123		186, 226, 247,
10:4	56, 123		250, 268, 271, 274
10:8–12	123	11:11–14	57
10:9–10	218	11:11–12	15, 161
10:11	115	11:11	96, 107, 113–14,
10:13	218		116, 118–20, 128,
10:14—11:15	123		141, 161, 182,
10:14–16	184		184–87, 191, 275,
10:15	226		285, 288
10:19	119	11:12–20	286
11	vii, xi–xii, xiv, xxii–xxvi,	11:12–15	183
	xxix, 13, 47, 55–57, 59,	11:12	15, 120, 187, 253,
	86, 103, 105, 107, 149,		274, 286, 289
	153–54, 156, 179–82,	11:13–32	13–14, 265
	197, 200–201, 206, 212,	11:13–16	75, 77, 81
	215–17, 220–21, 226,	11:13–15	107, 110, 121

Romans (continued)

11:13-14	16, 45, 184, 231, 269, 273, 289	11:25-32	14, 128, 142, 232, 266
11:13	xx, 14, 119, 121, 185, 259, 265, 286, 289	11:25-31	81
		11:25-27	114, 117, 146, 159, 162, 170, 175, 185, 208
11:14	60, 286, 289	11:25-26	59-60, 162-63, 174, 176, 250, 267-69, 273
11:15	15, 219, 253, 274, 286, 289		
11:16-24	114, 182	11:25-26a	146, 157-58, 163, 194
11:16	80, 124, 131, 159, 205, 286, 289	11:25	109, 116, 139, 142, 153-57, 159, 161, 164, 166-67, 169-72, 175-76, 193-95, 200, 221, 252-53, 270-71, 287, 291
11:16b	124		
11:17-24	14, 80, 108, 125, 157-58, 187-88, 220, 268-69		
11:17-23	290		
11:17-21	158, 160-61, 190-92, 206-7, 272	11:25ff	251
		11:26-27	14, 115, 146, 159, 163, 172, 194-95, 205, 273
11:17	xxvi, 126-27, 131-32, 134, 158, 161, 181, 190, 207, 211, 220, 275, 286, 289-90		
		11:26b-27	157, 291
		11:26	x, xv, xxvi, 68, 77, 109, 142, 176, 214, 217, 268, 271, 276, 287, 291
11:18-24	120		
11:18	133, 158, 286, 290		
11:19-21	127	11:26a	194
11:19	127, 134, 158, 190, 286	11:27	125-26, 162, 287, 291
11:20-26	253	11:28-36	77
11:20-24	127	11:28-32	137, 184-85
11:20-22	220	11:28-31	273
11:20-21	135	11:28-29	xv, 48, 56, 93, 104, 109, 116, 140, 143, 159, 161, 180, 185, 195-96, 201, 205, 217, 259, 271, 291
11:20	84, 127, 139, 158, 189, 286, 290		
11:21-28	287		
11:21	136-37, 191, 287, 290		
11:22-24	140-41, 158, 191-92, 207, 272	11:28b-29	179
		11:28	xxvi, 81, 110, 138, 181-82, 205-6, 208, 211, 215, 218, 225, 249, 275, 287, 291
11:22	58, 96, 127, 140, 191, 287, 290		
11:23-24	188, 207		
11:23	143, 220, 287, 290		
11:24-29	291	11:29—12:1a	288
11:24	137, 143, 205, 287, 291	11:29	80, 93, 180, 214-15, 224, 251, 288, 291

11:30–36	197, 208	14:4	95
11:30–32	109, 136, 159, 161, 186, 220, 266–67, 291	14:6–9	82
		14:6–7	89
		14:10a	74
11:30	288, 292	14:13	71
11:31	288–89, 292	14:13a	74
11:32	288, 292	14:14—15:4	72
11:33—12:3	281–82	14:14	90
11:33–36	219, 243, 267, 270, 278, 291	14:14b—15:3	57
		14:14b–23	56
11:33	288, 292	14:15	71, 80, 82
11:34	288, 292	14:16–18	32
11:35	288, 292	14:18	37, 47, 70–71
11:36	245, 288, 292	14:19–22	86
12–16	87, 98, 173, 182, 247	14:20	85
		14:22b–23	84
12–15	49, 51, 55, 110, 137, 146, 150, 186	14:22	85
		14:23	84–86, 97
12:1—16:27	80	15	55, 184, 266
12:1–21	266	15:1–33	78
12:1–5	246	15:1–3	75, 86
12:1–2	56, 59	15:1	68, 95
12:1	14, 75, 88, 146, 161, 182, 201, 266, 288	15:2–3	68
		15:4	45
		15:5–13	73, 175, 267
12:1ff.	207	15:5–12	49, 133
12:3	139	15:5–7	36, 72
12:6–8	32	15:7–12	75, 208
12:9–21	266	15:7	74, 77, 88
13–15	45	15:8–9b	78
13	xviii	15:9–12	77
13:1–7	32, 266	15:12	126
13:1–5	9	15:14—16:27	47
13:8–10	56	15:14	36, 47
14–15	viii, xx, 65, 69, 96, 115, 117	15:15–32	46
		15:15–16	13, 45, 73, 265
14	4, 10, 47, 55, 69, 97, 110, 186, 266	15:16	47, 29
		15:18–19	47
14:1—15:13	47, 49, 76, 80, 87, 117, 266	15:24	172, 194, 270
		15:25–32	14, 265
14:1—15:7	126	15:26–32	47
14:1—15:3	25	15:26–29	59
14:1–2	72	16	13, 32, 47
14:1	68, 71, 85	16:1	32
14:2	84	16:3–5	7, 32
14:3–13	72	16:3–4	47
14:3–12	89	16:7	32, 47
14:3b	74	16:11	47

Romans (continued)

16:17–20	47, 55
16:19	36
16:25–27	48

1 Corinthians

1:10—6:20	11
7:7–14	145
7:17–24	246
8–10	81, 107
8	viii
8:11–13	81
8:11	82
9	94
9:19–23	89–90, 255, 257
9:22	89–90
10:25–30	84
15:12–58	278
15:28	254, 278
15:50	278

2 Corinthians

2:5	171
3:14	156, 168
3:15	168
5:16–19	246
8:23	32
11:5	32
11:13	32
12:11	32

Galatians

1:13–16	106
1:13	259
1:16	289
2	94, 239, 244
2:1–2	92
2:8–9	289
3:1a-b	119
3:23	255
3:24–25	107
3:28	145, 246
6:15	246

Philippians

1:1	32
3	94
3:6	93
3:7	255

Ephesians

4:13	254
4:18	156

1 Thessalonians

2:14–16	255

2 Thessalonians

5:12–14	32

1 Timothy

3	32
3:2	32

Titus

1:5–9	32

Philemon

17	71

1 Peter

44

Hebrews

44, 181

8:13	258
10:25	45

James

44

2:2	45

DEAD SEA SCROLLS

1 QH

7:26–32	292

Index of Ancient Sources

RABBINIC LITERATURE

Tosefta

t. Zebaḥim

9:8	119

Talmuds

b. Menaḥot

53b	126

ANCIENT JEWISH WRITERS

Philo

On Agriculture

6	130

On the Cherubim

58	168

On the Contemplative Life

10	168

That the Worse Attacks the Better

22	168

That God is Unchangeable

93	168

On Flight and Finding

121	168
123	169

Who is the Heir?

76	168

Hypothetica

7.12–13	12

Allegorical Interpretation

3.91	168
3.231	168

On the Embassy to Gaius

14.107	31
20.132	43
23.155–58	43
23.155	31
23.156	43
23.157	44
30.206	31

On the Life of Moses

1.124	168

On the Posterity of Cain

8	168

That Every Good Person is Free

55	168

On Providence

2.20	168

On the Sacrifices of Cain and Abel

69	168

On the Special Laws

1.117	169
1.341	168
3.6	168

On the Virtues

7	168

Josephus

Against Apion

2.15	169

Against Apion (continued)

2.75-77 (or 2.6)	44
2.175	12

Antiquities of the Jews

1.267	169
4.280	169
12.138-50 (or 12.3.3-4)	43
14.184-89	203
14.185-276 (or 14.10.1—11.2)	43, 203
14.190-212	8
14.204 (or 14.10.6)	44
14.213-67	8
14.213-16 (or 14.10.8)	43
14.214-16	8
14.225-30 (or 14.10.11-13)	44
16.27-28 (or 16.2.3)	43
16.43	12
16.52-53	8
16.152-65	8
16.160-78	8
16.162-65 (or 16.6.2)	43
16.172	8
16.278-312	8
18.3.4-5	30
18.65	30
18.81-85	30
19.287-91 (or 19.5.3)	43
19.300 (or 19.6.3)	43
19.304-6	8

Jewish War

2.195-97 (or 2.10.4)	44
2.291	12
5.2	8
5.228	169
7.420	8

GRECO-ROMAN WRITINGS

Aristotle

Rhetoric

2.10.11	57

Celcus

De Medicina. Aretaeus 193

521	155
527	155
575	155

Columella

De arboribus 129

17.3	132
26.1-9	132

De re rustica 129

4.24.4-6	164
4.29.1-17	132
5.9.16	130
5.11.1-15	132
7.8.1-4	132

Dio Cassius 24, 28, 31

Historia Romanorum

60.6.6-7	10, 25
67.14	33

Epictetus

Dissertation (Diatribeai)

2.9.19-21	204
2.9.20-21	45

Euripides

Bacchae

1300	160

Galen

Ars Medica

1.387.18	155, 193

Commentary on Hippocrates,
De fractures

18b.398–401	155
18b.412	155
18b.429	155
18b.505	155
18b.531	155
18b.541	155
18b.789	155

Hippocrates

De alimento

53	155, 193

De articulus

14.17	155, 193
14.24	155, 193
15.6	155, 193
49.18	155, 193

De fractures

23.10	155, 193

Isocrates

Or.

12.24	160
15.68	160

Juvenal

Satirae

14.96–106	9

Marcus Aurelius

Meditations   144

Palladius

De insitione

53–54	130

Pausinias

Graeciae descriptio

8.40.2	127, 190

Plato

Cratylus

117e	160

Timaeus

76a	160

Pliny the Younger

Epistulae

10.96.1–10	9
10.97.98–117	9

Quintillian

Institutio oratoria

8.6.54	136

Suetonius   24, 28–30, 35

Divus Claudius

25.4	9, 25

Nero

16.2	11, 29

Tacitus   29–31, 35

Annales   31

15.44.2–8	35, 45
15.44.2–4	32
15.44	4

Historiae

5.4–5	9
5.5.9	31

Theophrastus

De causis plantarum

1.2.5.10	162
1.3–4	134
1.4.5	164
1.4.5.8	162, 194
1.5.5	166
1.6.1–10	132
1.6.1–4	134
1.6.3	164
1.6.8	164
1.6.10	129
1.7.2.7	162, 194
1.12.1–3	134
1.12.8–9	134
1.13.3.3	162, 194
1.13.9.6	162, 194
1.15.3–4	129
1.19.5.7	162, 194
1.20.3	127
1.22.2.8	162, 194
2.15.3	128
2.15.5–6	132
2.16.5.1	162, 194
2.17.5.12	162, 194
3.7.5–12	128, 132, 164
3.14.1—16:3	132
3.15.3.10	162, 194
4.16.1	128, 130
5.1.3–4	134
5.1.3	133
5.1.4	134
5.16.2	162, 194
5.16.4	164
5.17.3	128
5.17.5	132
5.17.6	128
5.18.4.3	162, 194
6.8.7	133
6.11.6–7	133
6.11.16	164
15.1.1–3	132
16.1.2	128

Historia plantarum

1.1.9	133
1.8.1–4	164
1.8.4	166
1.8.5	133
1.10.7	133
2.1.4	134
2.3.1–2	129
2.4.3	166
2.7.1	128
2.7.2	132
2.7.12	128
3.7.1	164
3.17.1.11	162
4.14.8	166
4.16.1	127
5.2	162, 164
5.3.1	165
5.6.7	162

Thucydides

4.35.1	160
5.72.1	160

Xenophon

Cyropaedia

7.1.33	160

EARLY CHRISTIAN WRITINGS

Ambrosiaster 35

Ad Romanos 4, 40

Barnabus

9.5	156

Index of Ancient Sources

Chrysostom

Hom. Romans

19	156, 171

Clement of Alexandria

Protreptikos

9.83.3.6	156

Stromateis

1.18.88.3.2	156
2.5	33

First Clement

51.3	156

Ignatius

To the Magneians

9.1	4

To the Philadelphians

6.1	4

Justin

First Apology

1.4	32

Dialogue with Trypho   44

Origen

Comm. in Evangelium Matthaei

11.14.68	156

Pseudo-Clementine

158.8	156

Second Council of Nicea

Canon 8   4

Shephard of Hermas   44

Mandate(s)

11.9–14	35
11:9	45
11:13	45
11:14	45

Similitude(s)

30.1	156
47.4	156

Tertullian

Apology

3.5	32

Theophilus

Ad Autolycum

2.35.23	156

First Clement   44

Ignatius   4

www.ingramcontent.com/pod-product-compliance
Lightning Source LLC
Chambersburg PA
CBHW020106020526
44112CB00033B/971